THE KINGDOM OF
MACBRAYNE

Nick S. Robins is a Hydrogeologist with the British Geological Survey, based in Crowmarsh, Oxfordshire. He is familiar with the Hebrides through his professional work on such schemes as Tiree's public water supply. He has written many widely-acclaimed books on the history of British shipping across the years, among them *The Evolution of the British Ferry* (1995), *The British Excursion Ship* (1998), *Turbine Steamers of the British Isles* (1999), *Ferry Powerful: A history of the modern British diesel ferry* (2003), *The Last Steamers* (2005), and *The Cruise Ship* (2008).

Donald E. Meek was Professor of Scottish and Gaelic Studies at the University of Edinburgh (2002-8), and Professor of Celtic at the University of Aberdeen (1993-2001). He is a native of Tiree, where he became an enthusiast for ships and boats of all kinds, local, national and international, but particularly those of David MacBrayne. The nineteenth-century Highlands and Islands are one of his main research interests. He has published an all-Gaelic account of West Highland shipping, *An t-Aiseag an Iar* ('The Passage West') (1977). He first made contact with Dr Nick Robins in December 2004, having read and greatly enjoyed his volume *Ferry Powerful*. The result is this collaborative venture.

*The **Claymore** (1955) entering Oban Bay, with the **King George V** (1926) in the background, by Gordon Bauwens [Copyright D. E. Meek]*

THE KINGDOM OF
MACBRAYNE

NICK S. ROBINS AND DONALD E. MEEK

*From steamships to car-ferries in the
West Highlands and Hebrides*

BIRLINN

This edition first published in 2008 by

Birlinn Limited

West Newington House

10 Newington Road

Edinburgh EH9 1QS

www.birlinn.co.uk

ISBN13: 978 1 84158 601 4

ISBN10: 1 84158 601 3

British Library Cataloguing-in-Publication Data

A catalogue record for this book is available from the British Library

Typeset by Sharon McTier

Printed and bound by Bell and Bain Ltd, Glasgow

Chaidh an leabhar seo a sgrìobhadh agus a chur ri chèile mar chomharradh spèis air na h-euchdan mòra a rinn ginealach an dèidh ginealaich de Sgiobairean, oifigearan, innealairean, seòladairean agus maraichean eile, ann an deifir chompanaidhean, ann a bhith a' frithealadh nan coimhearsnachdan air Taobh Siar Gàidhealtachd na h-Alba agus anns na h-Eileanan.

As aonais an dìchill-san, an teòmachd agus an gaisge, cha bhiodh e comasach do na coimhearsnachdan sin a bhith beò. Tha sinn a' nochdadh ar spèis dhaibh le buidheachas agus le mòr-urram.

This book has been written and compiled in appreciation of the outstanding services rendered to the communities of the West Highlands of Scotland and the Hebrides by successive generations of Masters, officers, engineers, sailors and other crew members in various companies.

Without their dedication, skill and bravery, these regions would not have been able to sustain viable communities. We salute them in a spirit of gratitude and admiration.

v

'As a ship is the noblest, and one of the most useful machines that ever was invented, every attempt to improve it becomes a matter of the greatest importance, and merits the particular attention of every British subject.'

Henry Bell, *Observations on the Utility of Applying Steam Engines to Vessels* etc.

CONTENTS

PREFACE

The earth belongs unto the Lord
And all that it contains,
Except the Western Islands,
And they are David MacBrayne's.

This verse – a parody of the opening verse of Metrical Psalm 24 – is quoted (and frequently misquoted in various forms by those unfamiliar with the Scottish Psalter) whenever reference is made to David MacBrayne. David's independence of the Almighty may be questioned by those sufficiently articulate in theology, if not in Psalmody, but there is no doubt that he is widely regarded as 'the uncrowned king of West Highland shipping'. His name (to echo the Metrical Psalms once again) has endured, and has done so for well over a century. As we approach the centenary of the great man's death in 2007, it seems appropriate to look afresh at 'The Kingdom of MacBrayne', which has assumed a virtual monopoly of Hebridean sea-services over the past century, and is now known even in the corridors of power in Brussels.

This is not the first book, and assuredly not the last, to be written about David MacBrayne. Its claim to attention is based, not on the unearthing of fresh information, though it contains some new material, but on a desire to display the Kingdom from two relatively neglected perspectives – that of wider British shipping developments on the one hand (covered by Nick Robins), and that of the Gaelic people on the other (covered by Donald Meek, who writes from an Inner Hebridean vantage-point, and does not attempt to cover the entire Hebrides). Existing, mainstream accounts of David MacBrayne do not interact with the Gaelic world in which the ships operate. Wider British developments also tend to be overlooked. Concern with individual ships and their technicalities, which is extremely important in its own place, operates (almost inevitably) to the detriment of social and human contexts. Other companies which supplemented MacBrayne's services – notably McCallum and Orme – are often treated only in the bygoing.

We try to redress these balances in this book. We let observers and travellers speak for themselves wherever possible, and – at the risk of bias and favouritism – we even ascribe some degree of character and personality to ships that we have known. We examine the need for the ships, the role they had in Hebridean life, and the reasons they were created as they were. We recognise the contribution of West Highland and Hebridean entrepreneurs, such as the remarkable John McCallum from Crinan, to the founding of several early companies.

The external influences which contributed to 'the making of MacBrayne' are given considerable space. From the very outset, West Highland and Hebridean steamships were produced by, or responded to, initiatives far beyond the Hebrides. In fact, there is a fascinating two-way interconnection between the owners and builders of these small vessels and the creators of the new steam liners sailing between the United Kingdom and North America. Expertise in business and construction, as well as managerial know-how, was often contributed by Clyde-based entrepreneurs whose chief, initial interest lay in the West Highlands and Hebrides. The Hebrides were central, not peripheral, to the exciting, wider world of nineteenth-century maritime adventure. In the twentieth century, new approaches to the design, building and propulsion of ships were applied throughout Britain, and these were readily accepted by David MacBrayne's successors. Indeed, David MacBrayne Limited was sometimes the pioneer, rather than the imitator, of such novelties, and the company exerted a formative influence on other British shipowners – a point often forgotten.

Hebridean shipping continues to respond to wider policies and patterns. We are aware of the current debate about the tendering, under EC directives, of Caledonian MacBrayne, and we take this opportunity to look at the patterns of the past in order to learn lessons for the future. Political debates and media assessments of Caledonian MacBrayne often fail to give credit where credit is due. We hope to supply some of the broader vistas which appear to be absent from the arguments of those who are more concerned to restructure the company, come what may, than to consider its role from the perspective of its Hebridean responsibilities across many years.

Our book aims to be easily read and understood by the legendary 'average general reader' rather than the die-hard specialist or shipping buff. It operates within a broadly chronological framework, but it pays attention to the types of ships which emerged within each period. It considers the impact of steamships, motor-vessels and car-ferries on island life, and concludes with an overview of 'The Kingdom of MacBrayne'. Those who may wish more detailed information will be well served by other books listed in the Bibliography. The wider sweeps, rather than technically comprehensive accounts of individual vessels, are our concern here.

Illustrations are used lavishly in this book. Many of those relating to the pre-1970 phases of the Kingdom of MacBrayne derive from a wealth of photographic and other kinds of memorabilia generously given to Donald Meek from boyhood by older collectors – pier-masters, tourists, passengers, Pursers, and even Captains. Their contributions are listed in the Acknowledgements. Photographs of post-1970 ships derive mainly from the camera of Nick Robins, in the course of many voyages on MacBrayne vessels and no less frequent visits to ports such as Oban.

The Kingdom of MacBrayne has inspired creativity of different kinds across the years. Artists and model-makers have responded to it, and they have been given their place in this book. The importance of art in recreating familiar scenes and ships from the past is emphasised by the cover, based on work specially commissioned by Donald Meek from the outstanding Scottish marine artist, Gordon Bauwens, whose fine paintings grace the new Cunard liner, *Queen Mary 2*. The book thus provides, and contributes to, a celebratory display of artistic endeavour and photographic evidence not normally accessible to the general public.

In surveying the Kingdom with a kind but critical eye, our overall aim is not to produce yet another company history of the conventional kind. Instead, we try to set David MacBrayne, the man and the legend, in his overall context, and to narrate clearly the course of the company before and after his death. We also aim to give just recognition to those other pioneers who have been overshadowed by 'King David', but who deserve their own memorials alongside his in the history of British, and specifically West Highland, shipping.

NSR and DEM
March 2006

Note to the Second Edition

We are delighted with the warm reception given to the first edition of this book. In the second edition, we have covered recent events (2005–8) by means of an additional chapter. We have also corrected minor errors of fact and typography, and updated the narrative where appropriate. Readers are reminded again that this is not a detailed account of each and every ship, but a broad-brush account of the MacBrayne 'Kingdom' from a particular perspective – that of the authors.

Our thanks are due to CalMac Ferries Limited, Captain John A. Gillies, currently Master of the MV *Isle of Arran*, Biggart Baillie LLP, Solicitors, and, of course, our enthusiastic publishers (and especially Andrew Simmons). We do, however, owe a particularly large debt to Dr Hugh Dan MacLennan, former Director of Communications at CalMac Ferries Limited, for his outstanding courtesy, warm support and provision of information.

NSR and DEM
July 2008

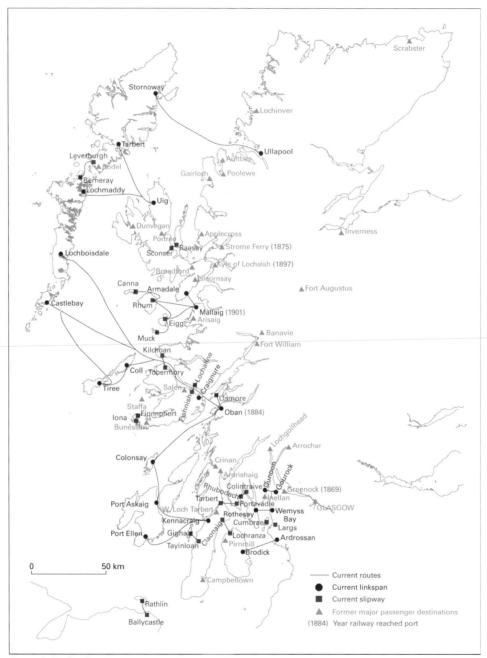

Scrabster

Stornoway

Lochinver

Tarbert

Leverburgh
Rodel
Berneray
Lochmaddy

Ullapool

Aultbea
Gairloch Poolewe

Uig

Dunvegan

Inverness

Portree
Raasay
Sconser
Broadford

Applecross

Strome Ferry (1875)

Kyle of Lochalsh (1897)

Lochboisdale

Isleornsay

Fort Augustus

Canna
Armadale
Rhum
Eigg

Mallaig (1901)
Arisaig

Castlebay

Muck

Kilchoan

Banavie
Fort William

Coll Tobermory

Salen

Lochaline
Craignure

Tiree

Staffa
Iona Fionnphort
Bunessan

Fishnish

Lismore

Oban (1884)

Lochgoilhead
Arrochar

Colonsay

Crinan
Ardrishaig

Dunoon
Gourock
Greenock (1869)

Colintraive

GLASGOW

Port Askaig

Rhubodach
Tarbert
W. Loch Tarbert

Portavadie
Rothesay
Cumbrae

Innellan
Wemyss
Bay
Largs

Kennacraig

Port Ellen

Gigha

Claonaig

Lochranza
Pirnmill

Ardrossan

Tayinloan

Brodick

	Current routes
●	Current linkspan
■	Current slipway
▲	Former major passenger destinations
(1884)	Year railway reached port

0   50 km

Campbeltown

Rathlin

Ballycastle

Drawn by Pauline Sapey

CHAPTER 1

IN THE BEGINNING

*The compact and modern car-ferry **Lochnevis** approaching Mallaig [NR]*

IN THE BEGINNING

*With a story stretching back to the advent of the **Comet**, David MacBrayne Ltd. has probably had more written about it than any other shipping company. Ardent admirers and indefatigable historians have all contributed their quota from the plethora of records still available.*
FROM AN ARTICLE BY EARNEST READER, *SEA BREEZES*, DECEMBER 1950.

The history of David MacBrayne's shipping operations has been well documented, and has been told many times. Perhaps the most frequently cited record is that of Christian Duckworth and Graham Langmuir in their foundationally important and much-respected book, *West Highland Steamers*, first published in 1935. The very best records of all, however, are the memories of youth, and the vision of the red-and-black funnel atop a smart steamer butting into the wind as she heads out to the islands. It is this vision that we still see behind the contemporary departure of the *Clansman* as she heads across Oban Bay, or the diminutive *Lochnevis* setting out from Mallaig. It is also this same vision and these same memories that demand yet another record of the MacBrayne Kingdom.

Watching the bulky, high-sided *Clansman* as she closes her bow visor, glides astern effortlessly from Oban's modern linkspan, and, controlled by her Master from a console on the bridge, swings round smoothly with the aid of her bow-thrusters, it is hard to imagine that her pedigree derives directly from the tiny *Comet*, whose well-constructed replica now graces Port Glasgow. Built for Henry Bell of Helensburgh, the *Comet* proved the viability of steam navigation in coastal waters as soon as she undertook her maiden voyage in 1812, and she gained a place in history as the first successful commercial steamship in Europe. She had reached Fort William by September of that year. In 1819, following service on the Forth, she initiated the steamer service from Glasgow to Fort William through the Crinan Canal.

Sadly, the pioneer ship was lost in December 1820. Her place was then taken by the steamer *Highland Chieftain*, built originally for the Dumbarton Steamship Company as the *Duke of Wellington* in 1817. Suitably renamed, this vessel joined the *Ben Nevis* and the *Commodore* on services to Inverness in 1824, as a new *Comet* had been commissioned

*The replica of Henry Bell's **Comet** (1812) at Port Glasgow [NR]*

EARLY STEAMSHIP PIONEERS

HENRY BELL, CREATOR of Europe's first commercial steamship, *Comet*, which took to the water in 1812, was also the first person to send a steamship northwards to the West Highlands from the Clyde. As Captain James Williamson relates in *The Clyde Passenger Steamer* (1904),

On the 2nd September [1812], the sailings of the *Comet* were extended *via* Tarbert and the Crinan Canal, to Oban, Port Appin, and Fort William, the return journey occupying four days. Before long, however, the steamer seems to have been transferred to Grangemouth, but in August, 1819, she re-appeared on the West Highland route. She continued that service till the following year, when, on 13th December, 1820, on the passage from Fort William to Glasgow, she was caught by the strong tide-race and easterly wind, and wrecked at the Doras Mòr, outside Crinan. The after part of the vessel drifted towards Corrievreckan, but the fore end, from which Henry Bell and the crew and passengers scrambled ashore, remained on the rocks, and from it the machinery was afterwards removed.

Henry Bell (1767-1830) was born in Torphichen, West Lothian. Trying his hand at various trades, including masonwork, ship-modelling and engineering, Bell became a builder in Glasgow in 1790, but by the end of the century his main interest lay in the development of a steamship. Successful steam navigation had already been introduced to Scotland by William Symington, creator of the *Charlotte Dundas* (1802), whose achievement in running his vessel on the Forth and Clyde Canal was well known to Bell. The wooden hull of the *Comet* was built by John Wood, Port Glasgow, and the engine was constructed by John Robertson, Glasgow. Originally the *Comet* had two paddle-wheels on each side, but she was lengthened and the number of paddles reduced to one per side. She could reach speeds of about five knots. Bell later held shares in other steamers, including the *Highland Chieftain*.

If Henry Bell can justly claim to be the father of the Scottish – and European – commercial steamship, Robert Napier (1791-1876) can claim, no less justly, to be the father of Clyde shipbuilding. A native of Dumbarton, Napier began his working life as a blacksmith, setting up shop in Glasgow in 1815. He turned gradually to iron-founding and engineering, and gained a high reputation for the manufacture of powerful engines for steamships. In the 1840s he became an iron shipbuilder, and worked closely with Samuel Cunard in the construction of the Cunard Line's iron steamships, including the *Persia* (1856), the first iron Cunarder to cross the Atlantic. She gained distinction by ramming an iceberg on her maiden voyage, and 'popped rivets for sixteen feet on the starboard side'. Unlike White Star's *Titanic* of 1912, she survived the experience, thanks to her particularly robust bow structure. Robert's cousin, David, was also an engineer, and the inventor of the steeple engine. He had been consulted by Henry Bell with regard to the *Comet*.

Both Robert and David Napier owned steamships. Robert had West Highland interests, and acquired the fleets of several other early operators during the 1830s. His ships carried red-and-black funnels. This colour-scheme was transferred to Samuel Cunard's vessels, and also to the Hutcheson and MacBrayne fleets. David owned the *Marion*, the first steamship to ply on Loch Lomond from 1818, and also the *Rob Roy*, which, in 1818, began steamship sailings from the Clyde to Belfast.

George and James Burns, two extremely capable businessmen, represented the ambitious new class of commercial shipowners who had developed alongside

for the Fort William service in 1821. Unfortunately, the new ship was wrecked in 1825, but Archibald McEachern had introduced the *Highlander* in 1822, and within ten years he had built up sufficient trade to allow two more ships to join the West Highland link – the *Staffa* and the *Inverness*. In due course, the ownership of the *Inverness* passed to William Young, originally a plumber to trade, for use on the Crinan Canal.

Thus, in a very short time, the irregular sailing-ship connections which linked 'remote' coastal communities to the Clyde were superseded by a more or less regular service direct to Glasgow. Gradually, a more predictable pattern of connections was extended to the islands, first to the more northerly of the Inner Hebrides (pre-eminently Skye), and then to the Outer Isles. Consequently, the cultural isolation of many of these communities began to erode, as the first small step towards globalisation had been taken. Elsewhere in the United Kingdom, the more successful, pioneering steam routes were also the coastal and cross-channel services.

The appearance of the *Comet*'s immediate successors – stocky, little wooden-hulled steamers with lofty, spindly funnels, propelled by paddles, and able to take advantage of the Crinan and Caledonian canals – coincided with, and contributed greatly to, the changing social profile of the Highlands and Islands. As these ships puffed clouds of black smoke from their tall stacks into the fresh air, they made their own contribution to the Highland mist.

the network of engineers, shipbuilders and proprietors established by pioneers like the Napiers. The Napiers had combined all of these roles, but as steamship enterprises developed rapidly after 1820, it made sound practical sense to separate such functions, and to diversify. As a result, the nature of Robert Napier's enterprise had changed considerably by the late 1830s. The Burns brothers, who were clearly well prepared for the challenge of shipowning, belonged to a family of considerable influence in various spheres of Glasgow life. Their father, the Rev. Dr John Burns, was minister of the Barony Parish, and their sister was the mother of the future West Highland entrepreneur, David MacBrayne.

The shipowning interests of George and James Burns were evident when James Burns became agent for the Glasgow-Liverpool company, Mathie & Theakstone, in 1824. He was joined by his brother George, when the latter acquired a half-share in six sailing vessels on the retirement of Mr Theakstone. This was the beginning of the company known as G. & J. Burns.

The expertise accumulated by the Burns brothers in the 1820s and 1830s, as well as by their former rivals on the Glasgow-Liverpool run, David and Charles MacIver, was of great value to Samuel Cunard. 'Messrs George Burns and David MacIver' had a half-share partnership with Cunard in the mail contract of 1839 'for Conveyance of Mails to Halifax', which laid the

foundations of what became the Cunard Line. Stephen Fox, author of *The Ocean Railway* (2003), records that George Burns 'looked after the construction and repair of the Cunard vessels by Robert Napier and various Clydeside shipbuilders', while the 'flinty personality' of Charles MacIver determined the predictably safe, but rather austere, style which gave Cunard ships the ultimate edge over their competitors. In such a policy, which put safety before luxury and speed, there may be a trace of the Hebridean heritage of the MacIvers, two highly influential individuals whose family origins lay in Lewis. It was a policy that was to be replicated, to a significant degree, in the approach of David MacBrayne.

In addition to their Glasgow-Liverpool and transatlantic interests, the Burns brothers had West Highland concerns, which went back to vessels acquired from William Young in 1835. These were handled through their Glasgow and Liverpool Steam Shipping Company until 1842, when the whole of their operation came under the name of G. & J. Burns. In 1840, the Burns brothers entered into a partnership which amalgamated their fleet with that of Thomson & MacConnell, who had taken over the West Highland interests of Rober Napier in 1838. In 1851, the Burns' fleet of West Highland ships – now part of an increasingly cumbersome maritime empire which had expanded its boundaries from Glasgow

to Halifax, Nova Scotia – was ceded to David and Alexander Hutcheson, who were already working with the Burns brothers. This set the stage for the acquisition, in 1878, of the West Highland fleet by the Burns' nephew and the Hutchesons' junior partner, David MacBrayne.

David MacBrayne's company, now associated indelibly with the West Highlands and Hebrides, thus had its roots in the complex nineteenth-century alliance of Clyde-based maritime entrepreneurs who laid the foundations of some of the best-known British shipping lines. In due course, David MacBrayne was to achieve the same kind of supremacy in Hebridean waters as Samuel Cunard had achieved in the Atlantic.

James Burns

They contradicted and complemented some of the most significant and radically transformative processes in the region. Their sooty contribution arrived just as the cult of 'Highlandism', warmed by the afterglow of MacPherson's 'Ossian', took hold.

Clan chiefs who had embraced the role of landlords after the '45 Rebellion, and who now strutted themselves on the aristocratic and imperial stages of British history, played their part in forming consortia and bringing the smoky barges to the Highlands, at the same time as they introduced and encouraged sheep-farming on their estates. Initially, the romantically-inclined among them, such as Glengarry, viewed the steamship with as much disingenuous ambivalence as they viewed the sheep-farmers, but they

realised soon enough that the ship, like the sheep, could yield profits. As a result of commercial estate policies, seasonal and long-term migration to the Lowland cities was in full swing, while emigration across the oceans was opening new horizons. Economic instability was aggravated by two potato famines, the first in 1836 and the second in 1846. The second, which was by far the more serious, was followed by extensive, and in some cases infamous, clearing and displacement of impoverished tenants, most notably in the Inner Hebrides.

The steamship was an important facilitator in all of these processes – bringing external visitors to view the romantic Highlands on Ossianic and other grand tours, depriving the region of its indigenous people, and connecting the rural north and west of Scotland with the increasingly industrialised Lowlands or with the tall-masted – and still wind-powered – emigrant ships awaiting passengers in ports such as Oban, Tobermory and Greenock. This had serious, and varied, implications for earlier ways of life.

At the beginning of the century, the West Highland steamship was a relatively high-brow utility, promoted by landlords and a confusing variety of small syndicates. It was patronised by the well-to-do, conveying the upper ranks of Highland society. By the second half of the century, however, as industrial investments and profits displaced inherited capital, the ship came to be owned by self-made, large-scale entrepreneurs such as the Hutchesons and David MacBrayne.

The grouping of individual ships into small fleets becomes a recognisable trend after 1830. Robert Napier, a key figure in Clyde shipbuilding, was among the first to take an entrepreneurial interest in serving the West Highlands and the islands. In December 1835, the McEachern fleet became Napier's, along with the *Brenda* and part-ownership of the *Shandon*, two vessels closely associated with the Crinan Canal and linkages to Oban and Glasgow. In 1838, ownership passed to Thomson & MacConnell, who were agents for the City of Glasgow Steam Packet Company, founded in 1831. Following an agreement of partnership in 1840, this enlarged fleet merged with that of its competitors, George and James Burns, two Glasgow brothers better remembered for their prowess on the Irish Sea routes as G. & J. Burns. Their business interests, however, extended much farther afield. With the award by the British government of the transatlantic mail contract of 1839 to Samuel Cunard of Halifax, Nova Scotia, George Burns, along with David MacIver (of Lewis extraction), became a half-share partner in the company later known as the Cunard Line. The Burns' role as shipowners was commemorated right up until Burns & Laird ceased trading in the early 1970s.

The merged West Highland fleet now included the Burns' steamers, the *Rob Roy*, the *Helen McGregor*, and the *Inverness*, all said to have been acquired in 1835. The Burns

brothers soon took over other competitors, among them William Ainslie of Fort William, and in 1845 the Castles Company, latterly known as the Glasgow Castles Steam Packet Company, along with seven 'Castles', one 'Maid' and one 'Vale'. The Burns' Western Isles monopoly was now complete, and the brothers also retained a strong hold on the Clyde estuary routes. Of their Highland business, one later commentator wrote rather poetically:

From this beginning they worked up a whole system of steamers for the day passage through the Crinan or the night passage round the Mull, gliding along canals or battling with the Atlantic, meeting at Oban, crossing and re-crossing, plunging into the lochs, winding along the sounds, threading their way among the islands, fine pleasure boats for the flock of summer swallows, stout trading boats summer and winter serving the whole archipelago, linking with the world the lonely bay or the outer islet, freighted out with supplies of all sorts and shapes, freighted in with wool and sheep, Highland beasts and Highland bodies: surely the liveliest service in the world!

In 1846, a Burns vessel was placed at the disposal of the Admiralty to convey Grand Duke Constantine to view the islands. When it was announced that Queen Victoria was to make the same journey in the following year, another vessel was found and furnished from the Burns' household. The journey through the Crinan Canal (known to this day as part of MacBrayne's and Caledonian MacBrayne's 'Royal Route') was given a regal touch by the gaily decorated tracking-horses on the tow-path, with their attendants dressed in gold and scarlet.

By 1851, the Burns' enterprise had become so unwieldy that they decided to concentrate on the Irish Sea and Atlantic services and to dispose of their Clyde and Western Isles interests. With the exception of five of the 'Castles', the fleet and its interests were transferred to David Hutcheson & Company of 14 Jamaica Street, Glasgow. The Hutcheson brothers, David (who had been employed by Burns since 1822) and Alexander (also a former employee of the Burns empire), were joined by George and James Burns' nephew

EARLY STEAMSHIP OWNERS IN THE WEST HIGHLANDS

IN THE FIRST half of the nineteenth century, West Highland steamships were owned by a perplexingly large and ever-changing number of companies, consisting of small groupings of individuals with shares in particular ships, or syndicates of interested parties. Initially, 'single-ship companies' were common. By 1840 several such companies were amalgamating within the larger enterprises of Robert Napier, Thomson & MacConnell and G. & J. Burns (see 'Early Steamship Pioneers'), but the adding of Highland interests to expanding companies resulted in unwieldy combinations. By 1851 and the dawn of the Hutcheson era, the 'large managed business' model of West Highland shipowning had emerged, creating a distinct West Highland fleet from the myriad of earlier ventures. This became the dominant mode of operation, but smaller companies, such as those associated with John McCallum and Martin Orme (see Chapter 4), maintained the older model, dependent on a small group of individual shareholders, long after 1850.

It was no easy task to maintain one steamship, to say nothing of several, in West Highland waters. This is reflected in the mosaic of owners who might be connected with one vessel. Certain vessels, such as the *Highland Chieftain*, passed through a bewildering variety of owners, including the Ben Nevis Steamboat Co., Robert Napier, Thomson & MacConnell, and latterly G. & J. Burns. A similar pattern is evident with the long-lasting *Maid of Morven*. Companies also amalgamated in order to increase their capital base, or to improve efficiency.

Such fluidity was doubtless encouraged by the nature of shareholding. Because of shareholding, and the resulting multiple ownership of a vessel, the distinction between 'owners' and 'agents', who acted for owners, is rather fine in this early period. Agents often owned, or part-owned, their own vessels, which could function within wider consortia or 'conferences'. They could also hold shares beyond their own companies – even investing in 'rival' enterprises, possibly to increase market share and/

or to maintain a more favourable environment for steamship enterprises more generally.

There was scope for ambitious and well-placed businessmen to capitalise on such ventures. John McLeod, an agent for Highland steamers, acquired the *Ben Nevis* of 1824 for the Glasgow-Fort William route. In 1835 Archibald McEachern, who succeeded McLeod in 1828, became Robert Napier's agent for his West Highland ships, having acted for the previous owner of these vessels. He was connected to the Tobermory Steamboat Co. and the Ben Nevis Steamboat Co., both named after their first ships. McEachern also represented the Glen Albyn Steamboat Co., builders of the *Glen Albyn* (1834), and was likewise a trustee in the Maid of Morven Steamboat Co., first owners of the *Maid of Morven* (1826). McEachern thus became a very powerful figure, foreshadowing the emergence of David MacBrayne later in the century.

Shareholding by different parties, creating a company managed by a group of Directors, seemed to work best in the West Highlands when vessels were primarily cargo-boats. Passenger vessels demanded a stronger managerial framework, to maintain regular timetables and to plan and oversee replacements. In such contexts, a single iconic leader, like David MacBrayne, might emerge and 'rebrand' the company. Larger ventures evolved from single-ship companies, including the (Glasgow) Castles Steam Packet Company, established in 1832, and absorbed by G. & J. Burns in 1845. Most of its ships (e.g. *Inverary Castle*) were named after prominent (mainly Scottish) castles. Such absorptions and 'tidying up' processes are evident across the years. In a sense, the making of Caledonian MacBrayne in 1973 was the last step (to date) in a process of pragmatic amalgamation going back to the earliest days of West Highland steamships.

It is very important to note that the initiative to create and to finance early steamship companies did not lie solely with Clydeside entrepreneurs. Several early ships and companies depended heavily on initial West Highland and Hebridean investment, commonly

by landlords, farmers and merchants. For instance, a body of 'enterprising gentlemen, consisting of landed proprietors, tacksmen and merchants connected with Mull, Morven and Ardnamurchan' built the *Tobermory* in 1836. James Matheson, proprietor of Lewis, built the *Mary Jane* in 1846, while Islay landlords, Walter Frederick Campbell of Islay, James Morrison of Basildon and John Ramsay of Kildalton, operated several vessels from the mid-1820s to 1876, when David Hutcheson purchased Ramsay's steamer, *Islay*. The Islay-owned ships included Northern Irish ports, such as Portrush, on their itineraries. A later venture involving Ramsay of Kildalton, namely the Islay Steam-Packet Company, incorporated in 1890, had over one hundred shareholders, of whom some 95%, ranging from landed proprietors to shepherds, were from Islay itself. The Western Isles Steam Packet Company, which operated from 1871 to 1881, owed much of its initial investment to farmers and merchants and other interested parties in Uist, Barra and Skye. In the early twentieth century, Lord Strathcona and Mount Royal, the owner of Colonsay, was a major shareholder in McCallum and Orme. By contrast, the shareholding of David MacBrayne Limited, from 1905 to 1928, was based in Glasgow, Edinburgh and Oban, and sustained mainly by large-scale entrepreneurs, such as the shipowner, George Service, and (latterly) the shipbuilder, William Denny & Bros.

The **Duntroon Castle** [DEM's collection]

David MacBrayne, who in 1851 had just turned 37 years of age.

That, in brief summary, is the complex and untidy background to what became the Kingdom of MacBrayne. But just what were those early days actually like, and what comforts did the ships offer?

The principal features and qualities of these first steamships, as well as people's reactions to them, are recorded in Gaelic and English literary compositions. Gaelic-speaking Highlanders were among the first to observe the ships. At the outset, they did so from a safe distance, but by the late 1820s they were able to gain first-hand experience of their many fascinating idiosyncrasies. Traditional Gaelic narrative genres were modified to express a mixture of feelings, which remained fairly constant throughout the nineteenth century, but with different emphases at different stages. Initially, the steamship could be seen as a marvel or a monstrosity, or a combination of both.

The steamships were first commemorated creatively in Gaelic verse. A number of eulogies on individual ships were composed by contemporary Gaelic poets. In most cases, these poems describe, in surprisingly graphic detail, the vessel itself, commonly known in Gaelic as *bàta-smùide* or boat of steam, the crew and the passengers. Allan MacDougall (c.1750-1828) from Glencoe made a specially significant contribution to 'steamship verse' of this kind, as he functioned as an unofficial poet-laureate or 'literary agent' to the new-fangled vessels when they arrived in the Fort William area in the 1820s. Officially MacDougall was poet to the archetype of romantic Highland chiefs, Alexander Ranaldson MacDonell of Glengarry.

Glengarry's life and death had close links with the first generation of Highland steamships, which he initially despised and even tried to ban from the stretch of water adjacent to Invergarry House. Glengarry disliked the Caledonian Canal as much as the vessels which used it. Ironically, he met his end as a consequence of the stranding of the *Stirling* (or *Stirling Castle*) in a hurricane in 1828 close to his own home. He and his two daughters were travelling on the ship. The rock on which he perished, as a result of his attempt to rescue one of his daughters, was subsequently known as *Sgeir Mhic 'ic Alasdair* (Glengarry's Rock). MacDougall had the sad duty of composing an elegy on the dead chief, in which he condemned *am bàta dubh toite* ('the black boat of smoke'), whose wrecking had resulted in Glengarry's untimely demise. He laments the deforming of his face in the grim accident:

> Do ghnùis àlainn ga dochann
> Leis a' bhàta dhubh thoite,
> Dan robh dàn a' mhì-fhortain,
> 'S am fear a dhealbh air a stoc i,
> B' fheàrr nach beirt' e bho thoiseach le mhàthair.

> *Your beautiful face being disfigured*
> *by the black boat of smoke,*
> *which was destined for misfortune,*
> *and the man who designed her on the stocks,*
> *it were better had he never been given birth by his mother.*

In celebratory rather than elegiac mood, however, MacDougall commemorated in fine style the distinguishing features of the new ships. His word-picture of the *Highland Chieftain* is illuminating, since it provides a rare insight into what contemporary observers found noteworthy in these steamers:

SLAN GUN TILL NA GAIDHEIL GHASDA
Oran don bhàta-thoite, den goirear an 'Ceann-fine'

Slàn gun till na Gàidheil ghasda,
Dh'fhalbh Di-màirt air sàil do Ghlaschu,
Leis a' bhàta dhìonach, sgairteil,
 Làidir, acfhainneach gu strì.

'S e h-ainm am Beurla 's an Gàidhlig,
An 'Ceann-fine measg nan Gàidheal';
'S thig i dhùthaich nam beann àrda,
 'S gheibh i càirdean anns gach tìr.

Nuair a dh'fhalbhas i gu h-aotrom,
'S luaithe h-astar na 'n gath-gaoithe,
Cha till fairg' i no sruth caolais,
 Ge b' e taobh don tig an t-sian.

'S ged a dh'èireadh muir gu buaireas,
Snàmhaidh i air bhàrr nan stuaghaibh,
Mar steud-cruidheach 's spuir ga bhualadh,
 Dhol san rèis a bhuannachd cìs.

Le cuibhleachaibh air gach taobh dhith,
'S i masgadh fairge le saothair;
Ioghnadh 's motha th' air an t-saoghal,
 A dhealbh clann-daoine rim linn.

Gu dol an aghaidh na gaoithe,
Le teine gun aon snàthainn aodaich,
Gun ràimh, ach a stiùir ga saoradh,
 Air muir a' taosgadh na glinn.

Sgioba fearail ri àm cruadail,
'S Caiptean Mac-an-Aba, an t-uasal,
Calum Dòmhnallach is Ruairidh
 'S MacCoinnich a tha suairce, grinn.

Caiptean Mac-an-Aba 'n t-àrmann,
A shìol nam fear a sheasadh làrach,
A leagadh aighean agus làn-daimh,
 Anns an fhàsach bràighe ghlinn.

Mu Urchaidh nam buinnean gailbheach,
Aig Eas-chaiteilig nan garbh-shruth,
'S tric rinn do mhorgha marbhadh,
 Air bradan tàrr-gheal fon still.

A SAFE RETURN FOR THE HIGHLAND GALLANTS
Song on the steam-ship which is called 'Chieftain'

A safe return for the Highland gallants
who went, on Tuesday, by sea to Glasgow
on the watertight, valiant vessel,
 equipped and strong to fight the tide.

Her name in English and in Gaelic
is the 'Chieftain among Gaels';
she will come to the Highlands,
 and win friends in every clime.

When she sails away so lightly
her speed is faster than a wind-blast;
no heavy sea or current will halt her,
 whatever side the squall may rise.

And though the sea should swell to tempest,
she will swim upon the wave-crests,
like a hooved steed spurred in earnest
 to run the race to win a prize.

On each side she carries paddles,
and she churns the sea with ardour;
of world's wonders, this is the greatest
 that man has devised in all my time

To sail straight against the wind-storm
with fire, and not a thread of sail-cloth,
without oars, while her rudder saves her,
 as glens appear in the surging brine.

She has a manly crew in time of hardship,
with Captain MacNab, the noble,
Malcolm MacDonald and Rory
 and MacKenzie, kind and fine.

Captain MacNab is the stalwart
descended from those who stand fast,
who would fell both hinds and stags,
 in the heights of the glen that's wild.

About Orchy of the terrible torrents,
at Eas-chaiteilig of the strong streams,
often your sea-spear, beneath the deluge,
 caught a white-bellied salmon on its tine.

This song is clearly a promotional 'puff' for the steamship, and its contents can be compared with those of an advertisement in English which appeared in 1820:

*The Steam-boat **Highland Chieftain**, has already gone as far as the Sound of Skye on this route, for a trial, and performed the passage in the remarkably short space of 35 hours from Glasgow – a distance of 235 miles, notwithstanding she had to stem currents which run so violently in the Sounds of Skye and Mull. She returned in nearly the same time, and encountered with great intrepidity, very severe weather. The track now proposed that this Steam-boat shall run, will be highly gratifying in the summer months, for an excursion.*

The renaming of the *Highland Chieftain*, formerly the *Duke of Wellington* when she was built in 1817, initiated a style of nomenclature which was soon to become characteristic of West Highland steamers owned by Lowland companies. Her new name reflected the prevailing romanticism, in which the Highland chief and his clan basked in the reflected glory of Macpherson's 'Ossian'. As a consequence, across almost two centuries, successive MacBrayne-styled companies have exploited Highland romanticism of this kind in the naming of their ships (as evidenced in the present-day *Clansman* and *Lord of the Isles*, owned by Caledonian MacBrayne). The romantic image of the sword-bearing Highlander has endured as an artistic motif and even as a quasi-figurehead or roundel on the bows of the most modern car-ferries. It is carried by the current *Clansman* (1998) and *Hebrides* (2001), for example.

MacDougall's poem about the *Ben Nevis*, which began to ply northwards to Inverness in 1824, includes graphic description of the ship, both inside and out:

*An early steamship (possibly the **Duke of Wellington**, later renamed **Highland Chieftain**) on the Clyde near Dumbarton, by William Daniell, 1818 [Glasgow University Library]*

Oran don Bhàta-thoite, dan goirear *Beinn Nibheis*

'S mòr an t-ioghnadh leo san rìoghachd,
'S iongantach ri innse an tràth-s' e,
Beinn Nibheis a dh'fhàs cho ìseal
A' falbh le innleachdaibh air sàile,
Eadar Inbhir Nis 's an Crìonan,
'S Glaschu mòr na stìopall àrda;
Cha till frasan, gaoth no sian i,
Braise lìonaidh no sruth tràghaidh.

....

Dh'fhàs i na darach 's na h-iarann,
'S a cliathaichean dìonach, làidir,
Staidhrichean gasd' air am fiaradh
A' dìreadh bho h-ìochdar gu bràighe;
Seòmraichean geala gu h-ìosal
Far an òlar fìon na Spàinte,
'S gach fear as urrainn a phàigheadh,
Gheibh e 'n-siud gach nì gu àilgheas.

'S àrd sna speuraibh chìthear smùid dhith,
'G èirigh suas bhon fhùirneis ghàbhaidh,
'S coireachan goileach a' spùtadh
Air cuibhleachan ùra pràise;
'S gach ball na com is mòr ioghnadh,
Riamh chan fhaca sùil an àicheadh,
'S ge b' e fear a dheilbh air tùs i,
Cò nach tugadh cliù gu bràth dha?

Nuair a thèid i ceart air ghluasad,
'S fada chluinnear fuaim a h-àlaich,
Fairge ga sgoltadh ma guaillean,
Sruth air cuartagan a sàileach,
'S cobhar àrd ga stealladh uaipe
A bàrr nan tonn uaine càir-gheal,
Le neart a h-onfhaidh ga fhuadach
Mu chlachan ruadha na tràghad.

....

'S feumail dhi 'n treun laoch ga stiùireadh,
Neartmhor, dùmhail, lùthsar, làidir,
Bonnanach, somalta, tùrail,
Anns a bheil cùram is nàire;
'S air àirdead 's gun èirich sùghain,
Nach cuir sumbaid às a làraich,
MacLachainn bhon chaisteal chlùiteach
Don dùthchas bhith 'n Earra-Ghàidheal.

Song on the Steamship, which is called **Ben Nevis**

It is a great wonder to people of the kingdom,
And it is strange to relate it at this time,
That **Ben Nevis** has grown so tiny
That it sails by ingenious means on salt water,
Between Inverness and Crinan,
And Glasgow of the lofty steeples;
No showers, wind or storm will turn her back,
Nor the strength of incoming tide or ebb-current.

.....

She grew as oak and iron,
And her sides are watertight and robust,
With fine staircases which curve
As they ascend from her bottom to her top;
White-coloured saloons are below,
Where one can drink the wine of Spain,
And the man who is able to pay it
Will find there everything to please him.

Smoke from her will be seen high in the skies,
Rising from the awesome furnace,
As boiling cauldrons spout [steam]
On to new flywheels made of brass;
Every item in her hull is a great wonder –
Eye has not seen anything to gainsay them –
And whoever it was who first designed her,
Who would not praise him for ever?

When she gets properly under way,
The noise of her propulson will be heard afar,
Sea being sliced about her shoulders,
And a current created by the eddies of her stern,
As she sends foam high and splashing,
From the tops of the green, white-crested waves,
Which is driven by the strength of her surging,
As far as the brown stones of the shoreline.

....

She has need of the brave hero to steer her,
Powerful, thick-set, energetic, strong,
Well-built, good-natured, sensible,
Who has a sense of responsibility and care;
And, however high the surges rise,
Who will not be knocked off his feet by a billow;
[He is] MacLachlan from the famous castle,
Whose native place is in Argyll.

Eiridh am fear-iùil na toiseach,
Nuair a chì e coltas gàbhaidh,
A' glaodhach ri laoch na stiùire,
'Glèidh do chùrsa mar a tha e;
Lean do ghabhail dìreach romhad,
Tha mhuir coimheach ruinn an-dràsda;
Cùm a ceann ri sùil an fhuaraidh,
'S cuirear tuilleadh guail san àmhainn.'

Feasgar anmoch tighinn bhon linnidh,
Dol gu caladh 'n ionad sàmhach,
A' leigeadh a h-acraichean sa ghrinneal,
Ceangal *Beinn Nibheis* le càbaill;
'S cridheil, sunndach, 's mùirneach gillean,
Sùrd air mire 's air ceòl-gàire,
Greis air òrain, òl is iomairt
Aig na seòid as binne mànran.

An Caiptean Bàn an sàr dhuin'-uasal,
Maladh gun ghruaim, gruaidh as àilte,
Sgiobair fearail ri àm cruadail,
Cridhe stuama, suairce, càirdeil;
'S an latha thachair sinn shuas ud,
Anns an uair sin ghabh e bàidh rium,
'S ged a bhiodh mo chceann air cluasaig,
Chuirinn mun cuairt a dheoch-slàinte.

The pilot will stand up in her bow,
When he sees a sign of tempest,
Calling to the hero at the helm,
'Keep your course steady as it is;
Maintain your passage straight ahead,
The sea is surly to us at the moment;
Hold her head directly to windward,
And let more coal be put in the furnace.'

Late of an evening coming in from the firth,
She goes to harbour in a peaceful spot,
Dropping her anchors in the bottom gravel,
Which hold **Ben Nevis** *with cables;*
Cheery, happy, hearty are the lads,
Full of energetic fun and laughter,
With spells at songs, and drink, and gaming –
Those heroes of the choicest conversation.

Captain Bain is the splendid gentleman,
With brow unfurrowed, and finest cheek,
A manly skipper in time of hardship,
With a modest heart, generous and friendly;
On the day that we met up yonder,
In that very hour he was well disposed to me,
And though my head were on a pillow,
I would circulate his health-drink.

The vignettes of the helmsman, who would have to be very strong to handle the tiller of such vessels, and the pilot are particularly illuminating. As early steamships were steered from the stern, usually by means of rudder and tiller or wheel, and not from a bridge placed amidships (which was a later post-1850 development), it was essential to have a look-out posted at the bow, who could advise the helmsman on any immediate dangers and the state of weather and tide. The word-picture of the *Ben Nevis* coming to anchor in a secluded harbour in the evening evokes a gentle, relaxing spirit, as does the allusion to the fun and good humour of her sailors. The esteem in which the Masters of such vessels were held is evident also. The poet treats Captain Bain as if he were a bardic patron from an earlier era, whose 'favour' was keenly sought, and who is described with the standard epithets used of clan chiefs. Master Mariners long remained the 'local heroes' of seagoing communities, fulfilling, alongside ministers and schoolmasters, the leadership roles of earlier clan chiefs and tacksmen.

Even if they were an alien intrusion into the region, and rendered acceptable only by the special pleading and rhetoric of the poets, the first steamships in Highland waters embraced features of Highland society which gave them a distinctive ambience. MacDougall, in describing the *Benlomond*, draws attention to the piper who played on board the ship:

'S binn sa mhadainn bhith dar dùsgadh
Le pìob mhòr nam feadan siùbhlach;
Uilleam Rothach nam meur lùthmhor
Chuireadh sunnd fo ghillean òga.

Sweet in the morning our being wakened
By the great pipe of nimble chanters;
William Munro of the energetic fingers
Who would make young fellows happy.

The piper was common on such vessels. He was, to some extent, the equivalent of the 'tannoy' of present-day ships, announcing the departure of the vessel and piping passengers on board, as well as intimating meal-times and other events in the ship's routine. The piper also had the ability to set feet dancing, and to evoke an atmosphere of joviality and celebration.

By 1828, the first steamships were reaching out to the islands on much more ambitious voyages, as confidence in their performance increased, though such confidence was not always fully justified, given the likelihood of boiler explosions and wreckings. Allan MacDougall provides an early indicator of a developing network of steamer services, which was to become an integral part of Highland life by the mid-century:

Chuir iad *Beinn Nibheis* do Leòdhas,
An *Ceann-cinnidh* sìos do Chrombaigh;
'S i *Beinn Laomainn* le siubhal fonnmhor
A choisneas an geall san Oban.

*They sent **Ben Nevis** to Lewis,*
*And **Chieftain** down to Cromarty;*
*It is **Benlomond** with her tuneful progress*
That will win the prize in Oban.

As regular services were developed, passenger numbers increased, and tourists began to take advantage of the opportunity to view the sublimities and peculiarities of the Highlands and Islands. There was, however, scant reporting in the English media of the early steamers' activities, other than in occasional advertisements, such as the following – aimed at tourists – from a June 1828 edition of the *Glasgow Herald*:

Highlander: *from Glasgow every Monday for Oban, Tobermory and Staffa;*

Maid of Morven: *from Glasgow every Thursday for Oban and Inverness;*

Benlomond: *from Tobermory every Monday for Strontian and the Spar cave in Skye;*

Ben Nevis: *from Glasgow Broomielaw every second Tuesday for Stornoway.*

Soon, even St Kilda was within the range of the larger steamships, as is indicated by a notice printed by the Glasgow publisher, W. R. McPhun, in 1835. It contains the following paragraph:

*All the Steam Vessels call at Greenock and Port Glasgow both going and coming. The **Glen Albyne** [sic], **Foyle** and **St Columb**, during the summer months make some delightful pleasure excursions round all the West Coast, stopping a few hours for the accommodation of tourists at each place. No person who comes to Scotland for pleasure should lose the opportunity thus afforded them of viewing at little cost and in little time the most delightful scenery in Scotland. These vessels touch at St Kilda, Iona, Caulin [sic] Hills, Spar Cave, Skye, Giant's Causeway, Campbeltown, Jura, Islay, Sound of Mull etc, etc.*

The *Glen Albyn* had reached St Kilda by 1834, and a West Highland 'cruise route', embracing the key sights of the 'Ossianic grand tour', had come into existence.

By the late 1820s and early 1830s, travellers like J. E. Bowman and G. C. Atkinson were venturing bravely northwards from the Lowlands and from England, and trying out the ships. Several recorded their impressions in diaries and contemporary journals, such as the influential Edinburgh publication, *Blackwood's Magazine*. Distinguished figures, such as the German composer, Felix Mendelssohn, the English artist, J. M. W. Turner, and the Lakeland poet, William Wordsworth, also took the steamer to Fingal's Cave, in 1829, 1830 and 1833 respectively, and they produced their celebrated reflections in their distinctive media.

IN SEARCH OF THE SUBLIME

THE WORD 'SUBLIME' is seldom used nowadays. When it is, it is usually in the sense of 'extremely beautiful, surpassingly splendid'. In the eighteenth and nineteenth centuries, however, the word meant much more than that. As defined by Edmund Burke (1757) and later philosophers, it encapsulated a way of responding to the world, and especially the wilder aspects of nature. 'The Sublime' was to be found in large-scale natural phenomena, such as volcanoes, mountains, cliffs, tumbling waterfalls and lonely landscapes. These inspired awe and, often, terror in the observer. The Sublime intermingled with 'primitivism', the notion that people at an earlier stage of development were noble beings, unpolluted by progress. The Sublime was at the heart of James Macpherson's presentation of the Highlands of Scotland in his 'translations' of Gaelic epic verse, featuring a hero named Fingal, king of Morven. Fingal's son, Ossian, was believed to have been a great, heroic poet. Macpherson's 'translations', published between 1760 and 1763, claimed to be the work of Ossian, and they are generally known nowadays as 'Macpherson's "Ossian"'.

Tourism in the Scottish Highlands and Islands began very largely in response to Macpherson's 'Ossian'. Visitors wanted to see the land where Fingal and his heroes had lived, and pre-eminently its remotest parts. The first tourists who patronised the early steamships were usually going in search of Ossianic sublimity. St Kilda and Staffa were much-favoured destinations, as their natural formations of towering cliffs and basalt pillars inspired the sense of awe which lay at the heart of the Sublime.

Steamships, however, were not a natural phenomenon. They were unnatural, in being man-made. They were also dirty and sooty, and thus contrasted with the purity and beauty of the Sublime. Gradually, however, the notion of the Sublime was transferred to engineering. By the mid-nineteenth century, engineers such as Isambard Kingdom Brunel were pursuing the Sublime in the building of very large steamships like the *Great Eastern*, which certainly inspired awe and wonder in her own day. The desire to build enormous objects intensified as mechanical skills developed in the course of the nineteenth century. Ocean liners were a key area in which human endeavour of this kind could be worked out.

By the late nineteenth century, the quest for the Sublime was influencing the shape and furnishings of ships, as well as their size. Ocean liners not only became huge and externally beautiful objects; they were also turned into floating palaces, initially by designers working for German companies. The concept of the cruise yacht, elegant and sleek externally, and beautifully equipped internally, was indebted to the Sublime. Ships were made to match the anticipated experience, because the senses were aided in conceptualising the Sublime by entering magnificent, sea-going castles or country houses, set apart from normal human activity. Cruise ships, large and small, are the consequence of a residual sense of the Sublime, though floating casinos, malls and cinemas are now more appealing than country style. Names such as *Ocean Odyssey*, *Chieftain*, or *Hebridean Princess* affirm the special nature of both ship and cruise.

The search for the Sublime in the Highlands and Islands was a key factor in opening the area to tourism, and it contributed to the development of steamships as a means of conveyance. Well into the twentieth century, the idea of the Sublime can be detected in the advertising materials of shipping companies active in the region.

Tourists usually offered a much less romantic view of the steamers than did the Gaelic poets. In 1825, J. E. Bowman was horrified when he encountered the *Ben Nevis* at Oban, and discovered chaos on her decks:

> Her deck presented such a scene of tumult and disorder that we were at a loss to assign the cause. She was altogether so unsteady, that her wheels were lifted alternately out of the water.

The author goes on to note that the ship's Master was drunk! The problem with the paddle-wheels was a hazard with all early paddlers, as adverse weather conditions could cause a ship to heel badly to one side or the other. On this occasion, the *Ben Nevis* was carrying 280 passengers – a remarkable number for such a small ship – because the second *Comet* was out of action with engine trouble.

George Clayton Atkinson from Newcastle, who visited the Hebrides in 1831 and 1833, encountered the *Highland Chieftain* on his second visit when she was moored at the Broomielaw:

> We also went down to the Broomie Law, a long, busy, crowded quay, like our own canny Quayside, to inspect **the Highland Chieftain** which is destined to convey us to Stornoway. To me it was an old friend, as I had partaken of its accommodation and dis-accommodation in visiting some of the Hebrides two years since, and I hinted to Cookson [his travelling companion] that his eye seemed engaged in looking for it among vessels of too magnificent an aspect – I was scanning the second and third rates. I ought to explain that as she takes the short cut to the Islands through the Crinan Canal, instead of round the

The celebrated painting, 'Fingal's Cave', by the renowned English artist, Joseph Turner, showing the **Maid of Morven** *smoking darkly to the west of Staffa [Yale Center for British Art]*

Mull of Kintyre, *she must of necessity be so small as to pass the locks of the canal…One consequence of her smallness is that she has no sleeping room, but lands her passengers every night at different stations for that purpose – a misery or not according to taste.*

Atkinson's own taste was severely challenged when he reached Oban, and found land and ship in unhappy contradiction of one another. He observed

a fine open bay…ornamented by a white picturesque mass of houses upon its shore at its centre…running out to the north is a fine woody point on which stands Dunally Castle!…Our vile, small undignified Steamer stopped here to renew its stock of coals, and we, hungry and dinnerless, rambled on shore, (and) the while(s) sketched

TURNER, STAFFA AND THE *MAID OF MORVEN*

THE QUEST FOR the Sublime put the Inner Hebrides firmly on the tourist map of Scotland from the late eighteenth century. A special place was afforded to the islands of Iona and Staffa, and both became an integral part of tourist itineraries from 1800 to the present. The basalt columns of Staffa were a particularly powerful magnet, attracting a remarkable succession of dignitaries and famous visitors in the 1820s and 1830s, including Queen Victoria in 1833. Leading musical, literary and artistic figures of the early nineteenth century were drawn strongly to Staffa. Among them were the German musical composer, Felix Mendelssohn, who visited the island by steamship in 1829, and subsequently composed his celebrated 'Hebrides Overture'; the poet William Wordsworth, who arrived in the island in 1833, and put his sentiments into verse; and the artist, Joseph Turner. For all three, Staffa was a source of inspiration and further creative endeavour.

Joseph Turner's depiction of the island is especially noteworthy. Turner visited Scotland in July 1830, at the request of Walter Scott's publisher, Robert Cadell, who believed that the collected edition of Scott's poems would be all the more successful if it contained illustrations by Turner. Turner was somewhat reluctant to visit Scotland, given the difficulties of travel, but he was gradually persuaded. The Ossianic 'grand tour' was attractive, and so too was the prospect of the steamship. 'When I get as far as Loch Katrine, I shall not like to turn back without Staffa, and Mull and all. A steamboat is now established to the Western Isles, so I have heard lately, and therefore much of the difficulty becomes removed…'

Turner was conveyed to Staffa from Tobermory by the steamship, *Maid of Morven*, and recorded his adventure thus:

> After scrambling over the rocks on the lee side of the island, some got into Fingal's cave, others would not. It is not very pleasant or safe when the wave rolls right in. One hour was given to meet on the rock we landed on. When on board, the Captain declared it doubtful about Iona. Such a rainy and bad-looking night coming on, a vote was proposed to the passengers: "Iona at all hazards, or back to Tobermoray." Majority against proceeding. To allay the displeased, the Captain promised to steam thrice round the island in the last trip. The sun getting towards the horizon, burst through the rain-cloud, angry, and for wind; and so it proved, for we were driven for shelter into Loch Ulver [*recte* Ulva], and did not get back to Tobermoray before midnight.

In 1832 Turner produced a well-known, impressionistic painting which relates very closely to his written account. It shows the *Maid of Morven* sailing to the west of Staffa, smoke belching from her tall stack and matching the stormy darkness of the sea as night closed in. By contrast, Staffa itself is portrayed as a source of radiant light, its physical shape only faintly delineated and almost losing its identity in the deepening gloom. As a romantic typical of his time, Turner evidently regarded the steamship as a dark intruder, useful to travellers but in conflict with the sublimely beautiful qualities of the region. This corresponds to the views of writers such as the Rev. Dr Norman MacLeod in his Gaelic account of the *Maid of Morven* – the only Hebridean steamer of the time caught by both the author's pen and the artist's brush.

> *blackguard children…till recalled to the boat by the most indefatigable ringing of a badly toned bell, and a long column of insurgent steam.*

It is only fair to note that both Bowman and Atkinson had happier experiences on other vessels – Bowman on the *Highlander*, which conveyed him safely from the Clyde to Staffa and Fingal's Cave, though her Captain too had difficulty in preserving 'the proper equilibrium' of the vessel, and Atkinson on the *Maid of Islay* in 1831.

Native Highlanders were likewise ready to provide their impressions. The Rev. Dr Norman MacLeod, a native of Morvern and minister of Campsie, and also the editor of the first Gaelic literary journals, penned an important description of a voyage in a steamship – the *Maid of Morven* which later conveyed Turner to Fingal's Cave. It was published in Gaelic in 1829, and is the fullest account known of a vessel of this kind. His work was much influenced by the genres in *Blackwood's*. MacLeod imagined a rustic passenger, Finlay the Piper, writing a Gaelic letter to his wife, and describing a voyage from Morvern to Glasgow on the *Maid of Morven*, built in 1826 for Archibald McEachern and the Maid of Morven Steamboat Company, but owned by Robert Napier from 1835. The piece was first published in *An Teachdaire Gaelach* in 1829. Among many other valuable insights, his pen provides an initial glimpse of a ritual later to be known on the Clyde as 'going to see the engines' (with implications of lubrication beyond the purely mechanical):

> *'Come with me,' [said Para Mòr to Finlay the Piper], 'to take a look at the guts of this very Maid, to see if we can understand how the ingenious device functions.' But if we went, dear Mary, what a kerfuffle we saw there! Iron beams and rods moving over and back, up and down, backwards*

and forwards, without ceasing, without stopping; pulleys and forks and notches responding to one another. Little wheels going full speed round the big wheels. A poor man down among the gear, perspiring steamily, where you would not imagine that a mouse could venture without being disfigured; but he was moving in the midst of the commotion as fearlessly as Para Mòr or myself would go among the sheep; greasing every piece of equipment, joints, swivels and ducts, with oil and butter. 'Poor man,' said Para Mòr, 'I certainly do not envy you your place; you earn your bread dearly.' 'Why?' said he, turning up his eyes which were swimming in sweat. Though the iron levering-rod that he had in his hand should have spoken, this would not have caused us greater wonder than when we heard this man speaking Gaelic. 'Did I not think,' said Para Mòr, 'that he was an Englishman, or an Irishman, or a poor Lowlander.' He came up, wiping the sweat from his face with a hemp rag which was in his hand, and he began to give us an opinion of the equipment. But, my dear, that was a complete waste of effort. 'Don't you think, Para Mòr,' said I, 'that there was real ingenuity in the head that first thought of this?' 'I have no time for himself or his ingenuity,' said Para Mòr. 'This ingenious device itself is unnatural and sinful, defying the current and wind of Providence, going against them without sail, without oar.'

The notion that this wind-defying, steam vessel and others like her were in conflict with the laws of nature, and consequently 'of the Devil', was commonly held at the time.

Among the *Maid's* motley collection of passengers, Finlay the Piper noted clan chiefs and upper-crust toffs, as well as the token 'rude' Englishman of such narratives:

Who was in the stern of the ship but Red-haired Alasdair Mac an Abraich, the Laird of Coll. He noticed me, and he beckoned to me – I did not dare to refuse him – there were many toffs down there with him on the quarter-deck of the ship: English folk, Lowlanders and French folk. Some of them reading, some sleeping, some yawning, some eating.

One of them [had] a long, fancy telescope to his eye, as if he were going to fire at Duart Castle; I noticed a tall, thin, sallow-complexioned man with a monacle on his nose and a red stick in his hand with which he was drawing a picture of the castle. There was a large, posh noblewoman among them with a poor, wee, hairy yapper of a dog on her lap, which she was fondling and kissing; and there were two young maids with her who wore something that I had never seen before, white trousers of linen, under the rest of their clothes. I myself brought out the pipes as they asked, but the first blast they gave, all of them fled except one big, fat Englishman who sat in front of me with his two fingers in his ears, and with a scowl as if I were going to eat him.

As this evocation of the *Maid of Morven* seeks to demonstrate, the early steamship is very much a microcosm of the stratified and class-conscious society of its own time. Passengers reflect the social scales and values within which the vessel operates, and these scales and values alter across the century. Some levelling of social distinctions is evident, even in 1829, as a clan chief converses with an 'ordinary' Highlander on the quarter-deck. Other differences, however, emerge. Tourists are already evident in 1829, but they are very obviously a different 'breed' from native Highlanders. Within a decade of its introduction, the steamship was opening the door to a new view of Highland scenery, but it was also facilitating social restructuring and new economic potential within the region.

Soon the steamship was appropriated conceptually by the 'ordinary' people of the Highlands and Islands, who, like MacLeod's rustic travellers, patronised it regularly in their desire to find employment in the Lowlands. As its economic benefits became apparent, Highlanders came to believe that they had some sort of controlling interest in it. As time passed, the people made it 'their' ship, serving 'their' part of the Highlands and Islands, for good or ill. The ship thus entered the deepest levels of Highland – and Gaelic – popular awareness.

Half a century of purposeful development was to pass

before David MacBrayne rose to prominence. By 1900, he had become a Highland hero, 'one of ourselves', worthy of a place in the pantheon of Highland benefactors, despite the Lowland affiliations of the successive companies which bore his name, and their ambivalent contribution to the social transformation of this economically volatile region. In 1850, however, David was only at the beginning of his career. The foundational glory for the creation of what became MacBrayne's West Highland fleet belongs to another David – David Hutcheson.

CHAPTER 2

ENERGY AND ENTERPRISE:
DAVID HUTCHESON & COMPANY

*The **Isle of Mull** enters Oban Bay, and passes the memorial on Kerrera to David Hutcheson [Rhoda Meek]*

ENERGY AND ENTERPRISE:
DAVID HUTCHESON & COMPANY

It is almost impossible to estimate the amount of good which has been conferred on the Highlands by the enterprise of the firm of which Mr. Hutcheson was the moving spirit. Not only has the value of property been increased, but the blessings of social improvement have been brought within reach of the thousands who people the shores of its beautiful bays and lochs, who also enjoy the advantage of convenient and economical intercourse between their once remote hamlets and the great centres of industry; benefits which will extend to the Highlands of the future a prosperity far more real and enduring than can ever be attained through the varied philosophies of Land and Socialistic Reform.
FROM *MEMOIRS AND PORTRAITS OF ONE HUNDRED GLASGOW MEN*

The formation of David Hutcheson & Company in February 1851 coincided with the beginning of a relatively stable period in the economy of the Highlands and Islands – an uneasy calm after a storm which still had sufficient residual energy to create strong, disabling eddies. The notorious 'Clearances' had been at their height during the first half of the century, and sheep were now grazing in many places where people and their subsistence plots once stood. After 1850, the tide of economic change was less severe, but the upheaval consequent upon the potato famine of 1846 had uprooted many islanders. This generated a steady stream of potential emigrants, awaiting their opportunity to re-establish themselves overseas, particularly in Australia.

This 'quieter' phase in Highland history was matched by a realignment of steamer services. Thomson & MacConnell had retired in 1850 from both the West Highland trade and their interests in the Irish Sea, leaving G. & J. Burns in sole charge. The Burns brothers in turn decided that their empire had become too unwieldy, and took the decision to shed the less profitable West Highland services in order to concentrate on the Irish Sea cross-channel and coastal routes. The new company was placed in the charge of the brothers, David and Alexander Hutcheson, and their younger partner, David MacBrayne.

For the Highlands and Islands, emigration was a double-edged weapon, depleting resources on the one hand, but stimulating new and beneficial support-structures of long-term significance on the other. Steamer operators were able to turn the adverse tide to their advantage. Once the immediate exigencies of the potato famine had been met and the disaster had bottomed out, the ongoing exodus of Highland people probably encouraged David Hutcheson to establish steamer services to, and particularly from, key areas of population displacement.

There were, as yet, no regular steamer services from the Scottish mainland to the Outer Hebrides. Services, such as they were, concentrated on the west coast and the more accessible islands, usually those nearest the mainland. Skye, for example, was comparatively well served by David Hutcheson's steamers from 1851, with the *Cygnet*, *Lapwing* and *Duntroon Castle* plying the West Highland route from the Broomielaw, and sailing via the Sound of Mull as far north as Portree. These vessels transported emigrants as well as other passengers in the early 1850s.

Emigration, it must be remembered, was assisted by landlords in certain districts, and the relationship between landlords and shipowners must have guaranteed a steady traffic for steamships. Some landlords themselves acquired ships which soon became part of the developing steamer network. James Matheson, proprietor of Lewis, built the iron paddle-steamer *Mary Jane* as his own yacht in 1846, but circumstances soon encouraged him to use her for the public good. In February 1847, Matheson employed the *Mary Jane* to transport, free of charge, seasonal migrants from the Hebrides to the Broomielaw – between 200 and 300 young men from Lewis, Harris and Skye. For such acts of generosity, Matheson was knighted. In 1851 Matheson sold the *Mary Jane* to the Glasgow & Lochfyne Steam Packet Company. Later, as Hutcheson's *Glencoe*, she was used

DAVID HUTCHESON (1799-1880)

DAVID HUTCHESON AND his brother Alexander were born in Inverkeithing, Fife. Their connection with the west coast of Scotland was formed when their father moved to Port Glasgow, where he established a cooperage. He died shortly thereafter. It is said that David's mother was 'a conscientious Scottish woman, who in the midst of a hard struggle gave him the rudiments of a sound education, which in his early manhood he improved and extended by his own love of knowledge.'

Initially David followed in his late father's footsteps, finding employment as a clerk in Steel's cooperage in Port Glasgow. In 1817, however, he made what was to be a strategically important decision to leave the cooperage, and join a shipping firm which owned two small steamships, *Industry* and *Trusty*, plying between Glasgow, Port Glasgow and Greenock. Several years later, Hutcheson accepted a position with the Glasgow and Leith Shipping Company at Port Dundas. Thereafter he was employed by a Mr Kid, who was agent to Mathie & Theakstone, owners of a fleet of Liverpool smacks. On Kid's death, the agency passed to the Burns brothers, who 'assumed Mr. Hutcheson as manager with a share in the profits.' In 1851 Hutcheson became the owner of the Highland

dimension of the Burns' fast-expanding business.

In addition to his skills in shipping management, David Hutcheson is said to have been 'a man of refined culture, courteous and genial, alike to the prince and the peasant; a lover of literature; a liberal patron of the fine arts; fond of music, and an enthusiastic admirer of our great national bard, whose songs and poems he used to recite.' He himself was also something of a poet, and recorded in verse his wish to be buried in the Oban area:

For I would wish my bones to lie
Among the scenes I loved so well;
The mountain glen, the gorgeous sky,
The wimpling burn, the gowany dell.
And where were sepulchre more sweet
For me than 'mong dear Oban's braes,
Where oft in contemplation sweet
I, rambling, tuned my simple lays.

On his death his wishes were respected, and he was buried in Pennyfuir cemetery, outside Oban. His wife (née Dawson) had connections with Linlithgow and Glasgow. She died in 1885.

Three years after his death, an obelisk in memory of David Hutcheson was erected on the eastern edge of the island of Kerrera, looking across to Dunollie Castle

and commanding the narrow entrance to Oban Bay, which has given passage to successive generations of red-funnelled West Highland ships. The memorial carries the inscription: 'Erected by a grateful public in memory of David Hutcheson by whose energy and enterprise the benefits of greatly improved steam navigation were conferred on the West Highlands and Islands of Scotland. 1883.'

(Summarised from *Memoirs and Portraits of One Hundred Glasgow Men*.)

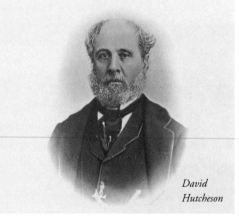

David Hutcheson

to transport emigrants from other parts of the Hebrides, including Tiree. At least partly as a result of island-mainland linkages by steamship, the number of emigrant ships which sailed overseas directly from Hebridean harbours, such as Portree and Tobermory, appears to have declined sharply after 1850, in favour of departures from more southerly mainland ports, such as Campbeltown and Greenock.

The poignant practicalities of the emigrant trade, assisted by steamships, were noted by contemporary observers. The Raasay House Weather Tables record the arrival of cargoes such as 'shoes for emigrants in a large package' on the *Duntroon Castle* in March 1852, and they note that emigrants from Raasay travelled on the *Islay* (May and June 1852), the *Cygnet* (June 1852) and the *Duntroon Castle* (July

1852). These emigrants were bound for Australia. Those who travelled in June and early July 1852 were almost certainly part of the large contingent who sailed from Greenock to Australia on the *Georgiana*. Others were to follow. On 6 June 1854, 'the *Chevalier* put into the bay at 4 pm and took on Board 129 Raasay People Emigrants to Australia'. The chill wind of emigration was now supplementng the hot air of Ossianic tourism, and something approaching a proper steamship network was coming into existence in the West Highlands and Hebrides.

This network was developed initially by means of the steamers which David Hutcheson & Company had inherited from the Burns brothers. This inheritance comprised the paddle steamers *Curlew*, *Cygnet*, *Dolphin*, *Duntroon Castle*,

Edinburgh Castle, *Lapwing* and *Pioneer*, and also the *Shandon* which had previously belonged to Thomson & MacConnell's City of Glasgow Steam Packet Company. Of these, the *Shandon* was of wood construction, with a primitive single-cylinder, side-lever engine. The remainder of the sea-going vessels had iron hulls and steeple engines. The *Duntroon Castle* excelled in having two cylinders rather than the simple single-cylinder arrangement. In addition, there were the two iron-hulled track-boats, *Maid of Perth* and *Sunbeam*, on the Crinan Canal in summer months, both being relatively young. It was the *Sunbeam* that had conveyed Queen Victoria along her Royal Route in 1847 in the charge of three horses ridden by 'scarlet-clad postillions'.

The deployment of the remainder of the Hutcheson fleet was as follows:

- The Glasgow-Crinan Canal-Inverness route via the Sound of Mull was serviced by the sisters *Cygnet* and *Lapwing*. They were peculiar-looking ships, with a rounded bow that could nose through the canal lock gates. They had sponsons which ran the length of the hull, and were designed to protect the paddle-wheels.
- The *Duntroon Castle* serviced the Glasgow to Oban, Tobermory and Portree route which seasonally also included the Gairloch.
- The *Edinburgh Castle* and *Curlew* were on the Caledonian Canal as part of the Fort William to Inverness mail-coach and steamer route.
- The summer-only Crinan to Oban service was undertaken by the *Shandon*.
- The *Dolphin* was based at Oban and her roster included the summer-only Iona

The **Chevalier** [NR's collection]

and Staffa round trips.
- The *Pioneer* was on the Glasgow to Ardrishaig service.

The new company decided to embark on a programme of fleet renewal during its very first season. This programme was innovative in the extreme, and soon led to the development of a series of crack steamers, the like of which the world had not previously seen. The company also had eyes on expanding its services to include the Outer Hebrides by the provision of a regular schedule.

The first of the new ships was the *Mountaineer*. She was launched at Govan in May 1852, and that summer took over the Ardrishaig service from the *Pioneer*. The *Pioneer* in turn displaced the *Shandon* at Oban; the *Shandon* was sold in 1853, and voyaged as far as Australia and North Asia before she was broken up in 1865. The *Mountaineer* was the first of a series of crack ships designed for the Ardrishaig tourist route. Her bow and stern were decorated with gilded carving work, and she was flush-decked, but, unlike earlier steamers, she had two imposing funnels. Her public rooms were finely adorned yet comfortable, and the new ship immediately became popular with the 'doon the watter' brigade. Although she was the last steamer in the fleet to be equipped with a steeple engine, she was nevertheless fit for 15 knots. Subsequent ships benefited from the increased power afforded by the simple oscillating engine. The compound engine, in which one cylinder exhausted into a second, bigger cylinder, did not appear until the late 1870s.

The first steamer with oscillating engines was the *Chevalier*, which followed off the stocks in 1853. She was designed with

HORROR ON A STEAMSHIP

STEAMSHIPS WERE USED as tenders to convey Highland emigrants to the large sailing-ships which were destined to take them to Canada and Australia. Because of her ability to sail in bad weather – a practice encouraged by agents who were determined to obtain their full complement of emigrants – a steamship sometimes added an agonising first stage to the uncertainties and dangers of the impending, long journey.

In December 1852, the paddle-steamer *Celt*, owned by the Campbeltown & Glasgow Steam Packet Joint Stock Company Limited, transported islanders to the sailing-ship *Hercules*, lying at Campbeltown and destined for Australia on what turned out to be a particularly dreadful voyage. The *Celt*, operating in conjunction with the *Islay*, made several trips to Skye and the Outer Isles. On the first of her trips, she was forced to seek shelter in Skye, before crossing to the Outer Hebrides. The dolefully-named James Chant, the officer of the Emigration Commission who arranged the voyage, writing from the Birkenhead Depot on 3 January 1853, recorded what happened when the *Celt* left the shelter of Skye:

> We weighed anchor on Monday morning at half-past 10, and proceeded on our voyage. The gale had not at all abated, and the sea was running very high. The steamer was kept head to wind for about eleven miles, to obtain an offing round Cocknehow Point, which caused her to pitch heavily and to ship some very heavy seas. One tremendous sea struck us on the starboard quarter, carried away part of the paddle-box, blew up the watercloset, carried away the binnacle, knocked the man from the wheel and broke two of his ribs, sent the water casks and everything else on decks adrift, and threw the pilot and myself under the starboard bulwarks.

The *Celt*, regarded by Chant as 'a capital seaboat', reached Lochmaddy, and then sailed north to Finsbay in Harris. Having loaded her first batch of emigrants, she returned to Lochmaddy. Chant wrote that he found 'all the emigrants (95) had been collected by Captain MacDonald of Rodil, Lady Dunmore's Agent, and that he had made every preparation in his power to facilitate the shipment of the people and their luggage. The embarkation was effected in boats in about three hours, during a heavy storm of wind and rain.' He further described the leave-taking at Finsbay for the benefit of the Emigration Commissioners:

> The leave taking was the most painful scene I ever witnessed[;] sturdy Highlanders grasped each other by the hand, whilst the muscles of their faces and bodies quivered with emotion. Women hung on the necks of friends, and were in some cases removed by force[;] to say they sobbed aloud would faintly express their sorrow. It would be difficult perhaps impossible, to describe it. As the vessel steamed out of the bay they stood on the poop, threw their arms in the air giving full vent of their grief, as they gazed for the last time on the black peaty glen and bleak rocky hills, over which they had long been accustomed to roam, and to which they were so devotedly attached.

Because of bad weather, and the possibility that the

50 sleeping berths for the Glasgow-Oban-Skye service, making numerous intermediate stops, including occasional calls at Stornoway. The *Chevalier* operated in partnership with the steamer *Islay*. The latter belonged to the Islay landlord, John Ramsay of Kildalton, and remained outside the Hutchesons' clutches until finally taken over in 1876. The *Chevalier* fared less well, being wrecked in the Sound of Jura in November 1854. She was succeeded by the first *Clansman* in 1855. This was the ship which put the Outer Hebrides firmly into regular Hutcheson schedules, by calling at the Long Island on her round trip from Glasgow via Oban and Skye, although the *Chevalier* had inaugurated the Stornoway call in 1853.

The growth and consolidation of West Highland steamer services in the 1850s are evident in the splendid account of a voyage on the *Clansman*, undertaken by Alexander Smith in 1865. Smith was yet another Ossianic enthusiast in pursuit of the Sublime, which he discovered in Skye. In his writing, the *Clansman* is presented without any sense of wonder at her machinery or design, and in this respect Smith's account contrasts sharply with that of the Rev. Dr Norman MacLeod forty years earlier (see Chapter 1). The ship is no longer a grotesque phenomenon, but a naturalised part of the west coast, providing an arterial highway for a range of travellers. She calls in at various ports, effortlessly crosses the Sound of Sleat, takes on wool in Loch Nevis, and jousts with the Mull of Kintyre on the final leg of her voyage to Greenock. Smith provides a cameo of the passengers and other occupants of her deck-space:

> *A lot of sheep were penned up near the bows, amidships were piles of wool, groups of pointers and setters were scattered about and at the breakfast-table were numerous sportsmen returning to the south, whose conversation ran on grouse-shooting, salmon-fishing and deer-stalking....*

Celt might not be able to return for remaining emigrants, Chant had to exceed the number of passengers (242) which the ship's sea-going certificate permitted her to carry. This was permissible under such circumstances, with the agreement of a ship's officer.

Chant related the ferocity and the consequences of the storm which struck the *Celt* on leaving Lochmaddy:

On Friday morning, the 9th of December, we left Lochmaddy at 10 o' clock, with 350 passengers of all ages, wind west-south-west blowing a gale with a heavy sea on the beam. In the course of a short time the people became very sick, especially the women, who were much alarmed at the rolling of the vessel, and they shrieked dreadfully every time the sea struck us. Depression of spirits and exhaustion, produced by sea sickness [and] brought on by hysteria, (and) rendered strong stimulants necessary. By the application of vinegar to the head, warm water to the feet and a liberal use of hot brandy and water, some soon recovered; but there were others who were unconscious for hours, and required mustard to the soles of the feet. Even this strong remedy was very slow in giving relief. At noon it blew a hurricane, and we were obliged to run for Canna harbour, which we made a little before dark. The women suffered greatly during the night, and required constant attention.

The weather was a little more moderate on Saturday morning but the sea was still running very high. We left Canna soon after daylight and made Oban at 5 o' clock in the afternoon. Here we were detained to replenish our coals. The people were all very sick again this day and required stimulants frequently. Many of the women voided blood which caused me great anxiety.

Eventually, on Sunday morning, the *Celt* left Oban, and she was in Campbeltown by 3.00 p.m. Chant wrote: 'The emigrants were transshipped, and arranged their berths before night, and expressed themselves very thankfully for the accommodation provided for them. The successful result of the first trip was very gratifying to me and I felt considerable relief that the most dangerous and difficult part of the duty had been accomplished.'

For the hapless emigrants, however, the 'result' was not exactly 'successful'. The ship's surgeon, unlike Mr Chant, saw a different picture when the emigrants reached Campbeltown: 'The greater proportion on imbarkation was exceedingly dirty and very many prostrated by excessive sea sickness.' Shortly after leaving Campbeltown on 26 December, the *Hercules* ran into bad weather, and had to make harbour in Rothesay. By 31 December, an outbreak of smallpox had been reported, 'supposed to have been introduced into [the] ship by a boy from the Isle of Skye'. As the illness spread, the ship was diverted to Queenstown (now Cobh, near Cork) in Ireland, where only half of her passenger complement (originally 756) re-embarked – 'this great diminution in the number to be attributed to death, those still sick at the hospital and the friends of those sick unwilling to leave without them.'

Leaving Queenstown on 14 April, the *Hercules* eventually reached Australia on 26 July 1853, after a voyage which has gone down in history as one of the worst of its kind. To this, the steamship *Celt*, and in particular the grim determination of the emigrant agents to transport their human cargo, come hell or high water, doubtless made a significant contribution.

SOURCE: W. B. Clarke, 'H.M.S. "Hercules": Scottish Emigrant Ship', published privately (Bicheno, Tasmania).

There were drovers going to, or returning from, markets; merchants from Stornoway going south; a couple of Hebridean clergymen, one of whom said grace; several military men of frank and hearty bearing; an extensive brewer; three members of Parliament who had entirely recovered from the fatigues of legislation; and a tall and handsome English Earl of some repute on the turf. Several ladies, too, dropped in before the meal was over…

The morning and forenoon wore away pleasantly – the great ceremony of dinner was ahead and drawing nearer every moment – that was something – and then there were frequent stoppages and the villages on the shore; the coming and going of boats with cargo and passengers, the throwing out of empty barrels here, the getting in of wool there, were incidents quite worthy of the regard of idle men leading for the time being a mere life of the senses.

An important new element has come into the picture, namely merchants and their purchases, chiefly sheep and wool. The steamship is now contributing not only to tourism and to 'Improvement' (by facilitating clearance), but also to the expansion of trading opportunities within and beyond the Highlands and Islands. Her stoppages at various harbours are closely connected to trade, as the region begins to 'industrialise' modestly. As traffic increases,

Punch*'s portrayal of passengers on a West Highland steamer in the nineteenth century [D. W. Stewart's collection]*

the accompanying traits of gawping tourists become ever more evident. Observing 'the natives' as they load and unload the vessel has already become a spectator sport for 'idle' travellers. It remained so until the advent of sophisticated car-ferries in the latter part of the twentieth century destroyed much of the delightful chaos and unpredictability of the mailboat in a Hebridean harbour.

Smith also draws attention to the 'reach' of the steamship. She now conveys 'members of Parliament' and 'English Earls'. The Highlands and Islands are being exposed much more obviously to external forces from the mainland, and even from London. A very similar message was conveyed two years later by Rev. Dr Norman MacLeod, minister of the Barony Church in Glasgow, in his *Reminiscences of a Highland Parish* of 1867. 'Norman of the Barony' was the son of the Rev. Dr Norman MacLeod who described the *Maid of Morven* in 1829. He lamented the arrival of the steamer and its consequences, and blamed Sir Walter Scott for what had happened:

But when Scott adopted the Highlands as the subject of romantic story and song…then began a new era of centred comfort…Steamers foamed on every Loch and banished water kelpies. Telescopes were substituted for second sight…Forty years ago steamers had not mingled their smoke with the mists of the hills, and the Highlands had not become as common as Vauxhall to the Londoners. It was then a land of distance and darkness.

Distances were certainly shrinking throughout the northern hemisphere, thanks to the steamship, and new opportunities arose unexpectedly as a consequence. Scottish shipowners with an eye to business on the far side of the Atlantic found that they could make a pretty penny by selling some of their ships to participants in the American Civil War, in which the Confederate State and the Union State were engaged between 1861 and 1865. This was to affect the destiny of two ships called *Iona*.

Their precursor, the *Mountaineer*, had been so successful in developing the summer tourist traffic on the Ardrishaig route that a larger and faster replacement was ordered only three seasons later. J. & G. Thomson at Govan, who had built the *Mountaineer*, was again asked to build the ship: a flush-decked beauty, with a canoe-shaped bow, square stern and twin funnels straddling the paddle-boxes. The newly-developed oscillating engines provided a service speed of 17 knots. This was the first of the three steamers to bear the sacred name, *Iona*.

The first *Iona* was hugely popular and hugely successful. She was flush-decked, but had a single, rounded front deck-house, extending from the foremast part-way to the stern. She could accommodate 1400 day-passengers in luxuriously-appointed, wood-panelled cabins, complete with bars, shop and the obligatory ship's pipe-band. (The piano-accordion was not to set sail on the Clyde until the next century.) The displaced *Mountaineer* adopted the secondary day-passenger excursion from Oban round Mull to Staffa and Iona – a service that remained popular until the retirement of the *King George V* in the early 1970s (see Chapter 7). After only six summer seasons – she was laid up in the winter – the pride and joy of the fleet was sold to an American agent acting on behalf of the Confederates. The intention was to use the *Iona* as a blockade-runner, taking men and supplies to the besieged army in the Unionist territory in the north.

Stripping the *Iona* of her panel-work and fine fittings at the end of the 1862 season, the Hutcheson company received an over-generous bounty for their ship as she set sail for her Atlantic crossing. But no ship carrying the name *Iona*, and the sacred connotations that go with it, could ever become a part of war, let alone a scuffle between northerners and southerners in the New World. Leaving Glasgow in the early afternoon of 2 October and loaded with coal for the journey, she parted the Clyde for the last time on her way to Nassau to be fitted out for her new role. Five hours later, Providence took a hand, when a steamer struck the *Iona* off Gourock, and sank the heavily ballasted ship in just a few minutes. Charitable to the last, the ship with the sacred name allowed all of her crew to leave unharmed.

David Hutcheson & Company now had a princely fee in the bank, but no ship to operate the Ardrishaig service in the 1863 season. J. & G. Thomson performed their magic once more, and a second, improved *Iona* was ready and on station towards the end of June the following year. This one could manage 18 knots, and was furnished with much of the panel-work and fittings removed from her predecessor, and much more. Little expense was spared – and why should it, when the Confederate Army was willing to pay for such an upgrade? Again, accommodation was laid out in two classes, but this time a dispensation had been given to incorporate

The majestic third Iona
[NR's collection]

a deck saloon without its counting towards gross tonnage, and the *Iona* became the first of the company's saloon steamers. First class featured white- and gold-fluted pillars and velvet curtains at the saloon windows. Many of the windows were sash-balanced, and could be dropped down in good weather. Steerage class, though slightly less adorned with upholstery and gold inlay, was nevertheless better than anything available elsewhere on the Clyde. There was even a Post Office on this ship. Surely the Hutchesons would call it a day with such a perfect vessel?

In late September, it was announced that the new *Iona* would be stripped of her fittings and finery, and would attend the Confederates' bidding across the Atlantic. Setting out in January 1864 to cross the Atlantic, the ship with the sacred name of *Iona* safely made the south of Ireland, whereupon she was sunk near Lambay Island during severe weather, her light construction having been designed principally for sheltered waters. Again, the Confederate money was in the bank, and, yet again, J. & G. Thomson was contracted to

build a new ship. This was the third *Iona*, launched on 10 May in time for the 1864 summer season, complete with many fittings from her earlier namesakes, and her design honed to eliminate the minor mistakes and errors inherent in the first two *Iona*s. This was the ship *par excellence*, and it was this *Iona* which, albeit displaced in 1879 to the Oban station, was to reap rewards for her owners, to the delight of her regular summer clientele, for the next seventy-two years.

The North Atlantic circuit had thus become a shipping thoroughfare that encouraged an unusual export trade. In a round-about way, this trade had facilitated the development of West Highland shipping. The misfortunes of contemporary Americans placed David Hutcheson & Company on a firm and well-founded financial basis. It also gave the company a brand-new, state-of-the-art, luxury ship, for which no serious competitor had yet arrived on the Clyde. The three *Iona*s were each the pride of the fleet, and although there was a price that satisfied the owners, no

The veteran steamship **Glencoe** *at Port Askaig, Islay [Courtesy of Pat Roy, Bowmore]*

the *Glencoe* plied the west coast trade until May 1931. She had been built of wrought iron and this was less susceptible to rusting than the early forms of mild steel that were later in use. This undoubtedly contributed to the longevity of the ship. Although she was reboiled twice, her original steeple engine lasted her whole life.

In addition to the *Clansman* and the three ships named *Iona*, all of which were paddle-driven, the Hutchesons commissioned screw steamers. The steamer *Fingal*, delivered as a running-mate to the *Clansman* in 1861, was the company's first screw-propelled vessel. The advantages of a submerged propeller in rough seas are obvious, and the propeller had come to stay on the longer and more exposed routes across the Minch and elsewhere. Unfortunately, the temptation to support the Confederate cause for a suitable price meant that the new *Fingal* retained her red-and-black funnel for only four months before she too set off across the Atlantic. Unlike the first two *Iona*s, this vessel actually reached the end of the journey, but she was captured and turned into a Federal gunship! A fourth ship, the paddle-steamer *Fairy*, also went to the Confederates. Plying on the Caledonian Canal, she was found to have too great a capacity for the traffic then on offer, and, as a consequence, she was dispatched across the Atlantic.

The *Fingal*'s replacement was a fine, smart-looking, screw-driven vessel named the *Clydesdale*. Another product of the Thomson yard, she was notable not only for her handsome looks, but also for her machinery, which included novel surface-condensing engines, later modified as compound engines. The *Clansman* was wrecked in 1869, and was

price would have been enough should their ship have been destined to appear next season under new colours at the Boomielaw. On the Clyde, however, service in the American Civil War was not seen as realistic competition.

As the Americans slogged it out, the Clyde estuary and its islands enjoyed a tourist boom, while processes of population displacement continued apace in the Highlands. The economic benefits of the new four-legged clansman, the sheep, were ultimately to favour those crofters lucky enough to have been left in place. The Hutchesons' new-building programme for both the Inner and Outer Isles services continued to match this upturn in potential trade. At the same time, the Hutchesons laid increasing responsibility for the running of the company on their younger partner, David MacBrayne. It was MacBrayne who made many of the strategic and policy decisions in the 1860s and who supervised the rebuilding programme and expansion of company routes.

While the three *Iona*s were enjoying their consecutive summers on the Clyde, other new ships were coming off the stocks or being bought into the company. This expansive programme made David Hutcheson & Company a monopoly that few could rival. In February 1857, the Glasgow & Lochfyne Steam Packet Company, which, prior to 1851, had been part of the G. & J. Burns empire, was taken over along with its three ships. Of these, the *Mary Jane* is noteworthy, as this veteran, built by James Matheson of Lewis in 1846, was transformed into the saloon steamer *Glencoe* in 1875. As the *Glencoe*, she lived long enough to be captured in a fine Gaelic word-picture from the early twentieth century (see 'Travelling on the *Glencoe*'). With her role as an emigrant barge long fogotten, she was described lovingly and romantically in Gaelic – thanks largely to her longevity and her old-fashioned machinery.

Minus her original clipper bow, which had been replaced by a gently raked stem,

THE LIFE OF THE *LINNET*

FEW TOURISTS WHO travelled on the Crinan Canal between 1866 and 1929 failed to comment on, or more frequently to wax eloquent about, the little steamship, *Linnet*, which connected the two ends of that waterway, Crinan to the north and Ardrishaig to the south. For most travellers, the *Linnet* was a curious, child-like exception within the MacBrayne fleet, as she presented the sharpest possible contrast, in shape and size, to other vessels. This perspective was to some degree justifiable. The *Linnet* was a tiny, twin-screw, iron steamship, shaped more like a single-deck mail-coach than a traditional steamer. A mere 86 feet long by 16 feet broad, she is often compared to a tramcar. She had a canoe-like bow, sharply honed to push its way into lock gates, and a blunt, rounded stern. Her superstructure was modest, consisting of a cabin which ran from the stern forwards to the beam, and extended the full width of the vessel. On the deck above the cabin was a tall funnel, and latterly a bridge with a prominent wheel. The deck railings carried some half-dozen lifebelts per side. Contemporary accounts make much of her prominent red-and-black funnel, her white superstructure and her black hull, and much too of the beautiful scenery through which she passed as she chugged up and down the canal. In such an idyllic setting, this pretty little vessel was the 'darling' of the romantic tourists of her day.

Yet disparaging adjectives such as 'quaint' and 'comic' are applied to the *Linnet*, even by such sober chroniclers as Duckworth and Langmuir. It is, however, misleading to categorise, or patronise, the *Linnet* in this way. She was, in fact, a pioneering vessel of a very specific kind – a canal passenger steamer – without parallel elsewhere in Scotland until the second *Fairy Queen* was built for service on the Forth and Clyde Canal in 1897. When set alongside the *Fairy Queen* and her consorts, such as the *May Queen* (1903) and the *Gipsy Queen* (1905), the *Linnet* can be seen in proper perspective. Strange she may have seemed alongside large, sea-going steamers, and even alongside the smaller paddlers which traversed the Caledonian Canal, but she was exactly what was needed to convey passengers back and forth on a canal. In design, she anticipated by thirty years the essential features of the steamers of the Forth and Clyde, and her longevity and usefulness far surpassed theirs. Her success is more than amply demonstrated by her lengthy period of service, spanning 63 years. In designing such a ship, David and Alexander Hutcheson were pioneers of canal transport, as well as of short-sea passenger vessels.

Displacing the horse-drawn track-boats, *Maid of Perth* and *Sunbeam*, the *Linnet* was a splendid witness to the manner in which steam power could be adapted to small vessels with a specific purpose. Her neatly-built steam engines consisted of two, two-cylinder units which were inverted, each driving a propeller shaft. Here we may note the beginning, not only of the sophisticated canal steamer, but also of the twin-screw propulsion of a later era. Such clever 'micro-engineering' meant that the *Linnet* could make full use of the Canal's narrow channel, as she was not hampered by sponsons and paddles. She also had what is nowadays called 'bridge control of engines', as her engine was regulated from the deck, and latterly from the bridge. She represented, in her own day, precisely the same sort of downscaling of technology (from 'large' to 'little') as we can see in the contemporary *Lochnevis* (2000) (see Chapter 10). Within her own context, she was brilliantly designed and constructed.

The *Linnet* had to navigate no less than thirteen locks on her journey through the Crinan Canal, which lasted some two hours. Passengers were able to disembark along the route, and some took advantage of the thirst-quenching services offered by such hostelries as the Cairnbaan Inn, until it ceased to provide *aqua vitae*. Local enterprise of other kinds was not lacking. The trade in milk, straight from the cow's udder, was such that the route was known by some as the 'Milky Way'. Souvenir shops too were well patronised.

The demise of the *Linnet* foreshadowed modern developments within the MacBrayne Kingdom, as faster and more economical road-transport replaced the shorter steamer routes. Following her sale in 1929 to the Glasgow Motor Boat Club, she was deprived of her engines, and anchored at Shandon as a clubhouse. She was destroyed by a gale in 1932. No small vessel better deserved to be preserved as an example of the consummate engineering skills of the nineteenth century. Beyond the printed page and the collector's postcard, only the Linnet Boathouse, on the Crinan Canal, keeps her memory alive to the present day.

*The **Linnet** at work in the Crinan Canal [DEM's collection]*

replaced by a namesake, a handsome screw steamer with a figurehead and curved prow, complete with traditional carved and gilded woodwork. Such ornate, sea-going vessels were at the opposite end of the scale to the little *Linnet*, a miniature twin-screw steamer which was built in 1866 for service on the Crinan Canal. Small she may have been, but she was a considerable engineering achievement in her own terms.

The last ship to be ordered by the Hutchesons was the culmination of the *Iona* class of swift day-passenger ships for the Clyde service. Another company had suddenly reared its

head, and had placed a handsome, fast and well-appointed steamer on the service between Glasgow and Inveraray in 1877. The new ship, *Lord of the Isles*, was not only a threat to the fourteen-year-old *Iona*, but she thoroughly outclassed her, poaching traffic at intermediate calls, as the two ships plied between the Broomielaw and Loch Fyne, albeit to different destinations. David MacBrayne, who was now virtually in charge of the Hutcheson company, was not going to be outdone, and he immediately placed an order with J. & G. Thomson, builders of all three *Iona*s, for a day-steamer that would outshine even the *Lord of the Isles*. Built at a cost of

*The beautiful **Columba**, perhaps the most famous of all MacBrayne steamers [Donald B. MacCulloch]*

THE BENEFITS OF STEAM:
AN ARGYLLSHIRE PERSPECTIVE OF 1878

'THE WEST HIGHLANDS have derived much benefit from the modern improvement of steamboat communication. The want of such means of transit was severely felt, and the Old Statistical Account is full of references to this grievance. Mr MacLeod of Morven, in the concluding part of the report on his parish, pointed out strongly the disadvantage under which that part of the country laboured, and even suggested Government bounty to sailing packets that would ply regularly between it and the south. However, he lived to see steamboats introduced, and his youngest son, still living in the manse of Morven, could tell a wonderful tale of what has been done through steamboat traffic in his day. The first steamer built in this country, the old *Comet*, was launched at Port Glasgow in 1811. She had her trial trip from Glasgow to Greenock on the 18th January 1812, and in September of that year her voyage was extended to Oban and Fort William.

'By means of the *Comet*, and other steamers, which immediately followed, when the great experiment of Henry Bell was seen to be a success, the traffic with the Highlands was kept up. The number of boats of all kinds passing through the Crinan Canal from the year 1822 to 1838 was 1346, and in 1875 it was 2117, and in 1876 it was 2293.

'The introduction of passage-boats on the canal, introduced in 1838, has made great difference on the passenger traffic. Large well-appointed steamers now receive the passengers at either end of the canal, and not only a speedy passage, but comfort and elegance are provided. Until the time referred to, only small steamers that could pass through the canal were used for [the] coasting trade, but these were kept up in a spirited manner. Messrs Thomson & MacConnell, the Messrs Burns and a few others, were the owners of these steamers, and conducted the traffic with great energy.

'The *Maid of Morven*, the *Highlander* and *Highland Chieftain* are still fondly remembered by those who knew them in early life; and at a later date, the *Rob Roy*, Captain Duncan; *Helen MacGregor*, Captain Turner; *Toward Castle*, Captain Macdonald; the *Dolphin*, Captain McKillop, were regular and welcome visitors.

The *Maid of Morven* was a great favourite, and was better known by her Gaelic name, *A' Mhaighdeann Mhorairneach*.

'About the year 1851 the steamboat traffic was handed over by the two large firms above mentioned, to Messrs David Hutcheson & Company, who have continued to trade with great success. That enterprising firm have conducted the business well and successfully, although they have had sometimes opposition to meet, and always an exacting public to satisfy. Their fleet of steamers, small and great, amounts to nineteen in number. They ply to many ports beyond the bounds of Argyllshire, but that county gets a full share of their services. The swift passenger boats can stand comparison with any in the world; but they are so well known and appreciated that it is needless to say more about them.'

(From Duncan Clerk [Writer, Oban], 'On the Agriculture of the County of Argyll', in *Transactions of the Highland and Agricultural Society of Scotland*, Fourth Series, X (1878), pp. 80-82.)

£28 000, the new ship was to be the doyen of Clyde steamers and the most famous of them all – the *Columba*. This 19-knot paddle-steamer was driven by oscillating engines which gave her a smooth, vibration-free passage through the water. George Stromier wrote in the *Scottish Field* magazine:

Her speed placed her among the fleetest of the Clyde greyhounds and her length of over 300 feet has not been equalled in the Clyde passenger fleet. Among her additional appointments were a post office and a barber's shop and in the former department the mail was stamped, sorted and delivered at the various calling points at a rate of over 100 000 letters a month. **Columba**'s *voyaging was confined to the holiday months and it was rare for her season to extend into even the first week of October. By that time she was snugly tucked away in Bowling Harbour and did not emerge until the following May had run its course.*

Such then was the magnificent vessel which took up the Tarbert and Ardrishaig sailing in 1878 and maintained it for 58 summers with scarce a break in routine.

The *Columba* was also something of an experiment, as she was the first ship in the fleet to be constructed of steel, and only the second Clyde steamer to use this radical material. Her long, fine lines were a good test of the steel hull, as amidships she carried twin-cylinder oscillating machinery and four heavy, Navy-type boilers. When these boilers were replaced in 1900 by two haystack boilers, her draft became five inches shallower, and with steam pressure increased from the original 50 to 55 psi, her speed also increased from 18 knots to over 19 knots.

Her accommodation was second to none. The first-class

saloon stretched the width of the ship. It was decorated to a standard that would satisfy even the landed gentry travelling to their shooting-lodges in the Highlands. Catering centred on silver service with gold-braided waiters in attendance, and it was reputed to be the finest in the Highlands. The Royal Route now served a train of international tourists from all over Europe, who enjoyed the traditional haggis, neaps and tatties, as well as lighter Continental dishes and salads. Gordon Ramsay would surely have had a restaurant franchise here, had he been born over a hundred years earlier!

David Hutcheson retired from the company in 1876, Alexander following two years later. David MacBrayne was now in charge of a monopoly that controlled all the key services between Glasgow and the Western Isles, as well as many of the mainland destinations that were poorly served by road or rail. His monopoly not only embraced the Inner Hebrides, but also firmly controlled the routes to the Outer Hebrides. By then, David Hutcheson & Company had become a force to be reckoned with. This was a company that had bolstered its income from opportunistic selling of vessels to war-torn America, had recognised the commercial needs of west-coast Scotland and its islands, had supported and developed the seasonal tourist traffic, and had assisted in the emigration of countless hapless crofters to new lives in both Australia and America. David MacBrayne clearly deserves credit for a large part of the foresight and vision that had embedded the company so firmly in Highland life, as well as for promoting innovation in maritime engineering.

The magnetic pull of the Highlands and Islands helped the company to achieve its success. Although the romantic stories of Ossian were the foundation of the tourist influx to Hutcheson territory, it is interesting to note that no Hutcheson ship bore Ossian's name. When naming its ships *Iona* and *Columba*, the company focused on the mystique of the sacred island of Iona, and on Saint Columba himself, reflecting the growing cult of Columba's island and its appeal as a tourist venue, close to Staffa and Fingal's Cave. The sacred ideal was complemented by the exaltation of icons of past secular glory, like Fingal, the father of the legendary Ossian. Names such as *Clansman* – and also *Lord of the Isles*, used by the company's rivals – harked back to the perceived former grandeur of Highland life, at a time when (paradoxically) the region was in the grip of economic restructuring which was far from sympathetic to older ways of life. This fascination with Highland custom in an earlier Golden Age enticed a loyal, Lowland clientele, without whose patronage the company would not have been viable.

In reality, given the social circumstances of the time, the *Clansman* would have been better named *Land Clearance I* or *New Opportunity II*, but these are hardly names which would be recognisable today as characteristic of, or appropriate for, West Highland steamers. The romantic ethos, built into the company's foundations by the Hutchesons, has endured robustly, despite the turmoils of more than a century. Indeed, three of the best-known Hutcheson names – *Iona*, *Clansman* and *Columba* – have been bestowed on twentieth-century car-ferries, as has that of the first *Columba*'s great rival, the *Lord of the Isles*.

Clearance and new opportunity were, of course, complemented by the stark reality of confronting an alien way of life in the Lowland cities or in the towering forests of Nova Scotia or in the Australian bush. The challenges of this contradictory and ambivalent era are well delineated by Dr Norman MacLeod in his description of the old *Maid of Morven* arriving at the Broomielaw back in the late 1820s, with Fionnlagh Pìobaire and Para Mòr as passengers:

Air an là màireach ràinig sinn Glaschu, àite ris an canar am Broomielaw; b' e sin ceidhe na h-ùpraid. Luingeas na smùide a' falbh agus a' teachd làn sluaigh, mar gum biodh an saoghal a' dol do Ghlaschu, agus an saoghal a' teicheadh às. O nach d'fhàs mi bodhar leis a' ghleadhraich a bha 'm chluasaibh, cha chùram leam gun caill mi mo chlaisteachd tuilleadh. Bha sreath dhaoine (portairean a' cheidhe) air an tarraing suas fa chomhair nan soithichean le ball cainbe mu ghuala gach aoin diubh, agus bràiste rìomhach air uchd. Bha iad seo a' smèideadh oirnn mar a bha sinn a' dol gu tìr, a h-uile beul fosgailte mar gum biodh iad a' cur fàilte oirnn; gach làmh sìnte, agus gach sùil siùbhlach mar gum biodh iad ag iarraidh luchd-eòlais. Bha aon fhear gu h-àraidh a shocraich a shùil orm fhèin, agus air dhomh amharc air gu geur, a dh'fheuch an cuimhnichinn cò e, chuir e làmh ra aid, agus chrom e cheann cho modhail, shìobhalta, 's nach b' urrainn domh gun an fhàilt a fhreagradh; ann am priobadh na sùla bha e air clàr na luinge, agus thog e leis bocsa mo phìoba agus màileid Phara Mhòir, cho èasgaidh 's a ghlacadh gàidsear Thobar Mhoire buideal uisge-bheatha, gun chuireadh, gun chead. Air d' athais, arsa Para Mòr. An cuala tu riamh, mo ghille math, mar a thuirt Clag Sgàin, "An rud nach buin duit, na buin da"? Leanaibh mis', a dhaoine uaisle, ars an duine, agus e falbh ceum romhainn. 'S ann sa bhaile mhòr fhèin, a deir mis', a tha 'm modh. Is fhad' on a chuala mi gum bi gill' aig an fheannig fhèin san fhoghar. Dh'iarr sinn air e gar toirt gu taigh Eòghainn Oig, far an d'rinn iad ar beatha gu cridheil.

The next day we arrived in Glasgow, [at] a place that they call the Broomielaw; that certainly was the quay of commotion. Steamships going and coming full of people, as if the world were going to Glasgow, and the world escaping from it. Since I did not become deaf with the clamour in my ears, I have no fear that I will lose my hearing ever again. A row of men (dock porters) were drawn up before the vessels with a hemp rope round the shoulder of each of them, and a fancy badge on his chest. They were waving to us as we were going ashore, every mouth open as if they were welcoming us; every hand stretched out as if they were looking for acquaintances. There was one man in particular who set his eye on myself, and when I looked closely to see if I could recognise him, he raised his hand to his hat, and he bowed his head in such a mannerly, genteel way that I could not but respond to his welcome; in the twinkling of an eye he was on the deck of the ship, and he took away my pipe-box and Para Mòr's bag as nimbly as the Tobermory gauger would confiscate a cask of whisky, without invitation, without permission. 'Take it slowly,' said Para Mòr. 'Have you not heard, my fine lad, what the Bell of Scone said, "The thing that has nothing to do with you, do not take anything to do with it"?' 'Follow me, gentlemen,' said the man, as he took a step ahead of us. 'It is in the big city,' I said, 'that one really finds manners. It is a long time since I first heard the saying that even the hoodie crow itself will have a servant in autumn. We asked him to take us to Young Eòghann's house, where they gave us a hearty welcome.

The description of the Broomielaw provides fair comment on the hustle and bustle of the famous quay, with steamships much in evidence. The reference to Eòghann Og acknowledges the existence of a colony of urban Gaels, whose members provide a 'home from home' for recent Highland immigrants. Of more significance, however, and much less friendly in tone, is the characterisation of the 'welcoming' shore-porters as exploitative and devious, always on the lookout for 'innocents' whom they can waylay. The contrast between the lowland city and the islands – between the new world and the old - is eloquently expressed.

Eventually, however, Highlanders made their peace with the smoky city. They also made friends with the steamship – thanks in large measure to the contribution of a man with a Highland surname, whose family had likewise left the Highlands and had sought its fortune in the deceptive streets and vennels of Glasgow. This was the Hutchesons' junior partner, David MacBrayne, who was about to take the helm in Hebridean waters.

STEAM ENGINES

THE BASIC PRINCIPLE of the steam engine is a cylinder in which sits a piston connected to a piston rod. The piston rod passes through one end of the cylinder through a stuffing box and is connected to the connecting rod which in turn connects with the crankshaft (Figure 1).

Superheated steam drawn via a throttle valve from the boiler passes into the cylinder via a slide valve. The steam trapped in the cylinder expands and forces the piston to move away from the top or bottom of the cylinder and this motion allows the slide valve to cut off the steam. As the piston nears the far end of the cylinder the slide valve allows the spent steam to evacuate the cylinder and new steam under pressure from the boiler to enter the cylinder at the opposite end, again expanding to push the piston back again. The slide valve is driven by an eccentric rod connected to an eccentric disk or sheave on the crankshaft so that the slide valve is consistently out of phase with the piston. Unlike a petrol or diesel engine in a car, which is single-acting, the steam engine is double-acting.

In Figure 1, the cylinder is vertical so that the crankshaft lines up with the propeller via the thrust shaft, tunnel shaft and tail shaft. The engine is called a **reciprocating engine** as the piston rises and falls ('reciprocates') back and forth within the cylinder.

The earliest form of marine steam engine was the **side-lever** engine, so called because the principal mechanism transmitting the power of the piston to the paddle-wheel was a lever at the side of the engine. This engine was an adaptation of the Newcomen 'beam engine', used to pump water from mines. The 'beam' was hinged on a central fulcrum, above the cylinder, and connected the piston rod to a flywheel. The side-lever, placed close to the bottom of the engine, replaced the beam. The upward and downward thrust of the piston crosshead was transmitted to the lever by side-rods which caused the lever to rock about its fulcrum. The other end of the lever drove the crankshaft which turned the paddles. Some engines

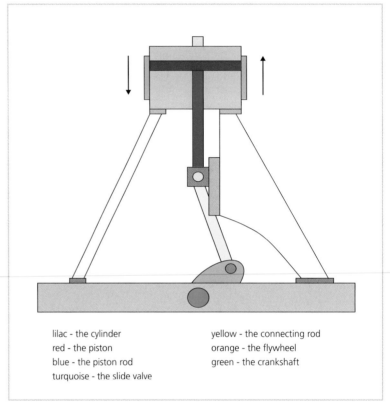

lilac - the cylinder

red - the piston

blue - the piston rod

turquoise - the slide valve

yellow - the connecting rod

orange - the flywheel

green - the crankshaft

Figure 1 The basic steam engine

had levers on both sides. The side-lever engine was characteristically British, as early American steamships retained the beam above the deck. This close variant of the original model was known as a 'walking beam engine'. The side-lever engine of *Comet II* can still be seen at the Clydebuilt centre of the Scottish Maritime Museum, Braehead, Glasgow.

The cylinder of the **steeple engine** (so called because of its resemblance to a steeple) was placed immediately below the crankshaft, and drove vertically upwards by means of two piston rods, connected to a longtitudinal crosshead on each side of the engine. Each of the crossheads was connected in turn to a transverse crosshead which travelled up and down in guides. At the top end of its stroke, this crosshead was well above the level of the saloon deck or engine-house, where it could be seen at work (as on the *Glencoe*, ex-*Mary Jane*, which had a single-cylinder steeple engine). The transverse crosshead in turn drove upwards and downwards to the crankshaft, which was connected to the paddles.

In an engine with **oscillating cylinders** the pistons were connected directly by their rods to the crankshaft, without connecting rods. Each cylinder was hinged (by means of 'trunnions') in such a way that it could move ('oscillate') with the crankshaft. The cylinders were usually mounted below the crankshaft which drove the paddles, and were thus at right angles to the centre-line of the ship. This type of engine was fitted in the best tourist steamers in the United Kingdom and on the Continent, as it was remarkably smooth-running and free from the surging of the single **diagonal** engine. Despite their compact nature and smooth-running, such engines always suffered from the difficulty of keeping the steam trunnion glands steamtight, and could be used only at relatively low steam pressures. The celebrated *Columba* had a mighty set of oscillating steam engines, whilst the *Gondolier* on the Caledonian Canal had a neat and almost miniature set, by comparison.

In the **compound** steam engine, the spent steam, as it expanded at decreasing pressure, was passed from a smaller cylinder to a larger cylinder, and the process in the second cylinder extracted more energy from the expanding steam. A third, even larger,

cylinder and a fourth, comprised the **triple- and quadruple-expansion** engine respectively. Some triple-expansion engines had two low-pressure cylinders of equal diameter which received steam in parallel. Compound two-cylinder engines and triple-expansion engines were the type normally used with screw-driven vessels. The arrangement of the cylinders on screw-deriven ships was vertical, and 'inverted', i.e. with the pistons driving down to the crankshaft. Screw steamers which were equipped initially with 'simple' two-cylinder engines were sometimes 'compounded' at a later date (e.g., *Dunara Castle*).

Later paddle-steamers often used compound or triple-expansion engines in which the cylinders were set **diagonally**, at an angle, with the piston rod pointing upwards towards the crankshaft (as on the *Waverley*). Consequently they were called **diagonal** engines.

The control levers of such compound-diagonal engines were set in a stand, and comprised an ahead/astern lever, a throttle ('speed') lever, a starting lever cotrolling impulse valves to admit steam to the medium-pressure and low-pressure cylinders to set the high-pressure piston in motion, in the event of stalling; and a set of 'drains', one per cylinder, to open valves which allowed residual condensate to drain away. Similar control arrangements were fitted to the engines of screw-driven vessels.

The **turbine engine**, invented by Sir Charles Parsons and seen powering the epoch-making, 34.5-knot *Turbinia* at the Spithead Naval Review in 1897, works by admitting high-pressure steam to a long, horizontal cylinder containing circular sets of blades mounted on a rotor. The diameter of the rotor and the size of the blades increase progressively within the cylinder, in order to obtain the same amount of horsepower from the expanding steam, since the steam loses pressure at each row of blades. The overall shape of the rotor and blades therefore resembles a horizontal cone. Three or more cylinders are often placed in 'parallel flow', on the principle of triple- and quadruple-expansion engines described above.

When exposed to high-pressure, super-heated steam, turbine blades revolve at great speed. In order to attain an efficient propeller speed, the rotors are connected to the propellers by a reduction gearbox,

which, in some instances, reduces the turbine revolutions from thousands of revolutions per minute to around a hundred at the propeller. As the main turbines are uni-directional, a reverse turbine, which is needed to drive the ship astern, is mounted on the rotor of the low-pressure turbine, and rotates in the opposite direction when astern movement is required.

Turbine engines are usually associated with very fast ships, like warships, passenger liners and cross-channel ships. They were also employed on pleasure steamers, such as the *King George V*.

In most steam engines (except those of very early ships such as the first generation of Scottish coasters known as 'puffers', which puffed their used steam directly into the atmosphere), the steam was returned to the boiler via the condenser, which returned the remaining steam back to a condensate by bringing it into contact with cold pipes. The pipes were cooled by sea water driven through them by the circulating pump. The condensate was sucked out of the condenser by an air pump which maintained a vacuum in the condenser. The condensate was returned to the boiler via the hot well tank and its pump and the feed heater and the feed pump. In this way the loss of feed water was minimised.

The side-lever engine of **Comet** *(II), on display at Clydebuilt, Scottish Maritime Museum, Glasgow [DEM]*

CHAPTER 3

THE COMING OF THE KING:
RAILWAYS, FOREIGN ASPIRATIONS
AND SECOND-HAND SHIPS

The **Grenadier** at Iona [Donald B. MacCulloch]

THE COMING OF THE KING:
RAILWAYS, FOREIGN ASPIRATIONS AND SECOND-HAND SHIPS

Although MacBrayne owned only small ships compared with the large vessels owned by other men on the Clyde, people had a knowledge of his name that they did not have of the names of those gentlemen who owned the great ships. There was no harbour or inlet or pier at which the red funnel of his ships could be seen, where people did not speak of him as a man with whom they had personal dealing and a personal relationship. Today MacBrayne has a place in the history and lore of the Islands that the Lords of the Isles do not have. He is placed shoulder to shoulder with Fionn and Columba. Many a person will claim that MacBrayne and the Crofters' Act were the two most efficacious wells that were ever opened in the Highlands.
REV. DONALD LAMONT, 'AN LUIDHEAR DEARG' ('THE RED FUNNEL') 1935

The rebranding of David Hutcheson & Company as David MacBrayne by the former junior partner of the company in June 1879 could be perceived as an act of arrogance, given the distinguished contribution of the Hutchesons to the development of West Highland shipping. It is, however, more likely to have been, firstly, a reflection of the passion that David MacBrayne had for the company with which he was now charged, and, secondly, the outcome of a desire to give the company a more appropriate Highland-sounding name, perhaps to acknowledge his own ancestral links with, and his benevolent concern for, the Highlands and Islands. Whatever the need for the change, the company vision, initially at least, remained steadfastly on retaining and developing the existing shipping services.

The days of bounties from the American Civil War and income from the carriage of emigrants from the islands were over. Although the Highland clearances had ended, their effect was keenly felt, and crofters were now determined to safeguard their interests against further exploitation. Agitation among crofters for security of tenure and fair rents began in the 1870s, and continued into the 1880s. The 'Battle of the Braes', which took place in Skye in 1882 over the grazing of Ben Lee, drew national attention to crofters' grievances and resulted in lowered rents, but not until 1887, following the passing in 1886 of the historic Crofters' Holdings (Scotland) Act. In the early 1880s steamships were sometimes obliged to carry military personnel and police *to* the Hebrides, rather than emigrants *from* the Hebrides. Several civilian steamships were also chartered to support the small flotillas of warships involved in the heavy-handed 'gunboat diplomacy' of the time.

In April 1882, following the initial stand of the Braes crofters against the estate authorities, the *Clansman* conveyed a small detachment of Glasgow policmen to Portree. Accompanying them was Sheriff William Ivory of Inverness-shire, who boarded at Oban. It was as Ivory and these policemen were entering the township of Braes that the celebrated 'Battle of the Braes' took place. The role of MacBrayne's ships in bringing sheriffs and police to Skye caused much resentment, because the vessels had predominantly Hebridean and Highland crews. Masters and crews were sometimes prepared to take a stand, even if that meant loss of jobs. The opportunity came when the 1876-built steamer *Lochiel* was chartered in 1884 as part of an expeditionary force to Skye – the first since the Jacobite Rebellion of 1745 – with the intention of suppressing any further unrest among the islanders. Captain Cameron and his crew, who were sympathetic to the crofters' cause, refused to comply, and it was only after a new Master and crew had been found that the *Lochiel* discharged the terms of her charter. Captain Cameron had to find employment with another company. Carrying Sheriff William Ivory, along with the Sheriff Clerk of Inverness-shire, the Chief Constable and a body of police from the mainland, the *Lochiel* accompanied the troopship, HMS *Assistance*, and two gunboats to Portree. In October 1886, it was the turn of the *Glencoe* to take the pugnacious Sheriff Ivory, the Chief

DAVID MACBRAYNE (1817-1907)

DAVID MACBRAYNE'S FAMILY roots lay in the West Highlands, and specifically in mainland Argyll. The MacBrayne kindred is regarded as a sept of the Clan MacNaughton, which held land and castles from Fraoch Eilean in Loch Awe to Dundarave on Lochfyneside. David's grandfather, Donald MacBrayne, who was said to have been 'the representative of the Macnaughtons of Macnaughton', migrated to Glasgow in the early 1700s, becoming a partner in the firm of Adam Good & Co., calico and linen printers in the High Street. The name of the company was later changed to MacBrayne, Stenhouse and Co., an alteration which in some ways anticipated his grandson's rebranding of the Hutchesons' shipping empire. The MacBraynes appear to have had a knack of building on earlier business ventures, and transforming them for their own purposes.

David, Donald's son, became the registrar of Barony parish, Glasgow. He married Elizabeth (Beth), daughter of Dr John Burns, minister of the Barony Church, and sister of the shipping pioneers, George and James Burns. David had three sons, J. Burns MacBrayne, an insurance broker, David MacBrayne, the future shipowner, and Robert MacBrayne, who became a member of the Glasgow firm, Black & Wingate.

Initially David was apprenticed to a printer and trained as a typefounder, but he then became a clerk with a shipping firm, probably that of his uncles, George and James Burns. Thereafter he was in partnership with David and Alexander Hutcheson, who acquired the West Highland interests of the Burns' firm in 1851, and he became principal partner on the retirement of the Hutchesons. In 1860 David MacBrayne married Robina Eckford Robertson, daughter of an Edinburgh banker, Laurence Robertson. They had two sons, David Hope and Laurence, and one daughter.

David MacBrayne's family home was at 11 Park Circus Place, Glasgow, where he died in 1907. This spacious residence was later gifted by the MacBrayne family to the University of Glasgow, becoming MacBrayne Hall, one of the university's student halls of residence.

David MacBrayne became a patriarchal figure in shipping circles. It is said that he was always present on the Glasgow dockside at the departure of his favourite steamship, *Claymore*, on her regular voyages to the islands. The preservation of his name in the company title to the present day has given him (rather than David Hutcheson) the status of the founding father of West Highland shipping. The historical record, however, suggests that he was, first and foremost, a far-sighted commercial manager who was alive to business opportunities and given to innovative, if risky, ventures. He served on the Clyde Navigation Trust and as a JP for Glasgow. Following his retirement in 1905, his business became a limited company, of which his son, David Hope, was appointed chairman and managing director.

(Sources: *Curiosities of Glasgow Citizenship*; Anthony Slaven, 'MacBrayne, David' in *Oxford Dictionary of National Biography*.)

David MacBrayne

Constable and a body of mainland police on yet another expedition to Portree. The men were welcomed with a 'perfect tempest of booing and groaning' as they went to their hotel. MacBrayne's ships were not, however, the only ones involved in these ignominious duties. The *Dunara Castle* (see Chapter 4) conveyed police to Dunvegan, and she also carried crofters from Skye to the mainland, in order to stand trial for their 'misdeeds'.

The Skye crofters, however, won the greater victory. As a consequence of the crofters' success, Ben Lee became a 'holy hill' to those who knew its place in Highland history. The Skye poetess, Mary MacPherson (1821-1898), known in Gaelic as 'Màiri Mhòr nan Oran' ('Big Mary of the Songs'), witnessed events first-hand, and she must have been as troubled as any by the manner in which civilian steamships with Highland and Hebridean crews were being 'commandeered'. Later, she observed how deeply moved passengers were when they saw the famous landmark from the deck of a steamship as they approached Portree:

Name	Year Built	Company originally built for	Year acquired	Year sold	Route
Lochness	1853	Loch Goil Company	1885	1885	Inverness to Fort William
Ethel, renamed *Clansman* in 1910	1880	A. McMullin, Ballymena, Ireland	1885	1916	Mainly Glasgow to Inverness
Handa	1878	William Lang (see Chapter 4)	1887	1917	Initially Oban based, Coll, Tiree, Lewis, Harris and Skye
Countess of Kellie	1870	Caledonian Railway	1887	1904	Coal carrier, Clyde north via Crinan Canal
Gladiator	1860	T. & J. Harrison, Liverpool	1887	Wrecked 1893	Foreign service
Udea	1873	South Wales owners	1888	Wrecked 1894	Coal carrier
Staffa	1861	Not known	1888	1909	Oban Outer Isles
Pelican	1850	City of Cork Steam Packet Company	1888	Wrecked 1895	Foreign service
Falcon	1854	City of Cork Steam Packet Company	1888	Wrecked 1890	Foreign service
Margaret	?	Not known	1889	1894	Coal carrier
Texa	1884	W. J. Mutter, Glasgow	1889	1917	General cargo duties
Loanda	1870	British & African Steam Navigation Company	1889	1897	Foreign service/coal hulk
Flowerdale	1878	Independent Marine Salvage & Steam Pump Company	1889	1904	Oban to Outer Isles
Hero	1858	Malcolm McIntyre	1890	1909	Greenock to Ardrishaig; renamed *Mountaineer* in 1892 for Oban summer excursions
Islay	1872	Larne & Stranraer Steamboat Company	1890	Wrecked 1902	Glasgow to Islay via Kintyre
Great Western	1867	Great Western Railway	1891	1904	Strome Ferry to Stornoway, renamed *Lovedale* in 1893
Gael	1867	Campbeltown & Glasgow Steam Packet Joint Stock Company Limited	1891	1925	Oban to Gareloch day service
Cygnus	1854	Weymouth & Channel Isles Steam Packet Company	1891	1896	Loch Fyne service, renamed *Brigadier* 1922
Carabinier	1878	London & South Western and London, Brighton & South Coast Railways	1893	1909	Oban to Tobermory and Loch Sunart
Hibernian	1875	Paul & Mackenzie, Dublin	1894	1894	General cargo, lost off the Isle of Man
Gairlochy	1861	Mckellar, Helensburgh	1894	1919	Caledonian Canal, destroyed by fire at Fort Augustus
Glendale	1875	London, Brighton & South Coast Railway	1902	Wrecked 1905	General duties and Oban to Gairloch

Table 1 *Second-hand tonnage bought by David MacBrayne between 1885 and 1902*

'S iomadh rosg a nì mùthadh	*Many eyes will soften*
Tighinn air bàta na smùide,	*As they come on the steamship,*
'S iad a' sealltainn len dùrachd	*And observe with affection*
Air bruthaichean Beinn Lì.	*The slopes of Ben Lee.*

Mary's songs were rooted in a deep affection for crofting communities in Skye and elsewhere, but she also had a remarkable capacity to appreciate the different roles of David MacBrayne's steamships, which she frequently mentions, and even celebrates. As this verse indicates, she was very much aware of the steamships' key contribution in encouraging tourism and in enhancing awareness of the splendid landscapes of Skye (see Chapter 11).

In the 1870s and 1880s, as crofters fought back, the tourist trade continued to thrive throughout the Hebrides. Indeed, one of the last acts of the Hutchesons was to take a leasehold of the island of Staffa, in order to provide an easy landing-place for visitors who wished to inspect Fingal's Cave. They had also bought the Loch Awe steamer, *Queen of the Lake* (which had a wooden hull), and they placed a new steamship, the *Lochawe*, alongside her in 1876. This enabled circular day-trips by road and steamer to be made from Oban via Crinan or Loch Awe. The swift steamer *Columba*, of course, provided ingress from Glasgow to Ardrishaig, and the onward journey to Oban could be completed likewise by either route.

Two key influences determined the next phase of company history, under David MacBrayne's management, and its overall vision was redirected accordingly. The first was the arrival of the coastal railheads and the award of the carriage of the mails to the railway companies. The threat of the railways was one which MacBrayne had to face, and he did so head-on. The steamship was no longer state-of-the-art technology, and its place was taken firmly by the steam train and the excitement of speed. Indeed, the railway had arrived at Greenock's Albert Harbour (later known as Princes Pier) in 1869, and this provided an option for passengers to embark there for Ardrishaig and thus to avoid the rather foul and smelly upper reaches of the Clyde. The arrival of the sewer and the sweetening of Glasgow in 1894 put the sparkle back into all-the-way sailings down the river!

The arrival of the first train at Strome Ferry in 1875 was initially viewed with scepticism by MacBrayne, but he soon realised that the fast overland journey from the Lowlands had the potential to increase the traffic to the islands rather than erode it. Two rail tracks gave access to the pier, and a succession of steamers owned by the Dingwall & Skye Railway – the *Jura*, the *Oscar*, the *Carham*, and the *Ferret* – provided connections from Strome Ferry to Plockton, Broadford, Portree, Raasay, Gairloch, Aultbea, Poolewe, Stornoway, Lochmaddy, Tarbert, Lochinver, Ullapool, Kyleakin, Balmacara, Glencoy, Isleornsay and Armadale. As the pier was never satisfactory from a navigational viewpoint, the railway company was obliged to mark the channel up Loch Carron by means of buoys and lights.

In 1880, David MacBrayne took over the mail services provided by the Dingwall & Skye Railway (later the Highland Railway) from Strome Ferry to Portree, and the last of their steamers, the *Ferret*, was sold. She eventually reached Australia, in dubious circumstances which involved a swindle by her purchaser and three renamings *en route*! MacBrayne inaugurated the Stornoway mail service from Strome Ferry in 1881, using the *Lochiel* and latterly also the *Staffa* and the *Clydesdale*. MacBrayne's late entry into the Outer Isles trade is accounted for by Duckworth and Langmuir as follows:

From the eighteenth century the mails for the Outer Hebrides passed through North Uist, and by 1840 those for Barra, South Uist, Benbecula and North Uist went via Lochmaddy, as also did those for Harris until 1840 from which time the latter had its separate packet, twice a week in summer, once in winter, from Uig. These mail services were provided by Government vessels such as the sloop **Perseverance***, plying fortnightly to Lochmaddy from Dunvegan, later increased to bi-weekly and tri-weekly by the* **Skylark***, and from 1876 daily by the cutter* **Dawn** *between the same ports. The early mail contracts to and from the Outer Islands, held initially by the Highland Fisheries Company Limited (who operated the chartered steamers* **Tartar** *and* **Holly***), passed to David MacBrayne in 1888, and* **Staffa** *was stationed at Oban for this service, first along with* **Clydesdale** *and along with the* **Flowerdale** *a few years later.*

Both the Portree and Stornoway services were transferred to Kyle of Lochalsh when the railway was extended from Strome Ferry in 1897. Kyle was then little more than a collection of peat huts. The railway company therefore had to provide facilities for its workers and its passengers, whereupon it became something of an Edwardian boom-town.

The arrival of the railway at Mallaig in 1901 was a considerable feat of engineering, with impressive cuttings and concrete bridges. It replaced the coastal steamer or the alternative rough hill tracks to the mail coach at Arisaig, which provided a seven-hour long trek to Fort William three times a week. From 1901 onwards, crofters could take their animals to market by train rather than walking them, and the fishermen of Mallaig now had an outlet for the herring fleet that fast developed at the new port.

As MacBrayne secured the onward mail contracts from the new railheads to the islands, his passenger routes began to change from Clyde steamer-Crinan Canal-transit and steamer onwards, to composite overland-by-rail and onwards-by-steamer services. The 'swift steamer' and the 'all-the-way steamer' were ultimately destined to be replaced. The railway arrived at Oban in 1884. The cargo services remained Glasgow-based, and a number of second-hand vessels were bought in to bolster these routes, but, being too large for the Crinan Canal, they travelled round the Mull of Kintyre.

The second key influence on the development of the MacBrayne fleet was the realisation that further expansion of the company could be achieved only by extending its sphere of operation. The desire to expand was buffered to a large extent by purchase of second-hand vessels, many of which were towards the end of their economically useful lives. This was a purchasing strategy that was designed to lessen the financial risk of failure for the new venture. However, second-hand ships were also bought in for the West Highland routes in preference to purpose-built ships.

Second-hand tonnage entered the fleet from 1885 onwards, when the paddle-steamer *Lochness* and the screw-steamer *Ethel* (renamed *Clansman* in 1910) adopted the red-and-black funnel. Whether this reflected the limited resources then available to David MacBrayne, and hence the cheap engines fitted to the later *Grenadier*, or merely financial caution, is not known. It may have reflected saturation in the West Highland core of the company and a desire to conserve funds, in order to promote expansion by developing a totally new product. Although the *Lochness* was bought for the Caledonian Canal-Inverness-Fort Augustus run, and the *Clansman* was placed alongside the *Cavalier* on the Glasgow-Inverness route, some of the subsequent purchases were bought with more exotic purposes in mind.

In later years, the *Ethel* and the *Cavalier* maintained the weekly cargo service to Inverness, navigating the canal in poor visibility in late afternoons and early mornings during the winter months. They arrived at Inverness around 6 pm, and left twelve hours later – no mean feat, when there was not, at that stage, a single light on the Inverness-Loch Ness Reach. The *Lochness*, which had no navigating bridge, was one of the last ships in the fleet to retain the gongs on either paddle box to communicate with the engineer: one stroke for stop, two for ahead and three for astern.

MacBrayne now realised that he could expand further only by developing new routes, as the West Highland services were operated on a monopoly basis, with dense coverage. If the Burns brothers could enjoy success in their collaborative transatlantic venture with the Cunard Steamship Company, why could David MacBrayne not aspire to greatness by operating vessels to Iceland, the Baltic and even farther afield? Four foreign trading-vessels were purchased, with the aspiration of starting a service to Iceland, and possibly also Scandinavia and the Baltic. The ships were:

Gladiator, built originally for T. & J. Harrison, and purchased in Hamburg in 1887;

Pelican and *Falcon*, both purchased in 1888 from the City of Cork Steam Packet Company;

and *Loanda*, purchased in 1889 from the British & African Steam Navigation Company.

Records show that the *Pelican* visited Iceland a number of times with livestock, loading at ports which included Liverpool and Oban. Other vessels, however, sailed much farther. The *Falcon* was lost on a voyage to the United States in 1890, and the *Gladiator* was also lost three years later off Mauritius. It is likely that these two ships were under charter to a third party at the time of their loss, but, with their passing, MacBrayne withdrew to the Highlands once and for all. The *Pelican* became a coal hulk at Portree, and was later moved to Tobermory, where she was wrecked in a storm in 1895. The *Loanda*, it seems, never sailed with a commercial cargo. She was used as a coal hulk from the outset, being scrapped in 1897. So ended the MacBrayne aspiration for a 'place in the sun'.

Purchase of second-hand ships continued throughout

"Fusilier" as built.

the 1890s. By 1902, the company possessed thirty ships, of which sixteen had been bought second-hand, so that the average age of the fleet was 32 years. The second-hand vessels are listed in Table 1 (p. 41), showing also their dates of building and acquisition. MacBrayne's reluctance to construct new ships indicates that he was canny in the extreme. He 'made do' with vessels that were fit for the purpose and nothing more, except, of course, on his premier tourist routes, where the crack steamers, *Iona* and *Columba*, continued to provide a deluxe service. His second-hand policy also meant that, at the end of the Victorian era, he had money in the bank ready to spend at the shipbuilders.

Many of the second-hand purchases were entrusted with key routes, such as the Stornoway mail service, while others plied less prominent cargo-only routes. MacBrayne also acquired steam launches for service on Loch Shiel and Loch Maree, and at Tobermory.

Thus, with MacBrayne at the helm, the rate of new building slowed down, and a brief period of consolidation ensued. A new ship for the Glasgow-Stornoway route was, however, delivered by J. & G. Thomson in 1881. This was the first *Claymore*, a particularly well-proportioned and handsome screw steamer. Construction reverted to tried and tested iron, and her twin scotch boilers and single two-cylinder compound engine enabled her at times to achieve 15 knots, although her service speed was little over 13 knots.

The *Claymore* was followed two years later by the straight-stemmed *Cavalier* for the Glasgow-Inverness service, and then, in 1885, by the paddle-steamer *Grenadier*, which turned out to be the last ship to join the fleet from J. & G. Thomson's yard. Built for the Oban-Gairloch route, the new paddler soon adopted the Staffa and Iona day-trip from Oban in summer, and the

*The **Fusilier**, as modified, with bridge ahead of funnel*
[Harold Jordan's collection]

Greenock-Ardrishaig service in winter. The Gairloch service provided a long day-out from Oban. Alternating daily on a clockwise and anti-clockwise roster, the journey included calls at Tobermory, Eigg, Arisaig, Kyle of Lochalsh, Broadford, Portree and across to Gairloch on the mainland, before turning south to Oban in the evening.

The *Grenadier* was built with a steel hull, but she was rather conservative in other respects. For propulsion, she reverted to oscillating engines which were by then obsolescent, although, unlike the machinery which drove the *Columba*, they were compounded with a low-pressure and a higher-pressure cylinder. The attraction of this machinery was that it was more fuel-efficient on longer runs, such as the Gairloch excursion route. The oscillating

engine operated at pressures up to 100 psi, as the steam glands could not tolerate higher pressures, and daily coal consumption was typically about ten or twelve tons.

The last new ship to be built for another 15 years (until 1903) was the *Fusilier*. A quasi-sister of the *Grenadier*, she was built by McArthur & Company near Paisley, and delivered in June 1888. At last, the old oscillating machinery was discarded in favour of a single-cylinder, condensing engine supplied by a haystack boiler. This arrangement was considerably cheaper to install than a compound diagonal engine, but its main drawback was the vibrant push of the cylinder on the paddles, giving an unpleasant pulsating motion. Her design-route was the Oban-Gairloch service. Although the ship had been built at a

favourably low cost, she was nevertheless a valuable unit which provided many years' service to the company. The hull of this ship was of composite construction, using both iron and steel, which suggests that McArthur & Company may not have had the confidence to build an all-steel hull.

Of the more memorable vessels of this era, apart, of course, from the *Iona* and the *Columba* and other ships dating from the Hutcheson days, the *Claymore* and the *Grenadier* became the favourites. The *Claymore* was the mainstay of the Glasgow-Stornoway route. Of classic design, with mainmast and foremast, single tall funnel, clipper bow and bowsprit, this ship survived the rigours of the Minch and a single stranding incident in Broadford Bay in 1910. In 1929, her very last duty was to trial the new grey livery that was to emerge in the 1930s (see Chapter 7).

It is probably safe to say that no other ship that served the Hebrides was given the place in the people's affections bestowed on the first *Claymore*. She was the elegant Victorian and Hebridean steamer *par excellence*, designed for the eye as well as for the job, and as a result she captured popular imagination. Gaelic poets eulogised her from the outset, as is evident in the verse of the Skye poetess, Màiri Mhòr nan Oran. About 1886, Màiri composed a spirited song which pursues the metaphor of the 'great sword' (Gaelic *Claidheamh Mòr*) in the ship's name. The 'great sword' was also borne aloft in the right hand of a magnificent Highlander in full kilted regalia, splendidly carved in wood and mounted beneath her bowsprit:

Seo [an] claidheamh as ainmeil'	*This is the most famous sword*
Air an cualas iomradh,	*Which has ever been heard of;*
A threabhas druim na fairge,	*She will plough the ridge of the ocean,*
Sgoltadh gharbh-thonn greannach.	*Slicing rugged, surly breakers.*
'S nuair a gheibh i gual	*And when she gets coal*
Gu riaghladh air a cuairt,	*For apportioning on her voyage,*
Cha seòl a-mach à Cluaidh	*There will not sail from the Clyde*
Aon tè as suairce, banail.	*One ship more attractive or womanly.*
Nuair dhùisgeas cuan a mheanmna	*When the ocean rouses its energy*
Fon aigeal le a gairbhinn,	*Under the deep, because of her surge,*
An aghaidh sruth' is soirbheis	*In going against wind and current,*
Dearbhaidh i bhith fearail.	*She will prove that she is manly.*
'S e rinn gnìomh a' choibhneis	*He who set her on the waves*
Chàraich air na tuinn i –	*Truly acted out of kindness –*
An t-uasal MacBrayne,	*The gentleman MacBrayne,*
'S gur ro-mhath thoill e onair.	*Who has well deserved such honour.*

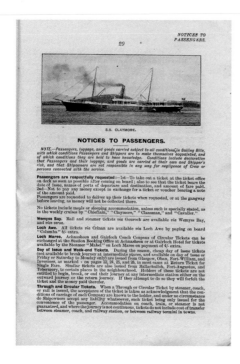

Even in the 1960s, the 'old *Claymore*' was well remembered by a generation brought up in the earlier part of the century, and familiar with her regular beat from Glasgow to Skye and Lewis. No contemporary observer, however, described her better than the Rev. Donald Lamont, a native of Tiree and editor of the Gaelic Supplement of the Church of Scotland magazine, *Life and Work*, when he wrote (originally in Gaelic) in 1935:

> Although the **Claymore** was built to carry cargo, she was just as handsome as the **Columba**, and, although it is a big claim to make, her like has not been seen going up the Sound of Mull since she herself ceased to go there. The **Claymore** ran for many years between Glasgow and Stornoway, and I heard someone saying last year that old David MacBrayne was so fond of her that she never left the Clyde without his being on the quay, to see her off. It was said that she was wet in heavy seas, but she was strong and safe and robust in her construction. If she had not been, she would not have lasted as long as she did,

fifty years, rounding the Mull of Kintyre in bad weather, and up to Stornoway, where the sea was even worse, and where she received, on many a bad night, a battering and a twisting that only strong ribs and gear could withstand. It was a fine sight to see the **Claymore** *leaving Tobermory on a summer evening, resplendent in paint and every inch of her copper or brass polished as clean as a new shilling, and a row of English folk standing at her gunwale, with a telescope in the hand or at the eye of each one, gaping at the seagulls of the shoreline and other wonders which they came to see in the Highlands. But, although the English folk were profitable to MacBrayne in the summer, the* **Claymore** *was not built to carry Englishmen, but to convey the people of the Islands and the West Highlands to and from Glasgow, and to transport cargo to many a township and harbour which had no other way of obtaining goods. If you have never seen one of MacBrayne's boats loading or unloading cargo, you have missed a spectacle as interesting as any in this world: bags of meal and boxes and baskets of bread, kebbucks of cheese and cement, wood and clay jars of whisky, calves and barrels of tar, all thrown on top of one another, and all the time pigs squealing so loudly and so angrily that the men pushing them cannot hear their own bad language.*

As both Gaelic poetry and prose suggest, the *Claymore* helped to establish David MacBrayne's reputation in the northern Hebrides. The *Grenadier* did likewise in the southern Hebrides and in the Clyde estuary. The *Grenadier* was a saloon paddle-steamer, with a clipper bow and bowsprit, two funnels and a foremast, and she exemplified everything that David MacBrayne stood for. Described by Duckworth and Langmuir as a pretty ship, she had been designed by Professor (later Sir) John Biles, Thomson's naval architect, who had recently designed the *City of Paris* and the *City of New York* for the Inman Line. She was enhanced still further when she was reboilered and given funnels of somewhat broader dimensions, but she was nevertheless a workhorse. Although she was designed for the intensive Oban-Gairloch roster, she made her name

on the Oban-Iona and Staffa day-trip service. She suffered various misfortunes, including a grounding in thick fog at Ashton in 1907, but none of these could compare with her tragic end at Oban in September 1927, when she caught fire and sank (see Chapter 6).

The ever-present risk of a ship-board fire was surpassed by the dangers of the sea. Travel by steamship in the confined and hazardous waters of the Western Isles remained difficult throughout the latter part of the nineteenth century. Even though many of the routes were popular with tourists in the summer, winter conditions were potentially dangerous. Ships were lost because of bad weather, navigational errors and mechanical breakdown. Human error did result in some losses, but considering the spartan navigational aids available at that time, the changeable weather conditions that prevail to this day, and the lack of seaway in the confined approaches to many destinations, losses were inevitable.

The catalogue of losses is extensive, and serves to demonstrate a risk (both from the insurance viewpoint and that of the passenger, human and animal) that would be deemed unacceptable by the post-war era of the 1920s. The list below excludes the foreign-service ships described above, but includes losses that occurred at a later date involving ships that were built or purchased under Hutcheson's or MacBrayne's auspices during the Victorian era, but lost after the MacBrayne rebranding in 1879:

Staffa (1863) wrecked off Gigha, August 1885;

Mountaineer (1852) stranded 27 September 1889 in poor weather off Oban. No loss of life but the ship later broke her back;

Udea (1873) wrecked off Jura, 7 April 1894;

Brigadier (1854) wrecked near Rodel, Harris, 7 December 1896;

Islay (1872) wrecked near Port Ellen, 1902;

Clydesdale (1866) stranded on the Lady Rock, 1904;

Flowerdale (1878) lost off Lismore, 1904;

Glendale (1875) wrecked at Deas Point, Mull of Kintyre, 1905;

SAILING ON THE STEAMSHIP *CLAYMORE*

DONALD MACLEOD, A Dumbarton resident and a prolific writer whose work appeared regularly in the *Dumbarton Herald*, travelled from Glasgow to Stornoway and back on the *Claymore* in 1888. He spent his summer holidays touring the Highlands and Islands on MacBrayne's ships, and his adventures furnished the material for several of his articles in the *Dumbarton Herald*. Here are some highlights of his voyage on the *Claymore*.

The steamship *Claymore* has all the comforts of a first-class passenger vessel, having been built and engined a few years ago by that eminent firm of shipbuilders Messrs J. & G. Thomson of Clydebank, the builders of the famous Inman and International liner, the *City of New York*. She is of goodly dimensions, having been built purposely for carrying a large amount of cargo to the West Highlands, as well as a large number of first-class passengers. The saloon, which is below deck, is handsomely fitted up, and is capable of dining with comfort at least 60 passengers. Ranged on either side are the state rooms containing sleeping berths, and snug little cabins they are. Coming on deck by the saloon stair you are met with a long row of deck cabins, all fitted in the same comfortable style as those below, while at the stern of the good ship is ample room for promenading and basking in the sun – when he makes his appearance, which, unfortunately, was not very often the case during my sojourn in the Highlands. From stem to stern of the vessel the passengers have a clear promenade, and none have cause to suffer from want of exercise.

After passing the historical rock of Dumbarton we begin to be propelled along at a greater speed, and in the course of half-an-hour reach the busy quays of Greenock. Our arrival at this port has evidently been anticipated. On the quay we see piled up immense packages of luggage, boxes, barrels, sacks of flour etc., while the edge of the quay is thronged with a large multitude of tourist-like persons. But surely they are not all coming on board? Yes, they are, every one of them, bound for the Highlands... During all this time the windlasses on board have been in constant motion, and by the time we are ready to call out "Let go there," our ship has sunk considerably nearer to the Plimsoll mark. We are soon off again, and rounding Battery Point, make our course straight for the Mull of Kintyre.

Our vessel is now going at full speed – 16 knots an hour – and we soon sighted Pladda Lighthouse, and kept on our course for the Mull...By this time the decks had become somewhat deserted of company, as well as by the rays of the waning moon, and it occurred to me that it was time to see about a place on which to rest my weary limbs. It would, no doubt, have been better for me had I looked into this matter sooner, as by the time I got into the reposing part of the ship, a sight presented itself to me which I will not readily forget. What was once a spacious dining-saloon had been transformed in a very short space of time into a huge bedroom, nothing but beds, beds, beds everywhere, tables, chairs, couches, and every available article having been transformed, with the assistance of bedclothes, rugs &c., into places of rest. The lights were low, the curtains drawn, and naught was to be heard but the peculiar sound of the propeller as it churned the water, mingled with the occasional thumping of the rudder-chain on the deck or roof of the saloon. Over and above those sounds came every now and again the deep snore of the weary voyagers – happy in the arms of Morpheus.

At the entrance to the Sound of Mull we stop for a few moments to allow of a ferryboat from Craignure discharging its cargo and taking on shore a few passengers for this rather lonesome spot. Lochaline is our next port of call....We then cross the Sound and touch at Salen Pier, Mull. During our passage from Oban I heard one of our female tourists, an American, as I afterwards found out, express great disappointment at not having seen any true specimens of the Highland race adorned in the picturesque costume worn in Eden, but at Salen the lady's wishes were gratified by the boarding of a gigantic Highlander *en route* for his shooting lodge near Stornoway. A most minute inspection, of course, followed. The question now arose, how was this immense piece of humanity going to stretch his

massive limbs in the small, confined space of the ship's berth? None of the passengers having the courage to put the question to the gentleman himself, the problem had to remain unsolved.

At Eigg a ferry came out meet us, and then we continued on our voyage, Isleornsay, Glenelg, Balmacara, Kyleakin and Broadford…are each touched at… [Leaving Broadford we] had to be most careful in our navigation, as the place abounds with sunken rocks. But our captain is a most capable officer, and we were soon again in the open, making for Portree, the capital of Skye. It was late when we arrived here, and the night being dark we contented ourselves with remaining on board and drowning the uncomfortable noises of the winches with the sweet strains of music which proceeded from the saloon. Fortunately we had on board some most excellent voices, male and female – the males, however, predominating to a too great extent – and we were not wanting either in accompanists for the pianoforte. Our concert was somewhat suddenly cut short by the appearance of some half-dozen of the steward's minions laden with bed clothes, and as this was the signal to clear out to let them prepare the berths for the sleepers, we – that is the male portion of the passengers – adjourned to the deck, and finished the concert there. There not being so many passengers on board, I was now delighted to hear from the steward that he had managed to find me a bed.

At four o' clock I was wakened up by the noise made by the propeller, which was whizzing round just at my ears, while over my head came every now and again the thud of the rudder chain as the ship was being steered. What sleep I had was refreshing, and we were all in the best of spirits when we met on deck in the morning. We breakfasted about seven o' clock this (Saturday) morning, and just as the first party finished, we arrived at Gairloch, one of the most charming places on the route. Here we were informed by the captain that we could walk to Poolewe, a distance of about seven miles, and be in time to meet the steamer when we got round to that place. Some thirty or forty of us started off, and the walk was well worth the trouble. About half-way to Poolewe we came in sight of Loch Maree, the scenery around which is simply magnificent. On arriving at Poolewe, we saw the steamer coming in the distance, and a few of the passengers indulged in a cold dip in the sea. We were once more on board, and our next place of call was Aultbea, another charming little spot…Our next place of call should have been our destination, Stornoway; but, having goods for Lochinver, we still kept hugging the mainland, and arrived at that place about three o' clock in the afternoon. We made a longish stay at Lochinver, in consequence of which we did not arrive in Stornoway until about eight o' clock on Saturday night.

At 2.30 on Monday afternoon we commenced our return journey for Glasgow. We sailed straight to Portree, where we arrived in the evening. We had a lively roll coming down the Minch, but by this time we were all good sailors, and stood the motion of the ship wonderfully.

On Tuesday morning at breakfast we stopped at Totaig, Loch Duich, and from there we sailed to Glenelg – in truth, a charming spot. Our next place of call was within the bounds of Loch Hourn. The scenery here is far and away the most beautifully wild that it has ever been my lot to witness in the Highlands. I cannot leave Loch Hourn without saying a word or two about the difficulties which a steamer has to encounter in coming into this narrow and island studded loch. On entering the narrows at a point which is called the Devil's Mouth – and not inappropriately – our ship had to go dead slow, while the helm was placed in the hands of the most experienced sailor. We soon discovered the reason for so much precaution. Looking over the side of the ship, we could see, just covered by water and no more, sharp projecting rocks that would have been our and the ship's doom, had we been badly steered, while stretching far away on the right we could see large banks of sand, which meant shallow water. In spite of all these enemies of the sea, our worthy and experienced captain took his ship in, got on board a goodly cargo of wood, and with the same dexterity piloted his vessel once more into the open, when the steam pipes were again let loose, and we sailed merrily along. The weather, which had been dull in the morning, brightened up most charmingly, and we repassed the places we had touched at in our up journey, and saw them under the most advantageous circumstances.

The trip to the Highlands by any of Mr MacBrayne's crack steamers is now more than ever popular, which is proved from the number who 'do' this route in the summer months.

The **Claymore** in Oban Bay [DEM's collection]

The **Claymore**, *showing her with gaff rig [DEM's collection]*

Pencil sketch of the **Claymore**, *by
D. E. Meek*

The figurehead of the **Claymore**, *now at the
Scottish Maritime Museum, Irvine [DEM]*

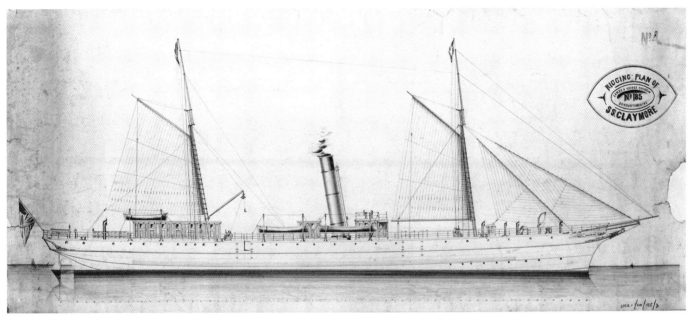

Rigging plan of the
Claymore *[Glasgow University Archives]*

The **Claymore** *coming up the Clyde [Glasgow University Archives]*

Lochiel (1877) lost at Portree, 1907;

Chevalier (1866) stranded on Barmore Island, north of Tarbert, in 1927, having had a long and productive career.

This, in fact, may seem an excessive list of disasters, but it was in proportion to the size of the fleet, and no different from the experience of other shipowners operating in the area, such as Martin Orme and John McCallum.

Despite the misfortunes which befell his ships in his heroic efforts to open new routes to the Highlands and Islands, and notwithstanding his conservatism and his extensive purchases of second-hand vessels, David MacBrayne was an astute businessman who laid successfully the mercantile foundations of the company that forms a major part of today's Caledonian MacBrayne. He was also innovative in the extreme, proving himself to be a pioneer and champion of new technology. For example, the first-ever repeating ship's telegraph was trialled aboard the paddle-steamer *Mountaineer*; steam-powered steering-gear was designed for, and developed aboard, the *Iona*-class of

paddle-steamer; the *Columba* was the first paddle-steamer designed with the saloon-housing carried out to the bulwarks, and the *Cavalier* was the first ship on the Clyde to be equipped with electric light.

In these and other ways, David MacBrayne left a potent and enduring legacy which, rightly or wrongly, eclipsed that of his predecessors and his contemporaries, and ensured that he would be numbered among the greatest Highland benefactors of all time. Nevertheless, it is apparent that MacBrayne did not succeed in providing a comprehensive network of services for the entire Highlands and Islands. There were serious gaps in provision, particularly in the carrying of cargo to and from many small, 'inaccessible' ports and harbours which lay off – and even on! – the main MacBrayne routes.

Unsurprisingly, therefore, short-lived attempts were made to create new ventures. In Islay, for instance, John Ramsay of Kildalton and other Islay landlords, along with several local distillery owners, established the Islay Steam-

THE *CLAYMORE* AND THE *ROTOMAHANA*

IN THEIR SEMINAL work, *West Highland Steamers*, Duckworth and Langmuir make passing and tantalising reference to a ship which they call the '*Claymore* of Australasia…the lovely S.S. *Rotomahana* of the Union S.S. Co. of New Zealand Limited, whose demise in 1926 was as much a blow to the people of the Antipodes as was that of her Highland contemporary five years later to those in the West of Scotland.' They note that the *Rotomahana* 'resembl[ed] her [i.e the *Claymore*] closely in appearance'. In fact, it is more probable that this resemblance – if it has any validity – operated in entirely the opposite direction, and that the *Rotomahana*, launched from the yard of William Denny and Brothers, Dumbarton, on 5 June 1879, could have contributed something to the design of the *Claymore*.

It must also be noted, however, that the prototype of the 'elegant' screw-driven steamship in West Highland waters was the *Clansman* (2), built for David Hutcheson in 1870. The *Claymore* could be regarded as an enhanced version of the *Clansman*, to which she was very similar, the main differences being the position of the *Claymore*'s bridge (forward of the funnel), and the more pronounced elegance of her line. One could conclude, not unreasonably, that a yacht-like type of Victorian steamer had evolved gradually, and of its own accord, by the 1880s. The parallels between the *Claymore* and the *Rotomahana* are nevertheless both interesting and tantalising. J.H. Isherwood describes the *Rotomahana* memorably:

> Denny's had turned out a little gem of a ship. She had a lovely clipper stem with a Maori princess for a figurehead. The sheer was pronounced forward and she sat the water like a duckling. With two well raked masts she was rigged as a brigantine, carrying only two yards on the fore. The funnel was rather well forward of amidships and the general proportions were those of a large yacht. She must have looked a magnificent sight in her dark green hull girdled by a gold band.

The *Rotomahana*, at 1,777 tons, was approximately double the size of the *Claymore*. She was 298 feet long, and powered by compound steam engines. She has her own place in shipbuilding history, as she is believed to have been the first 'large' vessel to have been built of mild steel and fitted with bilge keels. With accommodation for 140 first-class passengers, 80 second-class and 80 third-class, she was placed initially on the Wellington to Sydney service, which she maintained for fifteen years. For several months in 1894 she plied the Bass Strait, between Melbourne and Launceston, and she also undertook coastal services around New Zealand, performing the ferry run from Lyttelton to Wellington from 1897. She linked the North and South Islands for some twenty years. In 1907 she returned to the Melbourne-Tasmania service, remaining on the Bass Strait until 1920.

The *Claymore* differed from the *Rotomahana* in being built of iron, but the overall profile of her hull was very similar, with clipper bow, finely-wrought figurehead, a yacht-like sheer, a single tall, raked funnel, and holds fore and aft, served by derricks on the main and foremasts. The rigging-plan of the *Claymore* shows that she was originally intended to carry gaff-sails as required, as was *Clansman* (2). Sail-assistance was not, of course, uncommon at that time.

The *Rotomahana* was reboilered in 1901, with four new boilers in place of the original six, and averaged a speed of sixteen knots between Lyttelton and Wellington. Latterly, she was considered to be an expensive ship to maintain, because of excessive coal consumption at high speed. She was laid up in 1921, and sold to Melbourne breakers in April 1925, though her steel hull was still in good condition. She was partially dismantled before her hulk was scuttled three miles beyond Port Phillip Heads in 1928. The *Rotomahana*'s lifespan was therefore directly comparable with that of the *Claymore*, which gave some fifty years of service to the Hebrides.

J.H. Isherwood paid the following tribute to the *Rotomahana*:

> Let no one think that this beauty was in any way of the "pretty-pretty" variety. This had been no fair weather yacht but as tough a little steamer as could be found anywhere in the world. Her reputation was primarily one of 41 years of unbroken service, fair weather or foul.

A tribute in very similar words was accorded to the *Claymore* by such writers as the Rev. Donald Lamont, as we note elsewhere in this chapter.

Two more 'working yachts' of this kind were produced. These were the *Chieftain* (1907), built for David Hope MacBrayne, but sold in 1919 to the North of Scotland, Orkney and Shetland Shipping Co., who named her *St Margaret* (see Chapter 5); and the beautiful *St Sunniva* (1931), built by the same North Company. It is thus tempting to see a small 'family' of three rather distinctive and elegant steamships whose overall design may have been influenced originally by Denny's *Rotomahana*. If we cannot be certain about the matter, we can at least conclude that the elegant designs of David MacBrayne's *Claymore* and *Chieftain* rivalled those of ocean-going steamships, reckoned to be the finest in the world.

Information from Clydebuilt Ships Database www.clydesite.co.uk, updated by Bruce Biddulph from the original records by Stuart Cameron; and J.H. Isherwood, 'The Intercolonial Favourite', in *Sea Breezes*, No. 126 (June 1956).

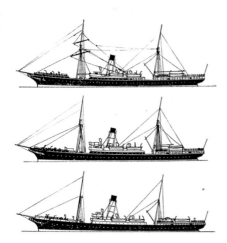

*Silhouettes of the **Rotomahana**, by John Isherwood [Courtesy of **Sea Breezes**]*

Packet Company, which was incorporated in 1890, for the 'conveyance of passengers, mails, goods … to and from, and between, Glasgow, Islay, Jura and other places in Scotland and Ireland'. It survived only until 1892, when it was dissolved following the death of John Ramsay. The attempt was, however, more significant than the achievement. It signified that there was indeed room for other operators, and that some well-placed businessmen were prepared to act purposefully to fill gaps or to improve existing provision. In years to come, dissatisfaction with MacBrayne's services to Islay – a route which never seemed to enjoy the best MacBrayne provision – would be crucial in challenging the company to change its ways (see Chapter 8). In the meantime, a couple of 'friendly' rivals, whose companies began at much the same time as MacBrayne's, were committed to reaching those parts of the Hebrides which, for whatever reason, even 'King David' could not reach.

The scrollwork on the bow of the **Lochness** *shows clearly in this photograph. [DEM's collection]*

CHAPTER 4

FROM LANCEFIELD QUAY TO VILLAGE BAY:
THE STEAMSHIPS OF JOHN McCALLUM AND MARTIN ORME

*The **Hebridean** coming up the Avon, and about to enter the Cumberland Basin, Bristol [G.E. Langmuir's collection]*

FROM LANCEFIELD QUAY TO VILLAGE BAY:
THE STEAMSHIPS OF JOHN McCALLUM AND MARTIN ORME

*When there were five thousand people in Tiree, not one ounce of the food that sustained them was imported to the island; it was taken from the soil or from the sea, but today, when it has only around eighteen hundred people, the bulk of the island's food is brought from Glasgow on the **Dunara**.*
REV. DONALD LAMONT, 'ATHARRACHAIDHEAN' ('CHANGES') 1933

David MacBrayne bestrode the Hebridean world like a colossus. In a much reconstructed form he still does, though his name is now little more than a facade covering a succession of new alignments, partnerships, mergers and government-backed capital-funding agreements. His iconic significance has obscured the contribution of several smaller operators who made a major contribution to maritime transport in the West Highlands, and none more so than the company known latterly as McCallum, Orme & Company Limited, which had its offices (in the 1930s) at 45 Union Street, Glasgow. Its best-remembered vessels sailed from Lancefield Quay to almost all of the Hebrides, as far out as St Kilda, with its line of cottages above Village Bay. These dwellings, now uninhabited, form a lasting and poignant memorial to an island community evacuated to the Scottish mainland in 1930.

McCallum, Orme & Company was formed in 1929 by the merging of two companies – that of Martin Orme & Company, which had an earlier existence as Orme Bros. & Company, reaching back to 1853, and that of John McCallum & Company, which is on record from 1876. Before merging, McCallum and Orme had operated on a broadly non-competitive basis, reflected in their schedules, which took account of the deployment of one another's vessels. Their companies were formed by syndicates, or cartels, of businessmen who acted as shareholders and agents for individual ships, which were apparently built or acquired to meet the needs of specific economic ventures in the Highlands and Islands, such as fisheries. This meant that the vessels were often disposed of relatively quickly, usually after two or three years, no doubt as the 'niche markets'

for which they were intended rose and fell. It was largely a matter of 'hit or miss' all round, with some unfortunate hitting (rather than missing) of submerged rocks in little-known Hebridean waters, which determined the untimely end of several worthy ships.

The first vessel owned by Orme Bros. was the *Queen* of 1853, 'an iron three-masted screw vessel of 275 tons gross, with figurehead, bowsprit and square stern'. She was capable of twelve knots. The Ormes' main interest from the outset was evidently in cargo-carrying, as the *Queen* accommodated only twenty-three passengers. Originally intended to reach Stornoway, the *Queen* was refused berthing by the Stornoway Harbour authorities, and operated briefly on the Islay, Oban, Tobermory and Portree service, before ceasing in July 1853. She was sold to Australian interests, and was in Melbourne by February 1854. Beyond the family circle, one of Martin Orme's partners was William Lang, from Kilwinning but latterly resident at Glengorm, Mull (a point which explains the appearance of the names, *Dunara Castle* and *Aros Castle*, both castles being in Mull). The *Queen of the Isles* (built 1860) was registered in his name. She served the Hebrides for only two years before being sold. Another partner, and also Martin Orme's Glasgow agent for a period, was William Dick, from Oban, who owned a small screw vessel *Lochfine*, which was in his service until 1850, when she was sold to G. & J. Burns.

Martin Orme's involvement in the short-lived (1857-60) Great West of Scotland Fishery Company illustrates the connection between economic ventures and contemporary steamship patterns. In 1858 the Fishery built the steamer *Islesman*, which was managed by Orme, and later (1860)

MARTIN ORME, JOHN McCALLUM AND GEORGE LENNOX WATSON

MARTIN ORME, 'SHIPOWNER', was a close contemporary of David MacBrayne. Born c. 1823 in Dumbarton, he was the son of John Orme, variously described as 'wright' and 'teacher of music', and Agnes Wilson. He lived in the Glasgow and Paisley areas. At the time of his marriage in 1866 to Helen McKechnie, daughter of Archibald McKechnie, Martin's occupation was given as 'Steamboat Agent', and he was living in Hill Street, Garnethill, Glasgow. From at least the time of the 1871 Census, when he was again designated 'Steamboat Agent', he lived at Hope Cottage, Bishopton, Paisley. At the time of his death, he was designated 'Shipowner'. His death occurred at Gilmour Street Railway Station, Paisley, in 1903, and was caused by heart failure at the age of 80. He had two sons, Archibald Lawrence (aged 1 in the 1871 Census) and John (who registered his father's death).

Initially Martin Orme was engaged in the steamship business with his brothers, James (1810-93) and Lawrence (1820-95), who were partners but not shipowners. By January 1853, they had formed Orme Bros. & Company. Martin pursued other commercial concerns, such as fisheries, which interacted with his shipping interests. Martin Orme's office in the early 1900s was at 20 Robertson Street, Glasgow.

After Martin's death in 1903, the family interest was maintained by his sons, Archibald Lawrence, who was a Director and shareholder of McCallum and Orme until his own death in May 1944, and John, a Chartered Accountant and a shareholder in the company, who died in 1942.

John McCallum, son of Robert McCallum, 'Seaman', and Christine McLachlan, was a native of Crinan, Argyllshire, born in 1842. By 1872 he was living at 7 Sedan Place, Paisley Road, Glasgow. Designated 'Seaman' on his Marriage Certificate, he married Jessie Paterson, daughter of Neil Paterson and Marjory Murray, at Kirk Street, Campbeltown, in December 1872. At the time of the 1881 Census, in which John is designated 'Master Mariner', the McCallums had three sons, Robert (aged 8), John M. (aged 4) and Neil P. (aged 2). The family had moved to Percy Street, off Paisley Road, by 1884. At the time of the 1891 Census, the McCallums were living at 6 Percy Street, and had a further three sons, Archibald (aged 7), Alexander (aged 3), and James (aged 1). Marjory Paterson, John's mother-in-law, was then living with them. By 1904 the family had moved to Whiteinch.

John McCallum obtained his Master's Certificate (Home Trade Passenger Ships) in Glasgow in 1865,

when he was only 23 years of age. He commanded the Catherine Hughes (1866-67), the Albert (1868) and the Corinthian (1871). Thereafter he is on record as commanding two of his own company's ships, the Lady Ambrosine (1874-76), and the St Clair (1877-78). He continued to be listed in Lloyd's Captains' Register (Guildhall Library) from 1880 to 1887, but no commands were reported, although there is evidence elsewhere (Michael Robson, St Kilda, p. 568) that he commanded other company vessels in this period, among them the St Clair (1879-80). In October 1885 he accompanied Captain McKechnie, then master of the Hebridean, on an emergency, out-of-season sailing to St Kilda (Robson, p. 600), perhaps acting as an additional 'St Kilda master' or pilot, in anticipation of bad weather in the area.

It is of further interest that John's brother, Archibald, who was born at Crinan in 1848, obtained his Master's Certificate in 1879, and went on to command the Lady Ambrosine in 1880. He was apparently the Master of the St Clair at the time of her wrecking later that year. He served as Master of the Hebridean in 1881. He too was listed in the Register from 1882 to 1887, but, once again, no commands were reported.

The dates of building of his principal vessels

acquired by William Lang, who instituted 'regular passenger services' to the Outer and Inner Hebrides, including the Ross of Mull (Bunessan), Coll and Tiree. Thereafter the Orme syndicate had a succession of short-term vessels, including the *Chieftain* (built 1860), which struck a rock at Arinagour, Coll, in 1861, but remained with Orme until 1863; the *Dunvegan Castle* (built 1868), which went ashore (appropriately enough!) at Dunvegan in 1874, and was sold out of the fleet a year later; and the *Talisman*, built by William Lang in 1871, in collaboration with Martin Orme, who had ten shares. The *Talisman* appears to have been quite exceptionally free from serious incident and self-destructive

tendencies, and was sold unscathed in 1874. The last of the smaller vessels in the fleet was the *Aros Castle*, built for William Lang in 1878. Following a grounding on Iona, she became one of David MacBrayne's many second-hand purchases in 1887. She was then renamed *Handa*, as better befitted her tubby, puffer-like profile, which was intended to allow her to use the Crinan Canal. Her ungainly shape later earned her the name of 'MacBrayne's Gladstone Bag'.

The origins of Captain John McCallum's company are difficult to ascertain, but they appear to lie in a network of steamship entrepreneurs, among them Andrew Ross, who owned a puffer-type vessel in 1871, and Andrew

indicate that John McCallum was at the height of his business powers in the 1880s and the 1890s. He is listed in *Lloyd's Register of Ships* (1894-95) as the owner of the *Hebridean* and the *Quiraing*. This may explain why he held fewer commands after 1880. As in the case of Orme Bros. & Company, it would seem that McCallum's company was to some extent a family venture, but that the McCallums were distinctive in being both Masters and owners of their vessels. However, they did not maintain their company interest as long as the Ormes, whose skills were essentially managerial.

McCallum's company traded under different names. The office of the Western Isles Steam Packet Company, with which McCallum was associated initially, was at 133 West George Street, Glasgow.In the 1880s, John McCallum & Company, 'steamship owners', were located at the Highland Steam Packet Office at 12 Ann Street. In the very early 1900s, the office of John McCallum & Company was at 10 Ann Street, though it appears to have moved to 36 Oswald Street by 1904-5, and to 87 Union Street by 1912.

Tragically, John McCallum (latterly residing in Oban) was drowned at St Helier, Jersey, on 17 June 1902, when acting as Mate on the *Hebridean*, then plying between Plymouth and the Channel Islands. His partners, William Young and Hugh C. Young, were chiefly responsible for maintaining the company thereafter

John McCallum's original connections with Crinan – a well-known base for Scottish yachting enthusiasts – may help to explain, in part at least, his close business dealings with G.L.Watson, to whom he turned for the designs of his two main ships. George Lennox Watson (1851-1904), the designer of both the *Hebridean* (1881) and the *Hebrides* (1898), was one of 'the foremost names in international yacht designing' and 'one of the Clyde's most prestigious designers' in the late nineteenth century. The son of a Glasgow doctor, Watson served his time in the yard of Robert Napier, and was skilled in both wood and iron shipbuilding. He was closely connected with T. B. Seath & Company, the shipbuilders who constructed the *Hebridean*. His designs rivalled those of the famous yacht builders, Fife's of Fairlie, and included *Britannia* (1893) for the Prince of Wales and *Shamrock II* (1901) for Sir Thomas Lipton. He was a member, along with William Fife, of the Royal Clyde Yacht Club. Watson was also noted for designing elegant steam yachts. In 1887 Watson became the first Consulting Naval Architect to the Royal National Lifeboat Institution. His name is commemorated in the Watson class of lifeboats, which he introduced to the RNLI, initially by producing a sailing lifeboat of foundational significance in 1890. In the words of Nicholas Leach (*Lifeboats*, in the Shire Album Series), the Watson sailing lifeboats 'pointed the way forward for the RNLI' after some serious

capsizes involving earlier designs. Later the Watson class boats were motorised. They were of different types, but their common factor was the design of their hulls. In addition to yachts and lifeboats, Watson designed twenty-two commercial vessels. According to the *Oxford Companion to Ships and the Sea*, 'all [Watson's] creations were notable for their elegance of line and their seaworthiness' – a splendid accolade which can be applied very justly to both the *Hebridean* and the *Hebrides*.

Martin Orme [Courtesy of the Orme family]

McKenzie Ross. Another venture, the Western Isles Steam Packet Company Limited, came into existence on 11 February 1873 'for the conveyance of goods in ships or boats between Glasgow and the West Highlands'. Four of its seven directors were Glasgow merchants, mostly in the wine trade, but twenty-five of its fifty-one shareholders hailed from South Uist (sixteen), Barra (seven) and Portree (two) – a highly significant development, which suggests a strong Hebridean desire to initiate steamship services, principally for cargo. John McCallum held two shares in this company, and retained these until it was dissolved in 1881. The company owned two ships, the *St Clair of the*

Isles (bought in 1873), and the *Lady Ambrosine* (launched in 1873). Both were sold in 1875, and the *Lady Ambrosine* was bought by her Master, John McCallum. At this point (in February 1875) the company contemplated voluntary liquidation, but it survived for another six years, possibly through McCallum's intervention and an alliance with his company, though this is not clear from the surviving records.

John McCallum & Company appears to have depended initially on the maritime skills of John and his brother, Archibald, who were both qualified Masters (Coastal Passenger Trade). The company was fully fledged by the

ST CLAIR OF THE ISLES

THE FIRST SIGNIFICANT vessel owned by the Western Isles Steam Packet Company Limited was the *St Clair of the Isles*, formerly the *Lisboa*. She was built in 1860, purchased in 1873, and in service until March 1875. The Inverness-based newspaper, *The Highlander*, provided detailed information about the ship and her cargoes, beginning in July 1873:

> We are pleased to announce to our friends in the west, that a new steamer, the "St Clair of the Isles", has just begun to ply between the Clyde and the Western Isles. The "St Clair" is a fine paddle-steamer, with splendid saloon accommodation, and berths, etc., for forty cabin passengers. Her figurehead is a Highlander in full costume – blue bonnet with feather, dark-green jacket, Stewart tartan plaid fastened at the shoulder with a gold brooch, his right hand is brought across his breast as if in the act of making for his claymore, on which his left hand is laid, and his face looks as if he were in earnest.

> Three weeks after her first voyage, the *St Clair of the Isles* struck a rock, and was temporarily withdrawn from service. Islanders were, however, more than appreciative of the new vessel, and tried to encourage the company despite the set-back. The Barra people expressed their support: 'We hope the company will not be discouraged for a moment; let them only persevere and they need not fear of success. The traffic to and

from the Western Isles has of late years so immensely increased, and is still increasing, that there is still ample room for two weekly steamers at the least.'

Likewise the people of North Uist expressed their gratitude for the *St Clair of the Isles*, stating that they regarded her charges as 'reasonable...compared with the exorbitant charges of the other steamers'. When the *St Clair of the Isles* reached Glasgow in mid-November 1873, having visited Barra, Uist and other islands, she unloaded 70 head of cattle, including two horses and two 'fine Highland bulls', 83 pigs, ten tons of cheese, dried fish, lobsters, wool and 87 passengers.

The launch of her consort, *Lady Ambrosine*, in December 1873 was also noted in *The Highlander*: 'She is an iron vessel, propelled by a screw, and is to have compound surface condensing engines of the newest description.' The paper stated that the two ships had been 'started for the patriotic purpose of stimulating the industries and supplying the wants of the Western Isles'. The *Lady Ambrosine* was sold to John McCallum in 1875, and served his company until 1890.

In March 1874 the Western Isles Steam Packet Company also mentioned that 'the proprietors are projecting a special trip to St Kilda, in June...Unless a certain number shall have made application for passages by the 15th of May, there is no certainty that

the vessel will be sent at all...We hope to have the Highlanders well represented if the trip takes place.' The trip, by the *St Clair of the Isles*, did not take place, despite interest from people in the north of Skye and tourists from the mainland cities and south. The challenge was taken up successfully by Martin Orme, whose *Dunara Castle*, built in 1875, made her first visit to St Kilda in July 1877.

(Information from Michael Robson, *St Kilda: Church, Visitors and 'Natives'*)

time it ordered the *St Clair*, a very trim little steamship which was built in 1876, though not to John McCallum's entire satisfaction (see 'Shipowner *versus* Shipbuilder'). The *St Clair* – a vessel rather similar to Lang's *Aros Castle*, but with a name reminiscent of the earlier *St Clair of the Isles* – seems to have been 'unlucky' from the start. Fate took a hold when she developed an extremely unfortunate habit of seeking self-destruction on treacherous rocks. Following two previous encounters and refloatings, the end of the *St Clair* was finally achieved in style when she struck the submerged reef of Raonabogh, at the southern entrance to the Sound

of Gunna in October 1880, and sank. Her crew were able to escape in a lifeboat. The incident was well remembered in Caolas, Tiree, until the 1960s. It appears to have been of some significance in encouraging the Commissioners of the Northern Lights to mark the Raonabogh rocks with a clearly visible, flashing buoy.

McCallum's replacement for the *St Clair* was the *Hebridean*, a highly successful steamship designed by G. L. Watson. Built in 1881, she remained with the company until 1917, and was well regarded in the Hebrides. She was modelled in wood, and even commemorated fleetingly in

Gaelic song at the time of the General Election of 1885, when she was chartered by the prospective candidate for Argyll, Donald Horne MacFarlane, to convey Tiree crofters to the polling booth in Tobermory. MacFarlane was elected to represent the constituency, and the island vote played its part. John MacLean, a bard from Balemartin, Tiree, offered a thumbnail sketch of the *Hebridean* (called *Eileanach*, 'Islander', in Gaelic) *a' gearradh geal nan tonnan dùbhghorm* ('cleaving the dark-blue waves into white') as she headed to Tobermory on a day of strong wind.

The *Hebridean* was chartered to other companies when business was slack at home. She served the Isle of Man Steam Packet Company periodically between 1912 and 1914, conveying mainly cargo but also some passengers. A particularly fine and very detailed photograph shows her to advantage as she negotiated the River Avon, possibly when operating for Bristol shipowners. She was a dapper vessel, typical of the time, with her straight stem, tall masts, and open bridge, which offered no protection for her officers other than canvas dodgers on the outer edges. The bridge carried telegraphs only. Her wheel may have been located below the bridge.

As the career of the *Hebridean* indicates, Captain John McCallum had a keen eye for business opportunities beyond the Hebrides. Late in 1890, as a replacement for the *Lady Ambrosine*, he purchased the *La Valette*, renamed her *Quiraing*, and employed her between Glasgow and Iceland in 1896, her last year in his service.

The Hebrides were, however, the mainstay of John McCallum and Martin Orme. Through their (often) locally-determined and rather informal approach to the carriage of Hebridean passengers and 'niche cargoes', such as whisky from distilleries like Talisker in Skye, McCallum and Orme forged flexible, but lasting, links with the Hebridean heartlands, even if their main offices were in Glasgow. MacBrayne's services, on the other hand, were more akin to a managed network, constituting a more obvious extension northwards of Clyde coastal operations, and dependent on stronger connections to railheads and ports on the western mainland. Again, unlike

MacBrayne, and long after the founders' deaths, McCallum and Orme were sustained by a small group of individual partners and shareholders, on the older nineteenth-century model of shipowning. Even after the merger of the two earlier companies in 1929, the single company lacked an iconic figure who could represent its constituent parts. The ships themselves were its key representatives.

John McCallum, Martin Orme and their successors were evidently shrewd businessmen. It was not until the 1920s, when economic circumstances were difficult generally, that the tracks of the two companies converged formally. They were incorporated as a single company on 1 July 1929, a year after David MacBrayne Limited had faced bankruptcy, and had been rescued by Coast Lines and the London, Midland & Scottish Railway. David MacBrayne (1928) Limited acquired 1,000 shares in the new McCallum and Orme company. In addition to MacBrayne, the partners in the post-1929 venture were Hugh C. Young; William Young; Lord Strathcona and Mount Royal, owner of Colonsay; Captain James Kitson, DSO, RN (Rtd); Archibald Lawrence Orme and John Orme, sons of Martin Orme, and William Ittington Young, son of Hugh C. Young; and latterly the three sons of Archibald L. Orme.

The principal shareholders from 1929, Hugh C. Young and William Young, had already taken over John McCallum and Company before 1917, evidently with the financial support of Lord Strathcona. The two Youngs also had a significant holding in Martin Orme & Company. The merger of 1929 was thus, to some extent, a legal streamlining of previous shareholding arrangements. Politics too played their part. The Transport Select Committee of 1928 desired the absorption of all West Highland transport companies into the new MacBrayne venture. Still acting as separate companies, both McCallum and Orme resisted pressure, and sought government subsidy to offset competition from the revitalised MacBrayne. The merger was partly a compromise, in which David MacBrayne (1928) Limited was also involved through shareholding.

The new arrangement provided a larger capital base,

SHIPOWNER VERSUS SHIPBUILDER:

JOHN McCALLUM & CO., STEAMSHIP OWNERS, GLASGOW v. STENHOUSE & Company, SHIPBUILDERS, DUMBARTON before Lord Rutherford Clark at the Outer House, Court of Session

IT IS OFTEN thought that delay in the delivery of new ships by the shipbuilders is a comparatively recent phenomenon, indicative of declining standards in modern shipbuilding. As this excerpt from the *Dumbarton Herald* of 15 March 1876 indicates, that is not so. John McCallum & Company felt justified in pursuing the builders of the *St Clair* in the Court of Session for delay in delivery and for not furnishing the ship with the best fittings. An earlier article in the same paper of 1 February 1876 claims that the 'price of the vessel and her appurtenances was fixed at £4500'. The telegraph fitted to the *St Clair* by the builders was regarded as 'second rate' by McCallum, who claimed that it had cost the company an additional £25 to install a Chadburn telegraph. The *Dumbarton Herald* reported finally as follows:

> Evidence was led in an action at the instance of John McCallum & Company, steamship owners, Glasgow, against Stenhouse & Company, shipbuilders, Dumbarton, in which pursuers concluded for payment (1) of £600; (2) £25, being the difference between the price of the telegraph fitted up for the

pursuers on board the steamship *St Clair*, and the price of the telegraph proposed to be supplied for the steamer by the defenders; (3) that the defenders should be ordained to fit up in the steamer a condenser of the kind and quality described in the specification, or otherwise for payment of £400. On 19th Nov. 1875, a contract was entered into between the parties for the construction of an iron screw steamship, and the defenders were to get the steamer classed as A1 at Lloyd's as an awning-decked ship, and certificated by the Board of Trade as a passenger ship of this description. The defenders further bound themselves to have the vessel with her appurtenances, fittings, furnishings and plenishings in all respect complete and ready for sea, and deliver her at Glasgow on the first day after the expiry of four months from the execution of the contract. It seems, however, that the vessel was not delivered to pursuers until 20th July, 1876. They say it was of great importance to them to get delivery at the time stipulated for in the contract, so as to enable them to catch the trade of the Western Isles. By the delay which occurred they missed that

trade, and were deprived of the use of the steamer for four months. They now estimate the loss thus occasioned at £600.

The defenders deny that they were responsible for the delay, and aver that the delay was caused by the pursuers themselves. The vessel, they say, would have been completed and delivered within the time specified in the contract had it not been for alterations required by the pursuers, and interference by them with the engineers, and for difficulties which arose in procuring a certificate from the Board of Trade. They further contend that the pursuers had not suffered damage by the delay.

After hearing evidence, the Lord Ordinary today gave decree in favour of the pursuers for £250 under the first conclusion, assoilzied the defenders from the second conclusion, gave decree on the footing of an understanding with respect to the condenser; and found the pursuer entitled to expenses, subject to modification. In giving judgement, the Lord Ordinary said he sympathised with the defenders, because he doubted very much if they fully appreciated the nature of the obligation that they had undertaken.

The **St Clair** [Mitchell Library, Glasgow]

*The **Hebrides** [DEM's collection]*

but not one that was significantly enhanced. Running costs soared in the 1930s. In December 1935, McCallum and Orme added to their operating challenges by acquiring the small business of Jack Bros. and their vessel *Challenger*, a former trawler bought by James Jack towards the end of 1929. Jack Bros.' vessels – the *Challenger*, the *Sagittarius*, sunk off Kintyre in 1930, and her replacement, the *Burnside*, which sank in March 1933 – sailed from Glasgow to Skye and the Outer Hebrides, and offered some considerable competition to McCallum and Orme. The venture ran at a profit in the late 1920s, but got into difficulties as costs rose in the 1930s. Largely through failure to acquire any subsidy, Jack Bros. succumbed to the overtures of the larger competitor, which bought it for £4 892, most of the money being expended on goodwill.

The Second World War brought more misery to McCallum and Orme, through rising costs and falling revenues, and it was forced to seek a subsidy greater than the £2 500 which it had been allocated. Its requests were not well received by government. Nevertheless, McCallum and Orme's canny business strategy enabled the firm to maintain an independent existence until 1947. The older family interests, particularly those of the Ormes, had ceased with the death of key partners in the early 1940s. The company went into voluntary liquidation, and its assets were acquired by David MacBrayne Limited in 1948.

At that point, the distinguished contribution of McCallum and Orme as steamship pioneers in the Hebrides was relegated to the obscure footnotes of the more prominent and headline-grabbing history of MacBrayne, where it tends to remain to the present. MacBrayne's greater prestige and larger operation notwithstanding, it deserves to be noted that, in terms of private enterprise and the capacity to survive in that sector in the longer term, McCallum and Orme enjoyed infinitely greater success than David MacBrayne. The company functioned, however, by maintaining a noticeably low-level operation, with ageing ships and without any major, new capital investment. This worked against it in the longer term, though it was able to pay all of its debts when the books were finally balanced, and a sum of £18 000 was transferred to David MacBrayne.

The principal achievement of McCallum and Orme was that, independently and latterly as a single company, they provided an arterial highway (with its business hub in the Glasgow docklands) to, from and between the entire Hebrides for well-nigh a century. As their knowledge of the western seaboard improved, and as the Highland economy stabilised after 1870, so also did the quality and size of their ships. In this, they were remarkably far-sighted. Rather than 'buying in' small, and often second-hand, vessels, they began to invest in much larger and stouter purpose-built ships with a remarkable capacity for stoic endurance, even in the face of the very worst storms and the most treacherous rocks that the Hebrides could put in their way. Indeed, if a prize were to be offered for the most faithful and consistent steamship service of all time to these islands, it would be won outright by the *Dunara Castle*, built for Martin Orme and William Lang to replace the *Dunvegan Castle* in 1875. In service until January 1948, she had an astonishing record of seventy-two years, surpassed only by the longevity of the *Glencoe* (built originally for James Matheson, and not David MacBrayne). Her later consort, *Hebrides*, built for Captain John McCallum in 1898, would surely take second place. She served the islands until 1955, and was displaced only by the arrival of the new, diesel-powered cargo-vessel *Loch Ard* in that year. Like the *Loch Ard*, the *Dunara Castle* and the *Hebrides* were primarily cargo-boats, but with significantly more accommodation for passengers (some forty or fifty) than the later motor-vessels. Their cargo-carrying role has

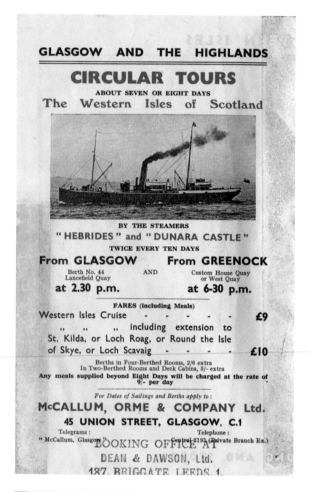

McCallum and Orme brochure from the late 1930s. Back and front covers [DEM's collection]

probably contributed to their relatively humble status, in contrast to the glamour associated with the Royal Mail steamers of David MacBrayne. The vessels of McCallum and Orme delivered mail to only three islands – Colonsay, Soay (off Skye) and St Kilda.

When the *Dunara Castle* first appeared from the yard of Blackwood & Gordon, Port Glasgow, in 1875, she was a stately, two-funnelled vessel, but she also carried some of the trappings of the age of sail. Early photographs, such as that taken by George Washington Wilson, show not only her two slender funnels, but also her sails, furled alongside her extremely tall masts. Her bridge was totally exposed to the elements, apart from canvas dodgers on its port and starboard extremities. There appear to have been three telegraphs on the bridge, one in central position and one on each wing. By the mid-1880s, a steering-wheel was positioned in a shelter below and ahead of the bridge, with an emergency wheel at the stern. The *Dunara* carried three white lifeboats, two to port and another (a large boat) to starboard of the engine casing. A deckhouse stood abaft the mainmast on the poop. In overall design, she was a modest three-island vessel, typical of that period, with holds fore and aft, served by derricks on each mast. The 'wells' were spanned by gang-planks which could be raised to allow full access to the tween-decks. Side-doors were provided for loading to and from ferries and flit-boats. Her straight stem was balanced by a finely wrought counter or 'elliptic' stern. She was often trimmed well down towards the stern, thus allowing her red boot-topping to show prominently towards the bow. The *Dunara*'s two-cylinder engine was compounded in 1882, and reboilering in 1894 eliminated one of her two funnels in favour of a single, stouter stack.

The *Hebrides*, designed by G.L. Watson and built in 1898 by Ailsa Shipbuilding, Troon, combined the best features of the *Hebridean* and the *Dunara Castle*. She was very similar to the *Dunara* – a quasi-sister, in fact – but with 'disguised' well-decks, which gave her a more elegant sheer, and much more modern machinery. The designer's specification for 'Screw Steamer, No. 370' envisaged a vessel of 170 feet 'between perpendiculars' and 28 feet in breadth, moulded. She was to be constructed

with straight stem and elliptic stern, full poop and topgallant forecastle, and with shelter deck extending over midship part of the vessel. Lightly rigged as a two-masted fore-and-aft schooner. Two holds with hatch to each; steam winch to each hatch and derricks on the masts. Crew berthed under main deck forward. Rooms for officers, w.c.'s, urinals, lamp-room, lockers etc. on main deck forward. Steerage on main deck forward. Cabin passengers in poop. Deckhouse aft, containing stair, clerk's room and deck cabin; and a small deck-house for chart-room amidships. Galley in casing amidships. Height from top of upper deck beams to top of main deck beams, 7 feet; from top of main deck beams to top of 'tween deck beams, 7 feet.

The paragraph on 'Sails, Covers etc.,' further illumines the appearance of the vessel. She was to have:

A complete set of sails to approved plan of No. 2 good ship's canvas, two tarpaulins for each hatchway on both decks, covers for sails, boats, binnacles, steering wheels, winches, skylights, with fastenings for the same. Weather cloths for front of bridge, also dodgers with stanchions for same. Awning for poop deck from mast aft, with awning stanchions, ridge poles, rafters etc., complete.

Although sails are mentioned in the specification, there is no known picture which shows sail of any kind on the *Hebrides*. The *Dunara*, however, was certainly equipped with sail-assistance. Even in the early 1900s, photographs show her with a furled fore staysail, which may have been used to hold her steady or to facilitate steering, and a sail furled vertically on the foremast. Both ships, in fact, had excellent machinery, and they were surprisingly fast. With a triple-expansion steam engine built by A. & J. Inglis, the *Hebrides* achieved 12.8 knots on trials, but her service speed is said to have been slightly slower than that of the slimmer *Dunara*. From the outset, the *Hebrides* carried a small wheel on the bridge, and had steam-assisted steering, but it is averred by some who travelled on her in the early 1950s that she was solely chain-steered by that stage.

ON BOARD THE *DUNARA CASTLE*

'IN THE EARLY years *Dunara Castle*, under her master Captain Archibald McEwan, was chiefly carrying cargo to the various and numerous west coast piers in remote places, but she was also fitted up to take a large number of passengers in diverse kinds of comfort to be found in cabins and staterooms, "second class" accommodation, and "steerage". Everyone could "promenade" along the quarterdeck, many could retreat into a "large retiring cabin" on the awning deck, and for those who preferred to stay under cover most of the time the saloon was "a large and tastefully furnished apartment" and "the ante-cabins are equally well fitted up". When the ship berthed in East Loch Tarbert, Harris, [at the time of the Census] in 1881 she had a crew of twenty-five including Captain McEwan, who, with twelve others all from the shires of Inverness and Argyll, spoke Gaelic. There were four stewards and a stewardess to attend to the wants of the passengers.

'One of the forty passengers aboard the *Dunara Castle* on a June afternoon at Glasgow's Finnieston Quay wrote of an experience which was typical of steamer voyages to the Hebrides. He had first of all watched the loading of the hold:

Presently Mr Donald, the ship's clerk, emerges from his deck cabin, and all is forthwith intelligent courtesy. The steward, Mr Kay, hurries up the companion-way, and assigns ourselves and our luggage to Norman, the under-steward, and Norman escorts us down to our state-room. The cabin accommodation of the steamer 'makes up' some fifty comfortable sleeping berths, including the ladies' state-room, numerous state-rooms for gentlemen, and the saloon. The 'bunks' in these state-rooms, with their neatly [draped] green curtains and snowy quilts and blankets, speak for themselves. But one cannot sufficiently admire the steward's resources at night, and the economy of space and packing power on board ship, when velvet

sofas and couches and dim stern recesses are deftly transformed into snug and airy, yet withal curtained and retired, sleeping-berths.

But now Captain McEwen is upon his bridge and before the red funnel. The steamer's final bell has rung, and the last passenger has stepped aboard. The gangways are hauled ashore and the hatches covered. 'Stand by there,' shouts the first mate, Mr Smith. The shore hawsers are eased, rat-tat goes the captain's brass handle rod down to the engine-room, and the man at the helm turns his wheel. The screw throbs slowly, and the *Dunara Castle* gradually cants towards mid-stream. Now she clears the Irish steamers lying ahead of her. 'Let go the hawsers down there.' Our good ship swings into the river, and drops down the Clyde at an easy rate for Greenock.

'The internal decoration of the *Dunara* was bright and cheerful, even sumptuous. "Marine self-adjusting lamps, swinging from the cupola, shed their soft light on the white and gold wainscoting and maple cabins and crimson velvet furnishings. The green baize of the central table relieved the silver and crystal with the aid of which, and Taliskar and steaming water, the national beverage was concocted by social groups."

'All, including the longer, somewhat erratic and unpredictable journeys, was very different from the generation of functional Hebridean ferries which was born nearly a century later, but there were certain similarities among the tourist travellers. There was that lady, "possessed by a passion for scenic beauty and sublimity. You will find her sitting upon the locker on the hurricane deck at all hours, gazing dreamily across blue sounds, or sequestered lochs, or wrapt in awe, as the steamer glides in stillness at the base of stupendous headlands, or past grisly peaks and cloud-capped scaurs." And there were the members of those "social groups" who sometimes made it ashore

and wandered about after rather too much of "the national beverage", loud people...

'So with the *Dunara Castle* in 1875 there was launched an invasion of tourists, romantics and adventure seekers of many kinds and from all sorts of places, who booked their passages so that they might, in summer and with some measure of comfort, look at west coast and island scenery and at communities with strange habits and a language different from their own. These communities therefore found themselves welcoming and gazing at a miscellaneous company of people, some of them still reeling from the effects of seasickness or of too much brandy and water, and just as odd in their behaviour and appearance as those they had come to see. Stimulated by the recent advertisements for steamer trips and by a variety of writers, many a would-be passenger considered that a visit to St Kilda had the greatest appeal in spite of, or even because of, the dangers and discomforts involved, and on safely returning they would make the final entries in journals and diaries logging their experiences and send off articles to a newspaper or occasionally write a book.'

(From Michael Robson, *St Kilda: Church, Visitors and 'Natives'*)

Pencil sketch of the **Dunara Castle**, *by D. E. Meek*

The **Hebrides** in Village
Bay, St Kilda, in 1938
[Robert Atkinson. School of
Scottish Studies Archives]

Even if they were the humble cargo-carriers of the
Hebrides, the two ships were comparatively well-appointed
for their passengers. The specification for the *Hebrides* was
very detailed in its recommendations for the saloon, and
especially for the sleeping accommodation to which it gave
access:

*Sofas round stern made with folding backs, so as to give
eight berths; and, if possible, six other berths to be got
above. Gentlemen's cabin, on port side, with four sofa
bunks, having folding backs, to hold eight. Ladies' cabin
with four standing berths and four sofa berths; separate*

*lavatory and water-closet. State-rooms (of which there
are six) need not be polished, but panelled in sound pine,
neatly grained and varnished. All furniture, however, to
be of polished mahogany – to have Smith's folding basin
in each, also in gentlemen's and ladies' cabins, and two
table-top basins at after-end of saloon, or Smith's fitted in
passage, as may be desired.*

Some passengers, however, were less than impressed
with the ship's accommodation. The Rev. Roderick Lawson,
who sailed to St Kilda on the *Hebrides* in 1902, wrote:

The chief drawback to sailing in these small steamers,

A TOURIST'S PERSONAL ALBUM:
MRS D. SEDDON MADE TWO TRIPS TO ST KILDA IN 1936–37

The <u>Hebrides</u> at Pooltiel, Skye [DEM's collection]

The <u>Hebrides</u> at Tarbert, Harris [DEM's collection]

The *Hebrides*
in Village
Bay, St Kilda,
1936 [DEM's
collection]

The village,
St Kilda,
1937 [DEM's
collection]

Captain Donald
MacMillan and
officers of the
Hebrides 1936-37
(above); Captain
MacMillan
and Mrs Seddon
(below left); Mrs
Seddon with the
radio operator,
Alasdair MacRae,
holding his gold
medal for Gaelic
singing (below
right) [DEM's
collection]

A pig being unloaded from the _Hebrides_ at Greenock [DEM's collection]

Flit-boats meeting the _Hebrides_ at Loch Eport, North Uist [DEM's collection]

A CURE FOR SEASICKNESS ON BOARD THE *HEBRIDES*

'I FOUND WHEN I was over in Lochboisdale [in May 1930] that the cargo ship, the *Hebrides*, from Glasgow took passengers and was going to St Kilda on the first journey since last summer. I was longing to go, and I was told to meet them at Lochmaddy the next day, and that it would cost me three pounds, ten shillings. So I hurried home with Angus John across the loch and when I got up to the cottage I was met by Mairi Anndra: "I hear you're going to St Kilda and it's going to cost you three pounds, ten shillings." The seagulls or something had got there before me, over that long distance, because it was nine miles by road from the hotel.

'I got my things together and went back with Angus John, took the *Lochmor* in the evening up to Lochmaddy, spent the night there and in the early morning joined the *Hebrides*. I knew the officers and crew, tall Captain MacMillan and the First Officer, Mr Clelland, the jolly rotund Chief Steward Mr Blair, and the wireless operator Alastair MacRae who was a real authority on birds and who had taught me the constellations by pinholes in brown paper held up to the light. The *Hebrides* was a lovely ship with her red plush saloon, the long dining table in the centre; everything was always bright and shining.

'Now you pass through the sound between North Uist and Harris, passing the lovely islands of Ensay, Berneray, and Pabbay, but once you get out into the Atlantic, there's always a huge swell, and this time it was an enormous oily swell, all the fifty miles across. I was on deck with my big Graflex camera and film and everything ready, but I began to feel worse and worse, and I thought, "This is terrible; I just can't face it." At last I had to go below to the red plush saloon and lie down. The steward came and he said, "Now if you eat what I give you, I can cure you." I said, "I'll eat anything to get over this." So he gave me a small slice of white bread soaked in Worcester sauce – Worcestershire, as we call it – and in no time I was completely cured and up on deck and never turned a hair again. I've since been told that this sauce contains capsicum, an ingredient of seasickness remedies.

'As we neared St Kilda, the sea-birds were absolutely extraordinary. Of course it was late May when there was always a tremendous number of them coming to nest. When the siren blew, they rose up in clouds – fulmars and puffins, guillemots and gannets. Near the entrace of the long horseshoe bay of Hirta, the main island, the cloud lifted and gave that vision of wild beauty that has so often been described. The small islands looked inaccessible, but Hirta itself was a most pleasing place with good pasture on its giant velvet green slope reaching to the summit of Conachair, the highest sea cliff in Britain. In the strange northern light every stone on the hillside appeared almost luminous. There was a row of houses with chimneys smoking and people with many dogs were hurrying to the shore…

'We were told that we mustn't touch a dog, because they were mangey. Nor were we to eat anything of their food. The St Kildans had had a severe winter and were terribly short, though fresh supplies were on the ship. A big rowing boat came out full of people who boarded the *Hebrides* to get news, supplies, and to talk, and we then went ashore.'

(From Margaret Fay Shaw, *From the Alleghenies to the Hebrides*)

Margaret Fay Shaw [Courtesy of Hugh Cheape]

in my opinion, is the poor character of the sleeping accommodation…they should put over the Cabin door – 'All ye who enter here leave Pride behind.' You had to crawl into your berth head foremost, and then **whummle** out as best you could.*

This was probably true of the 'sofa berths' which surrounded the saloons of all such steamers, and were also found in certain cabins. Even so, most passengers were content with what was offered, and both the *Hebrides* and the *Dunara Castle* built up a loyal following of tourists and travellers who were pleased to patronise them time and again. The ships were, however, three-class, and passengers who travelled in the steerage were offered only the most basic amenities.

The practical, down-to-earth nature and robust qualities of the *Dunara* and the *Hebrides* were enhanced by their long-term reliability. The *Dunara*, as she was – and still is – affectionately known by islanders, who always dropped the rather grandiose *Castle* from her name, saw several generations of MacBrayne vessels to the breakers, including the celebrated beauty, *Claymore*, of 1881. Given appropriate guns and camouflage, both the *Dunara* and the *Hebrides* went unscathed through two World Wars, the latter being transferred to the MacBrayne fleet temporarily by the Ministry of War Transport (in exchange for the *Lochgorm*) during the Second World War. Thereby she came to the rescue of David MacBrayne with an enhanced cargo-capacity at a critical time, when large aerodromes and airforce bases were being constructed in islands such as Tiree.

Part of the key to the long lives of the *Dunara Castle* and the *Hebrides* was their adaptability, within certain limits. They were regularly upgraded, and well maintained as very practical, unpretentious steamers. Their bridges were improved as time passed, and received wheelhouses during the Second World War. These were sturdy wooden shelters which afforded the officer-of-the-watch and the helmsman some degree of protection from the elements. Steering remained a challenge, nevertheless. The rudder was moved with the assistance of steam steering-gear located in the engine casing, and rods and chains on pulleys ran the length of the deck, connecting to a quadrant on the rudder stock. Despite steam-assistance, steering was heavy work, which required the moving of a couple of hundred feet of chain to achieve a change of course. The ships' even less welcome characteristics, such as their capacity to pitch and roll abominably in heavy weather, were not readily eradicated by any form of improvement or upgrade. Even when the *Hebrides* had her tall masts truncated to the height of the derrick blocks and ratlines in the early 1950s in an attempt to reduce her dreadful rolling, she still had the capacity to induce sea-sickness in her hardened crew. The trimming of her masts did little more than remove her majestic overall appearance, derived from the heady days of sail, though she remained a very attractive vessel to the end of her life, latterly sitting prettily in Kingston Dock in the berth opposite the *Loch Carron*, built in 1951 and soon to become another indispensable part of the Hebridean fleet.

Despite their rather functional style and their discomfort in bad weather, the *Dunara* and the *Hebrides* became an integral part of Hebridean existence. Their courses were deeply woven into the fabric of island life, in its happier and sadder moods. Indeed, they presided over key social events in the Hebrides. Both ships served St Kilda, and their presence in Village Bay – graphically portrayed in numerous emotive photographs, in which they are dwarfed by the surrounding expanse of sea and the serrated heights of Dùn – is perhaps one of the most poignant reminders that we have of the uneasy exchange between the Hebrides and the Scottish mainland. The *Dunara* has been immortalised as the vessel that undertook the final phase of the evacuation of St Kilda in 1930. She was, in one sense, 'the last ship out of St Kilda', when it was still – only just – an existing community. The *Hebrides* too played her part in this dispersal, and in other deeply symbolic departures. She conveyed the islanders of Soay (off Elgol, Skye) to new lives in Mull in 1953, and in the 1920s she acted as a tender to emigrant ships, notably the *Metagama*, the Canadian Pacific liner which carried a substantial number of Lewis people from Stornoway to Montreal in 1923. It could be argued that no two ships ever interacted so fully with, or contributed so markedly to, the lives of the Hebridean communities of the twentieth century. Yet, as their St Kildan contribution demonstrates, they increased the growing dependence of the islands on external assistance. In this way they exemplified, more obviously than any other vessels of their day, the deeply ambivalent role of the steamship in helping to weaken, as well as to preserve, the distinctiveness of island ways of life.

Like their predecessors in the fleets of McCallum and Orme, the *Hebrides* and the *Dunara* had intimate, first-hand knowledge of the geological structures of the Clyde and the Hebrides, through their friendly altercations with inconvenient rocks, their occasional groundings, and their capacity to 'sit it out' on the soft sands and mud of shallow bays until the tidal conditions permitted them to berth. The *Dunara* went aground at Fort Matilda, near Greenock, in August 1922, and in March 1947 she spent a week on the ground at Bunessan, Mull, eventually being refloated without assistance. About the end of the Second World War, the *Hebrides* scraped her bottom badly on a rock in the Sound of Gunna (between Tiree and Coll) when peforming a last, much-appreciated act of kindness for a funeral party from

*The **Dunara Castle** with two funnels [George Washington Wilson. Aberdeen University Library]*

*The **Dunara Castle** ashore at Fort Matilda in 1922 [G. E. Langmuir's collection]*

*The grand old steamship **Dunara Castle** being scrapped at Port Glasgow [School of Scottish Studies Archives]*

Caolas (Tiree) by delivering the remains of their relative to the inlet closest to the family home. In this manner, McCallum and Orme offered a personal service which would be ruled out sternly by today's safety regulations. It was not untypical of these vessels and their crews that they went out of their way (quite literally) to meet the varied needs of the community of which they themselves formed an integral part, and that they took considerable risks in the process. It says much for the fabric of the ships and the quality of their seamen that they lasted relatively unscathed until the late 1940s and (in the case of the *Hebrides*) the mid-1950s.

The extensive itineraries of the *Dunara Castle* and the *Hebrides*, coupled with their ability to push their way undaunted into secluded habours, gave them a very attractive selling-point. Tourists from far afield were enticed to sign up with McCallum and Orme, in order to 'Visit the Romantic Western Isles and Lone St Kilda', as the front cover of their brochure proclaimed. This was the so-called 'circular tour' of the Hebrides in the summer season. In a 'Notice to Passengers', the 1930s brochure stated:

> *The steamers 'HEBRIDES' and 'DUNARA CASTLE' have comfortable accommodation for Tourists. There are staterooms with two and four berths situated on the main-deck and on upper deck.*

> *Both Steamers are fitted with Wireless Equipment and carry an Operator. Radio Telegrams can be sent to these vessels (via Malinhead radio) from any Post Office, and vice versa.*

> *The fare, including meals, provides for*

> *Breakfast, Dinner and Tea, with Tea or Coffee and Biscuits at 9 p.m.; other meals, liquor, etc., are charged for at Tariff rates.*

> *The cuisine is of the best.*

> *During the summer months passengers are recommended to book their berths in advance, stating particularly whether ladies or gentlemen (Mr., Mrs. or Miss), and giving the name of each passenger.*

> *Passengers must take charge of their own luggage.*

There was an obvious demand for summer cruises of this kind in the inter-war years, and St Kilda – with its magnetic effect as the *Ultima Thule* of the Ossianic grand tour – was the centrepiece of 'The *Hebrides* Tour', as distinct from that of the *Dunara Castle*, which at that time centred on Skye and Loch Roag, Lewis. McCallum and Orme's 1930s brochure still played on the old concept of sublimity, while adding to modern, tourist-oriented romanticism the doleful note of recent desolation. It is also noteworthy that the 'elements' are seen to be the key factor in the fate of the island:

> *Ere morning is noon we reach St. Kilda and its crescent shaped rugged bay, now uninhabited during winter – for the elements won the struggle for supremacy. In the Island bay we see the village, a straggling line of grey stone cottages, across this vast mountain amphitheatre, awesome in its cliffs, solitude, and wheeling, screaming seafowl.*

St Kilda remained on McCallum and Orme's summer-season itinerary from 2 July 1877, when Martin Orme's *Dunara Castle* made her first visit, until 1939. McCallum

ELECTRIC REACHES ST KILDA

McCALLUM AND ORME'S ships, *Dunara Castle* and *Hebrides*, were the mainstay of the St Kilda service, anchoring in Village Bay during the summer season. Latterly, also, MacBrayne's *Clydesdale* included St Kilda on its itinerary. Other companies, quick to cash in on the early tourist boom, offered occasional voyages to St Kilda. These were in the nature of short cruises, intent on observing the human menagerie on the edge of the world, whose primitive habits contrasted with the sublimity of the setting, particularly that of Hirta, the main island of the archipelago. The island was first visited by the *Glen Albyn* in 1834, followed by the *Vulcan* in 1838, which was the first 'cruise ship' to reach St Kilda.

Fifty years later, in 1888, the steamship *Electric*, temporarily in the use of the short-lived West Highland Fisheries Company of Oban, took a shipload of tourists from Oban to St Kilda. One of these, Robert MacFarlan, recorded his visit in the columns of the *Dumbarton Herald*. The tendency of most such writers was to emphasise the backwardness of the 'natives' of this 'Outpost of Civilisation', as MacFarlan called it. In the main, twentieth-century authors of the ever-expanding 'St Kilda sequence' of popular (but not always accurate) books have regarded the literary efforts of MacFarlan and his kind as primary sources for the history of St Kilda, with the result that external biases and interpretations remain standard currency. For example, it is a common observation that the St Kildans were so ignorant of the outside world that they thought that the first steamship to visit the archipelago was a sailing vessel that had caught fire. In fact, such a perception of early steamships was not by any means restricted to the St Kildans. It can be found in other specimens of 'first encounter' with the new invention. Later writers who perpetuate these 'myths' forget that such 'primitivism' and 'ignorance' were typical of early nineteenth-century societies, including British society more generally. The authorial stance, which sees the 'prejudices' and 'humiliating condition' of others, but not its own, is reminiscent of that adopted by nineteenth-century writers on 'darkest Africa'.

MacFarlan's narrative is deeply prejudiced against the St Kildans, who are seen as unprogressive and unco-operative, despite their obvious ability to 'play the game' with tourists and 'make a killing' among the easy victims of primitivist delusions. The St Kildans are given confectionery and trinkets by the *Electric's* passengers, in much the same way as the 'natives' of other countries would be given beads and tobacco. They sell their goods in return. MacFarlan writes:

> On the following morning we joined the steamship *Electric* at Oban, and leaving there at half past ten, set off on the voyage to St Kilda. We (the 'we' now signifies about five ladies and forty-five gentlemen), passed through the Sound of Mull, and touching at Tobermory, Coll and Tiree, made for Castlebay, Barra, where we halted for an hour or two, during which we enjoyed ourselves in different ways according to the varied tastes of a promiscuous [i.e. motley, mixed] company. One gent was busy love-making, another took to the tap-room, while a third collected about a score of native children, and held a Gaelic concert on the pier, to the astonishment of the passengers, who were enchanted with the youthful singers of 'Mo Rùn Geal Dileas' and 'Mo Nighean Donn Bhòidheach' etc. Leaving Barra, we proceeded to Lochboisdale, and from thence to Lochmaddy, from which, passing through the Sound of Harris, we made direct for St Kilda, which we reached on Saturday at mid-day. Arrived in the bay opposite the dwelling-houses on the island, the ship cast anchor, and one of the small boats was lowered, and the passengers were taken ashore in groups of a dozen or more, the officers of the ship accompanying. Before we had got to shore, the natives had come down to meet us. They did not impress me favourably, and subsequent conversation and inquiry regarding them did not alter my first impression. Inclusive of three officials, viz. the minister, the teacher and the nurse, and of two babies (one ten days and the other ten weeks old), and a pair married on the Tuesday preceding our visit, the population of the island is 77, the females being in the majority.
>
> Passengers having confections, tobacco or spare money to dispose of were surrounded by knots of the islanders, who offered socks, sea birds (dead and alive), birds' eggs and wings for sale, and eagerly held out their hands for whatever was presented to them. The grown people have as a rule no English, but the younger folks have English as well as Gaelic. A pretty maid (from 17 to 20), the beauty of the island, received considerable attention from several of the handsome men of our party, who carried away her autograph in triumph, if they did not make havoc with her heart. She was in her best home-spun 'togs', for she, like the others, had learned of our expected arrival, and had made preparations to meet us. The names of the islanders are MacKinnon, Macdonald, McQueen, Ferguson and Gillies. The minister is the Rev. John Mackay, the teacher is a Macrae, and the nurse is Mrs Urquhart. The minister is prophet, priest, king, policeman, judge and final arbiter. His long residence on this lonely island has assimilated him to the people, who have pulled him down quite as much as he has lifted them up. He, it seems, encourages the poor folks in their peculiar delusions and prejudices. In particular, he incites them to remain on the island, rather than strike out into the world, and make men and women of themselves by getting rid of their present humiliating condition. Just now they appear to be not a great deal above the level of professional beggars.

MacFarlan failed to grasp the irony that the steamship and tourism had helped to create the society of 'professional beggars' which now confronted him. It was all the fault of the islanders, and not of the outside world.

The pier at St Kilda [School of Scottish Studies Archives, University of Edinburgh]

and Orme thus ceased its St Kildan cruises almost exactly a century after the Glasgow Steam Packet Company's *Vulcan* arrived at St Kilda on 28 July 1838, carrying both tourists and materials for twenty-one new houses. By combining cargo-carrying with an 'Ossianic circular tour' of the Giant's Causeway, Staffa, Iona, Loch Scavaig, Loch Coruisk and Lochmaddy, the *Vulcan* anticipated the later company's distinctive policy of conveying both essential goods and sight-seers in pursuit of grand scenery.

For tourists who had cameras in the first thirty years or so of the twentieth century, the 'out-of-the-way' nature of the McCallum and Orme cruises, which called at a large variety of islands, bays and inlets on their course to the sublime pinnacles of St Kilda, provided unparalleled opportunities for what has now become 'classic' old-style photography of Hebridean 'natives', maritime conventions and landscapes. Sets of photographs taken in this period show a consistently keen, if at times contrived, external interest in St Kilda. Tourists mingle with, and are eager to be 'snapped' alongside, the last inhabitants of this primitive insular paradise. Shots of St Kildan boats coming to meet the *Hebrides* and the *Dunara* are not infrequent, with the wooden simplicity of the St Kildans' small craft implicitly contrasting with the power and sophistication of the Victorian steamship. Photographs of other ports on this itinerary frequently portray the 'flit-boats' used to convey goods from the steamship to the shore. Some of these flit-boats were owned by McCallum and Orme (see Appendix B), in much the same way as David MacBrayne owned and utilised the well-known, small 'red boats' at locations where there were no piers.

Tourists were also anxious to stand alongside the heroic, up-to-date mariners who crewed the *Hebrides* and the *Dunara*. They took a particular pride in posing for the camera with their Captains, such as Captain Donald Clark (from Colonsay) on the *Dunara*, and Captain Donald (Dan) MacMillan (from Iona) on the *Hebrides*. Generally the officers and deck-hands of these vessels were from the Hebrides, while their engineers were from the Scottish Lowlands. The Masters of modern ships and machinery were, of course, the other side of the 'primitivist' coin of tourist currency.

Little wonder, then, that, in meeting the needs of islanders and tourists alike with such remarkable consistency and with a hint of their own intrinsic 'primitivism' as the years passed, the *Dunara* and the *Hebrides* became legends in their own lifetimes, sailing onwards in the popular mind to the present day. The *Dunara*, in particular, entered deeply into song and story, in both English and Gaelic, where she can still be encountered in a variety of roles. She was remembered warmly for going to the aid of wartime casualties, such as Hogarth's *Baron Renfrew*, which was damaged by aircraft bombing in 1941, but managed to reach the safe waters of Mull. According to the Ross of Mull bard, John Campbell,

'S i an **Dunàra** a shàbhail am Baran
  san àm,
O na sgeirean tha millteach aig beul
  Loch nan Ceall,
'S thoghaich gu tèarainte i do chaladh
  an àigh
Taobh a-staigh Chaolas Liathanaich
  beulaibh Loch Làthaich.

*It was the **Dunara** that saved the Baron*
  at that time
From the rocks that were deadly at the
  mouth of Loch nan Ceall,
And towed her safely to the splendid haven
  Inside Caolas Liathanach at the opening
  of Loch Làthaich.

The *Dunara*'s capacity to tow other boats, and to be offered a tow by them, became something of a set piece within the Gaelic story-telling tradition. She was also noted for her shrill and powerful whistle, which John Campbell likewise commemorates:

Gur th' ann aice tha 'n dùdach a
  dhùisgeas mo smuain,
A rifeid cho binn nuair a ghleusar i suas;
Air Ghalldachd 's air Ghàidhealtachd 's
  gu h-àrd 'n Abhainn Chluaidh`
Gu bheil trombaid an àigh aig Dunàra
  nam buadh.

She certainly has the whistle which will
  waken my thought,
Her reed is so sweet when it is tuned into
  form;
In Lowlands and Highlands and high up
  on the Clyde
*The **Dunara** of many virtues has the all-*
  surpassing trumpet.

In another song, composed at the end of the nineteenth century, she can be found rolling heavily round the Mull of Kintyre in an unseasonal storm which struck at the beginning of Glasgow Fair fortnight. According to the poet, Neil MacLaine, who was on board, her dreadful rolling knocked the airs and graces out of haughty young ladies who had forgotten their Gaelic, and had learned English and other affectations in Glasgow. The name of the *Hebrides* was less easy to blend into Gaelic verse, but she and the *Dunara* go together as inseparably and as indelibly as the *Queen Mary* and the *Queen Elizabeth*. A story about the one leads inevitably to a recollection of the other.

Time, however, caught up with these great, legendary liners, and also with the smaller, but seemingly everlasting, *Dunara Castle* and *Hebrides*. Having survived the Second World War, they had become maritime anachronisms, working museums of the late Victorian age, out of place in an unfolding new era which wanted to rebuild itself along progressive, post-war lines. The *Dunara* fulfilled her life cycle appropriately in 1948 by coming home to die at Port Glasgow, where she had begun her days in 1875. Photographs taken of her final weeks show her in shallow water, listing on her starboard side, largely devoid of rigging, with her forward derrick a mere lifeless pole without its tackle, and piles of her own gear and metal lying on the dockside. The robust construction and capacious holds of the *Hebrides* helped her to survive until 1955, when, with the arrival of the *Loch Ard* with her powerful profile and bipod mast, she too went to Smith's, the breakers at Port Glasgow. Black smoke and white steam from a red funnel, puffing its way from Mull to Tiree in the late evening, is the final, lasting memory of this gallant ship in the writer's mind. It was hard to imagine island life without her. Inevitably, however, the brave, new, post-war world belonged to the motor-vessels, and they in their turn became the maritime furniture of the islands. They were already trying to bang their way into the aspirational grandeur of the Edwardian era when the *Dunara Castle* and the *Hebrides* were still in the full bloom of youth.

DUNARA CASTLE REMEMBERED

'DURING THE SECOND World War, I used to travel fairly regularly on the *Dunara* from Tiree to Skye. I worked with the Air Ministry in Tiree at that time, and I would visit my close relatives in Skye in the summer. I would go on board the *Dunara* at Scarinish Pier, and I would waken up with the sun rising over Uig Bay the next morning. It was so beautiful. Sometimes we called at Loch Pooltiel on the way to Uig. I do not remember any noise from the engines when the ship was under way. My Aunt Flora would meet me on the pier at Uig. It was such an easy, convenient way to travel from one island to another. I would have a two-berth stateroom on the *Dunara*.

'Passengers would take their meals with the officers in those days. The officers were always ready to pull my leg, and to have a wee joke at my expense, as I was a Baptist and known to be rather fond of the Baptist minister in Tiree. It was such a happy atmosphere. The *Dunara* was always beautifully kept – she was immaculate – but she looked distinctly old-fashioned by that stage.

'We all loved the names of the *Hebrides* and the *Dunara* – they were household names to us, and we loved the ships themselves too. There were no ships like them. The islands depended on them for so many things. The *Dunara* was so reliable. You could set your watch by her. Just about everything you needed would be "coming on the *Dunara*" if it was not already in the island.'

Isabella Meek Ross, July 2005

Isabella Meek Ross [DEM]

THE NIGHT ON THE *DUNARA*

Neil MacLaine

I spent last night on board the vessel,
I spent last night on board the vessel;
I spent a night that was dark and stormy
on the sea west to the Gaels' homeland.

A year ago at last fair-time
when others were going home gaily,
I put my bag beneath my armpit
and I took my passage on the *Dunara*.

When we set sail from Greenock,
it was lovely, with the calm of seabirds,
and the lassies looked so pretty –
every single one was smiling.

Each one was so very pompous;
Tiree girls were talking English,
Mull ones and alas! Skye ones too –
all of them had lost their Gaelic.

A fellow began to tune his bagpipes
and on the lower deck the dancing started,
and if I'm honest in my story,
wasn't I myself among the dancers?

The young lassies were so sprightly,
bedecked in their attire so brightly,
every one was in her finest,
with high hats that sported feathers.

It rained, it blew, and it grew darker,
and the ocean swelled with anger;
there was never such a tempest
since the year the potatoes vanished.

When the ocean surged like valleys,
the English language soon departed;
each one would cry, 'Hold, hold me tightly;
my head is on the point of cracking.'

I heard a voice, sad and wistful,
from the Moss girl surnamed Currie,
saying then to Lucy Brogie,
'Lucky the one who's near her mammy!'

Before we reached Kintyre's Headland,
the whole scene was total chaos;
every single girl was levelled,
and her back was bent with retching.

Here and there would be seen scattered
false hairpieces on lower deck-planks,
and back-combs being smashed to pieces;
to me it was not a cause for laughter.

When we reached the rocks of Torrin
the wild sea in piles was rolling;
sighs could be heard in succession,
coming from those with towering hairstyles.

When at length we reached Bunessan,
and we were able to stand upright,
many a fine ribbon was creased then,
and many a suit in need of stitching.

The one who lost her Grecian curls
leapt across the deck so lightly,
to take a hold of a lifebelt,
but the cork could scarce assist her.

Those that night who were so haughty
that they would not dance a reel beside me,
by morning I'd not give a groat for them;
their boast remained, but their beauty vanished.

We reached the Low Island safely,
and I shall now conclude this ditty;
but I'll never lose my recollection
of that night of deluge on the *Dunara*.

'Low Island' – Tiree

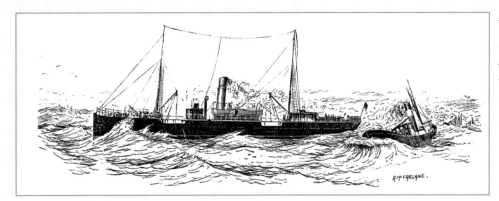

*A drawing of the **Dunara Castle**, by Alasdair MacFarlane.*

CHAPTER 5

THE EDWARDIAN SUMMERS:
CRUISE YACHTS AND PARAFFIN ENGINES

*The **Pioneer** (III), in West Loch Tarbert [NR's collection]*

THE EDWARDIAN SUMMERS:
CRUISE YACHTS AND PARAFFIN ENGINES

*It was 1911 when I first made the Oban-Tobermory run in the **Lochinvar**, when the glorious weather and magnificent scenery were discounted by the appalling roar of her motors, the vibration, and the playful habit of the thin exhaust pipes (which took the place of a funnel) in discharging blobs of paraffin and black carbon at frequent intervals. My friends in Mull were made aware of her daily coming by the splutter of her engines and whiffs of paraffin when she was yet only halfway down the sound. In placid summer weather she was a trial to voyage in, but one run in a cold gale, with lashing rain and a crowded deck cargo of sheep, was an ordeal in itself.*

FROM A LETTER TO THE EDITOR OF *SEA BREEZES* BY R. S. MCNAUGHT, FIRST PUBLISHED IN OCTOBER 1961.

In 1902, David MacBrayne, who was then an old man of 85, took his two sons, David Hope MacBrayne and his younger brother Laurence, into partnership. David Hope MacBrayne became Chairman of what was to become a new limited liability company in 1905, by which time Laurence had already left the company to plough another furrow. David MacBrayne, the elder, died in 1907.

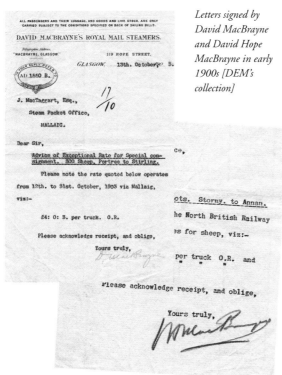

Letters signed by David MacBrayne and David Hope MacBrayne in early 1900s [DEM's collection]

The year 1902 was also a turning-point for the company, because the ageing fleet of steamers, half of which had been acquired second-hand, required to be replaced, and a renewal programme was commenced. Seven new ships were delivered between 1903 and 1905, four of them by Scott & Sons at Bowling, and the remainder by A.& J. Inglis. Three of them were near-sisters, rejoicing in bird nomenclature – *Lapwing*, *Plover* and *Cygnet*. Only the *Lapwing* was given a new set of compound engines. The *Plover* and *Cygnet* received the port and starboard compound engines and boilers from the *Flowerdale* respectively, engines which had been built some twenty-six years previously and which had been salvaged when the *Flowerdale* was wrecked off Lismore in 1904. The *Flowerdale* had been built with an odd arrangement of inward-turning screws. The port engine drove the propeller clockwise, the starboard engine counter-clockwise. These arrangements would have continued when the individual engines were transferred to the new ships.

The *Lapwing* offered limited cabin accommodation, but it was adequate for the Oban-Outer Isles service, which she shared initially with the *Flowerdale*, and latterly with the *Plover*. The *Cygnet*, however, had only limited passenger facilities, until these were improved after the Great War. The *Cygnet* also had a hinged funnel to allow her to berth at Glasgow up-river of the railway bridge while she was on the Inveraray service alongside the old *Texa*. All three new ships were excellent sea-boats, and served the exposed routes of the company well.

*The **Plover** [G. E. Langmuir's collection]*

*The **Cygnet**, coming into Tobermory [G. E. Langmuir's collection]*

The next new ship was the stately *Sheila*, built specifically for the year-round Kyle of Lochalsh-Stornoway service. Her distinction in MacBrayne history is that she was the company's first ship to be equipped with triple-expansion engines, which were relatively efficient, and, uniquely in the fleet, she was named after a character in a novel by William Black. Another new vessel was the little *Brenda*, which was destined to be the last Glasgow-based steamer to sail through the Crinan Canal *en route* for Mull and Inverness (latterly Fort William). Her use of this waterway continued until 1929, when the Crinan Canal route was abandoned. The sixth new ship was the paddle-steamer *Pioneer*, built as a shallow-draft vessel for the West Loch Tarbert-Islay mail service. She had compound diagonal engines, but, strangely, she was equipped with the haystack-type boiler which had been installed in ships such as the old *Glencoe*. However, this arrangement was relatively light in weight, and would have helped to reduce the draft of the ship as she sailed up and down the rocky shallows of West Loch Tarbert. It also allowed a paddle-wheel of smaller diameter and lighter weight to be fitted, but this came at the price of increased wear and tear. All the new ships had steel hulls.

The final new ship was the *Clydesdale*. She was designed for the Glasgow-Inverness service, but after only a few trips she was transferred to the Glasgow-Islay route in place of the *Glendale*, which was wrecked on Kintyre in July 1905, following confusion of the Sanda and Mull of Kintyre lights. This is the service with which the *Clydesdale* is best associated. The *Glendale* had arrived in the

THE CHIEFTAIN PASSING THE ISLE OF EIGG.

fleet only in 1902, having last been used by New Palace Steamers as *La Belgique* on their Tilbury-Ostende excursion service in 1897. She had been built in 1875 as the *Paris* for the London, Brighton & South Coast Railway. The *Clydesdale* was also used on the Stornoway mail service for two-and-a-half years, following the loss of the *Sheila* and prior to the delivery of the *Lochness*.

To crown the burst of new building, a rather special ship was commissioned in 1907 – the famous *Chieftain*, which was the company's only purpose-built cruise steamer. The cruise industry had developed slowly in the West Highlands since those first voyages of romantic curiosity in the early nineteenth century, and it was greatly enhanced with the arrival of the *Clansman* on the Glasgow-Stornoway route in 1870. Since 1881, the service had been maintained jointly with the *Claymore*, alternating on the six-day round trip, with Monday and Thursday departures from Glasgow.

These voyages had become firm summer favourites, and David MacBrayne had been quick to realise and develop the revenue-earning potential of seasonal-cruise tourist traffic. Although electric lighting had been installed in the ships in 1904, the *Clansman* in particular was becoming somewhat jaded, and her accommodation old-fashioned and uncomfortable. Besides, she was an iron-hulled ship, then 34 years old. The new *Chieftain* was her replacement – and what a fine ship she was!

The reason for the upgrade was simply that competitors had better-quality ships on offer. McCallum and Orme both added their unique flavour to the trade out of Glasgow, running their 'circular tours' as far as St Kilda (see Chapter 4), while the Leith- and Aberdeen-based cruises of the North Company on the east coast of Scotland were serviced by modern, purpose-built vessels, as were the Liverpool-based cruises offered by M. Langlands on the west coast.

*M. Langlands' **Princess Maud** leaving Oban [NR's collection]*

Coastal cruises from Liverpool and Ardrossan to the Western Isles were introduced by M. Langlands & Sons in 1870, using the screw cargo-and-passenger steamer *Princess Royal*, which had been built in 1863. In 1892, the *Princess Victoria*, a steamer of 1108 tons gross built by W. Thompson at Dundee, was designed specifically for seasonal West Highland cruises. She was a finely-appointed ship. The cargo spaces on the tween-decks were fitted with temporary cabin accommodation, which allowed the vessel to be converted for seasonal 'yachting' duties. After his first yachting season, Captain McNeill of the *Princess Victoria* reported to Mr Langlands that the profit on the bar more than covered the expense of the ship, and still showed a good round sum on the right side! Captain McNeill once clipped a rock in the Narrows in the Kyles of Bute, when

he found the main channel blocked by a yacht, and he was forced to take the winding Southern Channel, but none of his passengers were aware of the incident.

In 1901, the *Princess Maud* was commissioned by Langlands, with finely-appointed accommodation for 140 first-class passengers, and seating for 100 of these in the saloon, famed for its oak panelling and oak carving-work. By 1912, the company had commissioned another specially-built cruise ship, the *Princess Royal*, with berths for 200 first-class cruise passengers; but, alas, she was short-lived, becoming a war loss.

In 1886, the North of Scotland, Orkney and Shetland Company started offering cruises to the Norwegian fjords aboard the *St Rognvald* at £10 per head. The three-year-old *St Rognvald* normally served the Orkney and Shetland

ferry service. The cruises were so well patronised that the North Company built the world's first dedicated cruise ship, the 'steam yacht' *St Sunniva*, in 1887. Rather than displace the *St Rognvald*, the new ship extended the cruising season in subsequent years from May to September, and by 1889 had included cruises to Baltic and Mediterranean destinations, the latter on a charter basis. In addition, the Orient Line and other liner companies were assigning their best ships increasingly to seasonal cruising to ever more exotic locations.

David Hope MacBrayne's vision was to secure the West Highland cruising niche, and to do this he needed a purpose-built, attractive and comfortable cruise yacht. This was the *Chieftain*. Cleverly, he retained the *Claymore* on the route as a contrast in style, in which the berths opened on to the after saloon, where first-class passengers dined with the officers at one long table. The new *Chieftain* was state-of-the-art: triple-expansion engine, single screw, complete with silent-running steam winches, modern, airy first-class

SEASON 1907.

GRAND WEEKLY CRUISES
BY NEW STEAMSHIP
"CHIEFTAIN"
LAUNCHED, MAY, 1907).

Leaving Glasgow every Saturday, arriving at Oban same evening, remaining there over Sunday and sailing thence on Monday morning, visiting - - -

THE FINEST
LOCH SCENERY
IN THE
WEST HIGHLANDS
AND ISLANDS,

And arriving back in Glasgow on Fridays.

The "CHIEFTAIN," which has been specially built for the West Highland Tourist Trade, is more like a Yacht than a Tourist Steamer. The comfort of passengers has been fully kept in view in arranging the spacious Dining Rooms, Drawing Rooms, Smoking Rooms, Deck Cabins, State Rooms Bath Rooms, etc.

Electric Light and Bells throughout.

Passengers should book Berths, as long beforehand as possible, and state whether for Ladies or Gentlemen.

Full Particulars on application to the Owners

DAVID MACBRAYNE, Ltd.,
119, Hope Street, GLASGOW.

*Advertisement for the **Chieftain** from 1907 MacBrayne Timetable [DEM's collection]*

REMOTE AND ROYAL: TOURIST GUIDES AND TIMETABLES

THE PRINCIPAL STEAMSHIP companies serving the Highlands and Islands were very much alive to the tourist potential of the area. They themselves had to make a living from tourism, but their ships also helped people resident within the region to improve their circumstances by catering for tourists and visitors. It is noticeable that the last quarter of the nineteenth century, and the opening years of the twentieth, were something of a 'boom time' in the Highlands and Islands, as hotel proprietors built extensions and improved their properties to accommodate the increasing influx from further afield. Much of this was due to the steamship companies, and pre-eminently to David MacBrayne.

McCallum & Orme's front cover in colour (above left)
*The **Hebrides** passing Castle Moil (above right)*
*The **Dunara Castle** passing Iona (bottom) [DEM's collection]*

The companies had to 'market' their areas, as well as their own ships and amenities, as their survival depended on success in attracting business. A key component of their strategy was advertising, through posters bearing outlines of their ships, attractive timetables, and also tourist guides.

The style and format of these guides reflected the aspirations and relative affluence of the individual companies. McCallum and Orme produced very serviceable, but small and compact, brochures. These carried a principal 'marketing image' on their front covers – usually a fine Highland stag, standing high on a peak and grandly surveying a stretch of water, in which one of the company's ships can be seen sailing against a Highland landscape – latterly a silhouette of Village Bay, St Kilda. Colour was used initially, with paintings of the *Dunara Castle* and the *Hebrides* inside the brochure. By the late 1930s, a two-tone red-and-black format was used, with photographs of one or both of the ships on the back cover. The main text of the pamphlet was devoted to the ships' accommodation, and pre-eminently to summaries of their tours.

The tourist guides produced by David MacBrayne are among the ephemeral literary highlights of the period from c. 1880 to 1930. In their hey-day, these were produced as red-covered hard-backs, with gold tooling, carrying the title *Summer Tours in the Western Highlands & Islands of Scotland By the Royal Mail Steamers of David MacBrayne Ltd, Columba, Iona etc.* Engraved in gold on the front cover was the flagship of the fleet, the classic paddle-steamer *Columba*, bordered on the left by an elegantly curving thistle design. The cover also bore a golden crown, with the subscript, *The Royal Route*. Clearly, MacBrayne's principal selling-point was the company's association with royalty, whether through the Royal Mail or Queen Victoria's grand visitation in 1847, which gave the company 'a touch of class' and the genesis of its 'Royal Route'. In terms of symbolism and self-perception, this was indeed an ocean kingdom, with its own crown, sceptre and sword. The sword was borne aloft proudly in the hand of the ubiquitous, finely attired, plaided Highlander, who is the recurrent image of MacBrayne's sovereignty, in print, in plate and on prow – in short, the royal Highlander.

McCallum and Orme, on the other hand, catering for tourists to St Kilda, drew strength from their monopoly of the 'journey to the edge of the world'. They placed their marketing emphasis on remoteness and lonely beauty, which could be accessed (paradoxically) by means of their steamers. Their fine, front-page stag was a mutation of Sir Edwin Landseer's 'Monarch of the Glen' (1851), which had become the monarch of all he surveyed – a Highland 'royal' of another kind.

Both companies stressed the special qualities of their steamers. David MacBrayne was much more ambitious, distinguishing his 'Swift Passenger Steamers' from his 'Deep Sea Steamers'. The latter designation implied that the company was no mere estuarial outfit, serving the coasts and the nearest islands, but that it actually went 'deep sea' with strong ships – an emotive, and perhaps debatable, concept to Highland sailors who had travelled the globe on real deep-sea vessels. By ostentatious implication, MacBrayne was in the same business as Cunard, and passengers on his ships could expect the same degree of safety, luxury and maritime skill as those on Atlantic liners.

The aspirational grandeur of MacBrayne's Edwardian fleet reached its zenith in 1907, with the building of the majestic and heroically-named *Chieftain*. Her luxurious attributes were emphasised time and again in the guides and timetables of the period, with some excellent sketches of the ship herself, showing her fine lines to advantage. She was clearly the company's principal icon in terms of 'ship appeal' – the Hebridean and Edwardian equivalent of *Queen Elizabeth 2*. MacBrayne stressed that she had been 'specially built for the West Highland tourist trade', but that she was 'more like a Yacht than a Tourist Steamer'. The concept of the 'working yacht', already evident in the *Claymore*, had become even grander, offering greater luxury than ever before, including 'Electric Light and Bells throughout'. It was all (seemingly) sparkle and clink. One can almost envisage flowing evening dresses shimmering beside black ties on the great staircase as the guests go to dinner, and the vessel glides into Portree or Stornoway – to collect a cargo of sheep!

Such was the tempo of the times, in coastal waters and (truly) deep sea. This was the era of Cunard's

Lusitania and *Mauretania*, and White Star Line's triad of super-liners, *Olympic*, *Titanic* and *Britannic*. The principle underlying these three ships was that they should offer luxury beyond that provided by Cunard, and thus attract passengers. Sadly, the lives of two of the ships were cut short by tragedy, and the *Olympic* alone sailed the Atlantic until the 1930s. MacBrayne's *Chieftain* was also short-lived, but because of less dreadful circumstances. Like other ships of the 'yacht' type, she was difficult to handle and expensive to maintain, and had left the company by 1919.

The times were changing too, and so was the mode of propulsion. In 1910 the fleet-list in MacBrayne's *Summer Tours* admitted the company's three motor-vessels to the roll, but the compiler forebore to make any reference to them in the itineraries. They had come in sheepishly by the back door, so to speak, but in twenty years' time they were to emerge boldly at the front. In the meantime, McCallum and Orme's trusty vessels, *Dunara Castle* and *Hebrides*, kept plodding along.

In his guidebooks, David MacBrayne produced his own distinctive brand of Highland history in the manner of 'MacBraveheart'. High romance, filled with the deeds and derring-do of great Scottish monarchs like Wallace and Bruce, and the heart-stopping adventures of Bonnie Prince Charlie, was the staple diet. This emotive narrative was interspersed with homely, warmly-worded vignettes and thumbnail impressions of scenes. The shipboard traveller, guidebook in hand, was expected to observe the vistas and pick out the landmarks. A sense of 'fame' and 'achievement' was ever-present, even in potted biographies of near-contemporary individuals and references to modern industry:

On the right Onich Pier has beside it the manse of Onich, for many years the residence of the late Rev. Alex. Stewart, LL.D., famous under his literary name of "Nether Lochaber". The Celtic Cross beyond was erected to his memory. Nestling in a clump of trees near Cuilchenna Point, Cuilchenna House was for some years a resort of the Rev. Dr Norman Macleod.

In the direction of Glencoe, after rounding the buoy off the point, can be distinguished the upper workings of the celebrated Ballachulish slate quarries, the largest in Scotland, now wrought for over two hundred years, and away in the distance at the head of Loch Leven are the wonderful new works and town of Kinlochleven, seat of the industry of the British

Aluminium Company. To the left may be observed Ardgour House, and, shortly, passing through the narrows of Loch Linnhe, we arrive at Ardgour Pier. Fifteen minutes afterwards there comes in sight (on the left) Conaglen, seat of the Earl of Morton, at the foot of Conaglen deer forest. Close to the shore may be seen the rock on which Glengarry was killed in 1828, by rashly leaping overboard from the stranded steamer, *Stirling Castle*. There now appears, on the right, another view of Ben Nevis, while straight in front lies the Great Glen, through which ascends the Caledonian Canal, and in a few minutes we arrive at Fort-William.

MacBrayne's guidebooks employed a basic text which remained in place from at least 1895 to 1926, with appropriate additions, such as the reference to the British Aluminium Company in the 1910 volume. What changed most evidently, though, was the presentation of the book. In addition to the opulence of its covers, the pages of the 1910 edition were enhanced with miniature sketches of landmarks and steamers, birds, sheep, dogs, trundling omnibuses and pipers. The volume also contained several fine colour paintings of such scenes as 'Landing at Staffa', featuring the *Grenadier*, which complemented the rich description of Staffa and Fingal's Cave.

By 1926 the tooled boards of 1910 had given way to a creamy-buff paper cover, with a sepia sketch of a paddle-steamer in the Caledonian Canal. The 1926 edition offered excellent photographic reproduction on art paper – including a faked representation of the fast steamer *Columba* at Staffa! – but no coloured illustrations. Nevertheless, this was value for money at 1/6, compared with 1/- for the 1910 version. The work was, of course, subsidised by advertisements for fine food, drink and hotels.

This ambitious guidebook, in all its editions, shows clearly that 'getting away from it all' was a concept well known to, and brilliantly exploited by, David MacBrayne. As the introductory view of 'The Royal Route' states, the overall aim of a Highland tour by a MacBrayne steamship was to re-invigorate the individual:

A week of such voyaging, and one returns to the busy ways of men, not only with bronzed cheek and clear eye and new vigour pulsing in the veins, but with memories and impressions of the brave and beautiful Highland world that are never likely to be forgotten.

A good guidebook enriched the tourist's encounter with the Highlands and Islands, but by reading its pages he or she could also relive the 'memories and impressions'. Even today it is possible to capture something of the excitement of those heady MacBrayne steamship tours of the Edwardian and inter-war eras.

Front cover of, and pages from, **Summer Tours in the Western Highlands**, *1910, and back and front covers of 1907 Timetable [DEM's collection]*

accommodation, with electric lighting, and all the bells and whistles expected by the Edwardian cruise passenger. She had a main deck and a shelter deck, while the forecastle was raised by some four feet, and extended back to the deckhouse. The bridge was open. The first-class dining-saloon was forward on the shelter deck, and extended the full width of the ship. Aft of this were the entrance hall and the staterooms. She was also the largest steamer in the fleet, at a little over 1000 tons gross. Both the *Chieftain* and the *Claymore* were characterised by clipper bows and stately single funnels, which offered the classic appearance of the steam yacht.

The *Chieftain* was hugely popular, with repeat bookings taken on board for the following year. However, she was an expensive unit to run, as her winters were spent in lay-up, awaiting spring and the start of the summer cruise season. It was also found that she was largely unsuitable for carrying cattle and sheep, and her cargo-handling gear and hold arrangements made quayside duties laborious and slow. There was one main hatch forward, served by two deck-cranes, and two small hatches aft on either side of the shelter deck, just aft of the engine-room casing. These smaller hatches were found to be difficult to handle under normal operating conditions. The ship was also reportedly heavy on fuel, but, as fuel consumption is speed-related, it may be that her engine capacity was insufficient for some of the hard drives required when the ship had to maintain her schedule. Her design service-speed was 14 knots. Nonetheless, the *Chieftain* was the new, well-deserved flagship of the fleet, and most definitely served her purpose in securing the cruise market to the Western Isles.

Sadly, the cruise market could not be regenerated instantly in the austere post-war years, and the *Chieftain* was sold to the North Company in 1919, becoming their *St Margaret*. She was given slightly more top-hamper by the extension of her deck-house aft, and she gained a propensity to roll. Placed on the summer-only Leith 'west coast tourist service' to Stromness in Orkney and Scalloway and Hillswick in the Shetland Islands, she was

resold only six years later for use on the Canadian coastal routes, whereupon her clipper bow was removed and her appearance down-graded. She ended her days under the Panamanian flag, operating under dubious circumstances, allegedly with illicit cargoes and illegal immigrants! She was scrapped at Spezia in 1952.

David MacBrayne Limited continued in marine innovation, and became the world's pioneer of the internal combustion engine on inshore and coastal passenger services. Conscious of the time needed to prepare a steam engine for service, and of the cost of banking down fires in the evening, ready for early morning starts and full steam, the company bought its first motor-driven ship in 1907, at the time the cruise yacht *Chieftain* was arriving from the builder's yard at Troon. The motor-ship was a small vessel of 43 tons gross, and was given the pioneering name, *Comet*. Built by Robertson of Canning Town as the *Win*, she came into the MacBrayne fleet when two years old. She was equipped with twin four-cylinder paraffin-fuelled engines which had been built at Manchester by L. Gardner & Sons. Earlier experiments with petrol engines had given way to paraffin on the grounds of safety; although less efficient, the flash-point of paraffin is considerably lower than that of petrol. The marine diesel or oil engine was then, of course, only experimental.

The *Comet* had a straight stem and a counter stern. There were two separate deck-houses, with an open bridge above the after deckhouse, and there was ample covered accommodation below decks. However, the engine noise was tiresome, and in the early years, before improved silencing was fitted, the popping of the exhaust was intensive and obtrusive. The little ship was nevertheless highly successful. Her paraffin engines served her until 1928, when they were replaced during a major refurbishment which followed a serious grounding near Fort Matilda. Her new engines were also built by Gardner, and were more powerful, twin four-cylinder diesels. The little ship continued to serve her owners until 1947, when she was sold. Her hull is still in use as a houseboat at Shoreham. She had seen service on

The boxy, pioneer motor-ship **Comet** *in the Firth of Clyde [Harold Jordan's collection]*

a variety of inshore routes, including the Crinan Canal, but her main employment had been on the Clyde as the Lochgoil mail 'steamer'. Ironically, she was replaced by a steamer when she finally left the Clyde.

As a result of experience with the *Comet*, a full-size 'steamer', the *Scout*, was built to the order of the company in 1907, and she too was equipped with paraffin engines. These were built at Bristol by the Griffin Engineering Company of Bath, and were installed in the ship by her builders, the Ailsa Shipbuilding Company of Troon. Her twin engines had four cylinders. The *Scout* was altogether a much larger ship than the *Comet*, and had a gross tonnage of 82 and a length of 30 m.

The *Scout* worked the Ballachulish-Kinlochleven service. Outwardly she looked like the typical inshore steamer of the day, but only after a small funnel was added shortly after she entered service. She was particularly well endowed with promenade space, given her small tonnage. Unhappily, after a career of only six years, the *Scout* was destroyed by fire. This was the result of a serious blow-back from her engines which occurred in August 1913 – one of the first recorded marine accidents to have resulted from the malfunction of an internal combustion engine. The ship's two lifeboats were salvaged and fitted to the paddle-steamer *Columba*, where they remained until she was scrapped. Then they were transferred to the turbine steamer *King George V* (see Chapter 8).

The third motor-ship to join the MacBrayne fleet remains something of an unsung hero. This was the *Lochinvar*, built in 1908 by Scott & Sons, of Bowling, and engined by L. Gardner & Sons. This time, three six-cylinder, single-acting paraffin engines were used to drive the ship via three independent shafts. The *Lochinvar* was initially measured at 188 tons gross, and her required service speed was 8 knots. The new motor-ship was placed on the Oban-Tobermory mail service as a direct replacement for the elderly paddle-steamer, *Carabinier*. The dining-saloon sported a series of eight panels depicting the exciting life of young Lochinvar.

Originally the *Lochinvar* had one tall, very thin funnel near the stern, but this was soon replaced by three separate stove-pipes, one for each engine. These pipes were later diverted to a short funnel just ahead of the cargo hold, where there was an electrically-driven crane, the funnel being particularly short to allow the crane to operate over its top. Not a very attractive-looking ship, she was nevertheless highly successful on her daily year-round run up the Sound of Mull. Only very rarely was she called upon to relieve elsewhere.

The *Lochinvar*'s prototype, marine, paraffin engines were replaced in 1926, when she received three new four-cylinder Gardner 'heavy oil' diesel engines, coupled independently, as before, to her triple screws. Following the Second World War, the *Lochinvar* received a major refurbishment and a third set of engines, made by Davey-Paxman of Colchester. At this stage she was reduced from triple screw to twin screw, requiring only two engines. The engines were at last placed under an acoustic hood, somewhat akin to a large dog-kennel, and only when this was in place was it possible to travel on the ship without being overwhelmed by the dreadful noise of the engines.

The *Lochinvar* completed her last

*The **Lochinvar** with exhaust pipes, typical of early experimental motor-ships, before the fitting of a 'proper' funnel [St Andrews University Library]*

*The **Lochinvar** with wheelhouse and funnel, approaching Craignure [St Andrews University Library]*

run up and down the Sound of Mull in May 1960. She was then sold to the Thames and Medway Navigation Company, Sheerness, becoming their *Anzio I*. With a Class 4 certificate for 351 passengers, she ran between Southend and Sheerness until the end of 1963.

The *Lochinvar* and the *Comet* must be remembered as Britain's pioneer, motor-driven, sea-going passenger units. They were both immensely successful on the routes to which they had been assigned, but both suffered throughout much of their careers from excessive engine noise in the passenger spaces and on deck. The long service-life of both the *Lochinvar* (58 years) and the earlier *Comet* (40 years) is testimony to sound design and construction, although not to the quality of their original engines. The inadequacies of the paraffin engine, of course, had been highlighted by the premature loss of the less successful *Scout* at the tender age of only six years.

That David MacBrayne Limited was the first company in the world to introduce this form of propulsion demonstrates the company's important innovative role, and its influence over marine technology. Contributions made by Laurence MacBrayne to papers read at the Institution of Engineers & Shipbuilders of Scotland suggest that he was interested in the development of the motor-ship. Clearly, the railway companies would not take readily to engines of this kind, as they had abundant stocks of coal, bought at bulk-supply rates to maintain their locomotives. Nevertheless, the introduction of motor propulsion to coastal shipping remains an important maritime development, and it is significant that it was pioneered for, and within, the Scottish Highlands and Islands.

Three more steamers were commissioned before the war. These were the *Lochiel* for the Oban station, the *Dirk*, which was the last of the *Lapwing* type, and the *Mountaineer*, which was the very last paddle-steamer to be built for the company. The *Mountaineer*, as it turned out, was also the last ship to be built for David MacBrayne Limited, a company which fate decreed would spiral into terminal decline after the war in the depressed 1920s. Before the war, however,

the company was thriving, with over a third of its ships less than ten years old, a secure (or so it seemed) business plan ahead of it, and an operating environment which gave it an almost total monopoly.

Innovation continued with these last three steamers. The *Dirk* was the first coastal steamer to be fitted with a gyro-compass, followed closely by the *Lochiel*. The *Mountaineer* was fitted with deck windshields around the promenade deck, a feature that may have been attractive to passengers, but so greatly increased the windage of the ship that they were removed after the First World War.

The Edwardian summers were the halcyon days of coastal passenger excursions around the British Isles. Not only was West Highland traffic thriving, but so too were excursion steamers on the Thames, the South Coast, the Bristol Channel (with its distinctive Clyde flavour, offered by P. & A. Campbell Limited), and even at resorts such as Blackpool and Bridlington. On the Clyde, the *Iona* and the *Columba* enjoyed their hey-days, ploughing 'doon the watter' to Ardrishaig in summer, and retiring to Bowling harbour in winter.

The winter-season Greenock-Ardrishaig service was undertaken by the paddle-steamer *Grenadier*, which in summer maintained the tourist circuit from Oban to Iona, travelling round Mull, and calling at Staffa. A newsworthy incident occurred in 1909, when five young Suffragettes determined to abandon ship at Staffa in order to demonstrate their strength and resolve. When the steamer returned the next day, the ladies were severely reprimanded by the ship's officers for having pulled such a foolhardy stunt. The officers, it seems, had been concerned for the safety of the Suffragettes overnight on the island.

The tourist traffic never recovered in post-war years, when competition from the motor coach, combined with the lean years leading up to the onset of the Depression, inhibited trade. This was to be the death-knell of the once-thriving and profit-making company, David MacBrayne Limited. In the meantime, technological development had moved on. Not only had the triple-expansion engine and the internal combustion engine arrived in the MacBrayne fleet, but competitors were also beginning to place the turbine steamer on the long routes from Glasgow to the lower Clyde. The turbine steamer would have been out of place in the MacBrayne fleet at that time, as the company was conscious of its narrow operational margins, and was content with slower and older, although less economical, tonnage.

Turbine Steamers Limited was a new syndicate shared between William Denny, the Dumbarton shipbuilders, the engineering interests of Charles Parsons (1854-1931), the inventor and champion of the direct-drive marine turbine, and John Williamson, the established ship-operator and manager. The world's first commercial passenger turbine steamer was the *King Edward*, placed by the syndicate on the Glasgow-Campbeltown run in 1901, and followed in 1902 by the *Queen Alexandra*, which went into direct competition with the *Iona* and the *Columba* on the Ardrishaig route, and with the Lochgoil & Inveraray Steam Boat Company's paddle-steamer, *Lord of the Isles*, on the Inveraray route. The triple-screw turbine steamer, *Duchess of Argyll*, was built in 1906 for the Caledonian Steam Packet Company. These prototype excursion turbine steamers demonstrated the viability of the new propulsion system, and paved the way for a cross-channel revolution, with turbine steamers on all the fast cross-channel services around Britain within only a few years. They were also hugely successful, although there were occasional misfortunes. The *Queen Alexandra* was gutted by fire alongside the quay at Greenock in 1911, but she was replaced by a new ship of similar design and of the same name the following year. The turbine steamer would, one day, wear the MacBrayne funnel. In the meantime, it amounted to unwelcome competition, but, in a thriving down-river excursion trade, one which had made little initial impact on the existing operators. That would change.

Erosion of the Lochgoil trade by the turbine steamers was such that, by 1912, Turbine Steamers Limited, with additional funding provided by David MacBrayne Limited, was able to buy the Lochgoil company and its steamers. Thus, the *Lord of the Isles* became part-owned by MacBrayne, although she traded under the auspices of Turbine Steamers Limited. The Lochgoil company's elderly steamer, *Edinburgh Castle*, was replaced by the *Chevalier* in 1913.

The shorter Clyde routes, operated principally by the railway companies, were largely maintained by paddle-steamers, with the North British Railway restricted to their use by the shallow approaches to their base at Craigendoran. The Glasgow & South Western Railway, however, introduced the small, and relatively slow, turbine steamer *Atalanta* on the Ardrossan-Brodick service in 1906, but she was never an entirely successful ship, and eventually ended her days as a Blackpool excursion steamer.

At the onset of war in 1914, David MacBrayne Limited owned 32 ships (see Table 2), the oldest being the *Glencoe*, which was celebrating her sixty-eighth birthday! Through careful management, the business had been developed into a monopolistic carrier within the West Highlands and the islands, which none were willing to challenge. The railway companies were happy for the private company to run the specialist shipping services. Realising that the potential for competition was limited by the frugal winter business that was on offer, they did not compete for any of the mail contracts.

In addition to shipping services, MacBrayne inaugurated feeder bus services, the first between Fort William and North Ballachulish in 1906. Further bus services were introduced after 1910, with the result that the road network eventually blossomed into a major distribution service. Nevertheless, the Kingdom of David MacBrayne and his successor, David Hope MacBrayne, had reached its zenith.

Table 2 *The major units of the MacBrayne fleet and their normal service routes at the onset of World War I*

Vessel	Age in 1914	Normal service route
Mountaineer	4	Oban based and winter reliefs
Dirk	5	Oban-Coll-Tiree-Bunessan (Ross of Mull)
Staffa	6	Glasgow-Crinan Canal-Mull cargo service
Lochiel	6	Outer Isles routes
Lochinvar	6	Oban-Tobermory
Chieftain	7	Glasgow-Stornoway
Comet	9	Crinan, Clyde and Lochgoil services
Clydesdale	9	Glasgow to Islay
Pioneer	9	West Loch Tarbert-Islay
Brenda	10	Glasgow-Crinan Canal-Mull cargo service
Cygnet	10	Glasgow-Inveraray cargo service
Plover	10	Outer Isles routes
Sheila	10	Kyle of Lochalsh-Stornoway
Lapwing	11	Dunvegan to Harris and Lochmaddy
Countess of Mayo	17	Ballachulish-Kinlochleven
Fusilier	26	Summer Oban excursions an relief duties
Duke of Abercorn	26	Laid up with boiler trouble
Grenadier	29	Summer Oban excursions; winter Greenock-Ardrishaig
Texa	30	Glasgow-Ardrishaig cargo service
Cavalier	31	Glasgow-Inverness
Claymore	33	Glasgow-Stornoway
Clansman	34	Glasgow-Inverness
Handa	36	Glasgow-Crinan Canal-Mull-Loch Sunart-Loch Leven cargo service
Columba	36	Glasgow-Ardrishaig summer service only
Fingal	37	Oban-Coll-Tiree-Bunessan
Gael	47	Oban-Mull-Eigg-Mallaig-Kyle-Broadford-Portree-Gairloch
Linnet	48	Crinan Canal
Chevalier	48	Crinan Canal and occasional Clyde duties
Gondolier	48	Inverness-Banavie, Caledonian Canal
Iona	50	Glasgow-Ardrishaig summer service only
Gairlochy	53	Inverness-Banavie, Caledonian Canal
Glencoe	68	Various including Oban and West Loch Tarbert routes
	Average age 25 years	Total number of ships – 32 (plus several small units)

CHAPTER 6

WAR AND PEACE:
THE FIRST WORLD WAR AND ITS AFTERMATH

The **King George V** in Turbine Steamers colours [Donald B. MacCulloch]

WAR AND PEACE:
THE FIRST WORLD WAR AND ITS AFTERMATH

*Although there was not much shelter or comfort on the ships that MacBrayne sent out to the islands, they were usually good sea-boats. The **Dirk** was only small, but she was very lively, and she defied Cailleach Point and the Barra Minch for years. Her fate was to be sunk by a German mine in the last year of the war....The sea air in the west is so pure and healthy that many of MacBrayne's ships reached a great age. Some of them were so old that no living person could remember when they first put to sea.*
REV. DONALD LAMONT, 'AN LUIDHEAR DEARG' ('THE RED FUNNEL') 1935

Following the dramatic events that took place in Europe during the early summer of 1914, Britain finally declared war on Germany on 4 August. Within days, the rallying-cry of Lord Kitchener, the War Minister, was for 100 000 men to join the army, but, although the First World War was the last great infantry war, it was also a maritime war. Britain lost 9 million tons of shipping in the ensuing four years of conflict, during which new and deadly weapons were deployed, including the submarine and various types of mines.

Much of the MacBrayne fleet continued its vital trade, supplying the islands and bringing sheep to market, but some ships were requisitioned for active duty and others were laid up awaiting orders. Even some of the summer excursion services were maintained as morale boosters, save for the period 1915 to 1917, when the upper Clyde was closed to civilians, and services were, in any case, restricted by the defence boom which extended from the Cloch Light to Dunoon.

The *Dirk* was requisitioned, and converted to an armed trawler for escort duties in February 1915. HMS *Dirk* became one of two MacBrayne war losses when she was torpedoed off Flamborough Head in the closing days of May 1918. The next member of the fleet to enter active service was the *Grenadier*, which became the minesweeper HMS *Grenade* when she was requisitioned in July 1916. Her work was mainly in the North Sea. Happily, she brought her crew back to the Clyde, unscathed, in October 1919,

to revert to normal duties once again as the *Grenadier*. The *Lochiel*, requisitioned in January 1917, and stationed at Grimsby as the escort ship HMS *Lochiel*, became the second war casualty, when she was mined off Whitby in July 1918.

The *Plover* too had a brush with the enemy whilst on passage between Oban and the Outer Isles on 29 July 1918. Off Tiree, a submarine surfaced and attempted to shell the vessel. Intending to pursue the submarine and to attack her with his stern-mounted gun, Captain Neil MacDougall immediately sent his passengers off in the ship's boats. The submarine submerged before any further shots could be fired, but in the meantime the ship's boats were left to make their own way ashore. Happily there were no casualties. Following this incident, the decision was taken to paint the *Claymore* in camouflage colours, but the cessation of hostilities four months later prevented the scheme expanding to other company ships operating in the Minch, although they already wore drab wartime grey.

Many of the fast day-passenger steamers operating on the Clyde were requisitioned for war service. Turbine Steamers' *King Edward*, for example, became a troopship on the English Channel, and latterly voyaged to Archangel as a hospital ship. Many of the Clyde services were depleted, and a number of the slower (and much older) members of the MacBrayne fleet were chartered to fill the gap for much of the war. Thus, the North British Railway had the *Mountaineer* stationed at Helensburgh. The *Gael* was used

*The **Loch Aline** (ex-**Plover**), with gun and in wartime grey [Courtesy of Dr Bill Lind and the Ballast Trust]*

on the Caledonian Steam Packet Company's Ardrossan-Brodick route, having been laid up at the start of the war. For some time, the same company also had both the *Iona* and the *Chevalier* stationed at Wemyss Bay, on Rothesay and Millport duties. The elderly, but everlasting, *Glencoe* found herself being brought down from Oban to Ardrossan for a while, on charter to the Glasgow & South Western Railway. From a business perspective, these charters may sound attractive, but the war-time charter rates were not lucrative, and they barely covered the costs.

The shortage of shipping left on the Clyde forced the creation of Clyde Cargo Steamers Limited in August 1915, in order to maintain cargo services in the Lower Firth. This brought David MacBrayne Limited into partnership with several companies: Hill & Company, who had previously served Rothesay, Millport, Arran and Loch Fyne

ports; John Williamson, who had served Dunoon, Rothesay and the Holy Loch area; and the Minard Castle Shipping Company Limited, which was better known under its former trading name of Lochfyne & Glasgow Steam Packet Company. Hill's former Managing Director, John Rodger, took charge of the new company, which acquired the *Minard Castle* and the Hill steamers *Bute 4* and *Arran*. In 1918, the MacBrayne steamer *Lapwing* was given the black funnel of Clyde Cargo Steamers, but was soon requisitioned by the Shipping Controller, and placed under the management of the Hain Steamship Company. Initially rostered to maintain the Penzance to Scilly mail route, she also ran between Plymouth and the Channel Islands, but was returned to her owners in 1920.

Other ships in the MacBrayne fleet carried on their commercial duties as if there was no war. The *Columba* maintained the

Ardrishaig service, running from Wemyss Bay outwith the Cloch-Dunoon defence boom, save for much of 1915, when she was safely laid up in dock. Other main-line ships, such as the *Sheila*, *Clansman* and *Claymore*, went about their duties largely unaffected. The *Glencoe* operated a short season of Oban excursions in the summer of 1918, and some excursions had run in 1916.

A number of smaller units were sold during the war for further commercial service. These were the *Clansman* (formerly the *Ethel*), the *Staffa*, the *Texa*, the *Countess of Mayo* and the *Duke of Abercorn*, the latter pair having been acquired only in 1914. The *Handa* (formerly William Lang's *Aros Castle* (see Chapter 4)) was sold to Thomas W. Ward for scrapping and recovery of metals in 1917, but she never arrived at the yard, as she foundered in poor weather on Christmas Eve.

The Armistice was agreed at 11 am on 11 November, the eleventh month of 1918, and the Versailles Treaty was signed in June 1919. Lloyd George, the wartime Prime Minister, stayed at the helm until 1922, and business was set for a post-war boom, interrupted only by a short, sharp corrective slump in 1921/22.

David MacBrayne Limited emerged into peace-time a slimmer company than it had been before the war. It responded by cutting a number of services including the Ross of Mull (Bunessan) service from Oban via Tiree, and the Glasgow-Inverness route was cut back to Fort William, allowing the sale of the *Cavalier* in 1919. The company did receive one vessel, the *Devonia*, from the Shipping Controller in lieu of the two ships lost in active service. She was named the *Lochiel*, and placed on the Glasgow-Stornoway route, but provided only limited passenger accommodation. Her running partner was the *Clydesdale*, and the two ships were not dissimilar in appearance. The passenger certificate of the *Lochiel* was later withdrawn, after which she acted mainly as a livestock carrier on any route that demanded her services.

David MacBrayne Limited settled down to a period of consolidation and stability. However, the first summer of peace, 1919, was a difficult one for all the steamer operators, as ships remained in wartime condition awaiting refurbishment, and there were a number of mechanical failures that resulted from lack of parts. In 1923, the former accountant, H. T. Leith, who had become a Director of the company in 1915, was appointed Managing Director. His first duty was to retire the ageing steamer *Gael* to the scrapyard in 1924. The *Gael* had been built in 1867 for the Campbeltown & Glasgow Steam Packet Joint Stock Company, and was eventually purchased in 1891 by MacBrayne, following extensive service for a variety of owners in the south of England.

H. T. Leith

The diverse railway interests in Clyde steamer services received a boost when the railways were 'grouped' into four big companies in 1923. The result of this was to reduce competition by combining, and thus strengthening, the otherwise depleted fleets. Both the Glasgow & South Western Railway and the Caledonian Railway, along with their respective steamers, were subsumed into the newly-formed London, Midland & Scottish Railway, whilst the North British Railway became a part of the London & North Eastern Railway.

Until the Wall Street Crash of October 1929, the United States was riding high and the Roaring Twenties were in full swing. However, wages in the manufacturing industries in the UK were low, and in some areas were going down rather than up. Whilst the more affluent managerial classes enjoyed the Roaring Twenties, the working classes were spiralling into debt. David MacBrayne Limited, like most ship-owners at that time, had to cope with static business prospects and the inevitable decline in the mass excursion trade. However, the business acumen of old had slipped away from the Directors, and the trade had apparently changed at a faster rate than the company could cope with. Indeed, the tourist market was also under competition from the motor coach, and the level of pre-war steamer business could never again be attained.

The MacBrayne fleet gradually aged, with no new building or second-hand purchases, while the capital within the company slowly drained away. These were the last years that the West Highland services were run by an independent, profit-making company without government subsidy, and it is apparent that profits made in the summer were barely adequate to maintain the quiet winter-season sailings. The only unscheduled fleet deployments for the next few years were occasional charters of cargo steamers to help with the autumn livestock movements.

The MacBrayne institution remained steadfast throughout. The Kingdom at this stage is best summed up by a description of a summer holiday enjoyed in 1925 by the young E. C. B. Thornton, later to be the author of a series of

THE RESCUERS

JUST WHO WERE the London, Midland & Scottish Railway and the Coast Lines Group, and what were their respective philosophies?

The competing and overlapping services of the numerous railway companies that had developed in the late nineteenth century had been grouped into the 'big four' on 1 January 1923, in order to reduce losses and to 'secure the rail network for the nation'. The London, Midland & Scottish Railway was one of the big four railway companies, the others being the London & North Eastern, the Great Western and the Southern railways. The London, Midland & Scottish Railway was formed by amalgamating thirty-four companies, the main ones being the Scottish companies, Highland, Caledonian and Glasgow & South Western, and the English London & North Western, Midland, Furness and North Staffordshire railways. It was a very big company and was placed under the chairmanship of Sir Josiah Stamp, by all accounts an imposing and domineering man and a considerable force to be reckoned with.

Among the assets of the London, Midland & Scottish Railway were the Heysham/Fleetwood to Belfast overnight passenger ferry, plus the Clyde interests of both the Caledonian Steam Packet Company (a company that had been created to allow the Caledonian Railway to operate ships) and the Glasgow & South Western Railway. The former North British Railway fleet in the Clyde had become part of the London & North Eastern Railway, and remained so until the nationalisation of the railways in the desperate years following the Second World War. Thereafter, the entire Clyde railway fleet traded as the Caledonian Steam Packet Company, which later would become part of Caledonian MacBrayne.

The 1948 nationalisation of the 'big four' created British Railways. The 50% stake held in David MacBrayne Limited by the former London, Midland & Scottish Railway became the property of the newly formed British Transport Commission, although management of both David MacBrayne Limited and the Caledonian Steam Packet Company remained with British Railways (Scottish Division). In December 1962, the British Transport Commission was dissolved and ownership of the railway ships was vested in the British Railways Board. It was the British Railways Board that was to hand its interests in David MacBrayne Limited to the Scottish Transport Group in 1969.

But at the time of the rescue of David MacBrayne Limited in 1928, the London, Midland & Scottish Railway was well placed to invest in the West Highland services, knowing that the success of the MacBrayne operation could only bring benefit to the railway network by enhancing levels of traffic. At the same time, the railway company knew that there were no profits to be had in the sea-going operation, and it was, therefore, better placed as investor, saviour and guide to its part-owned and Government subsidised sea-going West Highland and Island wing. Not surprisingly, this was allowed to continue to trade under the MacBrayne banner, albeit with a punitive '(1928)' added for a few years.

The Coast Lines Group was of similar longstanding pedigree, although its interest was confined to shipping and a small element of road haulage in port hinterlands. The name 'The Coast Line' came into being in April 1917, when it was adopted as a brand name for Powell, Bacon and Hough Lines, which had been formed in 1913 through the amalgamation of these three respective coastal shipping companies. The company Chairman was Alfred H. Read, who was a dynamic young man and a contrasting personality to Sir Josiah Stamp (see 'Sir Alfred H. Read').

Read's progress did not go unnoticed. The huge Royal Mail Group needed a feeder service of coasting ships for its liner trades, and it soon purchased the entire assets and goodwill of Coast Lines against a price tag of £0.8 million. Blessed with the financial backing of the Royal Mail Group, Read was able to expand further, acquiring in quick succession the Belfast Steamship Company, the British and Irish

books on pleasure steamers, travelling with his mother. He wrote in the former Paddle Steamer Preservation Society's journal, *Paddle Wheels*, April 1972, as follows:

*We proceeded on our way by the **Columba**, and what a fine vessel she was! A real piece of Victoriana, no doubt, but her engines were fascinating with their huge oscillating cylinders and the cranks looking as if at some time in the not too distant future they must inevitably go too far and hit the roof, the clearance appearing so small. Then at Ardrishaig, we transhipped to the comic **Linnet**, with her red, match-stick funnel, for the passage of the Crinan Canal. Then the sight of our steamer, this day being the*

*Fusilier, with the sun shining on her brilliant red funnel, awaiting us at Crinan. What a terrible pity it is that for many years now it has not been possible to do this sail through the Crinan Canal and onwards to Oban through the gulf of Corryvreckan. From Oban we went around Mull to Staffa and Iona aboard the **Grenadier**. After a couple of nights at Oban we carried on by the **Mountaineer** to Fort William. A short rail connection took us to Banavie and as we approached this station we saw, from the train window, our steamer apparently standing in a field! It was of course the **Gondolier**, awaiting us at the top of the locks, and we embarked for the delightful sail through the Caledonian Canal and Loch Ness to Inverness.*

Steam Packet Company, G. & J. Burns and the Laird Line, despite a downturn in trade caused both by unrest in Ireland and the Coal Strike.

Although the Coast Line Seaway, as it became known, and its various partner companies flourished in the 1920s, the parent Royal Mail Line Group, under Lord Kylsant, was placed under increasing financial difficulties due to a general downturn in trade, notably with South America. Coast Lines took a number of measures, including significant bank loans, to insulate itself from the ailing Royal Mail Group, whose downfall was not helped by Lord Kylsant's refusal to refinance the company in 1922. The fall of both Lord Kylsant and the Royal Mail Group occurred in 1931, but Coast Lines and its associate companies, which now included a 50% share in David MacBrayne, had become financially distant from the parent, and were able to buy themselves out of the Royal Mail Group by 1936. The subsequent achievements of Coast Lines, as the one major independent coastal and ferry operator in competition with the railways, are legion. What might have happened to MacBrayne, had Coast Lines gone down with Lord Kylsant's sinking ship, is, happily, just a rhetorical muse.

In more recent years, and among many other acquisitions, Coast Lines bought the North of Scotland, Orkney and Shetland Shipping Company Limited in 1961 for a mere £1.1 million. The North Company was in trouble for having over-committed itself to conventional tonnage (much as Coast Lines itself was also doing at that time), rather than investing in container and roll-on/roll-off equipment.

In 1965, Coast Lines shared the ownership of the newly-formed North Sea Ferries, based at Hull, with a consortium which included P&O. This cleared the path for an eventual buy-out by P&O in 1971, when the Coast Lines Group, having sold its interests in David MacBrayne Limited two years previously, disappeared into the jaws of the mega-company for a mere £5.6 million. The Coast Lines' white chevron on a black funnel was seen no more, and the surviving ships of the remaining subsidiaries, such as the Belfast Steamship Company and Burns & Laird, were thereafter hidden under the ubiquitous corporate identity of P&O.

Coast Lines' motor-ship, **British Coast**, showing the company's distinctive chevron on her black funnel [NR's collection]

Stories and anecdotes of the steamers from this era, particularly the ever-popular Ardrishaig steamers, are legion. One of these was told by the late John Nicholson, whose artistic talent will continue to delight us for many years to come, when introducing his painting of the *Lord of the Isles* and the *Columba* racing to get to the berth at Rothesay:

> One of the many anecdotes associated with the **Columba** concerns a boy who embarked at Glasgow unaccompanied by an adult. He approached the purser and said that his mother had told him to be sure to ask to be told when they reached Dunoon. The purser promised he would do this, but at every pier the lad asked him 'Is this Dunoon?' Tiring of this, the purser eventually replied, 'No, don't bother me, I'll tell you when we get there'. However, at Dunoon there were large numbers getting off and on, and parcels to be put ashore, and in the commotion the purser forgot all about the lad until the steamer was leaving the pier and gathering speed for the run to Innellan. He dashed up to the bridge to tell the captain of his predicament and they decided that they had better put back to the pier. As the ship came alongside for the second time the purser found the lad and said, 'This is Dunoon'. 'Oh thanks,' said the boy. 'My mother said I was not to eat my sandwiches until we got there.'

Although building of new ships and maritime innovation bypassed David MacBrayne Limited in this period, other companies were innovative in the extreme. Turbine Steamers Limited, in collaboration with William Denny, Parsons' Marine Steam Turbines and Yarrow Boilers, determined to demonstrate the efficiency of high-pressure steam turbines (550 pounds per square inch at 750 °F). The result was the magnificent steamer *King George V*. E. C. B. Thornton in his book, *Clyde Coast Pleasure Steamers* (which is illustrated by John Nicholson), writes:

*Unlike the other turbine driven steamers which were direct-drive triple-screw vessels, the **King George V** had single reduction gearing to twin screws but had an extra high pressure turbine on the port shaft only. From the passenger's point of view, she introduced the principle of a glazed-in portion of the Promenade Deck and with a big Upper Deck above it occupying the middle half of the vessel. She was a most beautiful ship and became very popular. Mostly she ran between Greenock, Gourock and Inveraray, and also carried out what were known as 'turbine evening cruises' from Gourock frequently round Cumbrae.*

Her new high-pressure machinery was over-complicated, and the momentum of the gear-train inhibited rapid slowing down at the approach to piers. Sadly, a water tube burst in one of the boilers at the end of her second season, killing two members of the engine-room staff. She was reconfigured that winter with twin sets of conventional pressure turbines, one unit on each shaft. The *King George V* finally settled down as a

*The **Chevalier** at Crinan [DEM's collection]*

most reliable unit, destined in due course to spend the greater part of her career under the MacBrayne house-flag (see Chapter 7).

The fortunes of MacBrayne's, and for that matter the rest of the nation, were inhibited in May 1926 by the General Strike, which served to highlight low and declining wages in some sectors, including coal-mining. It lasted only a few days, but the coal-miners stayed out until November, putting industry on part-time, and causing coal-burning transport systems to contract. Many steamers were laid up throughout the summer and autumn, adding to the financial burden on David MacBrayne Limited, who forfeited much of its peak-earning summer season.

Without a doubt, the year 1927 was the Kingdom's 'Annus Horribilis'. Three major units in the fleet were lost in succession: the *Sheila*, the *Chevalier* and the *Grenadier*. The

trouble started in the early hours of New Year's Day, as the *Sheila* ploughed across the Minch from Stornoway on a routine voyage to Kyle. Her normal Master, Captain Cameron, was on leave, and, under the command of a relief Master, the *Sheila* may have missed the South Rona light and altered course towards Applecross too late. The ship went ashore just south of Loch Torridon; all the crew and passengers were lowered safely over the ship's side and on to the beach, but the ship was declared a total loss.

The *Chevalier*, a paddle-steamer dating from the Hutcheson era, was the next ship to be lost. When she was relieving on the Ardrishaig service on 25 March, the starboard paddle-wheel came adrift in heavy weather, and the little ship was immobilised off Barmore Island, near Tarbert. The battle to secure the vessel to windward of the island by means of the anchors rapidly failed, and

the *Chevalier* was blown on to the rocks. All passengers and crew, the mails and personal baggage were safely transferred to the ship's boats and landed at nearby Stonefield. The *Chevalier*, badly holed, had to stay on the rocks for several days before she could be recovered for inspection at Troon. Not surprisingly, the sixty-one year-old ship was declared a constructive total loss.

The third loss was the most tragic and seemingly unnecessary one of them all. Towards the end of the *Grenadier*'s season of excursions round Mull, via Iona and Staffa, the ever-popular paddle-steamer lay, as normal, overnight at the North Pier in Oban. With most of her crew asleep on board, and only the night watchman on guard, a fire developed and spread through the ship in the early hours of 6 September. The fire spread rapidly, so rapidly and violently that three of her crew, including Captain Archie MacArthur from Tighnabruaich, were

killed. Others were saved only by jumping overboard and swimming for their lives away from the ship. By the time the Fire Brigade arrived on the pier, the ship was ablaze, and all they could do was to cut the after mooring-rope to allow the ship to settle on the bottom, and let the in-rushing water extinguish the flames below. Later towed to Ardrossan for inspection, the *Grenadier* became the third declared loss for the company in one year.

Given the age of the vessels and their modest replacement value, the insurance money received by MacBrayne was unlikely to cover the cost of one replacement ship, let alone three. The company now found itself not only undercapitalised, but also ill-equipped to maintain its services, many of which it was contractually obliged to provide under the previously lucrative mail contracts that had been awarded to it. The longevity of many of the ships (see Table 3 for fleet list and disposition of vessels at the start

SIR ALFRED H. READ (1871-1955)

ALFRED READ (SENIOR) died at sea of fever in the Crimean war. His orphaned son, also Alfred Read, was introduced to F. H. Powell & Company in 1869 by a nephew of his mother. He became a partner in the company in 1881, by which time he had two sons and two daughters. The elder son was Alfred Henry Read, born in Liverpool in 1871. Alfred Read (the younger) served an apprenticeship with the Anchor Line, before joining his father's firm, and becoming a partner in 1893.

Alfred had a forceful personality and a persuasive manner. He was a restless young man who tended to act on impulse. It was Alfred who brought F. H. Powell & Company together with the coasting-liner companies, the Bacon Line in 1912, and the Hough Line the following year. In 1913, Read was in charge of the amalgamated fleet, with access to the Liverpool-London, the Liverpool and Preston to Wexford and the Bristol Channel routes of the Bacon and Hough lines respectively.

Read was both a pragmatist and a champion of innovation. He quickly bought a Liverpool cartage company, and applied for membership of the Irish Railway Clearing House, the latter being an attempt to woo the railway companies. He soon set about acquiring the British & Irish Steam Packet Company, a process crystallised by a soft loan to its Dublin-based Directors. In 1917, Alfred Read accepted an offer from Owen Cosby Philipps (1863-1937), the Welsh politician, estate-owner and shipping magnate. This brought the newly-formed Coast Lines Limited into the Royal Mail Group, with Read retained as Managing Director under Philipp's chairmanship. That year Read became Director of Home Trade Shipping, for which he received a knighthood the following year. Meanwhile, with the move to London, Read acquired a town house in Park Lane and an estate in Wiltshire.

Read maintained a degree of autonomy from his parent company, retaining offices in Liverpool and Belfast, and separate accounts from the Royal Mail Group. In 1922, Read stood up against Sir Owen Philipps, who had been ordering new ships without approval from the Coast Lines' Board, although this was much to the satisfaction of Group-owned shipyards. Philipps responded spitefully by calling in the company debt, but Read was able to issue shares to satisfy his loans, even selling his London and Wiltshire houses, and moving Lady Elena Read to rented accommodation in London.

The collapse of the Royal Mail Group led to the resignation of Philipps (now Lord Kylsant), and in due course to his conviction for allegedly making false statements over a share issue. Kylsant was jailed for twelve months in 1931. He received no sympathy from Read, who still remembered Philipps' callous actions nine years previously. The collapse of the mighty Royal Mail Group failed to take Coast Lines with it, due in no small part to the efforts of Sir Alfred.

Sir Alfred Read's leadership went from strength to strength. At the end of 1946, he relinquished the post of Managing Director of Coast Lines to M. Arnet Robinson. Read retired as Chairman in March 1950, and then moved to a modest home in Lisbon. He died on 8 March 1955, his body being buried at sea from the cargo vessel *Adriatic Coast*, a fitting end to the man who felt he once 'owned the Irish Sea'.

---

of 1928) was possible only through careful maintenance and continual care of the ships' structure and machinery, with extended overhaul periods, usually of not less than a month.

Sadly, when invited to tender for the renewal of the mail contracts during the winter of 1927/28, the Directors of David MacBrayne Limited were forced to decline. This immediately placed the old family firm in a terminal position, without any future prospect of continuing its business, and causing immediate discussion and debate in Westminster. Among the more amusing aspects of the parliamentary dialogue was reference to the youngest member of the fleet, the paddle-steamer *Mountaineer*, as the 'Flapper', the ship then being just eighteen years old!

A number of companies, including the railways, were brought into the debate, during which none were willing to step into the breach. For the first time in over a hundred years, it looked as if the Western Isles were in danger of losing at least some of the essential sea-connections which they had so long enjoyed with the mainland and Glasgow. It also looked as if the only salvation for the key services was for government to offer a subsidy towards future operating costs. Alas - too little too late! The old company had insufficient numbers of suitable ships with which to maintain the required services, and inadequate capital to acquire any new vessels. Discussion continued, and, in the end, with the promise of 'adequate' government support in the form of subsidies, the London, Midland & Scottish Railway, jointly with Coast Lines Limited, was persuaded to invest in, and develop, a new company to be called David MacBrayne (1928) Limited. The government set strict provisos regarding investment (see Chapter 7).

The formation of the new company is described in an article by Ernest Reader, which first appeared, under the title ''Twixt Highlands and Islands', in *Sea Breezes* in December 1950:

A major change in the fortunes of the company [David MacBrayne Limited] came in 1928 when they withdrew their tender for the conveyance of the mails and no other application was forthcoming. Finally, Sir Alfred Read, Chairman of Coast Lines Limited, and Sir Josiah Stamp (later Lord Stamp), President of the London, Midland and Scottish Railway, jointly came to the rescue and enabled the Government to maintain an adequate postal service over the routes by acquiring the fleet and trades of David MacBrayne Limited. A new company was registered, David MacBrayne (1928) Limited, and new head offices were acquired in Robertson Street, Glasgow. The new Board of Directors was formed with equal representation of shipping and railway interests, and a Director represented the Government. For day-to-day problems a local Board was also formed with equal shipping and railway representation.

At the same time, the new company was given extensive powers to develop road-feeder and connecting parcels services, as well as the authority to develop air services – an authority which was never claimed. With the new ships, which would be built as part of the investment package,

the MacBrayne Kingdom was back in business. However, the collective age of the ships comprising the fleet at the time of reconstitution (Table 3) illustrates the extent of the rebuilding programme that would be necessary in order to sustain the new company. It also reflects the meticulous care and attention given year by year to the ships, in order to sustain many of them into advanced old age.

Duckworth and Langmuir provide a rather sentimental summary of this fleet in their final chapter, 'General Notes on the Hutcheson/MacBrayne Steamers', a summary that is divorced from both the commercial plight of the former family-run company and the excitement of the establishment of the new enterprise created by its rescuers:

*...the MacBrayne fleet was a living museum of marine engineering. Reviewing the types of engine represented, there was the **Glencoe** with an ancient single-cylinder steeple paddle engine, the **Iona** and her two-cylinder simple oscillating engines, the **Linnet** with twin sets of two-cylinder simple screw machinery, all four cylinders being inclined together like an inverted letter 'V', **Claymore** having a heavy two-cylinder compound inverted engine, the **Fusilier** and her large single-crank diagonal paddle engine, **Pioneer** with the familiar two-crank compound diagonal type, the **Clydesdale** and her set of triple-expansion engines, the **Comet** with twin sets of four-cylinder oil engines, the **Lochinvar** having three sets of six-cylinder motors...*

We [Duckworth and Langmuir] can think of no other part of the world where such a state of affairs existed, and feel sure this must have been unique.

It is a wonder that the iron hull of the eighty-two year-old great-grandmother of the fleet, *Glencoe*, survived her daily buffeting off Skye at this late stage in her life. Unique the fleet certainly was, but that was surely no bad thing!

Table 3 *The major units of the MacBrayne fleet and their normal service routes in 1928 – note how the fleet has both aged and diminished in size since 1914 (Table 2)*

Vessel	Age in 1928	Normal service route
Mountaineer	18	Oban-based and winter reliefs
Lochinvar	20	Oban-Tobermory
Lochiel, ex-Devonia	22	Glasgow-Stornoway and general duties
Comet	23	Greenock-Lochgoilhead
Clydesdale	23	Glasgow to Islay
Pioneer	23	West Loch Tarbert-Islay
Brenda	24	Glasgow-Crinan Canal-Mull cargo service
Cygnet	24	Glasgow-Inveraray cargo service
Plover	24	Outer Isles routes
Fusilier	40	Summer Oban excursions and relief duties
Claymore	47	Glasgow-Stornoway
Columba	50	Glasgow-Ardrishaig summer service only
Linnet	62	Crinan Canal
Gondolier	62	Inverness-Banavie, Caledonian Canal
Iona	64	Oban and Fort William summer service only
Glencoe	82	Kyle-Portree mail service
Average age 38 years		Total number of ships – 16 (plus small units)

TRAVELLING ON THE *GLENCOE*

EARLY IN THE twentieth century, probably in the 1920s, a young man from South Uist by the name of Malcolm Laing travelled from Mallaig to Portree on the veteran steamship *Glencoe*. He recorded his impressions in a Gaelic story which was published in *Gairm* 193 (Winter 2000-2001).

At last the commotion of the harbour ceased. The cargo was evenly stowed down in the hold; the cranks of the iron man [i.e. the winch] fell silent; the derrick carrying the large hook was secured to the foremast; the gangways were taken ashore. Before the ropes were cast, we went below to view the wonderful engine that gave the *Glencoe* her motive power. If any others of the kind were to be seen, it was surely in the museum. The engineer was standing with a crowbar in his hands like a soldier with a musket. When the telegraph rang, he thrust the point of the crowbar through a hole in the end of a stout axle and he worked it against his shoulder with all his might until the shafts of the engine began to move in conjunction with one another's notches. That caused the mill-wheels on the sides of the ship to chew the brine. She had to go a small distance astern before her bow would point directly at the harbour passage. When the telegraph rang again, the man with the crowbar had to aim it successfully into the hole, stop the engine, and turn the axle in the other direction to propel the ship ahead.

When she got out past other ships, the *Glencoe* went at full speed. Seagulls followed us as if they were competing with us; curlews rising from the shore; a cormorant flapping his wings on top of a rock; a sea-trout or two swimming out of our way; the black smoke of coal belching out of the red funnel and weaving backwards in the air; the blue-grey mist of peat rising straight into the skies from a house on a moorland here and there, like strands of wool, smoothly carded. We stayed on deck from the time we left Kyle [of Lochalsh], looking at one of the loveliest scenes under the sun. It was a still, calm day in July….High on the mainland behind us stood the mountainous shoulders of Applecross, bidding us a farewell blessing…

To the south of us rose the notched battlements of the Cuillinn – Sgur Dhearg, Sgur Alasdair and Sgur nan Gillean – keeping watch over us. Happiness shone on every face on board. It was so easy for strangers to talk to one another and to the captain and his sailors. The bridge was on the top deck, where the tourists were pacing all together, like a single family on the move. There was not a sound or a sigh on the sea or a cloud in the height of the sky. In the breast of the ship the murmur of the revolving wheels lulled us with a harmony set in one arrangment, pouring through a tiny crack in the silence of the world. The brave iron engine kept time to the music, with well-oiled, fast, flexible joints; rugged calves and a nimble elbow showing through the ceiling and shining in the sun. She was a steamship as old as any still sailing, but she could travel just as quickly as the majority of those owned by MacBrayne today.

Anyway, she took us safely to Portree in mid-afternoon.

CHAPTER 7

REFLOATING THE KING:
NEW INVESTMENT AND THE COAST LINES' 'POCKET LINERS'

The innovative, diesel-electric motor-ship **Lochfyne** *[Donald B. MacCulloch]*

REFLOATING THE KING:
NEW INVESTMENT AND THE COAST LINES' 'POCKET LINERS'

Although David MacBrayne did great good for the Highlands in his day, it was not easy for him to keep people happy after the war, and they began to complain. The eventual outcome was that he sold his ships and that a new company sails them today under the old name. They have built new ships to go out to the islands, miniature Mauretanias which are so comfortable that you would be better to take a berth on board than go to a hotel in Oban. I do not know if they are paying their way – that is between the company and the government – but their funnels are as red as they have always been, and the appearance of captains and crews remains unchanged. May it long be so; without the red funnel by the side of the pier, Oban would be no better than Kingussie or Pitlochry.
REV. DONALD LAMONT, 'AN LUIDHEAR DEARG' ('THE RED FUNNEL') 1935

David MacBrayne (1928) Limited had various strictures placed on its new parents by government. In return for adhering to these requirements, government promised to maintain a dialogue regarding the need for, and value of, any ensuing operational subsidies due the company. Government, it seems, was primarily concerned about getting the mail through to the islands. Happily, Coast Lines was intent on the business of shipping, and the London, Midland & Scottish Railway, though also a significant shipowner, whose assets included the Caledonian Steam Packet Company, was more concerned about the carriage of people and goods. This combination of interests suited the new company perfectly. Collaboration between Sir Alfred Read of Coast Lines and Sir Josiah Stamp of the London, Midland & Scottish Railway in the north soon led to the formation of an Irish Sea cabal in the south, which included all the companies in the Coast Lines Group and the London, Midland & Scottish Railway, but not the London & North Eastern or the Great Western railways. It is said that Sir Alfred Read had a guarded respect for his new ally, the emphasis apparently being on the word 'guarded'!

The strictures of the 1928 deal required that the passenger accommodation on the Outer Isles services be brought up to accepted standards, and that the passenger- and freight-rates be capped, and, in some instances, reduced. This was coupled with an instruction that capital had to be provided to equip the company for the modern age, with four new major units provided within the first two years of operation. In addition, road services were to be provided as feeders for ship and rail in the form of a parcels network and a range of bus routes.

Before these arrangements could be implemented, the new company had to struggle on with existing mail contracts throughout 1928. The loss of three vessels in 1927 led to the redeployment of other members of the fleet. The *Iona* was sent to Oban to operate the Fort William excursions, while the *Fusilier* undertook the Iona run as best she could. The *Iona*'s place on the Ardrishaig mail service was taken by none other than the veteran Inveraray steamer, the *Lord of the Isles*. Under charter from Turbine Steamers Limited, who had acquired the ship in 1912, it proved to be the swan-song of the *Lord of the Isles*, which was condemned and sent to the breakers at the end of the summer season, complete with her two-cylinder, oscillating, single-crank engines.

The Glasgow-based cargo services to destinations such as Stornoway, Portree and Tobermory were also in difficulties, and new tonnage was urgently required. The Coast Lines' response was to cede the elderly steamer *Denbigh Coast* to the MacBrayne fleet as the *Lochdunvegan*. She had been built to the order of G. & J. Burns in 1891 as the *Grouse*, but she was able to assist her new owners with the West Highland cargo services from Glasgow until withdrawn for scrap in 1948.

The Coast Lines Group was well equipped to

*The steamship **Lochness**, dressed overall, approaching Stornoway [DEM's collection]*

administer the West Highland services required of David MacBrayne (1928) Limited. Not only had G. & J. Burns merged with the Laird Line in 1919 under the ownership of Coast Lines, but M. Langlands & Sons had also joined the expanding empire at the same time. Other acquisitions at that time included the Belfast Steamship Company. All four companies gained in financial security, and Coast Lines flourished during the 1920s, despite a downturn in Irish traffic before and after the Partitioning of Ireland in 1921. As time progressed, security became more tenuous as the mighty Royal Mail Group, which had bought Coast Lines as a feeder system for its various liner companies, became less and less viable in financial terms. By the time Lord Kylsant's mischievous accounting had come adrift, and his ailing Royal Mail Group had finally collapsed in 1931, the Coast Lines Group had gained partial financial autonomy, and was free to carry on its business independently.

The Royal Mail Group included three shipbuilders.

One of these was Harland & Wolff at Belfast, which was heavily committed to diesel machinery, and was building a succession of large passenger liners, each equipped with Burmeister & Wain-type engines, constructed locally under licence. Many of these were internal orders within the Royal Mail Group, and included ships for the Royal Mail Line, Union-Castle Line and the Nelson Line. In the late 1920s, the White Star Line's *Britannic* and *Georgic* were also in the design offices at Belfast. The commercial need for Harland & Wolff to demonstrate the viability of diesel power for fast ferries, and for the Royal Mail Group to retain the business of ship replacement in-house, was compelling. In March 1928 the twin-funnel, cross-channel motor-ferries of the *Ulster Monarch* class were laid down. These emerged successively from 1929 onwards, and were such an immense success that they were followed by numerous quasi-sisters for the Coast Lines Group. The notable point about the new, grey-hulled, twin-funnel ships was that

The **Lochness** in her original grey livery approaching Kyle of Lochalsh [DEM's collection]

they looked almost exactly like scaled-down versions of the *Britannic* and *Georgic*, or, for that matter, any of the Nelson Line or Union-Castle liners of that period. Even the choice of name, *Ulster Monarch*, reflected that of the recently completed Nelson liner *Highland Monarch*, and their grey hulls were akin to the lilac colour which adorned the Union-Castle liners. Diesel-powered mini-liners were now in vogue for short-sea routes.

It is therefore unsurprising that, of the four new ships to be delivered to David MacBrayne (1928) Limited, three were motor-ships. Although MacBrayne's innovative policy in the early 1900s had introduced the oil engine to passenger routes by means of the Edwardian vessels, *Comet*, *Scout* and *Lochinvar* (see Chapter 6), the company's post-1930 departure from steam was at the behest of Coast Lines, and not the result of previous successful operation of the early motor-ships.

The first ship, the *Lochness*, was urgently needed on the Mallaig-Kyle-Stornoway route, following the loss of the *Sheila*. She was completed with twin triple-expansion steam engines and oil-fired boilers at the Govan yard of Harland & Wolff, and was ready to take up her service in the late summer of 1929. Bunker oil was brought to Kyle for her by rail, and stored in a large tank above the quay.

Of conventional design, the *Lochness* is often described as MacBrayne's 'first modern vessel', and when she was delivered, with a liner-style grey hull and imposing red funnel, she looked impressive and powerful. She was a comfortable ship, although her second-class accommodation came under criticism as time went on. There was nothing lavish about the *Lochness*. Compared with contemporary cross-channel ships in the south, which had first-class accommodation in country-house style, she was only meanly furnished. The

Lochness maintained her design route until 1948, when she was transferred to Oban. She was sold on the arrival of the new *Claymore* in 1955. The first of the modern ships, but the last steamer to be built for the company, the *Lochness* was to be considerably outlived in the fleet by her diesel siblings.

The shape of the future became evident in 1929, with the building of the diesel cargo vessel *Lochshiel*. She replaced the *Brenda* on the Glasgow-Mull service, but she was too big to use the Crinan Canal. She was equipped with one engine of the same type as the pair of engines soon to be installed in both the *Lochearn* and the *Lochmor*. A sixth, identical engine was available to the company engineers, as a spare for any of the three ships.

The twins, *Lochearn* and *Lochmor*, which were designed for the Inner Isles and Outer Isles services respectively, were the first of MacBrayne's diesel passenger ships They were built at the Royal Mail Group's Ardrossan Dockyard, and were launched in April and May 1930. When viewed from the bows, they looked businesslike, but abeam and from the stern, they offered a solid central superstructure which, combined with their plump and ungainly cruiser sterns and grey hulls, persuaded Duckworth and Langmuir to liken them to a pair of wooden models in a toyshop window. They had twin sets of direct-drive machinery, which required to be shut down and started again, in order to reverse the propellers during manoeuvres. The engine in each case was started by compressed air which was stored in a bottle in the engine-room. Although the compressed air was replenished while the

THE EARLY MOTOR-SHIPS

OF ALL THE engineering innovation pioneered in the Hebrides, the early introduction of the oil engine in 1907 was both radical and bold. The petrol engine was first seen in a high-speed motor-boat at the Paris Exhibition in 1889, but paraffin was substituted for safer, but slower, use in barges and other harbour craft in due course. The three first paraffin-engined passenger vessels were the MacBrayne trio, *Comet*, *Scout* and *Lochinvar*.

Both the *Lochinvar* and *Comet* received new oil (diesel) engines in the late 1920s, as their original engines were found to be deficient, and they continued to serve their owners for many years. Paraffin, however, had not disappeared completely from the scene. The Girvan-based Ailsa Craig excursion boats, *Carrick Lass* and *Lady Ailsa*, were built with paraffin engines as late as 1934, and paraffin engines were still widely used on ships, large and small, to drive auxiliary equipment, both on deck and below.

The first reliable oil engines were built in the workshops of Mashinenfabrik Augsburg Nurnburg (MAN) in 1897. Early engines of this type were fuelled by naphtha, shale oil, and even household lamp oil. The first commercial applications of the oil engine were on tankers on the Caspian Sea. These ships depended on the distillates then available in the Caspian and Volga region, but the scarcity of suitable fuel oil hindered the introduction of oil engines elsewhere. The oil engines were initially based on steam-engine technology with open crank-cases, but the engines were greatly mistrusted by their engineers, who still preferred the hiss of steam and the smell of hot oil.

The oil engine gained acceptance only slowly. Its efficiency was greatly improved by the submariners' needs in the Great War, but it did not gain full acceptance for some time. Blame for this was ascribed partly to cheap coal, and an abundance of steam engineers. However, some liner companies, such as the Glen Line, built their last steamers as early as 1915, developing all-diesel fleets thereafter. Nick Robins writes in *Ferry Powerful*:

> In those early days, the motor ship was slightly more expensive to run than the conventional steamer, and successful operation depended on fuel oil being available at regular ports of call. Though more expensive, and also requiring a higher degree of training for the engine room staff, the motor ships proved their worth, as the engines and the bunker spaces were smaller and lighter, and more payload could be carried. A series of motor coasters built just prior to 1914 for Paton & Hendry, and given *Innis*-names, was doomed by the shortage of trained

engineering staff. However, by 1930 the average motor ship was using only one third of the fuel for the equivalent output of an oil-fired steamer, and its prospects for the coasting industry were greatly improved.

The building of the *Lochshiel* in 1929 reflected, through the Coast Lines link, the Royal Mail Group's interest in the oil engine, exemplified in its deep-sea liner trades and also in the new *Ulster Monarch* class of cross-channel vessels. The *Lochshiel* predated the introduction of cargo motor-ships (rather than cross-channel passenger and cargo ships) in the main Coast Lines fleet by four years. Truly a pioneer, she even had an oil-fired boiler to power steam-driven capstans and other auxiliary needs. The savings in being able to turn off the main engine on arrival, and start it up with compressed air on departure, were significant. The *Lochmor* and *Lochearn*, the first diesel-engined passenger and cargo ships in the MacBrayne fleet, provided the template right through to the *Claymore* of 1955. Paradoxically, the two early sisters did not live up to their design requirements, offering both inadequate speed and severe noise and vibration problems.

The design of the *Lochfyne*, built in 1931, attempted to address these problems by using an electric-drive coupling to the engines. This was a scaled-down version

White Star's **Britannic** *[NR's collection]*

Union Castle's **Carnarvon Castle** *[NR's collection]*

The **Ulster Monarch** *arriving at Liverpool in August 1966, near the end of her career [NR]*

of the turbo-electric system installed in the P&O liner, *Viceroy of India*, built in 1929 by Alexander Stephen & Sons, Glasgow, but the little ship still 'shimmied like a belly dancer', although the liner was as smooth as the ballroom dance-floor. The vibration problem was finally overcome with the *Lochnevis*, in which the two engines were mounted on bed-plates secured to the ship's frames via damping springs. The electric couple used on the *Lochfyne* and the *Lochnevis*, built in 1934, also allowed greater manoeuvrability, and overcame the need to stop and restart the direct-reversing engines used in the earlier ships.

The *Lochfyne* was the first diesel-electric passenger vessel to enter service in Britain, and as a result she attracted considerable interest in the technical press when she was built. She was also influential in the building of pleasure steamers for other companies. Her overall design, though not her propulsion, was replicated most obviously in the Thames pleasure-steamer, *Queen of the Channel*, built by Denny in 1935 for a consortium formed by Denny and the New Medway Steam Packet Co. According to Geoffrey Grimshaw, 'she was the first large pleasure vessel to be driven by direct-acting Diesel engines, and was the first vessel constructed for cross-channel cruising for twenty-nine years.' The basic *Lochfyne* model was developed still further in two more Denny-built vessels ordered by the General Steam Navigation Co., namely *Royal Sovereign* (1937), 'an enlarged edition

of *Queen of the Channel*' (Grimshaw), and the much more ambitious *Royal Daffodil* (1939), which differed from the *Royal Sovereign* in having her promenade deck extended to the stern.

The next MacBrayne motor-ship, the *Lochiel*, built in 1939, was the company's first vessel to incorporate geared drive. It was this technology, and the subsequent development of the variable-pitch propeller, that made the motor coaster the norm, and eventually sent the steamers to the ship-breakers. Also built in 1939 was the inter-island vessel *Earl of Zetland* for the Shetland services of the North of Scotland, Orkney & Shetland Shipping Company. In overall appearance, she was strikingly similar to the *Lochearn* and *Lochmor*, but she had much more attractive lines, with a yacht-like sheer, and remained in operation until 1975. Although she was the North Company's first motor-ship, as well as the first motor vessel to be built at Aberdeen by Hall, Russell, she still had direct-reversing engines. So too had many of the short-sea vessels built after the war, including MacBrayne's *Loch Seaforth* of 1947 and – remarkably – their *Claymore* of 1955. The latter was meanly engined with four-cylinder Sulzer diesels, although reduction gearing to high-speed diesels had become popular by the 1950s. The variable-pitch propeller was slowly introduced thereafter. A former Dutch coaster, later to become the MacBrayne cargo ship *Lochdunvegan*, was one of the first ships to be so equipped in the British register.

Given the company's reputation for running an elderly fleet of ships, it must be emphasised that MacBrayne contributed very significantly to engineering innovation, even innovation containing an element of risk. The company's leading role in pioneering the passenger motor-ship, and subsequently the marine diesel engine and its various means of coupling, is an important part of recent maritime history – not only Scottish maritime history, but also that of shipping throughout the globe.

*The Thames cross-channel excursion ship **Queen of the Channel** with the typical outline of a Denny-built pocket liner (above)[NR's collection]*
*The North Company's **Earl of Zetland** was modelled on the **Lochearn**-style of cargo, cattle and passenger carrier (below). [NR]*

*The **Lochmor** at Mallaig*
[DEM's collection]

*The **Lochearn**, with her original 'tall' funnel, and the **Lochbroom** in Tobermory Bay [Donald B. MacCulloch]*

*The **Lochearn**, with her shorter funnel, and the **Lochnevis** in Tobermory Bay [Donald B. MacCulloch]*

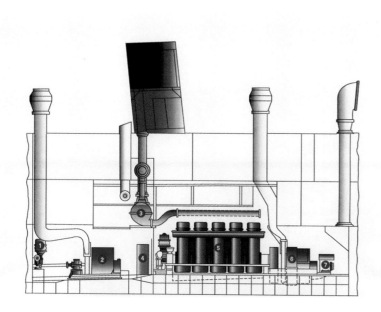

engines were running, the Master had to plan his ahead starts and reverse starts, to ensure that the bottle would not empty before the ship was alongside. Reversing gears were not yet available to suit the high torque generated by a diesel engine.

The actual design speed for the ships was over 12 knots, but in practice they could manage only just over 9 knots. Their lack of power was famously summed up by one of their Masters: 'They canna get oot their ain road!' In 1931, shortly after taking up service, the two vessels deeply embarrassed their owners by illustrating their lack of power and their clumsy manners before the watching public. The *Lochmor* grounded hard on a sandbank near Kyle of Lochalsh, and the *Lochearn* was summoned north to her assistance. She grounded likewise on the same bank, alongside her twin sister. The two new vessels, conjoined amidships, remained

fast until the eighty-five year-old veteran, *Glencoe*, paddled along to their rescue, and towed both motor-ships off the sandbank in fine style! To add to the company's grave embarrassment over the ignominious stranding of their 'advanced' pocket liners and their rescue by the oldest member of the fleet, a photographer associated with Kyle Pharmacy captured the occasion on camera. For some time, MacBrayne's tried to suppress the publication and circulation of the photograph, as it was 'bad for the image'. MacBrayne bosses may also have been aware that the plight of the *Lochearn* and the *Lochmor* was symbolic of the recent distress of the company itself, which had narrowly escaped a serious long-term stranding in 1928, when it was 'towed off' by Coast Lines and the London, Midland & Scottish Railway. As their modern vessels grounded, Lord Kylsant's great contextual empire was

itself on the rocks. They must have prayed earnestly that the Kyle incident was indeed a symbol of the past, rather than an omen of the future.

Another disadvantage that hardly endeared the two sisters to the travelling public was their extremely noisy machinery. There was no escape for passengers from the constant rattle of the engines and the thumping of the exhaust discharge. In 1948, however, the pair were re-engined with Paxman Ricardo diesels, which had the effect of dampening their noise somewhat and increasing their speed to around 11.5 knots, with a favouring breeze. The opportunity was then taken to attend to their unsightly first set of 'chimneys', which lacked rake and were too tall relative to the rather flat and boxy profile of their hulls, typical of motor-vessels of that type. They were given shorter and broader funnels of aluminium, which enhanced their appearance overall.

The *Lochmor*'s new funnel was set a little too low, and the *Lochearn* won the ugly sisters' beauty contest by a few sooty, black inches! Otherwise, the twins were almost identical, and from a distance they could be identified individually only by studying how they sat in the water. Overweight when launched, they were affected by long-term stability problems. The *Lochmor* appeared to be trimmed more heavily towards the stern, and to display a longer line of red boot-topping amidships than the *Lochearn*. The *Lochearn*, erring in the other direction, looked a little 'down by the bow', and tended to lie towards her port beam when at a pier, or loading or unloading into a flit-boat. The *Lochmor* also seemed a little 'squarer' than the *Lochearn* on the edges of her blunt and unimaginative cruiser stern.

Despite their external and internal novelties of design, the pair were well-appointed, with accommodation for 400 passengers. First-class cabins were equipped with a sink and hot and cold running water. The first-class public rooms featured a lounge and a smoke-room bar, and the dining-room offered the traditional-style waiter silver-service. The third-class public rooms were situated aft. The ships had a single hold forward which was served by an electric winch and derrick.

During the 1930s, the *Lochearn* was based at Oban, on the Barra, South Uist, Coll and Tiree mail service, whilst the *Lochmor* maintained the Mallaig and Kyle run to South Uist, North Uist and Harris, calling also at Eigg and Rum. Both vessels had a reputation for being somewhat 'bumpy' in heavy seas, doubtless because of their rather 'shouldery' profiles and short hulls, which disadvantaged them when riding out long swells, and led to 'ploughing'. Nevertheless, they were both remarkable sea-boats, and served their islands with distinction. One of the authors of this book has vivid recollections of seeing the *Lochearn* battering her way southwards from Barra through the Sound of Gunna about 8.30 a.m. on a grim and stormy September day in 1961, when nobody had expected a mail-boat to reach Tiree. Hardly visible through the mist, she wrestled with

the heavy swell, sometimes raising her red forefoot above the waves, and then plunging forward to the depth of her anchors. Navigating the Sound of Gunna in such conditions was a feat of the greatest seamanship, which was regularly undertaken as a matter of course by the Inner Hebridean mail-boats, sometimes in the teeth of south-westerly gales. The Masters of today's car-ferries, despite the electronic gadgetry at their disposal, are wary of taking their vessels through Gunna Sound in much more than a Force Six. By contrast, the Masters of the first diesel vessels to serve David MacBrayne, and also the first to establish diesel propulsion as a norm for short-sea passenger vessels in Britain, were frequently out in all weathers. Their Captains were trained by experience, and such 'training on the job' made them first-rate pilots and outstanding seamen.

There were, of course, occasional hidden 'snags', which caught even the best Captains unawares. From 1947, the *Lochmor* was in the charge of Captain Donald MacLeod. A brief article, which first appeared in *Sea Breezes*, December 1958, commemorating his retirement, recounts one colourful story of ship and Master:

*With a storm gathering strength, Captain Macleod in the **Lochmor** decided to leave Kyle and seek the shelter of Skye, but almost immediately was threatened with being blown onto a rocky shore. To prevent this he ordered the anchor to be dropped. Under the influence of wind and sea the anchor dragged and severed the underwater cable supplying Skye with electricity. The ship was saved, but Skye was without light, heat or power for three weeks!*

The final ship of the four was the first-ever, diesel-electric, coastal passenger ship – the *Lochfyne*. The *Lochfyne* was built by William Denny & Bros. of Dumbarton, the first

THE SHIPBUILDER'S INFLUENCE

NOWHERE IS THE shipbuilder's influence more apparent than in the case of the Dumbarton shipbuilder, William Denny & Brothers Limited, particularly on the design of the cross-channel ferry in the first half of the twentieth century. Denny was already an established builder of cross-channel steamers when the inventor of the marine steam-turbine engine, Sir Charles Parsons (1854-1931), approached the company with the idea of building a demonstration turbine steamer. This, of course, was the *King Edward*, which was completed in 1901, and followed shortly after by the first *Queen Alexandra*.

It was the success of the *King Edward* and *Queen Alexandra* as excursion steamers on the long-distance routes on the Clyde that persuaded the Board of Directors of the South Eastern & Chatham Railway to forsake their fleet of fast paddle steamers on the Dover and Folkestone to Calais and Boulogne services. The first replacement was the world's first fast steam-turbine ferry, *The Queen*, completed in 1903. She was followed by a further seven sisters by 1911, all built by Denny. The basic design was emulated by other builders for other owners, notably by Vickers Son & Maxim, John Brown, Fairfield Shipbuilding & Engineering, and Cammell Laird. From the mid-1930s, William Denny partnered the diesel manufacturers Sulzer, and products such as the *Loch Seaforth* and the *Claymore* were the beneficiaries of this liaison.

In the nineteenth century and the early twentieth, a shipowner would approach a shipbuilder with an outline specification. This would state the design speed, the required cargo volume and weight, the number of passengers and the trimmings, such as straight stem and counter stern or clipper bow and bowsprit. The shipbuilder would respond with a number of outline designs, and only when the owner had opted for one of these would the shipyard design-office set about the detailed design of the ship. Thus the shipbuilder and his designer had a great influence over the appearance and character of the ship.

The ships of the Laird Line and G. & J. Burns, which were amalgamated in 1922 under the Coast Lines umbrella, represented two different styles of construction. The Laird Line preferred as builders D. & W. Henderson & Co. and other companies such as A. & J. Inglis Ltd and the Ailsa Shipbuilding Co. at Troon, whereas G. & J. Burns preferred John Brown, Scott's and Fairfield's, although some ships also came from the Inglis yard. The difference in the two fleets is described by Nick Robins in *The Last Steamers*:

> The ships of the two companies had quite distinctive characteristics. The Burns ships had fine lines, well raked masts and funnels with a single derrick on the after side of the foremast and another forward of the mainmast; the saloon accommodation was aft and steerage was well forward. The Laird ships were more stately in appearance with shorter derricks fore and aft of the foremast and a short derrick aft of the mainmast. They were altogether broader vessels and accommodation was provided amidships for saloon passengers and aft for steerage.

In designing the Victorian fleet owned by the Hutchesons, and later by MacBrayne, the influential shipbuilder was J. & G. Thomson of Clydebank, the precursor of John Brown. Thomson was entrusted with designing and building all the key ships of the fleet, and parted company with David MacBrayne only when new building ceased with the delivery of the *Grenadier* in 1885. The ships were characteristically workmanlike and, for the day, efficient, but they were also embellished with a finish that signified something special – ornate gold scrolling, figureheads, clipper bows and bowsprits, which were of a kind clearly in keeping with the personal vision of David MacBrayne himself.

The Edwardian construction programme was entrusted to A. & J. Inglis and Scott & Company at Bowling. Their products were sturdy-looking vessels, which lacked the grandeur of the earlier Thomson-built ships, but were nevertheless efficient and fit for the purpose.

The new building consequent upon the 1928 redirection of MacBrayne's by the London, Midland & Scottish Railway and the Coast Lines Group was influenced very strongly by the design-offices of the Royal Mail Group's shipbuilders, Harland & Wolff and the Ardrossan Dockyard Company. The first passenger ship from this fold was the steamer *Lochness*. She had the mini-liner look characteristic of company policy, but she also had a powerful forebearing which made her look larger and more fleet of foot than she actually was. The twins, *Lochmor* and *Lochearn*, continued this trend, at least when not viewed from the quarter, an angle that the ships' designers apparently did not visualise until their products had actually taken to the water!

Thereafter, passenger ship construction was taken away from the Royal Mail Group and entrusted to William Denny & Bros. Denny produced a most innovative series of ships, diesel-electric and diesel passenger and passenger / cargo vessels, which were also some of the most attractive ever to be designed for island duties. Modelled on the motor-liners of the late 1920s and the early 1930s, all were built to the same basic design, and the series, which commenced with the *Lochfyne* in 1931, continued to appear after the war with the *Loch Seaforth* in 1947 and the delightful *Claymore* in 1955. Somewhat similar designs to those of the *Loch Seaforth* and the *Claymore* can be matched in cross-channel vessels likewise built by Denny around the same time.

The Denny-built ships were small enough to operate efficiently with the limited winter trade on offer, large enough to provide two-class accommodation and satisfy peak summer demand, and also capable of carrying specialist cargoes such as livestock, vehicles and, of course, the mails. Above all, the Denny stamp was on each ship. They not only looked the part, but they also played their part, becoming key members of Hebridean life and community.

*The **King Edward** in the Kyles of Bute [Donald B. MacCulloch]*

MacBrayne ship ever to be ordered from that yard. That the order was allowed to go to a company outside the Royal Mail Group reflects Coast Lines' increasing independence from Lord Kylsant's empire. Denny had also become a significant shareholder in David MacBrayne Limited in the 1920s. The cost of the new ship was £60 950, and she was handed over to her owners on 28 May 1931. Outwardly, the *Lochfyne* had a slightly raked stem, a cruiser stern and twin funnels, the forward one being a dummy. This was the ultimate 'pocket passenger liner', an intentional effect again highlighted by her grey hull. In overall appearance, but particularly in the set of her funnels with their horizontal tops, the *Lochfyne* was akin to a scaled-down version of the white-hulled passenger liner, *Reina del Pacifico*, built in 1931 by Harland & Wolff, Belfast, for the Pacific Steam Navigation Co. (British flag). In her later red-and-black livery, she resembled White Star's *Britannic* of 1930. The shipbuilders were different, but the underlying model was the same.

Although the *Lochfyne*'s external design reflected the prevailing fashion of the Kylsant era, her means of propulsion was highly innovative in a British context. Her novel power-units comprised two direct-current electric motors supplied by 520 volt direct current at a full load speed of 433 revolutions per minute. The motors were coupled directly to the propellers. The electric coupling was designed to overcome the difficulties of manoeuvring off coastal piers and jetties with strong currents. The main generators were driven by twin four-stroke, single-acting turbo-diesels, which were supercharged by blowing air into the cylinders at a faster rate than it could enter unaided. Auxiliary generators, which were driven by the main engines in tandem with the main generator units, supplied direct current for lighting, heating, cooking and capstan operation.

The main switch-gear was located at a control platform in sight of both the diesel engine starting-gear and the electrical controls. At the throw of a single switch, control could be given directly to the bridge, where a bridge controller, something like a normal telegraph, interpreted instructions regarding motor speed and direction by selecting the voltage and current supplied to the motors. Conventional engine-room telegraphs were also fitted, as certain of the more conservative Masters refused to use the bridge control due to its reputed unreliability in the early years. The daily fuel costs for the *Lochfyne* amounted to about £3 10 shillings, half that of a conventional vessel at that time, and she was able to maintain a service speed of 16 knots.

Sadly, the *Lochfyne* suffered from a serious vibration problem. Described more as a shimmering than a rattle, it was most intense when the main engines were running and the ship was stopped rather than under way. Waist-high observation hatches allowed passengers to maintain the tradition of 'going down to see the engines', but the ear-splitting roar emerging from the void, and the throbbing engine casings below, were a contrast to the old vision of sliding cranks and connecting-rods and the smell of hot oil. Ian Ramsay, Secretary of the Institution of Engineers and Shipbuilders in Scotland, wrote the following whilst peer-reviewing the book, *Ferry Powerful* (see the Bibliography):

*The **Lochfyne** suffered from horrendous vibration and airborne noise. The vibration was so bad that the compass bowl in the binnacle in the wheelhouse was mounted on damping springs as were the clock and the barometer, and the foremast continually whipped back and forth like a fishing rod about to cast a fly. The noise was not helped by the fact that the engine room had viewing windows along the length of the Main Deck and many were open for ventilation which resulted in the whole midship area of the ship being subjected to a deafening roar.*

It has to be said, however, that vibration was a common problem with most early diesel vessels, affecting even the largest. The mighty Royal Mail Lines' *Asturias* (1926) and *Alcantara* (1927), equipped at the outset with twin Burmeister & Wain diesel engines, both had to be re-equipped with more conventional steam-turbine engines in 1934, to make them more passenger-friendly and rattle-free.

Despite the noise and vibration, all went well for the *Lochfyne* until July 1939, when, as her main engines were running slowly while she was alongside at Oban, the starboard diesel engine suddenly exploded. Replacement parts and repairs took eight months, and the *Lochfyne* returned to service in March 1940.

Of the new ships, the *Lochfyne* was unique in that she carried only passengers. The accommodation was adaptable, and enabled her to operate as a one-class day ship in summer on the Oban-Staffa-Iona service, and later also on the Fort William excursions, whereas she became a two-class day ship in winter for the Ardrishaig mail service on the Clyde. There was no cabin accommodation. Her licensed passenger complement was 1200. The promenade deck suffered from obstructions such as ventilators, and passengers were obliged to be careful where they walked as they admired the passing views.

The *Lochfyne* established a small class of three vessels within the fleet. In 1934, the second of these, the lovely little *Lochnevis*, was delivered for the Portree mail service, which the *Glencoe* had left to the *Fusilier* three years previously. The *Lochnevis* was essentially a Mark II version of the *Lochfyne*, although she had both passenger accommodation and a large hold forward, served by a derrick which faced the bow (an exception within the fleet). The foremast, to which the derrick was attached, was mounted just ahead of the bridge. As on the *Lochfyne*, the wheelhouse was raised above the promenade deck to accommodate the switch-gear, again preventing passengers from seeing forward. The deck clutter was greatly reduced,

The **Lochnevis** *leaving Oban for Fort William in the summer of 1967 [NR]*

particularly as the ship had only one funnel.

Clutter and vibration were, however, the least of the company's worries. Replacing an outdated fleet was its most pressing challenge. With the arrival of the modern ships, several older vessels retired – and not before time. The *Brenda* and the *Cygnet* were displaced in 1929 and 1930 respectively. Following her withdrawal from the Crinan Canal in 1929, the elderly but much-loved *Linnet* was also sold. The long-overdue retirement of the *Glencoe* took place in May 1931. Before she was demolished, the *Glencoe* and the brand-new *Lochfyne* shared an open day alongside at the Broomielaw, and by all accounts the contrast between old and new could not have been greater. The difference between the simple machinery of the *Glencoe* and the sophistication of the *Lochfyne*, to say nothing

of their sharply differing profiles, must have presented an unforgettable spectacle to those privileged to see it. The two hulls, their equipment and their design, represented both ends of a century of immense change and progress in the development of West Highland shipping.

The *Claymore* was replaced in 1931 by the introduction of a stop-gap vessel, the *Lochbroom*. The *Lochbroom* was an iron-hulled ship, ten years senior in age to the *Claymore*, and built originally for the Aberdeen Steam Navigation Company, but refitted with a relatively young set of boilers. She operated on the Stornoway service for all but the darkest few winter months, since the business on offer during these months was insufficient for this large vessel. In 1937 she was herself sold for demolition. In the

*Separated by almost a century in their dates of building, the **Lochfyne** and the **Glencoe** lie together serenely at the Broomielaw in May 1931. [DEM's collection]*

meantime, she carried on the traditional role of summer cruise ship. The company said goodbye to its 'flapper', the *Mountaineer*, in 1938, when she was sold for demolition. At the same time, the old *Lochiel*, which had been awarded by the Shipping Controller in lieu of losses in the Great War, was sold for further service in the Channel Islands.

Rather than being consigned to the scrappers, some vessels were given a new lease of life. The *Plover* was taken in hand for a make-over as a 'liner look-alike'. She caused great surprise when she returned to duty in August 1934, wearing an all-buff funnel and a low white waist-line. Her promenade deck had been built out towards the stern, and she carried a new name, the *Loch Aline*. In this condition, she looked positively modern, while keeping in step with the pocket-liner image the company so cherished at that time. She was used as a winter relief vessel, but otherwise employed on excursions from Oban. It was not long, however, before the lid was off the pot of red paint, and the *Loch Aline* again carried the traditional corporate colours of MacBrayne. Also in 1934, the small but attractive excursion steamer, *Princess Louise*, was bought from Alexander Paterson of Oban. Although still maintained on excursions from Oban, she also ran on Loch Ness at a later stage, and was used for winter relief work on the Sound of Mull. She survived in the fleet a further five years.

For MacBrayne's, 1935 was a good year, since it demonstrated that the company was back on its feet – government subsidies and all – despite the rigours of the Great Depression. Its good standing was evident in what it was permitted to do. First, the company was

PATERSON'S EXCURSIONS OF OBAN

IN 1894, ALEXANDER Paterson of Oban took delivery of a small passenger excursion steamer named the *Princess Louise*. The little ship had a simple two-cylinder steam engine and was of modest proportions, being measured at only 66 tons gross. For the next four seasons she was used on day excursions out of Oban to a variety of destinations, including Kerrera, Loch Etive and Connel Ferry. In the spring of 1898 she was sold, whilst an order for a new and larger *Princess Louise* was placed with shipbuilders in Paisley. A stop-gap charter retained the business at Oban for much of the 1898 season.

The new *Princess Louise* was a smart little steamer with a compound steam engine and pleasant day-accommodation for excursionists. The ship developed a wide following, and a day trip on the *Princess Louise* soon became a 'must' for the Victorian visitor to Oban. A second ship was bought in 1901, the *Countess of Bantry*, which had been built seven years earlier for the Bantry Bay Steamship Company, a subsidiary of the Irish railway company, the Cork, Bandon & South Coast Railway. Both ships were used as auxiliaries in the war, but Paterson wisely parted with the older ship in 1919, anticipating declining patronage. The *Countess of Bantry* was then sold to the Orkney Steam Navigation Company for services between Kirkwall and the North Isles, until she was displaced by new tonnage in 1928.

The *Princess Louise* continued to ply her trade out of Oban. Tourist numbers did decline as the Great Depression crawled onwards, eventually forcing Alexander Paterson to look for a buyer. In 1934, he was grateful to the Board of David MacBrayne Limited for offering him just enough money to enable him to withdraw from the excursion industry once and for all. The little *Princess Louise*, neat and handsome to the end, finished her days in the Kingdom, acting both as an excursion steamer on the Caledonian Canal and elsewhere, and as a relief service steamer. Sold in 1939 for further service, the little ship was destroyed two years later by a direct hit during an air raid, whilst she was at Lamont's dry-dock in Greenock.

*The second **Princess Louise** at Colonsay*
[Hector M. Meek]

allowed to shed its reconstitution title, and to revert to its former name of David MacBrayne Limited. Second, it bought Williamson-Buchanan Steamers, including the assets of Turbine Steamers Limited, in collaboration with the London, Midland & Scottish Railway. The deal allowed the turbine steamers *Queen Alexandra* and *King George V* to join the MacBrayne fleet. The former, dating from 1912, was destined to replace the *Columba* on the Clyde, maintaining the traditional but oddly timed 'eleven minutes past seven' morning departure from the Broomielaw, whilst the latter replaced the *Iona* at Oban. Although there was a great hue and cry about the withdrawal of the elderly classic paddlers, they were well past their prime, and their replacements were worthy successors.

The deal gave the London, Midland & Scottish Railway the *King Edward*, the father of all the turbine steamers, as well as the brand-new turbine steamer *Queen Mary II* and the paddle steamers, *Eagle III*, *Kylemore* and *Queen-Empress*. These ships remained largely on their old services, and retained their former company's colours and house-flag. The *Queen Mary II* had been completed in 1933 as the *Queen Mary*, the suffix being added at the request of the Cunard Line, who completed their own distinguished *Queen Mary* in 1936. As the little 'Queen' was to outlive the big one by several years, the turbine steamer was later allowed to shed the suffix. The small *Queen Mary* now lies alongside the Embankment in London, where she has been reduced to static duties, while the great *Queen Mary* has been similarly reduced to static duties as a hotel at Long Beach, California.

Although the *King George V* entered service at Oban with a mere spruce-up, plus new funnel colours and two extra lifeboats formerly belonging to the *Columba*, the *Queen Alexandra* received a more thorough face-lift. Renamed *Saint Columba*, she emerged for the 1936 season with not two, but three, neatly stepped funnels. She was given a

WILLIAMSON-BUCHANAN STEAMERS LIMITED
AND TURBINE STEAMERS LIMITED

MACBRAYNE'S ACQUISITION OF the two turbine steamers, *King George V* and *Queen Alexandra*, in 1935, merits some explanation, as well as a sketch of their previous owners' background. In 1853 Captain Buchanan and Captain Alexander Williamson bought the paddle-steamer *Eagle*, which had been built speculatively by Denny of Dumbarton in the previous year. The little ship provided excellent service as a Clyde excursion steamer, but was sold as a blockade-runner in 1862. Thereafter the partners set up in competition, developing respectively Buchanan Steamers Limited and Alexander Williamson & Sons, the latter becoming ultimately John Williamson & Company, John being one of Alexander's four sons.

The other Williamson sons were James, who became manager of the Caledonian Steam Packet Company; Alexander (junior) who became manager of the Glasgow & South Western Railway fleet; and Robert who established a firm of ship repairers

at Newport on the Bristol Channel, having moved south with Captain Alexander Campbell, when he ran the Clyde steamer *Waverley* out of Bristol in 1888 following a successful charter to the area the previous year. Captain Campbell, of course, was joined two years later by his brother Captain Peter Campbell, whereupon the brothers set on course the Bristol Channel excursion fleet of P. & A. Campbell (The White Funnel Fleet), by using Clyde-built ships and Clyde operational experience. The exiled Scots produced some memorably contrived names for their steamers, including the *Glen Usk* and *Glen Gower*!

In 1901, Denny and Parsons created the Turbine Steamer Syndicate, Turbine Steamers Limited from 1902, to operate their innovative demonstration turbine excursion steamers on the long-haul Clyde services. The management of the new company was placed in the care of none other than John Williamson. So popular did these ships, the *King Edward* and

the original *Queen Alexandra*, become that the company was soon able to buy out the opposition on the Inveraray routes, including the teetotal paddler, *Ivanhoe*, and the famous Loch Goil paddle steamer, *Lord of the Isles*. The loss of the *Queen Alexandra* by fire in 1911 necessitated a replacement to broadly the same design and of the same name. The second *Queen Alexandra* was completed in 1912.

In the aftermath of the Great War, the Buchanan and Williamson fleets were amalgamated in 1919 to form Williamson-Buchanan Steamers Limited. The new company retained the close liaison with Turbine Steamers Limited which Williamson had enjoyed, operating a fully integrated timetable with a combined fleet which wore the famous white funnel with a black top, although the *Lord of the Isles* was graciously allowed to retain her old Loch Goil colours. The two companies were, however, financially independent.

*The **Queen Alexandra***
[NR's collection]

mainmast, and was painted in the style of a Cunarder, not unlike the liner *Queen Mary*, which was then nearly ready for her trials. The *Saint Columba* was converted to oil fuel the following year. MacBrayne once again led the way, as all the other Clyde steamers still burned coal. As a result of the desire that its ships should look like their larger ocean-going counterparts, the company had adopted an attractive grey hull for its earlier pocket liners, but found that it was expensive to maintain, and that it tended to camouflage the ships in half-light conditions. It was soon dropped in

favour of black, a colour against which many a rust streak could go unnoticed.

The flexibility inherent in the relationship between MacBrayne's and its new owners was shown in ship transfers. Two Coast Lines vessels were transferred into the MacBrayne fleet in 1937. The first of these was the *Lochgorm*, formerly the Burns and Laird Lines' *Lairdspool*, which, in her new guise, bolstered the Stornoway cargo service from Glasgow. The second was the *Lochgarry*, a more interesting ship which replaced the iron-hulled *Lochbroom*

In 1926, Turbine Steamers put their brand new experimental high-pressure turbine steamer, *King George V*, on the Greenock to Inveraray service. The original turbine steamer, *King Edward*, was then put on the Glasgow all-the-way service, displacing the old paddle steamer, *Lord of the Isles*, which was scrapped. In 1933, Williamson-Buchanan received an even finer new turbine steamer, the *Queen Mary*, for the Glasgow 10 o'clock departure 'doon the watter'. Like the old *King Edward* and *Queen Alexandra*, she reverted to the use of direct-drive turbines to avoid the drag of the momentum from the massive gear trains as she approached the numerous Clyde piers on her daily round.

The *King George V* was equipped with single reduction gearing to reduce the speed of the turbines to a more efficient propeller speed. Although her Yarrow water-tube boiler was removed in 1929, it was replaced by a Babcock and Wilcox water-tube boiler which was no more successful than the first. The water-tube boiler was not ideal for the service in which the *King George V* was engaged, with quick demands for full power from rest, after the fires had been damped back when stopped at piers. In 1935, the high-pressure, high-temperature experiment, which was an attempt to slow the inexorable advance of the diesel engine, was over, and the Babcock boiler and the extra-high-pressure turbine were taken out. The former was replaced by a double-ended Scotch boiler, operating at 200 psi. The characteristically slow approach of the *KGV* to the Clyde piers, and later to West Highland piers during her Oban-based cruises, was entirely due to the override caused by her gear trains, which prevented the ship from stopping in anything like the length of which the *Queen Mary* and her cohorts were capable.

The Great Depression finally took its toll of the Clyde excursion trade, and the end of the 1935 season left deficits in the accounts of both Williamson-Buchanan and Turbine Steamers. Thus it was that Williamson-Buchanan Steamers Limited passed into the ownership of the Caledonian Steam Packet Company, whilst Turbine Steamers Limited came under the ownership of David MacBrayne Limited. The *King George V* and the *Queen Alexandra*, now renamed and rebuilt with three funnels as *Saint Columba*, became the mainstay of the MacBrayne excursion trade, the former at Oban, the latter maintaining the Ardrishaig service. The *Queen Mary*, which had stayed on the Clyde routes of the Caledonian Steam Packet Company, although managed under the banner of Williamson-Buchanan Steamers (1936) Limited until the war, finally came into the amalgamated MacBrayne Kingdom in 1973, when the fleets of MacBrayne and the Caley were merged.

Williamson, Buchanan and Turbine Steamers together owned and operated a large part of the Clyde excursion fleet in direct competition with the railways. Other than the turbine steamers, perhaps the best remembered of their vessels are the Buchanan paddlers, *Isle of Arran* and *Eagle III*, and the Williamson paddlers, *Strathmore* and *Queen-Empress*.

*The Williamson-Buchanan steamer **Isle of Arran** was sold in 1933 to GSNC for use in the excursion trade on the Thames. [NR's collection]*

on the Stornoway and Outer Isles cruise circuit. The *Lochgarry* had been built as the *Vulture* for the Laird Line in 1898. Subsequent to the merger of the Laird Line with G. & J. Burns, the company nomenclature was eventually rationalised, so that the *Vulture* became the *Lairdsrock*. The *Lairdsrock* first came to the Western Isles on charter to MacBrayne in 1936, and was later transferred. Given an extensive refit the following winter, she re-emerged in January 1937 with a new and broader funnel, and neat white paintwork to main deck level. Her accommodation was reconstructed and modernised, and a particularly fine dining-saloon was created, ready to accommodate the traditional MacBrayne silver service. The *Lochgarry* immediately took up station with a weekly departure for Stornoway, offering seasonal round-trip cruises throughout the kinder months of summer. MacBrayne's 1939 brochure described her accommodation fulsomely:

This roomy and seaworthy vessel has been splendidly fitted and equipped for her particular service. Steam heating arrangements are of the most recent type. There are six

The regal, three-funnelled **Saint Columba** shows her elegant lines. [Donald B. MacCulloch]

single-berth cabins and forty-four two-berth cabins with hot and cold water. She has salt and fresh water baths, and sprays, a smoke-room lounge in pale blue with light-wood panelling and furnishings with a tea, coffee, ice and cocktail bar at your elbow, a lounge-writing room, sports and shelter deck, a capacious dining saloon – the ship is complete with everything that matters on a sea holiday.

Cruises had remained ever-popular, even at the height of the Depression in the 1930s. M. Langlands & Sons were not, however, able to resume their cruises after the Great War, but Coast Lines had been able to fill this void by deploying the former Irish ferry, now 'cruise yacht', *Killarney*, on West Highland cruises from Liverpool and Ardrossan from 1927 onwards. Earlier in the 1920s, the Burns & Laird steamer *Tiger* was taken off the Glasgow-Dublin route to operate summer cruises to the Western Isles. In the 1930s, two of the *Ulster Monarch*-class ships, the *Ulster Prince* and *Ulster Queen*, were also frequently deployed on long-weekend cruises to the islands. Iain F. Anderson, a journalist who became familiar with both the *Killarney* and the *Ulster Prince*, described both vessels in 1937:

*The **Killarney** is a large ship, as Hebridean ships go, of*

The miniature 'cruise liner', **Lochgarry**, approaches Tobermory. [Donald B. MacCulloch]

1,200 tons, and sails frequently on different itineraries, some of a week's duration and some extending to ten days or a fortnight. During the summer months you need never be surprised to see the grey hull and yellow funnels of the **Killarney** slip round some shoulder of land and gracefully steam across your track, either bound for Skye or the further north. I have seen the **Killarney** in many Hebridean ports and lochs, and remember on one occasion spending several hours with the wireless operator on my ship hoping against hope that I would again have another opportunity of meeting this delightful cruise ship, and having a yarn with her genial commander, Captain

Livingstone ... I have vivid recollections of a very happy cruise on board this ship and of the games, the dances and the very jolly company ...

The M.V. **Ulster Prince** is another frequenter of the Hebrides during week-ends. She sails from Liverpool on a Saturday afternoon, and as we waken on Sunday morning it is to look on the Sound of Jura or the Firth of Lorne. Her cruise is of short duration, but her speed carries one fast by night, and throughout the whole of Sunday we cruise up the Sound of Mull to Tobermory and then up Loch Linnhe to Ballachulish. The ship is a most popular one. That little *break when one can leave the desk on a Saturday, be transported for a day to the beauties of the Hebrides, and be back at one's work early on Monday morning ensures its popularity. The **Ulster Prince** is a miniature liner of the latest construction, and close on 3,000 tons, and her appointments of the very finest.*

Between 1935 and 1940, Coast Lines' passenger-cargo ships, the *Atlantic Coast* and the *British Coast*, called weekly at Stornoway on passage between Liverpool and Middlesborough. This too was an attractive summer-cruise opportunity. McCallum and Orme were able to maintain their long-standing and popular summer cruises to St Kilda until 1939 (see Chapter 4). Their itineraries continued to generate good copy for journalists and writers such as Iain F. Anderson, Alasdair Alpin MacGregor (who covered the evacuation of St Kilda in 1930), and Robert Atkinson.

While David MacBrayne Limited reinvented itself and cashed in on the inter-war tourist boom, other companies, reaching the end of their active lives with ageing ships, sought shelter within it. In 1937, the effects of the Campbeltown & Glasgow Steam Packet Company were absorbed, bringing the Clyde-based *Davaar* and *Dalriada* within the compass of the Kingdom, although managed separately. The *Davaar*, built in 1885, still had a classic clipper bow and figurehead, of the kind once so much loved by David MacBrayne himself. Whilst her running-mate, the *Dalriada*, was more modern, she too was no youngster. The *Dalriada* was one of the fastest single-screw steamers ever built, her four-cylinder, triple-expansion engine maintaining a service speed of 17½ knots. She spent her time running between Glasgow and Campbeltown, calling at Lochranza, Pirnmill, Carradale and Saddell. On Saturdays, she undertook a double run from Greenock, offering excursionists an afternoon at sea. She ran occasional cruises from Campbeltown. On a Steam 5 Certificate, she could carry 1294 excursionists.

Following the acquisition of this company, another spurt of new building brought the 1930s to a successful conclusion for David MacBrayne Limited. The novel Dutch water-bus, *Lochbuie*, was delivered from builders in

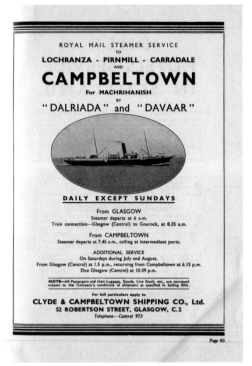

*Advertisement for the Clyde & Campbeltown Shipping Company, showing the **Davaar** [DEM's Collection]*

*The elegant **Dalriada** had a very tall funnel, shown conspicuously in this picture. [DEM's collection]*

CAMPBELTOWN & GLASGOW STEAM PACKET
JOINT STOCK COMPANY LIMITED

IN HIS BOOK, *Kintyre*, Alasdair Carmichael described the Campeltown & Glasgow Steam Packet as follows:

Road and air transport have between them relegated to fond memory the last two gallant, graceful, tall-funnelled old ships, *Davaar* and *Dalriada*, with which the Campbeltown & Glasgow Steam Packet Joint Stock Co. Ltd provided the main link between Kintyre and the outside world. The *Davaar*, built for this special service in 1885, was for long after her natural day a delight to ship-lovers, with her beautifully formed 'clipper' bow and her tall funnel. The *Dalriada*, launched in 1926 and capable of 17 knots, was regarded as being one of the fastest single-screw steamers of her day. These fine old ships sailed from Campbeltown for the Clyde on alternate days, with calls at Carradale, Lochranza, Gourock and Greenock. Since one was always on the homeward trip as the other was outward bound, their schedule did not allow the day-tripper a few hours either in Glasgow from Campbeltown, or in Campbeltown from Glasgow.

The company was formed by a group of Campbeltown merchants in 1826, with the four-year-old wooden paddle-steamer, *Duke of Lancaster*. She was joined by their first purpose-built steamer, *St Kiaran*, in 1835, and for a short while services were extended to Larne and Ayr. Concentrating on the core passenger and cargo service to Glasgow, the company built three more small paddle-steamers before trying their luck in the excursion trade. The *Gael* was purpose-built in 1867 for this traffic, and fitted out with pleasantly furnished accommodation on the main deck, yet capable of an impressive 16 knots. She was always charged with undertaking the twice-yearly shopping excursion from Campbeltown to Belfast.

The *Gael* was followed in 1868 by one of the most beautiful Clyde steamers of all time, the *Kintyre*, complete with a clipper bow and single funnel in the style of a steam yacht, and the first screw steamer in the fleet. A quasi-sister, the *Kinloch*, was delivered in 1878, but neither ship could match the *Gael* for speed. The *Gael* was sold in 1884, eventually joining the MacBrayne fleet in 1891 as one of their many second-hand purchases of that era. The *Kintyre* and *Kinloch* remained to deal with the summer excursion traffic.

The wonderful *Davaar* was commissioned in 1885 to take the place of the *Gael*. Running from Greenock whilst the other two ships ran from Glasgow, the *Davaar*, although not a fast ship, offered a seaworthiness fit for a small vessel which had to brave the elements of the Lower Clyde the year round. The *Davaar* very nearly came to grief in 1895, when she ran aground in Belfast Lough on one of the Belfast shopping trips. All personnel were safely taken ashore, but at low tide she looked a sorry sight with her graceful bows pointing skywards. Happily, she was pulled to safety two days later, but at the cost of one of the rescue tugs, which sank on striking the rocks.

Of course, the arrival of the big turbine steamer *King Edward* on the route in 1901 was a grave threat. The Campbeltown company was nevertheless able to continue more or less unaffected, despite the loss of much of the excursion revenue to the predator. Sadly, the *Kintyre* was run down and sunk off Fairlie in 1907, leaving the *Kinloch* and *Davaar* in charge of the route, the *Davaar* now also continuing through to Glasgow. The two thin funnels were replaced with one central funnel when the *Davaar* was reboilered in 1903, and the main saloon was widened to incorporate the side alleyways which were previously open to the elements. The funnel carried the unique, but classic, black with a broad red band, and the hull was black with pink boot- topping, in the same manner as the cargo-liners of T. & J. Harrison.

The *Kinloch* was replaced by the *Dalriada* in the company's centenary year. Although devoid of bowsprit and clipper bow, she was a handsome vessel with an over-sized funnel above the central accommodation block, the saloon still being on the main deck aft. Her arrival in service in 1926 reduced the passage time between Gourock and Campbeltown to three hours, allowing a second excursion run on summer Saturdays, or the opportunity for charter trips in the early season to places such as Carradale.

The two steamers were taken over by Clyde Cargo Steamers, in which David MacBrayne Limited was a partner, in March 1937. At the end of the month they became part of the MacBrayne Kingdom and by May they had red funnels topped with black, although they were retained under the ownership of the newly-named Clyde & Campbeltown Shipping Company Limited. Their tenure in the Kingdom was short-lived, as both ships were lost in the Second World War. The *Dalriada* was sunk while acting as a mercantile auxiliary in the Thames. The *Davaar*, intended as a blockship if needed at Newhaven in Sussex, was eventually broken up on the beach at the stately age of 58, her parts being of more use to the war effort than the ship herself.

The company name survived after the war, but the remaining cargo boats of the former Clyde Cargo Steamers fleet were soon subsumed into the Caledonian Steam Packet Company. The Campbeltown & Glasgow Steam Packet, however, retains a special importance, as, unlike David MacBrayne Limited, it was one of a very few successful Highland-owned and Highland-operated shipping companies.

The **Lochiel** at West Loch Tarbert [Harold Jordan's collection]

Amsterdam, in time for the 1938 season and her role as summer excursion ship at Fort William. One major new vessel, the *Lochiel*, came from William Denny at Dumbarton in 1939. Although similar in appearance to the earlier *Lochnevis*, and thus a descendant of the *Lochfyne*, the *Lochiel* was radically different in that she was equipped with twin shafts connected to diesel engines via a set of reduction gears. She was placed on the West Loch Tarbert to Islay run, after a short delay while the Tarbert pier was modified to accommodate her. The Islay service was designed to connect with the arrival of the Glasgow steamer at East Loch Tarbert, with a bus providing the link between the piers. The displaced paddle-steamer *Pioneer* moved to Oban to assist with excursion work, but was later used by the Admiralty in experimental submarine communication work. She was not scrapped until 1958.

The *Lochiel*, unlike the diesel-electric ships, was almost vibration-free. The earlier experience had led to investment in flexible engine-mountings to reduce both noise and vibration. The first-class accommodation was placed to starboard, the third class to port, and the respective dining-saloons and smoke-rooms were on the main deck, with the lounges, purser's office and ticket office on the promenade deck. As before, the bridge was raised above the boat deck to rail level, preventing passengers from seeing forward of the bridge, but affording the navigating officer excellent all-round vision. In common with the *Lochnevis*, she had a single hold forward, served by a derrick on a single, steel pole-mast.

As the building of the *Lochiel* demonstrates, David MacBrayne Limited had come through the depressed years of the 1930s with flying colours, carefully managed under the watchful eye of the Directors of Coast Lines and the London, Midland & Scottish Railway. The company had benefited greatly from a planned investment programme, receiving a mixture of purpose-built and recycled vessels, which placed it firmly as the sole possible contender to bid for the new mail contracts which were again issued in 1938. The outcome of this bid was that one new ship was to be supplied for the Islay service, the *Lochiel*, and a replacement for the Kyle-Stornoway route was needed to succeed the *Lochness*, the first of the quartet required to satisfy the 1928 mail contract. Before the *Lochiel* could settle into a routine, however, international events were leading rapidly to a confrontation. By September, Britain was once again at war. The new ship for the Stornoway service would have to wait until its conclusion.

At the outbreak of the Second World War, the fleet comprised seventeen ships with an average age of just 23 years (Table 4). Given that two vessels, both over 40 years of age, had only recently been transferred into the fleet, this low average fleet-age reflected the massive investment which the owners had undertaken since the 1928 agreement, when the average fleet age stood at 38 years (Table 3). Only the *Lochgarry* was lost during the war. She was replaced by the transfer of the *Ulster Star* from the Belfast Steamship Company in 1942.

A number of ships were requisitioned by the Admiralty, while others carried on supplying the islands, although the Portree mail service was suspended during the hostilities. Tiree became the site of a major RAF base, and this necessitated exchanging the *Lochgorm* for McCallum and Orme's *Hebrides* in 1942, in order to provide extra cargo and personnel capacity on the route. All the ships on civilian duties wore drab-grey. In the early years of the war, some were given black funnels with their white upper-works painted dull yellow. The *Lochearn*, for some unaccountable reason, managed to retain her red-and-black funnel right through until the Armistice.

There was much speculation as to which ships would be requisitioned for war service. The *Lochearn* and the *Lochmor* were very likely candidates. In the event, they were spared, partly because of the decision to requisition the *Lochgarry*. Both the *Lochgarry* and the *King George V* attended at Dunkerque, the latter with distinction. The former was then deployed on the Iceland supply route, and the latter on troop transfers on the Clyde. It was while employed on the Iceland service that the *Lochgarry* got into difficulties off Northern Ireland, and foundered in severe weather conditions, with the loss of twenty-six men.

The *Lochnevis* saw duty as the minelayer, HMS *Lochnevis*. She was returned to her owners in 1944, when she took up service alongside the *Lochfyne* on the Ardrishaig route, which was served from Wemyss Bay, below the Cloch-Dunoon defence boom. A number of ships remained on the Clyde: the *Loch Aline* as an inspection vessel at Rothesay, the *Saint Columba* as a naval depot ship at Greenock, and the little *Lochbuie* acting as an ambulance launch.

The two steamers of the former Campbeltown & Glasgow Steam Packet Company did not fare so well. The *Davaar* was taken south during the war for possible use as a blockship to be sunk at Newhaven, but was broken up on the beach in 1943, and the *Dalriada* was lost in the Thames estuary in June 1942, while working as a salvage ship.

Despite the economic instability of the 1930s and the challenges posed by the Second World War, David MacBrayne Limited had maintained course, and had gained no small distinction in the process. Modernisation of the fleet was the keynote of those years, and it deserves to be noted that this skilful achievement was of major significance to the economy of the Highlands and Islands. At a time when politically aware bodies and ginger-groups, such as the Highland Development League, were struggling, with relatively little success, to convince the government of the need to invest more meaningfully in the crofting areas, the alliance of Coast Lines and the London, Midland & Scottish Railway produced a model of well-managed, focused and purposeful action within a key public sector. It was without parallel elsewhere in the Highlands and Islands in the inter-war years. It also meant that, as far as sea transport was concerned, the region was well equipped to face, and to survive, the Second World War.

MacBrayne's forward-looking policy, which laid the foundations of the modern fleet that we know today, entailed risks. The introduction of the first diesel-powered, short-sea, passenger vessels to function in the United Kingdom was a very brave step, especially in the Hebrides. Diesel engines had yet to be tamed and domesticated, as their noise and vibration demonstrated all too clearly. Mistakes of all kinds were waiting to be made – in hull design and in propulsion, as well as in handling such vessels, particularly in heavy weather. It is greatly to the credit of the company's Masters, engineers and crews that it discharged its duties with so few mistakes. The new ships had an astonishingly good safety record, given that they operated in some of the most treacherous waters in the northern hemisphere.

The challenge of upgrading the fleet had been surmounted, but the rigours of post-war austerity and rebuilding now had to be faced by the successors of the Once and Future King.

BASHING MACBRAYNE'S RUST-BUCKETS

'FOR MOST OF the [1950s], however, anyone bound for Ardnamurchan came via Oban rather than Fort William, boarding at Oban a steamer which took him through the Sound of Mull to Tobermory. Disembarking at Tobermory he took a ferry back across to the mainland – if mainland be the right word for Ardnamurchan – stepping ashore this time at Mingary Pier, Kilchoan.

'The main potential trouble spot in this itinerary was the Tobermory-Kilchoan ferry, which was actually a small launch. If the Sound of Mull were at all stormy – and the sound here is more or less at an end and has widened into open Atlantic – the launch crew generally refused to make the run. It did not matter if the crossing, though rough, was yet possible; if they did not feel like it they did not stir and there was nothing one could do about it. Though supposedly tied in with the national transport network they had in actual practice a good deal of autonomy. Naturally, too, the launch skipper had – or adopted – a sea captain's authority in regard to his vessel and claimed to be the sole arbiter in all decisions affecting her daily running and risk.

'Once in a great while, on the other hand – I think when complaints became too loud and too prevalent even for those conveniently deaf to ignore – the same crew would display all the seafaring enterprise that one could wish, and perhaps a little more to boot. I have made the crossing on days when all was noise and welter, when the launch went from crest to trough like a bobsleigh and from trough to crest like a badly overloaded lift, when I had to wedge myself between bulkheads to avoid being hurled about the cabin and had to leap for my life when the vessel at last made a flying pass at Mingary Pier. But derring-do of that order was very much the exception rather than the rule....

'The launch was operated by MacBrayne's Ltd and that, to anyone who knows the region, explains a good deal. For longer than I can remember this company has had a stranglehold on West Highland transport, in all its ramifications, and has been notorious for its utter indifference to the welfare and comfort of its passengers. How clearly I recall from my childhood, how often, boarding the old *Lochearn* at Kilchoan, to return south with my parents after a holiday, and finding its scanty and spartan steerage accommodation already full of the Outer Islands poor, picked up at the start of the voyage. They would be sprawled out across every available foot of space, sick, white-faced and miserable after the long trip down from the Islands and the crossing of the dreaded Minch. There would be shawl-wrapped women with babies, men with shiny blue serge suits and soft hats, on their way to the Labour Exchanges of Glasgow, to the tenements, with their pathetic luggage, their possessions, piled around them.

'It was scarcely an advance on the emigrant ships of the nineteenth-century Clearances. Indeed MacBrayne's were all too often in the same line of business and operating about the same level of concern. Yet the *Lochearn* was a blue riband liner compared to earlier MacBrayne vessels. It is enlightening, and harrowing, to persuade old people in the Highlands to talk about such rust-buckets as the *Plover* and the *Cygnet*, where, frequently, one shared accommodation – if that is the right word for what was on offer; it was, at any rate, MacBrayne's word – with a herd of often-terrified cattle, plunging, bellowing and skittering.

'It should be noted that the doubtful privilege, granted post-War to Ardnamurchan passengers, of using Mingary Pier, was itself a revision of the earlier barbarous practice of embarking and disembarking in the open roads off Kilchoan. During my childhood the custom was for the steamer to anchor there (if the captain felt he had time for such minor diversions). One was ferried out and back from a small jetty in the village, in a tiny undecked boat that was invariably piled high with goods and luggage. The hazards of this operation in stormy weather may be imagined, especially if one were elderly or disabled.'

(From Alasdair MacLean,
Night Falls on Ardnamurchan (1984))

Table 4 *The major units of the MacBrayne fleet and their normal service routes in 1939*

Vessel	Age in 1939	Normal service route
Lochiel	0	West Loch Tarbert-Islay
Lochnevis	5	Mallaig-Kyle-Portree
Lochfyne	8	Oban excursions and winter relief Glasgow-Ardrishaig
Lochmor	9	Mallaig-Eigg-Rum-South Uist-NorthUist-Harris
Lochearn	9	Oban-Coll-Tiree-Barra-South Uist
Lochshiel	10	Glasgow, Mull and Loch Leven cargo service
Lochness	10	Kyle-Stornoway
King George V	13	Oban-round Mull-Staffa-Iona excursions
Saint Columba	27	Glasgow-Ardrishaig
Lochinvar	31	Oban-Tobermory
Comet	34	Greenock-Lochgoilhead
Clydesdale	34	Glasgow to Islay and Outer Isles
Pioneer	34	Oban excursions
Loch Aline	35	Oban excursions, winter relief vessel
Lochgarry*	41	Glasgow-Stornoway
Lochgorm	43	Glasgow-Stornoway cargo service
Lochdunvegan	48	Mainly Glasgow-Stornoway cargo service
	Average age 23 years	Total number of ships – 17 (plus small units)

* foundered in 1942 while on active service

MASTERS OF MACBRAYNE

MASTERS OF MACBRAYNE vessels were very commonly natives of the Hebrides, often hailing from the areas served by their ships. They were very well regarded in their local communities. Several were greatly respected as Gaelic tradition-bearers, possessing a rich knowledge of songs, tales and local history. They symbolised the islanders' mastery of the sea and their achievements in the Merchant Navy world-wide.

Outsiders frequently depicted MacBrayne Captains as 'characters', since some were known for their droll humour and curious turns of phrase (in English). Jokes about them, doubtless apocryphal in many cases, were part of common currency. For instance, it was claimed that one Captain, relaxing on his bridge at Oban, heard a cry for help from a yachtsman. 'We're sinking, we're sinking!', yelled the distressed mariner. 'And what are you sinking about?' responded the laid-back Captain, who, like many of his day, pronounced English *th* as *s*, and was nicknamed, the 'Souser'. Or, in still another such joke, the Captain announces to passengers that the ship has made a particularly fast crossing that day. 'Is that a record?' asks a passenger. 'No,' says the Captain, 'it is myself who is telling you.'

The closely localised connections between officers and their ship are very clear in the case of the *Lochmor*. The first master of the *Lochmor*, when she made her maiden voyage on 7 July 1930, was Captain Duncan Robertson, a native of Skye, and known more generally as 'Squeaky', apparently because of his high-pitched voice. He was allegedly given to droll sayings. On one occasion, it is claimed that he asked for a twisted railing 'to be bent straight'.

Captain Robertson was followed on the *Lochmor* by Captain Donald MacLeod, who had been an officer on the ship since 1930. Captain MacLeod, known to his own people as *Dòmhnall Màiri* ('Donald son of Mary') was a native of Caragraich, Harris. He had gone to sea as a deck-hand on the *Mountaineer*. He and his crew achieved distinction in the Royal Navy in the First World War, when they managed to sink a German submarine with the only small gun available to them. Captain MacLeod carried his decorations proudly on his MacBrayne uniform. After the war, he served on routes to Dublin, and then rejoined MacBrayne as mate on the *Mountaineer* in 1924. Serving as a Relief Master, he was promoted Captain of the *Lochmor* in 1947.

Captain MacLeod was succeeded as Master in his turn by Donald Joseph MacKinnon (*'An Iosag Ruairidh Iain Bhàin*, to give him his Gaelic pedigree), who was a native of Barra. He had previously served as Chief Officer of the *Lochmor* with Captain MacLeod. Captain MacKinnon was distinguished not only for his seamanship, but also for his interest in Gaelic songs.

As Finlay J. MacDonald noted in 1956, 'When he is not on the bridge, he can be found down in his own cabin, surrounded by books in which he writes every song and lyric he hears.' Captain MacKinnon was, and remains, very well known throughout the Gaelic world for his fine singing of traditional Gaelic songs. He too carried wartime decorations proudly on the breast of his jacket.

Masters from the Hebrides served alongside distinguished colleagues from other parts of the Highlands. The first Master of the *Lochearn* was Captain Robert ('Big Bob') MacLean, a native of Kintyre, who was one of only two officers in the MacBrayne fleet until the 1950s who possessed a Foreign-going Master's Certificate. Captain MacLean was Master of the *King George V* whilst on war service at Ostend, Rotterdam, Boulogne and Dunkerque, and was awarded the DSC for his efforts at the evacuation of Dunkerque. From 1947 until retirement in 1953, he was, as Commodore, in command of the *Saint Columba* in summer and the *Lochfyne* in winter. The other holder of a Foreign-going Master's Certificate was Captain Ewen ('Hugo') MacKinnon, a native of Skye, who was the first Master of the *Loch Seaforth*, and had also been at Dunkerque in command of the *Lochgarry*.

Several Hebridean Captains achieved the rank of

Captain Duncan Robertson

company Commodores, in charge of the flagships of the fleet. Captain Angus MacKinnon, for example, who was a native of Mull, was for many years MacBrayne's Commodore, in command of the flagship, *Saint Columba*. Between 1851 and 1969, there were only eight holders of this office, and from the early 1880s all were certainly Highlanders or Islanders, with surnames such as Campbell, MacTavish, Cameron, MacLean, MacKinnon and MacCallum. 'Royal Route' officers usually lived in Glasgow, a city with a long-standing reputation as a 'base' for MacBrayne employees – 'Davy's Navy' – whose homes were in districts such as Partick, Broomhill, Whiteinch and Govan, with their strong Highland and Gaelic-speaking communities.

The first car-ferries carried Hebridean Masters. Captain Colin MacDonald from Iona was the first Master of the *Columba* of 1964. Captain Archie MacQueen from Staffin, Skye, who was Second Officer on the *Claymore* in the 1950s, served as Master of the *Columba*'s sister-ship, *Hebrides*, and then of the *Hebridean Isles*. The *Loch Seaforth*, and thereafter the *Iona* and the *Suilven*, were served by Masters from Lewis and Skye, among them Captain John Smith and Captain Alasdair Matheson. The tradition continues on present-day ships.

The link between the native districts of the Masters and the ships which they served is very evident before 1970. Just as Masters from Lewis and Skye,

often with their homes in Stornoway, commanded the Outer Isles ships, men from the Inner Hebrides, whose homes were in Oban, were in command of ships which served these routes. Certain islands, such as Iona and Tiree, were noteworthy for producing sea-captains. In the mid-1960s, it was possible to undertake an evening circuit of the ships moored at Oban, and to find a Tiree man on the bridge of each one, beginning at the North Pier with the *Lochnevis* (Captain John Kennedy, Captain Sandy Campbell), and moving to the Railway Pier with the *Claymore* (Captain Neil Campbell, Captain John Lamont) and the *King George V* (Captain Neil Campbell). Tiree men, such as Charles Hamilton, were also prominent as officers and Captains on MacBrayne's cargo-boats. The latter group were frequently given humorous nicknames, including 'Hurricane Dan', who was supposedly wary of sailing in bad weather, 'Paraffin Dan' and 'Polaris', the last allegedly being the only Master who broke the officially-imposed radio silence at the time of the Cuban Crisis in the early 1960s. Like the officers and crews on the 'Royal Route', those serving on the cargo-boats were usually based in Glasgow.

Less commonly, islanders would serve as engineers on MacBrayne vessels, but several are on record. One of the *Lochmor*'s engineers in the 1950s was Donald MacDonald from Idrigill in Lewis, and islanders are to be found in the company's engine-rooms to the

present day. The company's engineers are often overlooked when the 'great men' of MacBrayne's ships are recalled, largely because their contribution was made below decks and was not obvious to passengers or to the general public. Consequently, Masters are frequently credited – wrongly – with achievements which would have been impossible without the skills of their engineers.

Whether they came from the Highlands or the Lowlands, however, or from much farther afield, the outstanding contribution of engineers to Hebridean and Clyde seamanship deserves to be noted, as it was indispensable to the work of the vessels. Capable and versatile men, their meticulous attention to their engines, and their ability to maintain them in pristine condition in all circumstances, lay at the very heart of the fine service which MacBrayne's ships gave to the Hebrides and the Firth of Clyde. Engineers had to respond to telegraphs very, very quickly, and they had to think on their feet on the spur of the moment, particularly if a vessel got into difficulties. Often, their dedication would become apparent only when their vessels were sold to other companies, with a subsequent succession of engine problems, previously unknown or unnoticed, because they were corrected by inspired engineering in the oily heat of the challenge.

Captain Donald Joseph MacKinnon (left) and Commodore Captain Angus MacKinnon (right)

CHAPTER 8

RATIONALISATION AND REBUILDING:
POST-WAR AUSTERITY, TWO CLASSIC MAIL-SHIPS
AND THREE FAT LADIES

Tower Bridge raised its massive bascules to grant passage to the **Clansman** *when she visited London to promote Scottish interests. [DEM's collection]*

RATIONALISATION AND REBUILDING:
POST-WAR AUSTERITY, TWO CLASSIC MAIL-SHIPS AND THREE FAT LADIES

The immediate post-war era was drab and grey. It was characterised by men's grey 'demob' suits, ruined city centres and damaged dock systems. Material shortages included basic foodstuffs and clothes – there was still a black market for ration cards – as well as coal, iron and steel. The Merchant Navy had survived, just, and there was a desperate need for replacement tonnage on both the deep-sea liner routes and the coasting services.

A lack of serviceable units in the aftermath of war led, in 1946, to the transfer of the *Robina* to David MacBrayne Limited from Coast Lines. This nomadic vessel had started life as a Blackpool excursion steamer in 1914, but later served as a passenger tender at Belfast in the 1930s. Coast Lines bought her, intending to use her for excursions out of Falmouth, but transferred her to Oban to run alongside the *Lochfyne* on excursions, while the *King George V* was on the Clyde maintaining the all-important Ardrishaig service. The *Robina* relieved the *Lochiel* in the autumn, and then retired to winter lay-up at Ardrossan. The following summer, she maintained the Gourock to Lochgoilhead route, but, as this was discontinued at the end of the season, she was sold, reverting to tender duties and occasional excursion work at Southampton. While under MacBrayne management, the *Robina* wore green, rather than red, boot-topping, and had cream rather than white upperworks. She nevertheless wore her red-and-black funnel with pride.

Pre-war obligations began to be implemented. Plans for the new ship for the Mallaig, Kyle and Stornoway service, as demanded in the 1938 mail contract, were finally displayed before the Provost of Stornoway and his councillors in February 1945. William Denny was contracted to build the ship, which was to benefit from a long-standing agreement between Denny and Sulzer Diesels. Some eighteen months later, on 19 May 1947, following protracted delays caused by shortages of materials, the new vessel, *Loch Seaforth*, finally entered the water. Her maiden voyage was further delayed during fitting-out, but eventually took place on 6 December.

The new mail-ship was a distinctive and imposing vessel for her size, and had an impressive service speed of 16 knots. Her high, white forecastle, similar to that of the *Lochness*, together with her wide, white deckhouse (accommodating the first-class lounge) below the varnished bridge, harked back to the grander, more robust era of the *Ulster Monarch*. Her hull had a touch of old-time elegance, with its long lines, graceful sheer and attractive cruiser stern. Only her funnel — somewhat squat in profile, and fixed directly to the boat deck — detracted from her appearance, as it was rather too low, and tended to be 'lost' behind the bridge and deckhouses when she was observed from the bow or beam. Its black top was also an uneasy fit, as it

*The **Robina** offered what is best described as rustic charm to the excursion services at Oban in 1946. [Keith Abraham]*

*The launch of the **Loch Seaforth** [DEM's collection]*

*The **Loch Seaforth**'s squat funnel was obscured by the bridge structure. [NR]*

*The **Loch Seaforth** sets out
from Mallaig for the Outer
Isles in August 1970. [NR]*

never seemed to be exactly the right size relative to the hull, and its depth varied across the years. On balance, the *Loch Seaforth* looked better with the deeper black top. Briefly, at the outset of her career, she had a small derrick ahead of the foremast, serving a fore-hold. Its removal left her a little bare, as it was evidently part of the original design. In general, her profile was broadly consistent with Denny style for that period, but her high forecastle, squat funnel and defiant angularity could be paralleled most readily in motor-vessels built in the mid- to late 1940s for Irish Sea crossings, among them the *Lairds Loch* (1944) and the *Hibernia* (1948).

Accommodation, for 500 passengers in two classes, occupied the after two-thirds of the vessel. The first-class lounge was particularly attractive, with large windows looking forward from the boat deck. There was a total of 680 cubic metres of cargo space, including 36 cattle stalls. A very fine sea-boat, well matched to her gruelling Outer Isles remit, the *Loch Seaforth* maintained her design route faithfully throughout the seasons. She was the first of the MacBrayne fleet to be equipped, in the late 1940s, with a radar set, though this did not give her immunity from occasional mishaps. She was off-service briefly in 1966, following a grounding at Kyle of Lochalsh, in which she was held hard by the bow. The accident attracted considerable media attention because of the difficulty of towing her clear.

As the *Loch Seaforth* began her distinguished service

*A sketch of the **Loch Seaforth**, by her Purser, Colin Tucker [DEM's collection]*

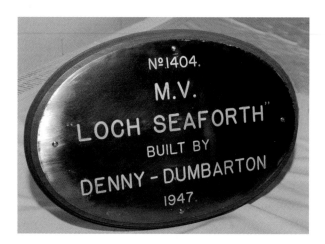

*The builder's plate from the **Loch Seaforth**, presented by Caledonian MacBrayne to An Lanntair, Stornoway, on the occasion of the 2005 Mod [Caledonian MacBrayne]*

from Mallaig to Lewis, realignments and absorptions of other companies were under way. The year 1948 was memorable in that McCallum, Orme & Company formally became part of the Kingdom, and finally lost its unique and much-loved identity (see Chapter 4). Its two ships, the *Hebrides* and the *Dunara Castle*, were integrated into the MacBrayne fleet, but their services were slowly rationalised by increased use of road connections and the development of a number of inter-island causeways. The *Dunara* returned to the Clyde from her last West Highland voyage on 27 January 1948, and, with neither fuss nor regret, was consigned to the breakers shortly afterwards. The *Hebrides* still had a few years' service to give, but was reduced to cargo and cattle runs, until, in 1955, she too was laid up, and later sold for scrap.

David MacBrayne Limited itself felt the impact of rationalisation in 1948. Post-war economics, combined with six years of war, had forced the government to take the railway system into state ownership, through the nationalisation of the four big railway companies. In this way, the 50% ownership of the company belonging to the former London, Midland & Scottish Railway became the property of the state, and David MacBayne moved another step towards complete state-ownership, retaining Coast Lines both as 50% private owner and much-needed mentor.

Soon significant changes occurred within MacBrayne management. H. T. Leith, whose son C. B. Leith would assume his father's role ten years later, was succeeded as General Manager in 1949 by H. S. MacLauchlan.

MAIL STEAMER HARD AGROUND OFF KYLE OF LOCHALSH

The Loch Seaforth aground off Kyle of Lochalsh yesterday.

Tug's hawser efforts fail

The MacBrayne mail steamer Loch Seaforth remained high on the rocks at Kyle of Lochalsh last night after two unsuccessful attempts to pull her off.

Hundreds of local people watched as a tug from Greenock got a strong steel hawser aboard the steamer — but when the tug backed up to take the strain, the line broke. Another attempt was made, and again the hawser broke.

An emergency service was main-tained yesterday by the cargo vessel Loch Dunvegan, which sailed from Kyle of Lochalsh over-night and arrived at Stornoway yesterday morning.

Until Saturday the Loch Ard, which had been diverted from her regular cargo service to assist the Loch Seaforth, will maintain the freight service of the Storno-way mailboat. Passengers will be taken across Skye to Uig, then to Tarbert, Harris, by the car ferry Hebrides, and to Stornoway by road.

*The **Loch Seaforth** began to develop a liking for rocks in the mid-1960s, as this newspaper cutting shows. [DEM's collection]*

MacLauchlan had joined the company in 1930, having learnt his trade with Burns & Laird Lines. One of his first duties was to dispatch the cargo steamer *Ulster Star* to the breakers. Service provision was also examined. The Oban-Lismore mails were reviewed in 1949, resulting in the purchase of a wooden hospital launch, which became the *Lochnell*. Ironically she had worked alongside the Dutch-style water-bus *Lochbuie* during the war, but the *Lochbuie* had already been sold by 1947. Likewise, in 1949 the Kilchoan (Ardnamurchan) call of the *Lochearn* was discontinued, and the second *Lochbuie*, a motor-launch built as an Admiralty high-speed vessel in 1942, initiated a service between Tobermory and Mingary. This was supplemented by the *Lochnell* between 1965 and 1968.

Cargo capacity was the company's principal concern in the late 1940s and the early 1950s. The fleet desperately required new cargo tonnage to maintain the Glasgow-based services, particularly in the light of the scrapping of the veteran *Dunara Castle*. The 'C' Type wartime standard coaster, *Empire Maysong*, was acquired in 1948 as she lay at her builders, Scott & Sons, Bowling. She was towed to the Ardrossan Dockyard, and her original triple-expansion steam engine was replaced by a new Polar diesel engine. The bridge was rebuilt aft, as was all the crew accommodation, and she was given the name *Lochbroom*. The company also bought its last steamer, essentially to act as sister-ship to the *Lochbroom*. This was the *Ottawa Maycliff*, formerly a Canadian-built 'C' Type standard coaster, which had been taken into the Dutch registry before coming to Scotland (with a Coast Lines cargo on board) as the *Loch Frisa*. The *Loch Frisa* retained her steam engine, and initially ran alternate Stornoway sailings with the former McCallum and Orme steamer, *Hebrides*. In 1963, the *Loch Frisa*, representing the last triple-expansion engine steamer in the fleet, was sold for further service under the Greek flag.

To supplement the cargo services, the Swedish motor-vessel *Örnen* was purchased in 1950. She had the distinction of being the first vessel in the fleet, and one of the first under the Red Ensign, to be equipped with a controllable-pitch propeller, allowing full control of the speed of the ship from the bridge. The only modification made to the ship before entering service from Glasgow was the addition of a radar set, the application of the corporate livery and the name *Lochdunvegan* applied fore and aft. A new ship, the *Loch Carron*, was delivered in 1950 by the Ardrossan Dockyard. This vessel brought a number of new features to the fleet – she was the first to be built with a cellular double bottom, she was equipped with hydraulic deck and steering machinery, and she was unique in offering 'heavy lift' capability, with derricks rated at 5 and 7 ½ tons.

Re-engining of existing ships became an urgent matter. The original engines of the *Lochmor* and *Lochearn* had become unreliable during the war, and had to be replaced

The **Loch Carron** approaches Scarinish, Tiree, in the mid-1970s. [DEM]

as soon as suitable machinery became available. The new engines that were fitted to these vessels had originally been destined for Landing Craft (Tanks), and, as they were high-speed and uni-directional, the ships were equipped at this time with reverse/reduction gears. The noise of the engines in the passenger accommodation was an improvement on pre-war days, but it was never possible to escape completely from their roar, which had to be inhibited by portable, acoustic, dog-kennel-shaped covers. Both ships also received a shorter and slightly dumpier aluminium funnel than before (see Chapter 7).

The *Lochinvar*'s prototype marine paraffin engines were replaced in 1926, when she received three new four-cylinder Gardner 'heavy oil' diesel engines coupled independently, as before, to her triple screws. Her new engines were similar to the original engines fitted in the *Lochearn* and *Lochmor*. Following the Second World War, the *Lochinvar* received a major refurbishment and a third set of engines, which had been made by Davey-Paxman of Colchester. At this stage she was reduced from triple screw to twin screw, requiring only two engines. These were six-cylinder engines, which were connected to the shafts via reverse/reduction gearboxes. The engines were placed under an acoustic hood (yet another large 'dog kennel') and only when this was in place was it possible to travel on the ship without being overwhelmed by the dreadful noise of the engines.

The no less noisy *Lochfyne* received new engines in the spring of 1953. The vibrations, characteristic of her first set of engines, were as bad as ever, and strengthening bars had to be added to the bed-plates. In time, the engine vibration lessened, and towards the end of her career it had become less obtrusive.

As the early motor-vessels were tamed and domesticated, further significant route contraction took place in the early 1950s, especially to the north-west mainland ports. Where possible, services were replaced by road haulage and bus connections. The company operated more than 100 buses at this time. These arrangements allowed the *Lochshiel* to be sold in 1952 for further commercial service, although she was scrapped only two years later. The elderly *Clydesdale* was withdrawn from the Glasgow to Stornoway cargo service shortly afterwards; at the age of 48 she was consigned to the breakers. In many ways, the *Clydesdale* was the last vessel in the fleet to represent the period of ascendancy of the MacBrayne heritage, having been built for the Glasgow-Inverness passenger and cargo service at the behest of David Hope MacBrayne. MacBrayne's buses were taking over a variety of small, generally poorly-equipped bus operators on Skye and Mull. The company was also expanding the road deliveries service under the banner of MacBrayne Haulage, largely as a substitute for the complex network of small ports that had previously been visited by the cargo ships. In addition, it was proposed to serve Coll and Tiree with the Inner Isles passenger vessel.

Cruises to the Hebrides, closely connected to cargo-carrying, also contracted,

as the new cargo vessels were permitted to carry no more than twelve passengers. Although MacBrayne's could no longer offer the 'round trip' cruise from Glasgow, Coast Lines were able to reinstate cruises from Liverpool to the Western Isles in 1947. The pre-war cruise yacht, *Killarney*, which dated from 1893, had survived the war, but she was deemed unworthy of investment and had been sold in 1947. Her successor was the former Belfast Steamship Company's *Patriotic*, built in 1912 and subsequently used by the British & Irish Steam Packet Company for their Liverpool-Dublin service under the names, *Lady Leinster* and, later, *Lady Connaught*.

Somewhat confusingly renamed the *Lady Killarney*, the new cruise yacht was given the buff-coloured hull and yellow funnel of the cruise liner, and placed under the command of her war-time master, Captain Peter Mullan. The light-coloured hull proved an impracticality and became green after only three seasons, and in 1952 it reverted of necessity to the black-and-white livery of Coast

Lines. The *Lady Killarney* offered a 100-seater restaurant on the main deck, a spacious entrance area combining the staircases to the main and promenade decks, a card room on the lower deck and a timbered smoke room on the boat deck. The old ship was withdrawn, much to the anguish of her regular clientele, in 1956. However, it was planned to use the relatively new *Irish Coast* (delivered in 1952, and the penultimate of the *Ulster Monarch* class) on the West Highland cruise programme in 1957. Alas, this was foiled by the delayed availability of a sister-ship which was covering for refits, and, even though adverts picturing the vessel in a Scottish loch appeared in *Punch* and other journals, the cruises never took place.

Cruises were resumed in 1958 by British Railways, using the Heysham to Belfast steam turbine ferry, *Duke of Lancaster*. She took on the role of cruise ship in spring and autumn, and roamed as far south as Portugal and as far north as Norway. Captain J. B. Wright from the Belfast Steamship Company, and former master of the *Lady Killarney*, usually

accompanied the *Duke of Lancaster* as pilot whenever she was in the Western Isles. The *Duke of Lancaster* completed her last cruise to the Western Isles in 1966. Thereafter, regular cruising opportunities to and around the islands were not available until 1989 (see Chapter 10).

The excursion market was, however, retained throughout all the post-war change, principally by means of the turbine steamers, *Saint Columba* and *King George V*. The *Saint Columba* sailed six days a week from Gourock to Ardrishaig and back, maintaining the link with the Islay service via Tarbert east and west. The up-river departure from Glasgow was not resumed after the war, and a rail connection from Glasgow was provided instead. The *King George V* undertook the Iona and round Mull excursion

from Oban, clockwise three times and anti-clockwise twice per week, with one day devoted to Fort William cruise passengers. However, at the end of the 1958 season, the retirement of the veteran *Saint Columba* was announced with the promise that her place would be taken by the *Lochfyne*, which would maintain the Clyde service winter and summer.

Steam power was, by now, associated primarily with the older excursion ships. Apart from the *Loch Frisa*, MacBrayne's workaday fleet was diesel-driven. In this respect, MacBrayne's was remarkably progressive and far-sighted. Neither British Railways nor, for that matter, the Isle of Man Steam Packet Company, had yet made any serious effort to progress from steam to diesel. Whereas

CRUISING ON THE *KING GEORGE V*

'IT WAS AN unforgettable September day in 1965. The skies were as clear as one ever sees them in the Inner Hebrides; feather-shaped wisps of cloud, driven by a light northerly breeze, occasionally stole the warmth of the sun. Standing on the wooden bridge-wing of the *King George V* – David MacBrayne's splendid but increasingly elderly pleasure-steamer – as her razor-sharp bow cut through the Sound of Mull at an effortless eighteen knots, I could hear the squawk of seagulls, the hum of the turbines and the splash of the bow-wave; astern, I could see the steamer's elegant wake, fanning outwards from the propellers until the curdled surf gave way to gentle ripples which seemed to touch the shores of Morvern to starboard and those of Mull to port.

'On the decks was a rich assortment of humanity, with vacuum flasks and sandwiches, throwing desultory scraps to voracious seagulls whenever the magnetic magnificence of the landscape permitted the eyes to wander. Some were hanging on to the deck-rails, lost in the tourist's abandonment of the cares of life, while others were viewing the world through binoculars and Pentax lenses. Lismore lighthouse, tree-clad hillsides, precipitous slopes, Ardtornish Castle swishing past, Ardnamurchan Point to starboard, and Tobermory hard to port, nestling in its concentrated and superbly sheltered bay ... the *King George* carried us majestically on our course, with the pennant of David MacBrayne, the uncrowned king of West Highland shipping, barely holding its own at the peak of the main-mast. Once round the Cailleach headland, she began to roll, with the balance of the high-masted, narrow-beamed turbine-steamer; any feelings of sea-sickness were dispelled by the anticipation of landing on Staffa and ultimately setting foot on Iona. But would we be permitted to step ashore? The heavy swells of the past couple of weeks had made landing difficult at both points...

'I too was among the tourists, having been invited by the Master of the *King George V*, Captain Neil Campbell, to accompany him on the regular Saturday day-trip to Iona. The fare? It would suffice, said Captain Campbell, if I helped the crew to wash the dishes. Captain Campbell hailed from Tiree, my native island, and was one of a long line of sea captains produced by the island. Several Tiree men commanded MacBrayne steamers, and both their seamanship and their kindness have justifiably become part of the maritime folklore of the Hebrides.

'I had only recently moved to Oban, in order to continue my education at Oban High School, and the prospect of a trip on the *King George*, that masterpiece of Clyde engineering, was particularly appealing to someone with an innate love of West Highland steamers. But it was also an opportunity to visit Iona, an island which lay only a few miles to the south-east of Tiree, and could be seen on the horizon as the final low-lying eminence at the nose of the Ross of Mull.

'Soon we were at Staffa, with its towering basalt pillars. Yes, we could land on the island, but, because of rock-falls, Fingal's Cave was off the itinerary. We clambered into the red ferry-boat which had come to meet us from Iona, and looked around briefly, before rejoining the ship and steaming southwards.

'By mid-afternoon the *King George V* was in the Sound of Iona, giving her turbines a temporary rest and rolling quietly as she tugged at her rusty anchor-chain. The 'red boats' which were used to ferry passengers from the steamer to the island were butting their way through the water, laden with inquisitive tourists. Having landed on the jetty, we walked through the village, passed the medieval nunnery, paused at St Oran's Chapel and Rèilig Orain ('Oran's Burial-ground'), and arrived at the restored cathedral, magnificent in its setting among the green fields. Across the narrow

Sound of Iona, glittering in the sunshine, was white-shored Fionnphort, the ferry terminal on the Ross of Mull. The *King George* looked particularly majestic in the middle of the sound.

'In what seemed a remarkably short time, the day's batch of tourists was being shepherded down to the 'red boats', and back to the *King George*. The bridge telegraph was ringing 'Stand by' in a matter of minutes, and the ship began to surge forward once again, cleaving the sound on the inward journey to Oban. Passengers made for the restaurant. I ate a hearty meal in the crew's quarters, and duly paid my fare by assisting a sailor to wash the dishes.

'By eight o' clock we were gliding into the tranquillity of Oban Bay, and the *King George V* was soon berthed at the Railway Pier. Captain Campbell rang 'Finished with engines', went to his cabin, and exchanged his gold-braided cap and uniform for his suit. As he walked down the gangplank, I thanked him for his kindness, and for what had been a splendid day.'

(From Donald E. Meek, *The Quest for Celtic Christianity*)

GEMS FROM THE 'GEORGE'

HAROLD JORDAN, FORMERLY PURSER ON THE *KING GEORGE V*, LOOKS BACK

The balance-sheets

'One fact about the *KGV* which was shrouded in secrecy at the time was just how profitable she was to MacBrayne's in the 1960s. The worst season for weather and passenger numbers was 1967 (and a dire season it was), but after all expenses, including wages and overhaul, were met, the net profit of the *KGV* was £20 000 – a small fortune in those days. I believe that the 1963 profit was in six figures – MacBrayne's Chief Accountant went out of his way to tell me that they were delighted by the 1963 results. This, for him, was completely out of character, so the results must have been quite spectacular.'

The ship's cat

'In 1966, on the 40th Anniversary of the Maiden Voyage, as the steamer left Iona, the bells of Iona Abbey were rung forty times. The Glasgow Office had sent orders, "vessel to be dressed". Many passengers enquired why all the flags were flying, and the *George*'s perennial Chief Officer, John MacCallum, who did not care for such events, replied in his droll manner, "The cat had kittens". The steamer did have a ship's cat, Daisy, which from time to time produced a litter of kittens.'

The steamer enthusiasts

'We were leaving Fort William one evening for the return to Oban. As the gangway was hauled aboard, one of the more outlandish steamer enthusiasts started waving his arms above his head, shouting, "Goodbye to the queen of coastal craft!" Spotting John MacCallum, he loudly enquired, "I say, what tonnage are you?"

"About twelve stone eight," replied John.'

*The **King George V** cuts the tranquil waters of the Sound of Mull. [Donald B. MacCulloch]*

*The little **Loch Eynort** arriving at Portree in 1964 after a rough passage from Kyle. [NR]*

Coast Lines and MacBrayne's had been largely diesel-driven since the early 1930s, the railways and the equally conservative Board of Directors of the Manx company had shunned the new technology in favour of oil-fired steam-turbine equipment. There was a penalty in due course, as the escalating price of fuel oil in the mid-1970s rapidly put most of these relatively inefficient steamers out of business.

MacBrayne's patterns of operation were firmly laid down by 1940, and diesel ruled the roost. By the early 1950s, new tonnage was required by MacBrayne's for both cargo and passenger routes. Another Mail Contract was issued in 1952, valid for ten years, and requesting one new cargo ship and one new mail ship to be commissioned within three years. The cargo ship was the *Loch Ard*, a development of the *Loch Carron* design, but fitted also with heavy lifting gear to deal with bridge sections and other engineering units needed for road development in the islands. She could also accommodate heavy vehicles as deck cargo, and was responsible for bringing a new fleet of red and olive-green MacBrayne buses to Islay. Although

mainly associated with the Glasgow to Islay cargo service, she was used wherever heavy lifts were required. She also had removable stalls for up to 130 head of cattle, and this facility was required on a variety of routes in the peak autumn months of cattle sales.

The new mail-ship was the *Claymore*, built in 1955 for the Oban-Coll-Tiree-Barra-Lochboisdale route (see Chapter 9). The *Claymore* represented the culmination of Western Isles mail-ship design, being a development of the *Loch Seaforth*, but using post-war innovations and design features to produce a much more modern-looking vessel with lighter and more open accommodation. Ornamentation included Highland wildlife marquetry panels and large glass doors to the dining saloon, featuring the MacBrayne Highlander, whose image also adorned the ship's bows and those of the *Loch Seaforth*. The ship was, however, rather meanly equipped with two vibration-inducing four-cylinder engines, which were direct-reversing.

The arrival of the *Claymore* from the builders, William Denny, displaced the *Lochearn* from general relief duties to service in the Sound of Mull. Consequently, the veteran motor-ship, *Lochinvar*, was assigned to winter relief duties and summer excursions at Oban, as well as a short and unpopular spell on the Portree link from Kyle. The *Lochinvar* was sold in 1960, and later saw summer excursion service as the *Anzio I* on the Lower Thames, running between Southend-on-Sea and Sheerness until Sheerness Harbour became unavailable to the service. Following a period of lay-up at Tilbury, she was sold to a company which wished to develop a service between Inverness and Invergordon. On the way north early in April 1966, she was driven ashore by a ferocious storm off Spurn Head, and her entire crew of thirteen, some of whom had close connections with Oban, were drowned. It was a particularly tragic conclusion to the *Lochinvar*'s career, which had been so closely associated with Scotland. She was literally on the way home when the disaster occurred.

The *Lochinvar* had served the Isle of Mull loyally for over fifty years, in the days when the Craignure call was

The **Loch Arkaig** arrives at
Mallaig on the Small Isles
run in May 1976. [NR]

dependent on transferring passengers and cargo to a 'wee
red boat'. In the late 1950s, MacBrayne's began to rethink
their policy for more out-of-the-way services. Instead of
depending solely on linkages by means of the 'wee red
boats', plying between the larger ships and harbours without
appropriate piers, some intermediate-size vessels were
acquired: the *Loch Toscaig* in 1955, the *Loch Arkaig* in 1959
and the *Loch Eynort* in 1961. In their previous existence,
they had been fishing vessel, inshore minesweeper and pilot
boat for the Irish Commissioners of Lights respectively. In
their new roles, they supported the Kyle and Toscaig ferry,
the Mallaig-Small Isles service, Kyle to Raasay and Portree
service (downgraded from an all-year-round mail service to
a seasonal summer service for passengers and goods only

from 1958 onwards), plus short excursions. By all accounts,
the wooden hull of the *Loch Arkaig* was increasingly prone
to leaks, and even required the replacement of her entire
sternpost.

The 1960 route listing for David MacBrayne Limited
was as follows:

Passenger services:

- Gourock-Dunoon-Innellan-Rothesay-Tighnabruaich-
Tarbert (and Ardrishaig, summer only) [*Lochfyne*]
- Port Ellen-Gigha-Tarbert and Tarbert-Port Askaig-
Colonsay [*Lochiel*]
- Oban-Lismore (small vessel)
- Oban-Craignure-Salen-Drimnen-Tobermory
[*Lochearn*]

LOCHIEL – 'INN AT THE QUAY'

FOR THIRTY YEARS, the *Lochiel* (1939) sailed from West Loch Tarbert to Islay, calling on certain days at Jura and Colonsay. At the time of the Oban cattle sales, she would be diverted occasionally to Tiree, to take animals to market.

Donald Meek has a vivid recollection of cycling five miles from his home in Caolas to Scarinish Pier on a Saturday morning in the early 1960s, to view the *Lochiel* for the first time when she was on a cattle run to Tiree. His parents had spent some years in Port Ellen, Islay, in the 1940s, and they had come to know the *Lochiel* particularly well before they returned to Tiree in 1949. As she glided towards the pier on a calm spring morning, the *Lochiel* looked very dapper and well-maintained. She resembled the *Lochnevis* overall, but her foremast and derrick were in 'normal' position, and her prominent funnel was set further aft. Her accessible tween-decks were well suited to the conveyance of cattle, and she loaded her cargo very quickly through her port side-doors. By mid-day the Captain was back on the bridge, the telegraphs were ringing, and her bows were swinging out of Gott Bay *en route* for Oban.

Twenty years later Donald caught up with the *Lochiel* again, this time in the unlikely setting of Bristol docks – much to his astonishment. Said by her owners to be suffering from 'derangement of machinery', the *Lochiel* had long since ended her ill-starred 1970 venture to the Isle of Man as the *Norwest Laird*, and had been acquired by Courage Breweries. She was moored close to Bristol city centre, where she attracted a clientele very different from Hebridean crofters and their cattle. Her intoxicating role doubtless resulted in much further 'derangement of machinery' before she was scrapped in 1995. The following extract comes from an article which Donald penned in Gaelic when he rediscovered the *Lochiel* in December 1984. It was published in *Gairm* (Vol. 132) in 1985:

I had only just begun my tour [of Bristol docks] when my eye alighted on a ship that I knew very well at one time, when she used to sail in the Hebrides. This was none other than the *Lochiel*, which had spent most of her life sailing under the MacBrayne flag between Tarbert Loch Fyne and Islay. The self-same lady gave the Islay folk many a nasty tossing – but today she lies peacefully in the middle of Bristol! She has undergone a complete and utter transformation. In place of the red and black colours which were customary for David MacBrayne, she is now painted from stem to stern in red and white; her lifeboats have been removed; and, to judge by how high she stands in the water, her engines have been taken out too. Nevertheless, nostalgia compelled me to step on board. I went up to the bridge, and I looked in through the door of the wheel-house. There was no sign of a compass or a wheel, or of the telegraphs which used to chime out loudly whenever she entered a harbour or departed. Not a sound was to be heard but the tinkle of glasses here and there, and, in place of the gallant Highland sailors who used to handle the ropes, chefs with tall hats would appear on the deck every now and then. The *Lochiel* is now a pub, and it would seem that she raises steam of a different kind in Bristol. When she left the Islay run, the *Lochiel* went south, and she was eventually bought by a company who own a number of pubs throughout England. Although the ship's appearance has been changed, this means that the *Lochiel* has remained in Britain, and I was glad to see that she is still afloat. Most of MacBrayne's surviving old ships are in foreign parts, and one has to go as far away as Greece to get another glimpse of some of them.

- Tobermory-Mingary (small vessel) [*Lochbuie*]
- Oban-Tobermory-Coll-Tiree-Castlebay-Lochboisdale [*Claymore*]
- Kyle of Lochalsh-Armadale-Mallaig-Eigg-Rum-Canna-Lochboisdale-Lochmaddy-Rodel-Tarbert-Scalpay [*Lochmor*]
- Mallaig-Loch Scavaig (summer only) [*Loch Arkaig*]
- Mallaig-Armadale-Glenelg-Kyle of Lochalsh-Raasay-Portree [*Loch Arkaig*]
- Mallaig-Kyle of Lochalsh-Stornoway [*Loch Seaforth*]
- Oban-Staffa-Iona-Tobermory or Fort William (summer only) [*King George V* and *Lochnevis*], also on Loch Shiel
- Kyle of Lochalsh-Toscaig [*Loch Arkaig*]

Cargo services (*Loch Ard, Loch Carron, Loch Frisa, Lochbroom* and *Lochdunvegan*):
- Glasgow to Skye and Lewis; to Mull, Coll, Tiree and Outer Hebrides; to Islay and Jura.

The MacBrayne fleet fared well in the 1950s and 1960s, with only relatively insignificant groundings and collisions. There were, for instance, two minor accidents involving the company's flagshps. In 1953, the *Saint Columba* ran aground in fog at Ettrick Bay, Bute, where she was high and dry for about ten hours. Again in fog, in June 1957, the *King George V* grounded on Scarba on her way north at the start of the season. She was in danger of capsize at low tide, but this was averted. The only collision between vessels was the head-on encounter of the *Claymore* with the coaster *Druid* at Tobermory in 1961. The *Claymore*, with a deep right-angle dent on her bow below the waterline, had to flee for repair to James Lamont's Greenock yard. The worst incident occurred in October 1960, when the *Lochiel* struck a submerged rock in the confined approaches to the pier at West Loch Tarbert and partially sank by the bow. All personnel were safely taken ashore, and the ship abandoned. Later raised and taken to Greenock, she was repaired and refurbished, and was back on station in March 1961 as a one-class ship with increased capacity for sixteen cars (lift-on/lift-

off). Her absence during the winter was covered by the *Lochearn*, operating out of Oban.

The increased car-capacity of the refurbished *Lochiel* was a straw in the wind. Car-capacity required to be increased throughout the fleet, but this had implications for capital investment. A significant development was announced at the commissioning of the *Loch Arkaig* in April 1960. It had been established that adequate capital for new tonnage could no longer be raised directly from the Coast Lines partnership with government, and that the financial onus must, in future, lie with the latter. When three new passenger and car ferries were planned, the question of funding was finally clarified with the announcement that the ships would be built to the order of the Secretary of State for Scotland, under powers newly vested in him within the Highlands and Islands Shipping Services Act (1960). These vessels were to accommodate up to 50 cars via side-loading hoists of the type pioneered by the Clyde ferries *Arran*, *Bute* and *Cowal*, and the Ardrossan-Brodick ferry *Glen Sannox*. Three new car ferry routes were visualised:

1. Uig to Lochmaddy and Tarbert (Harris)
2. Mallaig to Armadale
3. Oban to Craignure and Lochaline (Morvern)

Routes 1 and 2 together, combined with an overland connection via the much improved roads in Skye, was intended to replace the conventional Outer Isles service offered by the *Lochmor*. Route 3 was an obvious response to the increasing demand of vehicular traffic for Mull. The invitations to tender for the three ships were issued in June 1962, with a budget of £2 million assured by government. In the meantime, various engineering works were commenced at the respective piers and jetties, so as to accommodate the new ships. These included a 15 metre extension to the pier at Uig, which was already government-owned.

The order for the three car-ferries was won by Hall, Russell at Aberdeen. The first to be delivered was the *Hebrides*, making her maiden voyage from Uig on 8 April 1964. At the same time, the *Lochmor* closed the Outer Isles service, and moved to the Mallaig-Armadale crossing.

The new car-ferry carried in her lounge the bell of the McCallum and Orme steamer *Hebrides*, as a reminder of the distinguished pedigree of the name. The new *Hebrides* was highly innovative, but small by today's standards. It puts her garage deck into contemporary perspective when we note that its headroom was a mere three metres. The types of vehicles which she could carry were therefore restricted to cars, light vans and caravans.

The next ship to leave Aberdeen was the *Clansman*, which relieved the *Lochmor* of the Armadale-Mallaig service in June. The *Lochmor* then went to join her sister, the *Lochearn*, on the Oban-Craignure and Lochaline route, where, for the first time, the two elderly sister-ships worked together. Their task was hopeless, as they were the stop-gap car-ferry service; the ships' derricks were costantly in use lifting cars on and off at each destination. The two veterans were finally displaced at the end of July 1964 when the third car ferry, the *Columba*, arrived on station at Oban. Revival of this most cherished of names was recognised with a small Celtic cross placed on the *Columba's* fore jackstaff.

These new ships had several unusual features. One of these was that, like a number of other vessels in state ownership (e.g. the Heysham-Belfast, steam-turbine ferries, *Duke of Lancaster*, *Duke of Rothesay* and *Duke of Argyll*), they were equipped with an external water spray-system capable of washing radioactive particles from the vessels, should the need arise. The Cold War, it seems, was very much on the government's mind at this time. Another was that the owner of the ships, Michael Noble, the Secretary of State, sat in Edinburgh, and his ships, although managed by David MacBrayne Limited of Glasgow, were initially registered at Leith.

There were also design faults. The three rather beamy car-ferries were found to be difficult to manoeuvre at close quarters to piers, and, at an early opportunity, their rudders were modified to overcome this problem. Nevertheless, they were versatile vessels. Their accommodation was licensed for 600 passengers in summer, but reduced to 400 in winter. Garage space could be converted for the carriage of cattle, and, of course, the traditional MacBrayne wheeled 'container' was the means of handling all cargo and baggage on to and off the car deck.

The success of the three car-ferries was immediate. By December 1964, the *Hebrides* had shipped over 11 000 vehicles, the *Clansman* had taken nearly 14 000 over the sea to Skye (many *en route* for the *Hebrides* at Uig) and the *Columba* had dealt with 7 600 on the Sound of Mull. 'Three fat ladies' they may have been, but they were set to revolutionise the sea routes of the Western Isles.

Despite such success, however, the future was not to be plain sailing. In 1968 something unprecedented happened. A serious competitor appeared on a key route. The MacBrayne Kingdom had always been very careful to absorb, sooner or later, any rival company that might threaten its business, although it treated McCallum and Orme to the last as a complementary company 'in conference', rather than as a direct threat (see Chapter 4). The fact that a new company had been created specially to take on 'Mighty MacBrayne's' must have been irksome in the extreme. This is precisely what happened when Western Ferries Limited was formed to start a new drive-on / drive-off vehicle ferry service between Port Askaig and Kennacraig, a new terminal built on the southern shore of West Loch Tarbert, some 5 km nearer to the sea than the old West Loch Tarbert pier used by the *Lochiel*. A brand-new vessel, the *Sound of Islay*, initiated the service in April 1968, and was joined by a second, larger ferry, the *Sound of Jura*, in July 1969.

W. Paul Clegg reported in *Sea Breezes*, October 1969:

*MacBrayne's competitors on the Islay service, Western Ferries Limited, appear to be going from strength to strength. Their new ship, the **Sound of Jura**, made her inaugural trip on the West Loch Tarbert to Port Askaig route on 27 July. Costing £300 000, the new ship is the first drive-through vessel to operate in the Western Isles, was built in Norway, is one class, has a speed of 14 knots, and can take up to 40 cars or a combination of cars and commercial vehicles. A carpeted observation lounge on the Boat Deck has seating for 50 passengers and the maximum*

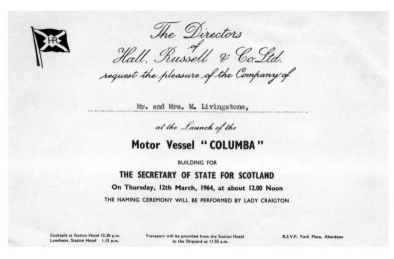

The **Clansman** still registered at
Leith in August 1970, leaving
Mallaig on the Armadale service
[NR]

*An invitation to
the launch of the*
Columba *[DEM's
collection]*

The **Clansman** *enters the water in
Aberdeen. [DEM's collection]*

*The **Hebrides** backing away from the pier at Uig in September 1974 [NR]*

*The **Columba** approaching Tobermory in July 1987 [NR]*

ON BOARD
THE *COLUMBA*

[Richard Danielson]

WESTERN FERRIES ↗

Kennacraig - Islay
Islay - Jura
Clyde - Cross

SUMMER 78 Commencing
May 1

NOTE: All times and charges shown in this timetable are provisional. Changes may have to be made at short notice.

*Western Ferries show the way: vehicles disembarking from the **Sound of Islay**. [DEM's collection]*

Western Ferries' **Sound of Islay** at Campbeltown in August 1970 [NR]

The larger and better appointed **Sound of Jura** approaching Kennacraig [NR]

is 200. Among the features are a saloon, with smoking and non-smoking sections, a small shop with vending machines for refreshments, play pens for children and a private room for mothers with small children

Western Ferries' first ship, however, had been much less ambitious, and her earlier record was not without blemish. This was, in fact, the *Sound of Gigha*, a much smaller, landing-craft type of vessel, which the company placed on the Port Askaig-Feolin link with Jura when the larger *Sound of Islay* arrived. Originally named *Isle of Gigha*, she had been built for John Rose, who lived in Oban and had established Eilean Sea Services. She had appeared, somewhat mysteriously, in her blue and white colours in Oban in the early summer of 1966, whilst the *Claymore* and other vessels were tied up at the quayside because of the seamen's strike. Later described by a Board of Trade Inspector as little more than 'a square pontoon, with shaped bow and stern', she was not the most sightly or stable of vessels, and capsized in November 1966 with the loss of two lives when sailing from Gigha to Port Ellen, Islay. She was, nevertheless, the very first commercial vessel in the Hebrides with bow-loading facilities. Following an extensive overhaul after her capsize, she passed into Western Ferries' ownership, and performed successfully on the Port Askaig-Feolin sevice for thirty years.

The *Sound of Islay* and the *Sound of Jura* were so radically different from the *Lochiel*, and so well suited to vehicles, that they quickly creamed off the vehicle traffic from the traditional carrier. The *Lochiel*, of course, retained the foot-passengers and parcels service which linked Islay with Gourock through East Loch Tarbert. Western Ferries caused further alarm bells to ring, especially when it was learned that the new company had more than attained first-year targets, and that it was likely to be in profit well before the planned date. Even more alarmingly, the new company had no access to any form of operational subsidy, either from central government or from the local authority.

The government subsidy due to David MacBrayne

Limited had risen slowly from £360 000 in 1952 to £600 000 in 1968. Not surprisingly, the government created a new umbrella organisation to manage its wholly- and partly-owned Scottish transport interests. This was the Scottish Transport Group, which came into being on 1 January 1969. David MacBrayne was, for the moment, retained as a separate entity from the other partners, the Caledonian Steam Packet Company and the Scottish Bus Company. MacBrayne's road-transport interests were subjected to an immediate, but phased, withdrawal, with the buses becoming largely part of the Scottish Bus Company, and MacBrayne Haulage being assigned to other national carriers.

Coast Lines retained their 50% interest in David MacBrayne while negotiations took place between the Scottish Transport Group and the Board of Coast Lines. These were completed by the following July, when Coast Lines sold their holding in the shipping interests of David MacBrayne, which then became wholly state-owned. A statement issued at the time stressed that 'close liaison would continue on matters of common interest between MacBrayne and Coast Lines', although Coast Lines was no longer the force that it once had been.

The Caledonian Steam Packet Company had been state-owned since the formation of British Railways and the Scottish Region in 1948, and it was logical that the two companies should merge in order to lessen overheads, and to present a single corporate identity. It was also logical that rationalisation of the combined fleets would enable some units to be disposed of, thus reducing running costs.

So it was that, on 30 September 1969, the *Lochfyne*, which had been suffering recurrent mechanical problems, was retired from the Ardrishaig route and replaced by the Clyde paddle-steamer, *Caledonia*, and from 6 October by the small passenger motor-ferry, *Maid of Skelmorlie*. The *Maid* was a far cry from the standards set so long ago by the Victorian *Columba*. Passengers sat in the lounge of the *Maid* on bus-type seating, all facing forward as if waiting

SCHOOLBOY SUMMERS IN THE 1960S

THE 1960S WAS a relatively relaxed era. The Jumbo Jet was on the drawing-boards at Boeing, the Beatles were in the Cavern, North Sea Oil was still under the North Sea and the word 'devolution' had yet to enter the English language. The authors of this book were then at school, one an Islander in exile at Oban High School, the other an Englishman at the cathedral school in Manchester.

The Islander was able to spend occasional happy Saturdays aboard the *King George V* circumnavigating Mull. This privilege was recompense for helping to wash the dishes in the galley! He also had the privilege of starting and ending term aboard the *Claymore*, as he relates in Chapter 9.

The Englishman, however, could only sit at home planning, in meticulous detail, summer tours on the Clyde and West Highland steamers. In due course summer holidays started, with arrival at Glasgow Central in time to get down to the river to see the morning Burns & Laird Lines' arrivals, the *Royal Scotsman* from Belfast and the *Irish Coast* from Dublin. Armed with a Scottish Region Railrover Pass, which allowed access to the Clyde steamers but not the West Highland routes, the journey down river aboard the *Queen Mary II* provided access to the remainder of the Caledonian Steam Packet Company's fleet. The highlight was boarding the shiny red-and-black funnelled *Lochfyne* at Rothesay bound for Tarbert, leaving the Caledonian boats behind in their muddy waters in the upper Firth. At Tarbert, the dash across the peninsula to the pier at West Loch Tarbert was rewarded by the sight of the *Lochnevis* loading for Port Askaig.

Every summer Tuesday the *Lochnevis* left the *Lochiel* in charge of the Islay service, later to rejoin her the following Friday. This allowed the *Lochnevis* to carry out mid-week excursions at Oban and provided the opportunity for combined coach and steamer trips via Tarbert, clockwise on Tuesdays and anti-clockwise on Fridays. As the *Lochnevis* sailed down West Loch Tarbert in the early afternoon, the English school-boy asked the Purser for half an excursion fare from Tarbert to Oban, but missing out the coach ride from Oban to Tarbert. Rather flummoxed and with other duties to attend to, the Purser raised an eye-brow, saying 'Come back later, laddie, and we'll see what we can do!'

Leaning over the rail on the promenade deck at Port Askaig, watching the comings and goings of cargo, parcels, tractors and their trailers, and passengers and their baggage, provided a memorable sense of security. Although the ship might yet sail without someone or some item of goods still on the pier, it could not sail without the watcher, who was secure and isolated from the hustle and bustle below. Returning to the Purser's Office, as the last call for High Tea was made, revealed the sorry news that a single from Tarbert to Oban was listed in the book as an unlikely £10 (the full excursion fare was only £5 or thereabouts). 'But I only have £10 in my pocket to last the remainder of the week.' The Purser's rejoinder followed a brief silence and a Gaelic shrug of despair, 'Go away, laddie, and mind you make yourself scarce.'

When the schoolboy met the Purser two days later, striding down the Railway Pier at Oban, he cheerily wanted to know if he had yet done the trip to Iona aboard the *King George V*.

Later, as he sat and relaxed on the train heading back south to Queen Street, the Gaelic warmth and hospitality became a heartening memory. But at Carlisle, the Scottish Railrover Pass became void, and the return ticket to Manchester was once again valid; Port Askaig was worlds away.

*The first picture of the holiday: the **Irish Coast** in the Clyde, arriving from Dublin on 30 July 1967 [NR]*

for some show to start. They could peer through forward-facing windows beneath the wheelhouse to admire the view – well, not exactly, as all they could see from their seats were the windlass and the bulwarks surrounding the forecastle. By the end of the year, both the *Lochnevis* and the *Lochiel* had been withdrawn as well. Rationalisation was in full swing.

For the moment, the mail-ships, *Loch Seaforth* and *Claymore*, were secure on their respective Outer and Inner Isles services. However, the *Claymore* was becoming too small to maintain the Oban-Coll-Tiree-Barra-Lochboisdale service, while the *Loch Seaforth* was beginning to suffer from decay of the poor-quality steel used in her construction, which was all that had been available in post-war Britain when she was built. A number of other celebrated ships were afflicted with deteriorating frames and hull plates in much the same way, the most famous being the Elder Dempster liner *Aureol*, which had to be withdrawn from service prematurely, although she survived many years subsequently in a static role.

Meanwhile, the *Hebrides*, *Clansman* and *Columba* were creating their own revolution – and the scene was now set for major change. The *Claymore*, the company's last mail-ship, and the last of the post-1930, passenger motor-vessels, represented the end of an epoch. In the hope of preserving the memory of such vessels, all of which would merit individual treatment by those who knew them well, Donald Meek recalls in Chapter 9 her unique character and her interaction with the life and people of the Inner Hebrides.

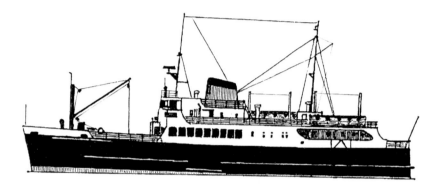

CHAPTER 9

HEBRIDEAN VIBRATIONS:
REMEMBERING THE *CLAYMORE* (1955)

*The **Claymore** at Tobermory, with matching Art Deco on ship and shore and an astonishing array of (presumably empty!) casks [Donald B. MacCulloch]*

HEBRIDEAN VIBRATIONS:
REMEMBERING THE *CLAYMORE* (1955)

An awareness of the sea and an interest in ships come naturally to any islander from the Inner Hebrides. Island crofts – small farms with white-washed dwelling-houses – fringe the island shorelines, thus giving direct access to the sea. Boats and fishing are part of life, and so too are the ships which serve the islands. Our croft was in the township of Caolas in the east end of Tiree. The croft house was called 'Coll View', as it enjoyed fine views across Gunna Sound to the island of Coll. Gunna Sound was a busy stretch of water, mainly because it was the key passage-way for vessels sailing north from Tiree to Barra and the Outer Hebrides, and frequently returning by the same route on the inward voyage to Oban and Glasgow. Regular users of the Sound in the 1950s and 1960s were pre-eminently the MacBrayne mail ships, *Lochearn* (1930) and *Claymore* (1955), and the cargo-boats, *Loch Carron* (1951), *Loch Ard* (1955), and (occasionally) *Lochbroom* (1945) and *Loch Frisa* (1946). The lighthouse vessel *Hesperus* serviced the Raonabogh buoy marking the southern approach to the Sound, and also that marking the eastern edge of the deep-water course through the Sound itself. From time to time, the *Hesperus* would appear on the horizon, crawl warily into the Sound, and draw slowly alongside each buoy. She would spend some time refuelling it or winching it from the water and replacing it (or its moorings) with a new version.

Puffers, fishing-boats, Army landing-craft (travelling to and from the South Uist rocket range and St Kilda) and fishery patrol vessels were also commonly seen in transit – but none of these vessels, however unusual, could match the thrill of seeing the *Lochearn*, and latterly the *Claymore*, travelling northwards about one or two o' clock in the afternoon, en route for Castlebay, Barra, and Lochboisdale,

on Mondays, Wednesdays and Fridays. On windy days – and hardly a day passed in Tiree without some wind – the *Claymore* would pass through the relatively sheltered waters of the Sound, and then begin to buffet her way through the troubled stretch of water known locally in Gaelic as *Am Bun Dubh* ('The Black Bottom'). From the highest window of the croft house, she could be seen burying her bow heavily in the grey swells. White sheets of spray would sweep across her bridge and, in the worst weather, the spray would temporarily obscure her large, domed, red-and-black funnel, which set her apart from all the other ships of the MacBrayne fleet. She seemed incomparably splendid as she wrestled with the waves, and it was tempting to envy the Barra folk who had the privilege of the long, seasick sail north to Castlebay.

The *Claymore* would indicate precisely when she would pass through the Sound, as there was a regular exchange between her radio-operator and the keepers of Barra Head lighthouse. On the Marine Band after one o' clock, the operator would call up the lighthouse – '*Claymore* calling Barra Head, *Claymore* calling Barra Head....' – giving the time of departure from Tiree and the estimated time of arrival in Castlebay. Information about wind and weather was exchanged. Then the *Claymore* herself would come into view, rounding the island's southern shoreline, passing Milton, and turning northwards into the Sound of Gunna at Roisigil. A narrow channel of water was sometimes employed to enter the Sound more quickly, if tidal conditions were right. The channel was accessed by traditional navigational methods, which required alignments of features on the island of Gunna and the islands in the south of the Sound. As the *Claymore*'s officers were usually Tiree men, they knew these waters intimately, and piloted her with great skill through the shallow stretches. On a good day, one could gain a grandstand view of the *Claymore*, edging as close as possible to the Caolas coast, as she headed north. An exciting bows-on view, with her sword-bearing Highlander displayed on the figurehead, would yield to a long side-elevation, and finally her port quarter, with its gentle tumble-home and elegant sheer, would pull northwards. Her throbbing Sulzer diesels would echo across the blue-green water – her rhythmical vibration audible in the rising and falling pulse of her engines, with their distinctive sound. A ribbon of foam rose at her bow, covering her red boot-topping, as she left a white swathe behind her cruiser stern, and seagulls

wheeled and cried overhead. The few vehicles stowed on the hatches below her derrick and her thick, yellow samson-post, were clearly visible, as were the men on the bridge and the passengers on the benches which doubled as life-rafts, alongside the varnished boats with their green tarpaulins. The MacBrayne pennant flew on her fore jackstaff, and the house-flag on her mainmast. She was a majestic ship, with her distinctive funnel and stunted, modern appearance. To this island lad, she had no equal – and he has not changed his mind more than forty years later!

My first view of the *Claymore* was, in fact, in the Sound of Gunna, as she passed through on the day of her maiden voyage in the early summer of 1955 – Monday 20 June.

*A far cry from the stormy Minches: the **City of Hydra** (ex-**Claymore**) cruises elegantly in the Aegean sunshine. [Tom Robertson]*

For some reason, schoolchildren had been given a half-day – perhaps to celebrate the arrival of this new vessel. Having walked home hurriedly from Ruaig Primary School in early afternoon, I reached the top of Croish in Caolas, just in time to catch sight of her, dressed overall and taking her first dip through what would become very familiar waters for her over the next twenty years.

My last encounter with the *Claymore*, unlike my first, was not in Tiree, but in the East India Harbour in Greenock, where she had been laid up prior to her departure to Greece. Determined to bid her a personal farewell, I went early in 1976 on a special mission to photograph her on what would assuredly be my last opportunity. I also wanted to thank her

– as if she were a sentient being – for the many safe and supremely happy passages that I had enjoyed on her as a boy. She looked much the same as ever, and it was hard to believe that she was now out of service. I felt like crying as I left her to face her future among the Greek islands. Shortly afterwards her 'real' name was blacked out, and *City of Andros* was painted in white on her stern and in black on her forward bulwarks. When she arrived in Greece, in the ownership of Cycladic Cruises, she was rebuilt and altered radically. Her new curved bow and canoe stern and elegantly extended upper deck, to say nothing of her creamy white colour, were in the sharpest possible contrast to the bumped bulwarks, the black, rust-bespattered hull

*The **Claymore**, still looking surprisingly pristine, in the East India Harbour, Greenock, prior to her departure to Greece in 1976 [DEM]*

and the battered belting which I knew so well. To the outward eye she was but a shadow of the earlier *Claymore*, retaining only the latter's distinctive bridge and funnel, but flattened off on top and given additional 'wings'. Renamed *City of Hydra*, she operated until the early 1990s from Piraeus to the Cyclades, before being laid up and sinking as a neglected, damaged hulk in the 'ship graveyard' at Eleusis Bay in November 2000. On reading of her demise, I suffered a sense of bereavement, as if a family member had passed away, but I consoled myself with the observation that, for me at least, she had ceased to be the *Claymore* as soon as she left MacBrayne ownership in 1976.

The thought that the *Claymore* might ever sink was far from the mind of this Tiree boy in the 1950s and 1960s. She was a model of stalwart service, successfully battling storms and gales of all kinds, though she was comparatively slow at twelve knots, and seemed relatively underpowered with her two four-cylinder, direct-reversing Sulzer diesels. She was also distinguished for her excruciating vibration, with its distinctive and unnerving rhythm. Her vibrations would 'wind up' to a crescendo, and then sink away to relative calm before recommencing the cycle. Any attempt to rest one's head on the woodwork of the second-class lounge, and catch a moment's sleep because 'the vibration had gone away', was doomed to failure, as the rattling and shaking began

anew. Tom Robertson, the *Claymore*'s former Chief Engineer, ascribes the vibration to her having four-cylinder Sulzer diesels, instead of five- or six-cylinder versions, which would have ensured much smoother running. Splendidly constructed under licence by her builders, William Denny, Dumbarton, her engines were extremely reliable, and, at 600 bhp each, adequate for the required service speeds. Their size was determined by overall efficiency, particularly when slow-running on the inward overnight run from Barra to Tiree. An unsuccessful attempt was made to reduce her vibration by placing heavy tie-rods between the two engines.

Despite her faults, the *Claymore* had her own potent magic, not least in her design. Her superstructure, streamlined bridge and funnel reflected the styles of the early 1950s. She bore a fascinating general resemblance to the French Line's steam-turbine liner, *Flandre*, which sailed on her maiden voyage to New York in July 1952, barely a month before the *Claymore* was ordered, in accordance with the Government White Paper of that year, stipulating the mail contract with MacBrayne, and providing for the building of a new passenger vessel and a new cargo vessel. The *Flandre* sported a similarly front-vented and domed funnel, crowning her rather broad-beamed hull. The *Claymore* also echoed the profile of the new generation of cross-Channel 'ferries', such as the Denny-built *Normannia* (1952), in what seems to have been a brief revival of maritime Art Deco, soon to be snuffed out by the ambiguous angularity of car-carriers. The naval architects who worked for William Denny were evidently responding to wider

IN PRAISE OF THE *CLAYMORE*
FROM THE 'GLASGOW LETTER' OF THE *OBAN TIMES*, AUGUST 1973

'THE WEATHER CLERK must have taken a dim view of my staying in Tiree for longer than the customary "Fair Fortnight", for no sooner had my fellow Glaswegians departed than the stormclouds began to gather.

'It was, admittedly, a gradual process, starting with a heavy mist, followed by light rain which became torrential by midweek, and finally built up to a good-going gale by Friday. However, my credit could not have run out entirely as the run to Oban on Saturday proved to be a pleasant one, despite the rather gloomy forecast.

'I have from time to time said some pretty uncomplimentary things about the *Claymore* and certainly never visualised a time when I would say "God bless her". [However,] I not only said it, but I feel rather proud of her and her crew. While the primadonnas of the Caledonian MacBrayne fleet, the *Clansman* and the *Iona*, were causing consternation on the Stornoway-Ullapool and Oban-Craignure runs respectively, the Cinderella of the fleet, the *Claymore*, was bravely attempting to maintain an impossible time schedule on the Oban-Tiree, Oban-Barra and Oban-Colonsay runs.

'As I fitfully dozed in the lounge still carrying the label, "First Class Passengers Only", it seemed that every creak, groan, rumble and shudder from this social outcast screamed defiance at the misguided souls who had only last year agreed to dispense with her services.

'Temporary the reprieve may be, but she has earned the respect, if not the love, of many holiday-makers this summer. God bless her and those who have kept her going virtually non-stop during the height of the holiday season.

'One is supposed to return from holiday full of exhilaration, refreshed and ready to resume work with gusto – I do not find it so. Such being the case and being reluctant to inflict my gloom on readers of the "Glasgow Letter", I will refrain from further comment on transport to the Western Isles.'

Alasdair Kennedy,
Glasgow Correspondent of the *Oban Times*

CLAYMORE TO THE RESCUE:
CHIEF ENGINEER, TOM ROBERTSON, RECOLLECTS THE SUMMER OF 1973

'I REMEMBER THE period mentioned in the "Glasgow Letter" of the *Oban Times*. We were certainly kept busy.

'On one occasion, maybe more, I recall leaving Colonsay overnight to Oban. We left immediately for Tiree and Coll. Then we went direct to Mallaig/Armadale, Lochboisdale, Barra, Tiree, Coll, Tobermory, Oban and Colonsay. This was the long way round for any passengers going to Barra. We were running twenty-four hours a day for a time!

'Even on our normal summer timetable then, Colonsay was tacked on to our normal Tiree, Coll, Barra and Lochboisdale sailing. We berthed at Colonsay in the evening and spent the night there, departing again at 06.00 for Oban and our normal service.

'On a Friday we returned from Colonsay to Oban in the late evening. We were in Oban at midnight, and departed again at 01.00, going direct to Tiree and Coll, and back to Oban via Tobermory. We reached Oban about 12.00, and departed at 13.00 to do the whole lot over again, arriving back in Oban at midnight!

'There was no rest on the Sabbath. The main engine pistons had to be pulled and new piston rings fitted as required. The cargo winch, though not essential for sailing, was essential for cargo! It was hard worked, and electrical controllers and contactor gear had to be serviced regularly.

'On one occasion the capstan motor burnt out, and had to be uncoupled, hoisted on deck and sent to Glasgow for repair. The windlass gearbox also fractured, and was temporarily repaired. Eventually we had to proceed to Gourock for a new gearbox.'

Tom Robertson at the engine controls of the
City of Hydra (*ex-***Claymore***)*

European designs in this period, and applying them to their own ships.

Old and new were, however, riveted together rather incongruously in the *Claymore*, making it evident retrospectively that she sat uncomfortably on the boundary between the earlier *Loch Seaforth* and the forthcoming triad of modern car-ferries, *Hebrides*, *Clansman* and *Columba*. Indeed, one can almost forgive the Greeks for determining to give her a complete revamp, while preserving waterline length, and for imposing an understandable uniformity of design on the *City of Hydra*, even if they destroyed her original character. The Greeks – shrewd recyclers of other nations' maritime cast-offs – realised that, behind the restrictive corsetry of the *Claymore*'s conventional features, there was another, much more modern ship 'trying to get out', and they rebuilt the hull to conform to the model implicit in the futuristic bridge and funnel. A radical overhaul of this kind, which made her look more like a shapely motor-yacht than a rugged passenger-cargo vessel, was the only way to prolong the ship's life. Such rebuilding was beyond the penurious purse of the newly merged Caledonian MacBrayne, which had arrived on the scene in 1973, with dire consequences for older members of the MacBrayne fleet.

The external peculiarities of the *Claymore* – rugged rivets, old-style gear and gentle lines, combined with flowing Art Deco curves in her superstructure – were part of her character. Her cargo-handling machinery likewise nodded towards a new era signified by the samson-post and derrick, but it was firmly linked to the old order of block and tackle. She was, for many people, the archetypal MacBrayne 'steamer', conveying passengers and cattle, sheep and foodstuffs, cars and coffins, to the islands. To view her loading and unloading by means of her derrick was an unforgettable experience, slow and ponderous, with a nerve-tingling element of suspense (in every sense). This was the principal reason for her early dispatch in 1976. By then she had been superseded by the above-mentioned car-ferries, which had begun to appear in the islands by 1964.

Modern though she was in overall design, her samson-post and derrick, and relatively small size, made her somewhat inflexible and hard, if not impossible, to convert to car-carrying when the new era finally struck the islands in all its power. She paid the price, but sailed in modified form for another twenty years.

The *Claymore*'s internal design offered similar contrasts, combining old-time graciousness in her décor with emerging modern utilitarianism and significant departures from traditional arrangements. Novel features included the positioning of the first-class bar on the promenade deck, the location of the crew's quarters aft on the promenade and main decks, and of the officers' accommodation in the deckhouse immediately below the funnel. Her novelties, however, did not extend to an easier layout. She had a labyrinth of steep stairs and passage-ways, which sometimes caused mild disorientation and confusion, especially if passengers were kept on board for prolonged periods in bad weather.

At the end of a particularly stormy week in 1974 or 1975, for instance, during which the *Claymore* had made several brave attempts to reach Tiree from Oban, she ventured north to Barra where she was storm-bound – but not for long, despite the persistent gales. In fact, islanders were astonished to see her lights coming through the narrow and difficult waters of Gunna Sound around 5 a.m. Berthing at Tiree in the windy darkness of the early morning was an heroic feat in itself, indicative of the immense skill of Hebridean Captains. Captain Donald Gunn was on the bridge, wrestling with the telegraphs and shouting (through a megaphone) to car-drivers to extinguish their headlights, as he tried to bring the ship's stern on to the outer edge of Tiree pier, and then swing her round with the help of windlass and capstans. The tide was high, with heavy swells, and the ship herself looked huge on the dark waves, her navigating lights, mast lanterns and deck illumination accentuating her robust overall profile. Eventually she berthed successfully, her propellers churning the black water to white, while nylon ropes groaned and squeaked with the immense strain.

Climbing the almost-vertical gangway, I struggled downstairs to the *Claymore*'s lounge, only to be confronted by a ghostly, female passenger who emerged shell-shocked from a cabin, and requested to know the place, the time and the day! She had been on board since the ship had left Oban the previous week!

Like that unfortunate passenger but for better reasons, I was soon lost in the *Claymore*'s atmosphere, her warmth and conviviality contrasting with the storm outside. Rugged staves of accordion music from the bar, interspersed with weary, inebriated, Outer Isles voices singing Gaelic songs, the smell of sheep-dip and kippers, bacon and egg, diesel oil and hot tea, and whiffs of Archangel tar, still mingle in my mind as I recollect her then. The more enticing fragrances led to the restaurant, with its fine wood panels and paintings, where tables were set out grandly with silver cutlery, large silver teapots and dazzlingly white linen. The *Claymore*'s accommodation was second to none for a vessel of that class.

The *Claymore*'s good qualities were enhanced by the kindness of her crew. For most of her time with MacBrayne, her Masters were Tiree men (a point of which I was particularly proud!), commencing with Captain John C. MacKinnon, MBE, who was followed by Captain Neil Campbell, who was followed in his turn by Captain John Lamont. Her last Master was Captain Donald Gunn, from Harris. The generosity shown by these skippers to their passengers deserves to be chronicled at greater length than is possible in this chapter. John C. MacKinnon, for example, would make a regular round of his passengers on leaving Tiree. His progress through the ship could be 'charted' by means of his booming voice and hearty laughter, as he shared a joke in Gaelic with a fellow-islander, and puffed out clouds of tobacco smoke from his ever-present pipe.

As a youngster, I travelled regularly to Oban, and onwards to Glasgow, for eye treatment. The highlight of the journey was to be called up to the bridge by Captain MacKinnon. There I was introduced to other members of the crew, who did not object to the 'boy on the bridge', and who continued to be close friends in later years. Subsequent Captains always gave me the opportunity to travel to and from Tiree on the bridge. Kindness was shown in other ways too. It was not uncommon for the Captains to offer their cabins to passengers who were also close friends, to allow them to sit, chat or rest in considerable comfort. On a visit to the Outer Hebrides in the early 1960s, I slept on the settee in the Captain's cabin on the inward voyage to Tiree. I felt that I was the Commodore of the Fleet, as I made my way from the Captain's cabin to the bridge, by means of the heavy metal door (with its loosely-fitting handle!) which secured the wheelhouse.

The panoramic vistas of the Inner Hebrides and the adjacent mainland to be gained from the bridge of the *Claymore* are still etched on my memory. So too are the grandstand views of local maritime dramas, such as the *Claymore*'s regular rendezvous with the Coll ferry-boat in the days before that island gained its own pier in the mid-1960s. In the first stage of the rendezvous, the ferry was moored at the *Claymore*'s side-door (on the port side). As both vessels rolled on the swell, passenger-transfer needed careful supervision. Passengers had to judge the moment when the gunwale of the ferry was level, or likely to be level, with the bottom of the *Claymore*'s side-door, and to engage in some smart foot-work, particularly when boarding the larger ship. As the faint-hearted put their best foot forward, two burly crewmen were waiting on each side of the door to pull them to safety. When passengers had been embarked or disembarked, the ferry was eased ahead, so that she aligned reasonably closely with the *Claymore*'s derrick. The non-human cargo was then transferred. The Coll ferry could accommodate a car or a tractor in addition to passengers, and it was especially exciting to see such a large item being raised or lowered. Usually the cargo consisted of mail in slings and animals in cages or boxes. When the process was completed, the little red boat cast her moorings, and drifted to leeward of the *Claymore*. She then engaged full power, and, dipping and heaving in the cold morning air, headed for Arinagour, doubtless to the great relief of all concerned. The *Claymore*'s next stop was Tobermory, where she would berth for about half-an-hour, before heading out to Oban. Tobermory was always attractive, with its myriad yachts in the harbour, and its steep, wooded slopes towering above the pier building bearing the name of David MacBrayne.

From time to time I would have the thrill of steering the *Claymore* on a safe stretch of water, usually the Sound of Mull. I was closely supervised, of course. I learned to keep a sharp eye on the rudder indicator, above the main wheelhouse window, to ensure that the good ship maintained a straight course. I came to understand compass bearings and readings, by listening to the officer of the watch as he gave orders to the helmsman. 'Nor'west by west a half west' was the regular course on rounding the north-east point of Mull on the way to Coll. Following the officer's instruction, the helmsman would repeat the command, and cap it with

a polite 'Sir', or, depending on the command, he would answer simply, 'Aye, aye, Sir'. Although officers and crew were generally Gaelic-speaking, and were often close friends, sometimes from the same island, course bearings and other commands were given very respectfully in English, but ordinary conversation would lapse naturally into Gaelic.

With officers' permission and sometimes under escort, I also had the privilege of moving around the ship and enjoying parts of the *Claymore*'s deck normally out of bounds to passengers. One of my favourite stances was under the forward jackstaff, where I could stand on the bollards, lean over the bulwark, look across the top of the Highlander on the quasi-figurehead, and watch the vessel's tapering stem cutting a fine wave of spray through the blue-green surface of the Sound of Mull. On a sunny day it was a glorious and even exciting experience, as old-timers like the *Lochinvar* tried their flagging paces against this greyhound

FUN WITH THE FERRIES
AS REMEMBERED BY HAROLD JORDAN

Improving the *Claymore*

'The overnight train from Glasgow arrived in Oban around 5.00 am, and passengers could board the *Claymore*, and, if they could rouse Donnie Stewart, the Night Steward, then tea and toast could be obtained in the dining-saloon. Donnie, a seasoned veteran, must have been in his late 60s, and the Chief Steward, Davie Samson, a real "character" and a genuinely nice man, in his early 60s. One morning Davie got up as the train arrived, and went round the lounges, announcing that tea and toast were being served in the dining-saloon. Eventually Donnie Stewart wandered into a packed saloon.

"What's this?" he exclaimed.

"This, my friend," said Davie Samson, "is initiative and youth at the helm."'

'In a burst of interventionism, C. B. Leith, General Manager, and Catering Superintendent, Jack Whittington, decided that the deck linoleum of the *Claymore*'s saloons should be painted with a varnish-type polish known as *Gleem*. This was perhaps a goodish idea for the untrodden decks of a new ship, but it was not recommended for well-worn decks, and Davie Samson knew it, but his protests went unheeded. Eventually the wretched stuff began to peel and turn black, where dirt penetrated. It took gallons of paint remover and many hours' overtime to restore the linoleum to reasonable appearance, and the cost was a sore point with MacBrayne's management. Some months later, on one of his unannounced inspections, C. B. Leith observed to Davie Samson,

"Perhaps, Samson, a little polish would improve the appearance of the deck."

"Oh! You mean *Gleem*, sir?" replied Davie, with affected innocence. C. B. Leith fixed him with an icy stare.

"Not necessarily," he managed to spit out, and stormed ashore.'

Life on the *Lochmor*

'Captain Dougie MacLean of the *Lochmor* (1930) was a very likeable but droll character. Following the foundering of the Railway car-ferry *Princess Victoria*, shipowners had to be circumspect about ordering Masters to sail in bad weather. In really frightful conditions, Dougie tied up the *Lochmor* at Lochmaddy for three days, and refused to go near the office phone. In Glasgow, the Grey Wolf (Marine Superintendent) was becoming puce with rage. Eventually Dougie was coaxed to the phone in Lochmaddy office. "What's keeping you there, MacLean?" thundered the Grey Wolf.

"Six ropes aft," replied Dougie, and hung up.'

'Sometime in the 1940s, the Earl of Cadogan travelled on the *Lochmor*, and struck up a budding friendship with "Squeaky", her Master. The following summer, the Earl came off the train at Mallaig, and eagerly made his way to the wing of the *Lochmor*'s bridge, where he was met with a blank stare from "Squeaky".

"I don't think you remember me, Captain," said the Earl.

"Ah, no!" replied "Squeaky". "You see that many queer faces."'

'Another well-known Captain of the *Lochmor* was the "Souser", so-called because he could not pronounce initial or internal *th*. The *Lochearn* used to relieve the *Lochmor* for annual overhaul. The Second Mate of the *Lochmor*, John Harvey, always transferred to the relieving vessel, to provide local knowledge. He would then transfer back to the *Lochmor*. After the *Lochmor* had returned from docking, the skipper of the departing *Lochearn* asked the "Souser", "Have you got everything, then?"

"Ach, yes! As long as I have the essentials – John Harvey, and the horsebox and the parallel rulers!"'

of the West, rattling along at all of her stunning twelve knots. Looking astern from this vibration-free vantage-point – possibly the only one on the ship – I could see the streamlined, white wheelhouse with its elegant wings and centrally-placed builder's plate, the foremast with its tripod and radar, and the large domed funnel with its deep front vents, emitting its characteristic 'lull-lull-lull' engine noise.

Officers and crew were very well versed not only in the ways of the sea and their ship, but also in Gaelic language and culture. I learned a great deal about my native Gaelic language and about other Hebridean islands during my wheelhouse conversations with the helmsman or officer, or with the Captain in his cabin. Angus Morrison, a genial native of Harris with a wry smile on his handsome, weather-beaten face, was frequently at the wheel, and he would test my knowledge of Gaelic by reciting words and idioms from his own island.

Attending Oban High School as a teenager between 1965 and 1967, I found that the *Claymore* and her crew offered me a 'home from home', where I would frequently spend a Saturday afternoon, watching the crew or participating in the routine of the ship, and sometimes enjoying the fun of salvaging one of her anchors from the entanglements of Oban Bay. (Lacking a bow-thruster, the

M.V. OR S.S. *CLAYMORE?*
TOM ROBERTSON RECALLS SOME MARITIME ADVENTURES

'ON A VERY stormy crossing between Tiree and Barra, I was called urgently to the engine-room. On entering on the top platform, I was confronted with clouds of steam. Were the engines overheating? A check of the fresh-water-circulating header-tank showed normal level and temperature. When I descended to the control platform, the Second Engineer, Rennie (Dick) Thomson, confirmed that all was normal, apart from the steam clouds. It transpired that a big sea had broken on the port boat deck, sending gallons of water cascading into the engine-room via the open skylights. This collected in the save-alls, or deep gutters surrounding the fuel-oil service tanks, filling them with gallons of water. Every time the ship rolled, more water spilled over, contacting the hot cylinder-heads and exhaust manifolds, and instantly turning into steam!

'The bridge was contacted, and we turned head-to-sea to reduce the rolling, closed the skylights, and removed the excess water from the save-alls. After sorting ourselves out, we resumed our course to Barra.

'I then proceeded to the bridge to inform Captain Donald Gunn that we were now OK down below. It was a very wild day indeed, and Donald said, "What are we doing out here on a day like this?" The only reply I could make was, "We had no choice but to go with you!" We eventually arrived at Barra, where Donald said, "That's it, we're here for the night." This was one of the very few times that Captain Gunn did not sail because of the weather.

'At least, the overnight stay in port meant that our Chief Steward, Davie Samson, got a decent night's sleep. Davie's cabin was in the port, or working, alleyway, directly opposite the engine-room door. On a night crossing, if we were rolling heavily – with no stabilisers in those days – when we rolled to port, the heavy engine-room door would swing open against the self-closer. At the same time, the generator diesels would lose suction momentarily for the lubricating-oil pumps, causing the low-pressure alarm siren to sound. A few seconds later, the same thing would happen to the main sea-water cooling-pump, causing the low-pressure alarm to sound. This was a "Monitor" air-alarm which gave off a piercing scream. As we rolled the other way, the engine-room door would close, and peace would descend until the next roll. Davie would complain that it was like trying to sleep in a fairground ghost-train!

'One night we were tied up loading cattle. As Davie sat in the dining-saloon, working on his accounts, he was rudely disturbed. The door between the tween-deck and the port alleyway had been left open in error, and a stirk saw its chance to escape down the alleyway into the saloon, to be confronted by Davie. Discretion being the better part of valour, he locked himself in the cash kiosk. Fortunately, no diners were present, and no tables set; so there was no damage, except to the polished deck. The stirk was eventually rounded up by the sailors and drovers, to be returned to the tween-deck, and Davie was released from his sanctuary!

'Never a dull moment on the old *Claymore!*'

'No Call at Coll', by Tom Robertson

Claymore often had to use the port or starboard anchor, to hold the bow and ensure a successful docking against adverse wind and currents.) Captain John Lamont and his family showed me great kindness on Saturday evenings; and I got to know the Purser, Donald Edwards, latterly on the *Clansman*; and the Chief Engineer, Tom Robertson, who is now well-known as a skilful marine artist specialising in portrayals of MacBrayne and Caledonian MacBrayne ships – with a particular talent for painting the *Claymore*! Walks along the Railway Pier on Sundays, when I would often encounter crew members like Calum Brown from my native Tiree, mending his Morris Minor van, allowed me to study the ship's hull in detail, every stud and rivet, and to view her propellers and rudder in the translucent waters of Oban Bay. It was sobering to think how many island communities owed their continuing existence to the skilful use of these hidden pieces of engineering.

The *Claymore* was a floating community, full of character, fun and friendship. We grew up together, and she was bonded into my being, where she remains to this day. She was as essential to my boyhood as she was to the life of the islands, conveying me to the mainland for medical care or to visit relatives, and to many new places and experiences. She and her crew helped to fix my sense of place in the Hebrides and in the wider world, and they contributed significantly to my general education.

'No matter the weather ... John MacKinnon will bring her in'

MEN WHO RULE THE ISLES OF THE WEST

by ALLAN DOUGLAS

Captain MacKinnon, his wife and daughter, after his investiture at Buckingham Palace.

'The earth belongs unto the Lord and all that it contains.

Except the Western Islands for they belong to MacBraynes.'

CLAYMORE AT CASTLEBAY

TOP—Captain MacKinnon on the bridge. ABOVE—Fishing boats at Castlebay, on Barra, are dwarfed by the Claymore as she pulls in to unload passengers. On the left is Kisimul Castle, stronghold of the MacNeils.

*The old **Weekly Scotsman** carried this tribute to Captain John MacKinnon, MBE, in the early 1960s. [DEM's collection]*

Unquestionably, too, the *Claymore* had an identity which is hard to replicate on contemporary slab-sided car-ferries. She belonged to another era, now largely vanished, when life on land and sea was more relaxed, less 'managerialised', less constricted by oceans of detailed regulation, less enslaved to 'turn-around times', but less casual in other ways. Unlike modern travellers in jeans, shorts and tee-shirts, islanders dressed up in their Sunday best to travel on the *Claymore*. In contrast to the leisurely *Claymore*, present-day 'ferry powerful' specimens of marine engineering dash from one island to another, scarcely resting for more than half an hour, and thereby reflecting the pressures of the profit-driven lifestyle from which stressed-out tourists are trying to escape. They offer their brief tannoy messages from the largely invisible Captain, broadcast their raucous, pre-recorded 'Safety Announcements' when leaving every harbour, and provide a generally bleak and impersonal approach to passenger

SERVING IN THE AEGEAN

THE STURDY QUALITY of the new ships built for David MacBrayne, after the company had been taken over in 1928 by Coast Lines and the London, Midland & Scottish Railway, is reflected in their long lives, which in some cases were extended for a considerable period in the warmer waters of the Mediterranean. Two of these ships (*Lochness* and *Claymore*) achieved an active life-span of about forty years. This, however, is considerably shorter than the active life-span of the pioneering *Lochinvar*, which served for fifty-two years in Hebridean waters, and for a further three in the Thames estuary, before she was wrecked as the *Anzio I* in 1966.

The first of the new post-1928 vessels, the 1929 steamship *Lochness*, was sold in 1955 to Italian operators, who renamed her *Valmirana*. In 1958 she was bought by Greek owners, who renamed her *Myrtidiotissa*. She served the islands of the Aegean until she was broken up in 1974. Apart from the removal of her bridge cabs, she remained largely unaltered, and was still eminently recognisable as the old *Lochness*.

She was followed to the Mediterranean by the 1930 twins, *Lochmor* and *Lochearn*, in 1964. Their voyage in sisterly tandem from Ardrossan to Piraeus, beginning on Tuesday, 1 September 1964, has recently been described vividly in *Sea Breezes*, Volume 78 (October 2004) by Bob Phillips, a Chief Engineer with David MacBrayne, who sailed on the *Lochearn*. He was matched on the *Lochmor* by John McCabe, also a Chief Engineer with MacBrayne. Prior to sailing, the *Lochmor* and the *Lochearn* were renamed *Amimoni* and *Naias* respectively. Photographs show their derricks resting on their cradles below the bridge – a sure sign that their Hebridean labours were at an end.

Bob Phillips informs us that, at Land's End, 'the two little vessels were at maximum speed enjoying a race' (hardly a concept familiar to those who knew the vessels in Hebridean waters), and that, with the vessels within hailing distance, 'the two Greek captains used rolled up charts as megaphones to call to each other. The cone call became a morning feature for the rest of the voyage....the *Lochearn* rolled heavily as she completed the journey through the Bay of Biscay.' *Lochmor* had problems with her engine cylinders, which received attention from the crews of both vessels at Port of Lisbon, and for a period she sailed on one engine.

Bravely enduring a storm in the Gulf of Cadiz, the vessels passed through the Straits of Gibraltar on 10 September, and reached Piraeus, via the Corinth Canal, on 19 September. By the last few days of the voyage, the *Lochmor* was sailing well, and both ships were logging speeds 'that probably exceeded the top speed recorded during their sea trials many years ago'. During the voyage, the ships' funnels were painted yellow with a blue band.

Their service in Greece was apparently short-lived. The *Lochmor* was broken up in 1969. According to Alistair Deayton, the *Lochearn* 'appears never to have operated in Greek waters, and was probably broken up by the early 1970s'. She disappears from Lloyd's Register in 1968, when she is described as a 'private yacht'. It is highly likely that the design of both ships made them somewhat difficult to convert to other, more practical roles. The *Claymore* (1955) was the next ship to reach Piraeus, arriving in 1976 (see Chapter 9).

The impending arrival of the *Isle of Mull* in 1988 displaced the *Caledonia* (ex-*Stena Baltica*), which had provided the Oban-Craignure service from 1974. At the end of her 1987 season she was sold to restaurant operators in Dundee. When this venture failed to materialise, she was purchased by Italian (Bay of Naples) operators, Linee Lauro. Renamed *Heidi*, but otherwise largely unaltered, she plied latterly between Pozzuoli and Ischia, carrying the green and yellow colours of Traghetti Pozzuoli. Laid up in 2004, she sank at her moorings in 2005.

The *Glen Sannox* (1957), originally a member of the Caledonian Steam Packet Co., served both the islands of the Firth of Clyde and the Hebrides following the creation of Caledonian MacBrayne. First renamed *Nadia* and then *Knooz*, she was sold in 1990 'to Red Sea operators, and although long laid-up, survives as *Al Basmalah I*' (Russell Plummer, *Ships Monthly*, Volume 40 (September 2005)).

The **City of Hydra** (ex-**Claymore**) at Hydra
[Tom Robertson]

comfort, more in keeping with a jumbo-jet than a ship. On many vessels, there is an almost total absence of interaction between passengers and crew, except when following the standard routines, going to the shop or having a meal in the paper-and-plastic cafeteria (not the restaurant now!). Back in the 'old days', when ships were ships and not 'ferries' (a term applicable in my early days only to open-decked 'flit-boats' or turntable vessels), I knew virtually every member of the crew of the *Claymore*, and I was known by them.

Today one can travel completely unnoticed, lost in faceless, modern anonymity, on the *Lord of the Isles* or the *Clansman*. Security concerns now dictate that bridge-visits are rare, and not as freely available as they once were on these vessels. Only once have I been ushered into the plate-glass control-centre of the *Clansman*, with its endless array of dials, switches, buttons and diagrams. The *Clansman*'s monitors and screens, her autopilot and satellite positioning system, are a far cry from the wooden wheel and compass, echo-sounder and radar set, of the unassuming 1955 *Claymore*. They seem much less exciting, much less human.

Undoubtedly, such new 'ferries' can offer a service which is much more reliable than, and technically superior to, what the *Claymore* could provide. Nevertheless, as the last of a long and distinguished succession of mail-ships in the fleet of David MacBrayne Limited, she will retain her place in the memory of many islanders long after her present-day successors have passed into oblivion.

*The **Claymore** heads away from Tobermory and down the Sound of Mull [Donald B. MacCulloch]*

CHAPTER 10

THE GREAT END-LOADING RUSH:
CAR-FERRIES AND THE MAKING
OF CALEDONIAN MACBRAYNE

*The **Hebridean Isles** is captured splendidly as she leaves Port Askaig, Islay, with the Paps of Jura in the background. [Philip Kirkham]*

THE GREAT END-LOADING RUSH:
CAR-FERRIES AND THE MAKING OF CALEDONIAN MACBRAYNE

By the summer of 1969, as the *Claymore* and the *Loch Seaforth* battled bravely with increasing traffic, the time-honoured course of their maritime world was about to change. A new hand was on the helm of the old company. Rumour abounded that, at the end of the season, the newly-formed Scottish Transport Group would dispose of the three MacBrayne diesel units, *Lochfyne*, *Lochnevis* and *Lochiel*, and the paddle-steamer *Caledonia*, belonging to the Caledonian Steam Packet Company. A Scandinavian roll-on/roll-off car ferry was being considered for possible use at Ardrossan, a new drive-through ferry was to be built for Islay, there were ideas of a new Ullapool-Stornoway service, and there was even talk of a new vehicle ferry for the Mallaig-Castlebay service and for that to Coll, Tiree and Lochboisdale.

It was also announced that the remaining steamers, *King George V*, and (from the Caledonian fleet) the *Queen Mary II*, *Duchess of Hamilton* and *Waverley*, would be systematically withdrawn, as their five-year surveys were due. This caused such a furore that, when the large, elderly turbine steamer *Duchess of Hamilton* was withdrawn at the end of the 1970 season, the *Queen Mary II* was upgraded to Clyde cruise-ship, supported by the one remaining paddle-steamer, *Waverley*. For the moment, the *King George V* also seemed safe at Oban, and she was even given a special passenger certificate to make a day excursion from Ayr to Bangor, County Down, at the start of the season.

The combining of the Caledonian and MacBrayne fleets allowed considerable flexibility in the deployment of vessels. In January 1970, the *Clansman* moved to the Gourock-Dunoon ferry service, and the Clyde-based side-hoist-loader *Arran*, complete with red-and-black funnel, transferred to West Loch Tarbert in place of the *Lochiel*. The *Lochiel*, meanwhile, had been sold, and renamed *Norwest Laird* by her new owners, Norwest Hovercraft Limited, with the intention of running day trips from Fleetwood to the Isle of Man. The ship, now separated from the tender, loving care of her MacBrayne engineers, was plagued with mechanical problems, and the Board of Trade insisted that the *Norwest Laird* should hug the Cumbrian coast, thus increasing the crossing time to six hours. She spent much of the summer in the Fish Dock at Fleetwood.

Three significant events happened at the end of May in quick succession:

1. The former *Stena Baltica*, a Scandinavian drive-through car-ferry, started between Ardrossan and Brodick under the new name, *Caledonia*, having been converted for her new role at a cost of £100 000.

2. The new drive-through and side-loading ferry *Iona* began on the Gourock-Dunoon service, relieving the *Clansman*, which was then able to return to Mallaig.

3. The side-hoist-loading ferry *Cowal* commenced a Fairlie-Brodick-Tarbert car and passenger service, to provide the connection with the *Arran* and onwards for Islay.

With the arrival of the car-ferry *Caledonia*, the former Arran ferry *Glen Sannox* was free to be converted to stern-loading for eventual use at Gourock and Wemyss Bay. One other development was that the *Loch Seaforth*, in between her Stornoway duties, ran one trip per day from Mallaig to Armadale for vehicles. In addition, the Skye ferry *Portree* was brought down to the Clyde, and put on the Colintraive crossing to Bute, her place at Kyle being taken by the new

ferry, *Kyleakin*. These exciting developments were driven
to a large extent by the Chairman of the new Scottish
Transport Group, Major P. M. Thomas. The order of the
day was the introduction of end-loading ferries on as many
routes as possible, with initial emphasis on the Clyde.

Co-ordinating the introduction of new end-loading
ferries and shore-based link-spans was difficult, not least
because many of the piers were owned by local estates
and other private companies. The arrival of the new Islay
car-ferry, *Iona*, illustrates this. A new development-site
was earmarked in the lower part of West Loch Tarbert
at Redhouse, but negotiations with the landowners were
seemingly exhausted and concluded without agreement.
When delivered, the *Iona* had a flower-pot funnel which
was painted red, but on arrival at Gourock this was changed

to yellow, and the much-trumpeted, revolutionary ship
commenced her duties as a cross-Clyde ferry, having no
suitable terminal to allow her to function on the Islay route,
for which she was intended.

Introduction of the *Caledonia* and *Iona* revealed another
problem. Although the vehicle decks could be loaded and
unloaded in fifteen to twenty minutes, a large complement
of foot passengers could not. Side gangways and doors
needed to be enlarged, in order to speed up the embarking
and disembarking of passengers. As always, all the changes
and improvements received some praise, a modest amount
of thanks – and a lot of criticism. W. Paul Clegg reported in
the November 1970 edition of *Sea Breezes*:

*On the Clyde, the new Arran ferry **Caledonia** has come
into a great deal of criticism, which has even reached the*

Sunday Express. Catering and litter seem to have been the subjects of greatest comment, but there have also been allegations of un-seaworthiness which have been hotly denied by both captain and owners.

For the moment, this diverted attention from Western Ferries at Kennacraig. On 7 May, their original and smaller vessel on the Islay route, the *Sound of Islay*, was transferred to a new Campbeltown-Red Bay, County Antrim, service (for which the single fare was a paltry 14/-), leaving the larger *Sound of Jura* in charge of the Kennacraig-Port Askaig service.

Progress in 1970 was marred by only one bizarre incident. The Iona flit-boat, *Lochshiel*, had come down to the Clyde, via the Crinan Canal, for routine pre-season maintenance at Shandon. On passage to Shandon, her fuel pipe severed, and the two-man crew launched flares to attract attention. Shortly after midnight on the morning of 29 April, the Dutch coaster *Kamperdyke*, which was on passage from Glasgow to Belfast, came alongside and radioed for a tow for the *Lochshiel*. The coaster then continued on her way. However, before help could arrive, the *Lochshiel* was run down and sunk by a vessel that was never identified. The two men were able to scramble on to a life-raft. They were later picked up by an Ayr fishing boat and taken to hospital suffering from exposure.

The following year, 1971, was much quieter. The *Iona* was still languishing on the Clyde, amid late-season rumour that she was shortly to go to Kyle to replace the *Loch Seaforth*, which, in turn, would take over the duties of the smaller, but younger, *Claymore* at Oban. Three of the MacBrayne fleet were sold, the cargo ships *Loch Ard* and *Lochbroom* going to Greek flag operators, and the little *Loch Eynort* being bought for use in the film industry. However, on her delivery passage south, the *Loch Eynort* was found wallowing off the Isle of Man, and was towed into Douglas with water rising in the engine room.

January 1972 witnessed the transfer of some of the MacBrayne bus network to Highland Omnibuses Limited and other units of the Scottish Bus Group, although a couple of private bus operators benefited as well. Significantly, the port of registration of the three side-loading car-ferries was changed during the year from Leith to Glasgow.

At the end of March, the *Loch Seaforth* was replaced on the Stornoway service by the *Clansman*. For the moment, the *Loch Seaforth* retired to Greenock, but by the end of May she was sent to Oban to take over from the *Claymore*, then no longer able to cope with the traffic on offer on the Lochboisdale route. The *Loch Seaforth* broke down after only four days, and the *Claymore* was reinstated. On the return of the bigger ship, the *Claymore* stayed at Oban a few days in anticipation of further problems with the *Loch Seaforth*, but the *Claymore* was soon retired to the Clyde, emerging only for occasional relief duties. Meanwhile, on the Clyde, the first of eight little landing-craft type ferries, the *Kilbrannan*, arrived to take up service between Largs and Cumbrae Slip, and later moved to the Lochranza-Claonaig route. During the next winter, she was followed by the *Morvern*, for the Fishnish-Lochaline service.

In turn, the *Clansman* was displaced from Mallaig by the *Iona*, the latter finally being released from the waters of the Clyde by the newly-converted and now stern-loading *Glen Sannox* and the *Maid of Cumbrae*, which together took over the Dunoon service. The *Clansman* went to the Ailsa yard at Troon to be converted into a drive-through ferry, with garage space for 50 cars and 14 lorries, the garage having a headroom of 4.3 metres. The transformation included raising the superstructure and lengthening the ship.

At the end of 1972, the *Arran* was taken from West Loch Tarbert, and the service was suspended until Easter whilst she was converted to stern-loading. Following £100 000 worth of work, she re-emerged in 1973 to take up a thrice-daily service from West Loch Tarbert to Port Ellen only. Jura was now served by the Western Ferries connection at Port Askaig. An unsuccessful attempt was made in the autumn of 1972 by the Scottish Transport Group to buy out Western Ferries. In the event, the company was sold to a consortium of owners for exactly the same sum as was offered by the Scottish Transport Group - £531 000.

*The **Clansman** after her 1972 transformation into a lengthened and raised drive-through ferry [NR]*

January 1 1973 was the day the Kingdom finally passed into the history books – or very nearly so. David MacBrayne Limited and the Caledonian Steam Packet Company were put under a single administration called Caledonian MacBrayne Limited with offices at Gourock. David MacBrayne Limited remained the registered owners of eight ships and managers of their respective routes, which were deemed to be subsidy-seeking services. These were as follows:

Loch Seaforth, Oban-Colonsay and Oban-Coll-Tiree-
    Castlebay and Lochboisdale;

Claymore, in reserve;

Iona, Mallaig-Lochboisdale-Castlebay, Mallaig-Armadale;

Lochdunvegan and *Loch Carron*, cargo services from
    Glasgow;

Loch Arkaig, Mallaig-Small Isles, Kyle-Portree;

Loch Toscaig, Oban-Lismore;

Lochnell, Tobermory-Mingary.

The designated Caledonian MacBrayne routes which were deemed to be self-supporting, apart from all the Clyde services, were:

Columba, Oban-Craignure;

Clansman, Ullapool to Stornoway (resuming in June 1973 after rebuilding);
Hebrides, Uig to Tarbert and Lochmaddy;
King George V, Oban excursions;
Arran, West Loch Tarbert-Islay.

Of these, the 'three fat ladies' (*Hebrides*, *Clansman* and *Columba*), the *King George V* and the *Arran*, along with the Clyde-based vessels, were placed in the ownership of Caledonian MacBrayne Holdings Limited.

Since the mid-1960s, the standard 'railway steamer' colours of the Caledonian Steam Packet Company had been enlivened by the addition of a Scottish red lion rampant to the upper dull-yellow or buff part of the funnel, and the hulls had been painted in monastral blue. This was the time when the railway ferries around the UK appeared with red funnels, and the white twin-arrow device, but also with their distinctive, dull, blue/green hull colour. During winter refits from 1973 onwards, the combined Caledonian and MacBrayne fleet, apart from the eight ships retained by David MacBrayne Limited, was given the new corporate colours. These comprised the placing of the red lion in a yellow disc on the red of the MacBrayne funnel, and the Caledonian fleet reverting to black hulls, with red boot topping and a white line. The paddler *Waverley* initially had a yellow band rather than a yellow disc, but this was changed quickly. Progress with adopting the new colours was inhibited only by the availability of red lions to bolt on to the funnel casings!

Meanwhile, on the Clyde, three of the small, utilitarian *Maid*s had been sold, curtailing calls at Craigendoran (the old North British and subsequently London and North Eastern railhead), Innellan and Arrochar. Among the more interesting early exchanges between traditional Highland and Clyde vessels were the *Hebrides*' service at Ardrossan in the winter, and the Clyde side-loader *Bute*'s period as relief-ship for the *Columba* at Oban.

Suddenly, in the midst of selling off the old stock and introducing the new, a maritime drama of (by now) relatively rare West Highland type engulfed David MacBrayne Limited, and brought reporters in droves to Tiree to witness an all-time 'classic' event. Under Captain Donald Gunn, on her normal Thursday morning return run from Lochboisdale and Castlebay to Oban via Coll and Tiree on 22 March 1973, the *Loch Seaforth* ran aground on Sgeir Uilleim, Gunna Sound, between Coll and Tiree, sending out a Mayday call just after 0515 hours. The 28 crew and 11 passengers took safely to the ship's boats, some transferred to the Tiree fishing-boat *Harbour Maid*, but all were safely in the Scarinish Hotel 90 minutes later. In true *Titanic* style, the 'owners' were aboard at the time of the stranding. John Whittle, Executive Director, and Morris Little, Chairman of CalMac, had joined the ship at Lochboisdale, having finished (in record time) their business in South Uist regarding ownership of Lochboisdale pier. Exhilarated by their success, they decided to sail to Oban on the *Loch Seaforth*, rather than fly back the next morning. They could not have anticipated the adventure that lay before them.

The *Loch Seaforth* was refloated with tug assistance later that morning, and towed to Scarinish, where she settled on the bottom in 6 m. of water the very next day, when the port-side cattle-door became submerged. At this point, it was found that some of her bottom plates were all but perished, the divers claiming that they could push their fists through the plates in some places. True or not, it was known that the ship suffered from decay of the poor-quality steel used in her construction. Though possibly somewhat embellished by local gossip and the press, the divers' comments may not have been too far off the mark.

The *Loch Seaforth* was later raised by floating crane and beached, so that she could be made seaworthy for a tow to Troon, where she was declared a constructive total loss, and sold for demolition. Coincidentally, the cargo vessel *Loch Carron* also went aground, this time at Lochboisdale, four days after the *Loch Seaforth*. The *Loch Carron*, however, was salvaged, and quickly put back into service.

While the *Loch Seaforth* sat on the bottom at Scarinish, Tiree pier was out of service for other vessels. Although the

Claymore was readily pressed back into service, her calls at Scarinish were made via flit-boat, a novelty that was not welcomed by the islanders. With almost Freudian perfection, the timing of the loss of the *Loch Seaforth* predated by just two days the final closure of her old service, which she had maintained so faithfully – Mallaig-Kyle-Stornoway. The *Iona* was then transferred to Ullapool, where she commenced on Monday 26 March, and the newly lengthened *Clansman* took over when she was released from the Ailsa shipyard in late May. The *Iona* then moved to the Oban-Craignure service, displacing the side-loader *Bute*, which then returned to the Clyde.

On the Clyde, an important new vehicle-ferry service was initiated in the spring by Western Ferries, when the former Swedish ferry, *Sound of Shuna*, was put on the route between new terminals at McInroy's Point (below Gourock) and Hunter's Quay (Dunoon). This provision was an instant success, and a second ex-Swedish ferry joined the service, followed shortly by the former Isle of Wight ferries, *Lymington* (one of the first Voith Schneider cyclical-propulsion vessels in UK waters when completed in the late 1930s) and *Freshwater*. The service suffered a set-back in the first autumn of operation, when the McInroy's Point terminal was damaged by gales, and put out of action for two weeks.

The frantic, and somewhat ungainly, race to put end-loading ferries into service had been precipitated undoubtedly by Western Ferries' Islay service. It was also seen as a major reason why subsidies were still required, and it was firmly believed by some that, once all routes were served by end-loading vessels,

Caledonian MacBrayne would then become a profit-making company which government could some day float on the Stock Market.

The year 1973 was the first for which a combined Clyde and Western Isles brochure was produced. Emphasis was on the carriage of cars, and the new Port Ellen and Stornoway services were marketed under the banner 'Hebridean Highways', featuring the converted stern-loaders, *Arran* and *Clansman*. The excursion business was played right down, although special folders were produced for the *King George V* at Oban, and the *Queen Mary* and the *Waverley* on the Clyde. The *King George V* maintained her usual Iona and Fort William excursions, plus a Sunday 'Six Lochs Special' throughout the summer, with her well-known purser Donald Maclean shepherding his many daily

tour-groups as best he could. The *Waverley* completed her last sailing on 30 September 1973, and was laid up pending disposal. Happily, she was gifted to the Paddle Steamer Preservation Society two months later for the princely sum of £1, and her subsequent and glorious history as the 'last seagoing paddle-steamer' is well known.

The passing of the traditional Mallaig-Kyle-Stornoway link, and the transfer of services to Ullapool, was the cause of much CalMac-bashing throughout the year. The newly converted *Clansman* arrived at Ullapool to take up duties on 30 June. Three months later, the Glasgow-Stornoway cargo service via Tobermory ceased, and the cargo vessel *Lochdunvegan* was put up for sale. This left the *Loch Carron* to maintain a ten-day round-trip out of Glasgow, which included regular

*The **Jupiter** sporting her career aspirations on her sides, seen at Gourock in June 1974 [NR]*

STERN-LOADING AND DRIVE-THROUGH FERRIES – THE LINKSPAN ARRIVES VIA RICHBOROUGH, DOVER AND LARNE

ALTHOUGH MANY ESTUARIAL, roll-on/roll-off ferries were developed to serve the Tay, Clyde and Forth, and areas such as the Mersey and the Isle of Wight, the first sea-going stern-loaders were train-ferries. The first end-loader was, in fact, Scottish, namely the train-ferry *Leviathan*, connecting railway lines at Granton to those in that other Kingdom, at Burntisland in Fife, from 1850. Cross-Baltic services started in the 1900s, followed in 1917 by the first cross-Channel service between Richborough in Kent and Dunkerque, where their main use was the transport of special army wagons to supply military operations. In due course, these same ferries were put to civilian use by the Great Eastern Train Ferry Company, and the concept of roll-on, stern-loading ferries was firmly established. The first proper double-ended ferry to the Isle of Wight started in 1927. Even earlier than that, tow-boats with removable transoms had been used on Isle of Wight services to convey wheeled vehicles.

The first sea-going, stern-loading car-ferry was the Townsend ferry *Forde*, converted from a minesweeper in 1929. Linkspan bridges were not forthcoming at either Dover or Calais until the early 1950s, and the *Forde* was deprived of use as an end-loader for much of her commercial career. Only when the French were on strike was the ship able to reverse quietly against the quay at just the right stage of the tide to allow her wheeled cargo to drive ashore!

The next development was in 1933, when a trio of identical passenger train-ferries inaugurated the through 'Wagons Lits' services between London and various continental destinations. For the famous 'Night Ferry' service, a trough was built into the train ferry deck to receive the waste from the toilets on the train, requiring periodic flushing with sea water! The anthracite stoves aboard the coaches had to be dowsed down before boarding. The Train Ferry Dock was designed like a dry dock, so that it could be pumped down to a set level to provide the long-wheelbase passenger coaches with a horizontal track-bridge to the ship.

The first operational stern-loader was the Stranraer-Larne ferry, *Princess Victoria*, built to the order of the London, Midland & Scottish Railway by Denny at Dumbarton. Delivered just before the outbreak of the Second World War, her call-up saw her converted to a minelayer, using the stern doors to discharge her deadly cargo. However, she herself was mined in 1940. She was replaced by an almost identical ferry in 1946, and the new *Princess Victoria* was an instant success. Unlike modern ferries, she had a pair of low, hinged stern-gates that opened inwards to allow the shore linkspan to be dropped on to a pin set in the ship's deck. The garage deck could accommodate 40 cars, but had only a few small scuppers, which were later found to be too small to discharge water from the deck, should significant ingress occur. The *Princess Victoria* foundered, with the loss of 135 lives, on the afternoon of Saturday 31 January 1953, when her stern doors were battered inwards during a fierce storm. The nation listened to wireless reports of her failing condition, with free surface water on the car-deck, which could not be discharged through the scuppers.

The tragedy had a profound delaying-effect on the development of the roll-on, roll-off ferry throughout the United Kingdom. It was only in 1957 that a replacement for the *Princess Victoria* was even considered, and it was 1961 before the new ship, *Caledonian Princess*, now preserved as a static feature beneath the Tyne Bridge at Gateshead, finally arrived to take up service at Stranraer. At Dover, the *Lord Warden* had been delivered before the accident, but it was 1959 before the next purpose-built car-ferry, *Maid of Kent*, was commissioned.

Given this set-back to the railway fleets, it took the private company, Townsend Ferries, to show the lead. Their innovative, newly-built vessel, the stern-loader *Free Enterprise*, revolutionised the Dover-Calais crossing when she started work in 1962. She had two vehicle decks, and there was a turntable at the stern to reverse large vehicles on boarding, ready for departure at the other side of the Channel. Three years later, the *Free Enterprise II* arrived on the scene, and she was the first British drive-through vessel, complete with bow-visor access to the car-deck, as well as the normal stern door. These ships were really still car-ferries, although coaches and small lorries could be carried. It was only when the *Free Enterprise IV* class came out in 1969 that the vehicle-decks were designed with sufficient headroom to accommodate the larger freight vehicles of the day.

Purpose-built freight-ferries started with the *Bardic Ferry* and *Ionic Ferry* of the Atlantic Steam Navigation Company, first deployed between Preston and Larne in 1957. These ships were stern-loaders, with a vehicle deck headroom of 4.4 metres and top-quality accommodation for 50 drivers. The idea of mixing freight vehicles with private cars was, however, pioneered by the *Free Enterprise IV*-class of ship.

Given this background, the arrival in 1964 of 'the three fat ladies' of the *Hebrides*-class, with side-loading hoists, may seem a conservative response to contemporary developments in naval architecture and design. However, there were no linkspans on the islands, and the cost of providing them was not yet warranted, given the limited traffic on offer, compared with the needs of services between Dover and Calais, or Stranraer and Larne. The Isle of Man Steam Packet Company also built its first car-ferries in the 1960s – the turbine-steamer *Manx Maid* in 1962, and her sister *Ben-My-Chree* in 1966. Both vessels served the island until 1984, using side-loading ramp systems unique to the company's ships, as Man had no linkspans at that stage. Inter-island services in Orkney and Shetland went roll-on/roll-off in the 1980s, but services to the Scilly Isles remain to this day lift-on/lift-off.

The construction of the drive-through and side-loading MacBrayne ferry, *Iona*, in 1970 demonstrates that the Scottish Transport Group had responded with vengeful vigour to the jolt given to it by Western Ferries and their drive-through ferry, *Sound of Jura*. The *Iona* was an innovative, state-of-the-art vessel, requiring only that shore facilities be upgraded in order to sustain her end-loading capability. The *Pioneer* (1974) and *Claymore* (1978) were more conservative stern-loaders, not unlike oil-rig supply vessels, which served to develop the roll-on/roll-off trade to the islands. The *Lord of the Isles* (1989) forms the link between these early ferries and the modern, drive-through vehicle-ferries which are the mainstay of the present-day CalMac fleet.

Once prompted by Western Ferries, Caledonian MacBrayne rose to the new loading technology, and developed it to suit its own needs and levels of traffic. At the same time, the company had to develop linkspans and vehicle-marshalling areas at all of its many and varied ports, in order to support the vehicle ferries. Although never at the forefront of roll-on/roll-off development, the company has been quick to learn, and currently offers a modern fleet of drive-through ferries on nearly all its services.

The **Pioneer** arriving at West Loch Tarbert Pier on Wednesday 14 August 1974 on completion of her maiden round-trip to Port Ellen [NR]

The **Suilven** leaving Ullapool in August 1985 [NR]

calls at Stornoway. Like the *Claymore*, the cargo ships were technically still owned by a mythical enterprise called David MacBrayne Limited, and, as such, still wore pristine red-and-black funnels.

The fruits of several years' planning appeared during 1974. The first was the arrival from her builders of the new stern-loading ferry, *Jupiter*, for the Gourock-Dunoon link, starting on 19 March. Lest she have ideas of shunning her route for deeper seas, the ship's hull carried the words GOUROCK DUNOON FERRY in very large white letters. The vessel was highly manoeuvrable, being equipped with Voith Schneider cyclical propulsion units. For her size, she was also well-equipped with two lounges, originally a blue lounge and an orange lounge, the latter with a tea counter. She was joined by sister *Juno* in February 1975.

The new stern-loading ferry *Pioneer* arrived, via Oban, at West Loch Tarbert on 16 August, to replace the *Arran*. One of the authors was lucky enough to travel on her that same day, despite rain and leaden sky, which prevented photography. The impression was of a warm and airy vessel, completed with modern, easily-cleaned and readily-maintained finishes. She was, however, a big ship to navigate up to West Loch Tarbert, and her Master must have been conscious of the fate of earlier voyages in smaller vessels up and down the loch. The *Pioneer* suffered a minor fire alongside at West Loch Tarbert in October 1975, requiring the *Arran* to return on duty for a short while. The chain reaction of ships deputising one for another ended with the *Claymore* coming out of retirement one last time, before being sold for further

*The **Iona** heads
northwards through the
Sound of Mull. [DEM]*

service in the Eastern Mediterranean the following year (see Chapter 9).

The next new ship was the *Suilven*, which arrived at Gourock on 19 August from her Norwegian builders. She had been bought by Caledonian MacBrayne on the stocks for £2.25 million, and proved a good investment, quickly attracting some praise on the Ullapool service, which she took over from the *Clansman*. The latter then became something of a nomad, although Ardrossan-Brodick was her normal beat for some time.

The veteran turbine steamer *King George V* did not emerge from winter lay-up in 1974. The following year, she was sold to owners in Cardiff, and laid up. Regrettably, she was destroyed by fire in 1985, while being prepared for a static role on the Embankment in London as a replacement for the paddle-steamer *Caledonia*, which had also been destroyed by fire while in use at London. The other turbine steamer, which reverted to her original name of *Queen Mary* in 1976, was maintained in service until the end of the 1978

season. She was moved to London in 1981, and in 1988 finally opened as a restaurant, pub and conference centre opposite the Queen Elizabeth Hall. Although currently adorned in unpleasant shades of green and other pastel colours, she remains alongside the Embankment – minus her steam-turbine machinery. Clyde cruising was continued with the former Tilbury to Gravesend ferry *Rose*, acquired in 1967 for the Largs-Millport service and renamed *Keppel*. She was sold in 1992, but, when not required elsewhere, the *Pioneer* picked up some of the Clyde cruise venues in the 1990s.

In the winter of 1975/76, the subsidy required to maintain the *Loch Carron* in service on the Glasgow cargo routes was increased to £350 000 per year. She made her final sailing to the Western Isles on 7 November 1976, as it was stated that the improved ferry timetables would be able to cope with any additional goods traffic. Almost overnight, the cost of fuel shot up to giddy heights in Tiree, because the *Iona*, then on the Tiree-Coll-Barra-Lochboisdale service, could not land fuel-tankers at Scarinish pier. The disgruntled islanders complained to the highest authority to whom they could gain access, and for several evenings there was a rebellious air in the well-known 'Lean To' (bar) of the Scarinish Hotel! A puffer had to be chartered once a month to relieve the island by means of fuel carried in barrels. Normally, Tiree received its coal in puffers, but now petrol and diesel were also coming by this traditional means. A similar arrangement had to be made for Barra. The great shipping revolution was momentarily going in reverse.

The *Iona* finally came of age in 1976, when she was sent to Robb Caledon at Leith for the addition of 16 berths on the bridge deck, the extension of her engine exhaust uptakes aft, and the removal of the quaint, flower-pot, dummy funnel which perched precariously on the after edge of the bridge. The exhaust uptakes were painted in the company colours, instead of being concealed as part of the white superstructure. What a difference it made! At last, the *Iona* resembled a businesslike ferry, with her appearance verging on the attractive.

The next innovation on the Clyde was the introduction by Western Ferries of the 27-knot catamaran *Highland Seabird* on commuter services based at Rothesay. Two previous high-speed initiatives had already failed: eleven years earlier, when Clyde Hover Ferries' small hovercraft was found not to be equal to the autumn gales, and again in 1970, when Caledonian MacBrayne flirted with an HM2-011 hovercraft at the Dunoon station. Western Ferries' attempt also failed. Either commuters were very conservative or the schedules were not quite right, but the Clyde duties of the *Highland Seabird* proved loss-making, and depended on summer tourists to maintain loadings. The *Highland Seabird* later saw service at Oban and elsewhere, finally being withdrawn in 1981.

Western Ferries' larger unit, the *Sound of Jura*, was sold in the autumn of 1976 leaving the original smaller vessel, *Sound of Islay*, on the Kennacraig-Port Askaig service. The *Pioneer* closed the old pier at West Loch Tarbert once and for all, with a final departure on 25 June 1978. Thereafter,

she shared the Western Ferries Terminal at Kennacraig with the *Sound of Islay*. Access to the linkspan at Kennacraig had finally been granted to Caledonian MacBrayne when Western Ferries were obliged to give up their lease on the terminal. This situation was quite unjust, as Western Ferries, who undoubtedly had the lion's share of the Islay business until 1974, were being ousted from their route by the state operator supported by a government subsidy. The matter was summed up in a letter addressed to the editor of *Sea Breezes* by A. G. Wilson, then Director of Western Ferries (Argyll), pointing out an error in an article which had appeared in the December 1987 edition of the magazine, written by one of the authors of this book. Written by a fair-minded Englishman, the article mistakenly suggested that both operators were due a subsidy (see Appendix B). History has told us many times before that Highland wars are not conducted on level ground! Not surprisingly, the *Sound of Islay* was withdrawn on 30 September 1981, leaving Caledonian MacBrayne once again in charge.

One of the key changes that hastened the demise of Western Ferries' foothold on the Islay service was the set of new rules for the government subsidy required by the Scottish Transport Group. From 1975 onwards, the subsidy was dispensed as a single sum of money per year to the operator to support all of his services collectively, and was no longer allied to a particular route or service. This meant that a subsidy could be attracted by the state operator, even though, in this case, he was operating in direct competition with the private sector. This had led to the earlier sale of the *Sound of Jura* and the return of the relatively poorly-equipped *Sound of Islay* (previously used on the Red Bay, County Antrim, to Campbeltown service) – and the inevitable withdrawal of a most enterprising operator from the service.

The company (or its associate Western Ferries (Argyll) Limited) was yet to gain a victory, and success may be sweet if it takes over the vehicle service from Gourock to Dunoon in the near future. Caledonian MacBrayne actually threatened withdrawal of the Dunoon ferry in 1981, when

*The **Claymore** departing Gott Bay pier, Tiree, on a crisp November morning in 1984 [NR]*

*The **Lochmor** setting out from Kyle on a rainy day in April 1984 [NR]*

the subsidy for the route was about to be passed to Western Ferries, and it was planned that the *Highland Seabird* would provide a passenger-only service to Gourock thereafter. In the end, a compromise was reached.

A new double-ended ferry, the *Isle of Cumbrae*, took up station at Largs in February 1977. The much-delayed *Saturn* finally took up duty at Wemyss Bay in February 1978. Similar to the earlier *Juno* and *Jupiter*, she had her bridge one deck higher to improve vision aft, and the words ROTHESAY FERRY were painted along her hull. She replaced the *Glen Sannox*, which had been maintaining the route since May. The last season for the Clyde excursion steamer *Queen Mary* was 1977, and she was replaced on Clyde excursion duties in 1978 by the *Glen Sannox*. That year, children usually left the ship at the end of the day adorned in stickers, proclaiming, 'I've been on the *Glen Sannox*', and the ship herself carried not one, but two, thin white bands on her hull to signify her importance on the Clyde. The *Glen Sannox* maintained a summer excursion and winter relief role until the early 1980s, when the summer excursions were withdrawn. Her thirtieth anniversary was publicised by a commemorative pictorial booklet, and there were special sailings, but at the end of the 1987 season the *Glen Sannox* was withdrawn from service.

In December 1978, the new ferry *Claymore* was delivered to Gourock from the Robb Caledon yard at Leith. Under the command of Captain John Gray, she took over the Oban duties from the *Iona* on 2 January. Once again a ship named *Claymore* was sailing daily into Scarinish *en route* for the Outer Isles, although calls at Lochaline

*The **Lord of the Isles** arriving at Oban on 7 June 2005 [NR]*

ceased in 1980. Then, following a refit at Troon, the *Iona* went to Kennacraig, releasing the *Pioneer* so that she could sail to Leith for the fitting of a side-loading hoist, ready to take up duties between Mallaig and Armadale. The *Iona* had finally arrived on her design route – eight years after she had been commissioned! During the customary winter storms, the former Oban to Lismore ferry, *Loch Toscaig*, which had been sold to owners in London in 1975, but had subsequently returned to the Clyde to give fishing trips out of Gourock, broke away from her moorings, and after smashing into both the *Saturn* and the *Arran*, promptly

sank in the middle of Cardwell Bay.

Time was running out for the smaller, wooden-hulled motor-vessels remaining in the fleet. The *Loch Arkaig* sank at Mallaig Pier on the night of 28 March 1979. A hole the size of a football was found in her wooden hull, apparently matching a projection from the quay that fitted perfectly. The *Loch Arkaig* was raised and put up for sale, ending her days in Dubai and eventually lost off Cadiz in 1985. Not a moment too soon, the *Lochmor* emerged from her builders at Troon in mid-summer 1979 to take up the Small Isles

THE POST-1970 CAR-FERRIES

FROM 1973, THE Caledonian MacBrayne fleet underwent rapid transformation, thanks to the acquisition of significantly more capital than was available in the 1960s. The first phase of the new programme witnessed the departure of virtually all the older pre-1970, non-vehicular vessels by 1976. Ship types were reduced from six to three, and finally to two by the 1990s – 'Major Vehicle Ferries' and 'Small Vehicle Ferries'.

The 'Major Vehicle Ferries' differed radically in appearance and design from the motor-ships which had served the Hebrides prior to 1963-64, when the Hebrides, Clansman and Columba made their appearance (see Appendix A). These vessels, with their high slab-sides, broad beams, and rather squat and ungainly profiles on the water, incorporated design principles which were, and remained, fundamental to ships of that kind. These principles have been enunciated by Ian Ramsay, in the course of reading the first draft of this book:

The overall design of the modern CalMac car-ferry is primarily determined by the maximum length, height and loaded weight of the largest vehicle that can use our motorway system. The maximum height determines the tween-deck height of the garage, and the required mix of private and commercial vehicles in turn determines the length and breadth of the ship. The breadth has also to be sufficient to give adequate stability when loaded with the maximum and most demanding cargo deadweight, as the cargo is all carried above the waterline. The above established breadth and associated length are usually sufficient to give the maximum required displacement on a draft that is limited by the available depth of water alongside the piers and harbours that the vessel's routes require.

Because of the height of the garage deck, the passenger accommodation is perched on top of it at a considerable distance above the waterline, and the fairly wide beam means that large spatial areas for passengers and facilities are available. This is all quite at odds with the design concept of the mail-boats like the Loch Seaforth and the Claymore.

This height of topsides and breadth of ship comes at a price – violent rolling – and, if ships on the more exposed routes were unstabilised, there would arise a loud cacophony of complaint.

The harbinger of the new-style car-ferries for the Hebrides was the Iona (1970), which differed from the Columba and her sisters by having bow-, stern- and side-loading facilities, the side-loading facilities having been placed aft of the main superstructure. The Iona, with her somewhat slimmer look, had a much more 'metallic' feel to her than the earlier triad of car-ferries. With their wooden decks and top-rails, and their varnished internal finish, the older vessels preserved something of the style of the mail-boat era. The Iona was steered by a gyro-compass and autopilot, in contrast to the traditional wheel and compass of her predecessors. Gyro-compass and autopilot became the norm for all such vessels thereafter.

The Iona was followed by a second new ship for Islay, the Pioneer (1974). The Pioneer had a noticeably 'straight-lined' hull, with little or no sheer, which gave the impression that she was sailing permanently 'bows down'. The Pioneer's improved half-sister, the Claymore (1978), with her lofty forward superstructure, had better lines, and she was somewhat less stark internally than the Iona. Her passenger space, however, seemed restricted. The combination of cafeteria and saloon was cramped, and not conducive to relaxation. The handsome, Norwegian-built, drive-through vessel Suilven (1974) was much less of a 'skyscraper'. In layout, she was also closer to the traditional Hebridean motor-vessel, with a separate saloon and cafeteria. She was a 'warm' ship in terms of her atmosphere, and a very good sea-boat, as her later adventures in colossal waves on the Cook Strait, New Zealand, have confirmed.

The 1980s witnessed a maturing of design for the second generation of post-1970 car-ferries. These have been given much more attractive layouts and longer, more balanced superstructures than the cramped and rather 'front-heavy' profiles of the Pioneer and the Claymore. They offer drive-through facilities and much improved passenger accommodation, mainly because they are much larger ships. The improved Pioneer

class comprised the robust and chunky Hebridean Isles (1985), and the neatly constructed and very personable (though rather small) Lord of the Isles (1989), both of which have bow-, stern- and side-loading facilities, and the twin exhaust-vents characteristic of the class. The Hebridean Isles has a very distinct and hospitable 'personality', and has been particularly well maintained over more than twenty years.

These ships were complemented by the Isle of Mull (1988), a handsome one-funnelled vessel without side-loading, designed for drive-through operation between Oban and Craignure. Originally overweight, the Isle of Mull was given a midships section to remedy serious deadweight problems. This demonstrates that, even in the late 1980s, it was still possible for shipyards to make surprising – and presumably very costly – mistakes with regard to the essential ratios in car-ferry design. The Isle of Mull was much enhanced by her lengthening, and came to resemble the Suilven, with a fine cafeteria and a sense of 'spacious living'. Her general design appears to have been copied in the Caledonian Isles (1993), built specifically for the Ardrossan-Brodick run (see 'Little and Large'). All three ships – Hebridean Isles, Isle of Mull and Lord of the Isles – give excellent service, and are still capable of performing very effectively on all the main CalMac inter-island routes, and further afield.

The third generation of car-ferries began in 1995 with the very large Isle of Lewis (6,750 tons gross – over five times the size of the 1955 Claymore!). Spacious and fast (18.9 knots), she is a much enhanced version of the Lord of the Isles, but twin-vented and thus still representative of the basic Pioneer class. She has proved herself to be a very capable vessel, providing (in summer) two sailings per day from Ullapool to Stornoway, and she is well regarded by passengers. The Isle of Lewis appears to have been influential in the design of NorthLink's three fine, new car-ferries, Hjaltland, Hrossey and Hamnavoe, which were built with funding from the Royal Bank of Scotland, as a 50% partner with Caledonian MacBrayne in the first NorthLink venture. These vessels have particularly excellent passenger accommodation.

The Isle of Lewis was followed in 1998 by the new

Clansman, built for £15 million to a superbly efficient design, particularly well suited to the conveyance of vehicles. More streamlined and less sharply angular than the improved *Pioneer* class, but rather bluff at the bows (which produce a very large and impressive bow-wave at 16.5 knots), the *Clansman* resembles a cross between the earlier *Suilven* and the current *Isle of Mull*, with the *Lord of the Isles* as a key 'link' in the design. Instead of the two biscuit-tin side-vents which have been a rather starkly functional feature of the *Pioneer*-class vessels from the outset, the *Clansman* was given a wedge-shaped, elongated funnel, unfortunately obscured to some extent by large lifeboats on either side. The funnel also acts as a plinth for her skimpy and perfunctory after-mast, in a manner similar to that of the *Suilven* and the *Isle of Mull*. By contemporary standards she is an attractive ship, seen to best advantage when observed directly on her port or starboard beam. When viewed from the bow or quarter, she tends to look rather high and overweight, with somewhat contradictory lines.

Despite her innovative features, however, the *Clansman* was spoilt by several design faults. Apart from the observation lounge forward, she had a rather cold and bland 'formica finish' in the seating areas. This, together with a lack of passenger deck-space, suggested that not enough thought had been given to the needs of the travelling public, or that safety-railing for the spacious and greatly under-utilised bridge deck had proved too costly. Considering her position in the evolution of the motor-vessel, she had a surprising amount of vibration, which disappointed many passengers, as it was particularly evident in the observation lounge and the cafeteria. In the latter area, it was initially so bad that cups of tea would develop 'water-spouts' and spill their contents on to the table. This fault has now been rectified to some extent, by providing better fixings for tables and chairs, and by mechanical improvements, particularly to her rudders, which caused considerable problems in late 1998 and early 1999. Significantly, however, the *Clansman* is 'quietest' and least liable to vibrate when she is fully laden, suggesting an underlying problem in the deadweight-to-engine-power ratio. Since 2003, her external passenger space has been extended, though not significantly increased. Notwithstanding her design faults and teething-troubles, the vessel

has become a highly successful and reliable member of the fleet, much appreciated by car-drivers and truckers. When she has to be withdrawn from service for annual overhaul or repair, she is certainly missed.

The *Clansman*'s design problems were eradicated in the building of her very well-appointed sister-ship, *Hebrides*, for the 'Hebridean triangle' in 2001. As reported in *Sea Breezes* in October 2001, the *Hebrides* is 'the first new CalMac ship to feature accommodation designed by an internal design architect. The result is a pleasing arrangement with attractive décor that concentrates on a combination of dark reds, various shades of brown and creams, together with contrasting colours such as the blue found in the seating of the café. Fitting out of the accommodation was undertaken by Ferguson's own joinery department and the finishes are of a very high standard.' The *Hebrides* has a cleaner look aft, largely because she does not carry bulky lifeboats, which in turn allows more deck space for passengers. She is equipped, instead, with the latest chute-operated Marine Evacuation System. Her hull carries the tell-tale connecting-lines by which her life-rafts would be towed by two fast rescue craft in the event of an emergency. She is also slightly different from the *Clansman* in the design of her bow. She carries the bell of the first *Hebrides*, built for John McCallum & Co. in 1898.

A particularly fine example of modern 'customised' shipbuilding is the delightfully compact 'mini-ferry' *Lochnevis* (2000), built for the Small Isles service. As is the case with the *Hebrides*, her performance and general suitability to her design route are greatly appreciated by islanders.

The larger vessels are complemented by the 'Island' and 'Loch' classes of 'Small Vehicle Ferries', which, in one form or another, have undertaken the shorter island-mainland 'hops' very effectively for some thirty years. The 'Loch' class is far from pretty, but it is highly functional. The use of these 'Major' and 'Small' ferries gives Caledonian MacBrayne great flexibility across a varied network, which has been gradually upgraded on-shore by the installation of new linkspans.

*The **Lord of the Isles** prepares to turn on the knuckle of Tiree pier in May 2006. [DEM]*

*The **Isle of Lewis** approaches Ullapool. [Rhoda Meek]*

*The **Hebrides** leaves Uig, Skye, in July 2006. [DEM]*

*The **Claymore** at Tiree [NR]*

service out of Kyle and Mallaig. This had been provided by the small landing-craft type ferry, *Morvern*, since the sinking of the *Loch Arkaig*. The islanders, however, judged the new *Lochmor* a spartan vessel, although she maintained her duties reliably and almost without missing a sailing.

In 1980, the name of David MacBrayne Limited finally disappeared, and the company became dormant, when its remaining assets, the *Iona* and two motor launches, were transferred to Caledonian MacBrayne. This was a consequence of steeply-rising fuel-oil prices at this time, as well as the realisation that Caledonian MacBrayne could never be free of subsidies. There was little point in keeping the subsidised routes separate under the MacBrayne banner. MacBrayne Haulage survived a little longer, however. Following criticism in the 1983 Monopolies and Mergers report of preferential rates for the Caledonian MacBrayne subsidiary, MacBrayne Haulage was finally sold out of the company in 1985.

Following the transfer of David MacBrayne's assets, Caledonian MacBrayne, with Colin Paterson at the helm as Chief Executive, and Sandy Struthers as Chairman, undertook a huge investment programme, which was at its height in the 1980s, and led to the building of a number of innovative, drive-through ferries. These were the *Isle of Arran*, originally for the Arran crossing, launched in 1984; the *Hebridean Isles*, for the Uig triangle, launched in 1985; the *Isle of Mull*, launched in 1987, for the Oban-Craignure crossing; and the *Lord of the Isles*, launched in 1989. The *Lord of the Isles* was a revision of the basic *Pioneer*-type of design, much enlarged and improved, with accommodation vastly superior to that of the *Claymore*. Early in life, she had to have a replacement engine (commandeered from the *Caledonian Isles*, then building at Lowestoft), and her other engine required to be rebuilt. In terms of Darwinian evolution, economies of scale and inevitable increase in capacity as time goes on, the immensely successful *Lord of the Isles* provides the link between the *Pioneer*-type ferry and the subsequent *Isle of Lewis* and younger ferries. The large *Caledonian Isles*, which made her maiden voyage on 25 August 1993, replaced the *Isle of Arran* at Ardrossan;

*The **Hebridean Isles** started work at Oban when first delivered. She is seen there on 10 March 1986. [NR]*

and the largest ship yet built for Caledonian MacBrayne, the *Isle of Lewis*, launched in 1995, took up the Ullapool-Stornoway service.

The most recent additions are the *Clansman,* which has maintained the Oban-Coll-Tiree and Oban-Lochboisdale services since 1998, and the *Hebrides,* which has been on the 'Hebridean Triangle', between Uig, Tarbert and Lochmaddy, since 2001. The building of the new vessels attracted significant European Union grants. For example, £3.3 million was given towards the building-costs of the *Isle of Mull.* Typically, the bigger ships require two crews of just under thirty, who work on the basis of two-weeks-on and two-weeks-off.

The new car-ferries did not arrive problem-free, and some had significant teething-troubles. Within her first year of service, the *Hebridean Isles* required the installation of 60 tonnes of ballast in her stern to improve her handling. Worse still, the *Isle of Mull* suffered serious deadweight problems when new, and during her first season in operation she was unable to carry anything like her design load. In the autumn of 1988, she was sent to Middlesbrough, where an extra 5.4 metre section was inserted just forward of the funnel, in order to increase her net tonnage. At the outset, the *Lord of the Isles* suffered recurrent difficulties with propeller-shaft bearings, and the *Clansman* required several dockings to address rudder deficiencies.

The complete rebuilding of the fleet – unparalleled since the days of Coast Lines and the London, Midland & Scottish Railway in the 1930s – was, however, well under way. As had happened fifty years before, the older ferries were displaced, one by one. The three original side-loading ferries went first. The *Clansman* was sold in 1984 to Torbay Ferries, but resold to Maltese owners because of berthing restrictions at Torquay. The *Hebrides* actually saw service on the Torquay-based Channel Isles service between 1987 and 1991, and the *Columba* was sold in 1988, after acting as the CalMac reserve vessel for a number of years.

Remarkably, the *Columba* was converted into a very up-market cruise ship – not a role that any islander who saw her struggling with sheep, cattle, cars and boxes could possibly have envisaged for the 'fat lady'. Her unexpected elevation was perhaps foreshadowed, when, in May 1979, she ran the first (non-landing) excursion to St Kilda. The trip was repeated for a number of years, although in 1987 it had to be postponed from May to August because of gales. Another pointer to the future can now be seen – retrospectively, of course! – in the chartering of the *Columba* to Howard Doris in May 1983. On that occasion, the ship – which berthed at Howard Doris's pier at Strome Ferry, MacBrayne's former terminal (1880-97) for sailings to Skye and Lewis – carried the Prince of Wales to the Phillips Petroleum Group's platform, *Maureen,* moored at the mouth of Loch Kishorn. Disembarking from the *Columba,* the Prince named and toured the platform, which Howard Doris had recently completed.

When the *Columba* was upgraded, Justin Merrigan reported in *Sea Breezes,* July 1989:

> The former Caledonian MacBrayne ferry **Columba** was renamed **Hebridean Princess** by the Duchess of York at Great Yarmouth on 26 April and in turn the Duchess was presented a bouquet by Louise Maclean, aged nine, from Inverness. Louise won the title 'Hebridean Princess' for the day after her grandmother entered her in a competition to find 'a special little Scottish girl'. Louise had twice given bone marrow to save her sister's life and now she gets a cruise aboard the **Hebridean Princess** for herself and her family.

> With a certificate for just 45 passengers, the **Hebridean Princess** started cruising in May 1989 from Oban to Mull, Skye, Arran, Eigg, Harris, Jura, Colonsay and St Kilda. Captain Ian Cameron, a former Chief Officer with Union-Castle and latterly serving with Caledonian MacBrayne, has been appointed master of the ship.

Ownership of the *Hebridean Princess* passed to Hebridean Cruises plc in 1998. By then her accommodation had been modified in the style of a five-star, country-house hotel, and her remaining vehicle deck space had been taken up by new crew cabins. This was a further luxurious make-over for the

NEW
ROLES
FOR OLD
FERRIES

The **Pentalina-B**, formerly the **Iona**, spent four years laid up at St Margaret's Hope in Orkney before being recommissioned for a new service across the Pentland Firth for Pentland Ferries. [NR]

Sea Containers' **Claymore** was placed on a new and short-lived service between Campbeltown and Ballycastle. She also is now owned by Pentland Ferries and works alongside the **Pentalina-B**, still with her original name. [NR]

former 'fat lady'. Now she required 37 crew to serve her own needs and those of her final passenger complement of 49. Although her external appearance has not altered greatly, it remains a challenge for those familiar with the earlier *Columba* to believe that this glamorous 'royal' is still the same ship. As if to remove any doubt, the royal status of the *Hebridean Princess* was more than amply confirmed when, in August 2006, Her Majesty Queen Elizabeth sailed on the little vessel for her eightieth birthday cruise to the Hebrides. This 'rust to riches' story – from car-ferry *Columba* to *Hebridean Princess* to Royal Yacht – is quite probably unique in maritime history.

To the present, the *Hebridean Princess* graces the Western Isles, gliding at her characteristic, leisurely pace, as she sails across calm summer waters to a quiet overnight anchorage. She makes occasional longer forays to Ireland, around Britain and even to Scandinavia and Iceland, but most of the more distant destinations fall to her international consort, the *Hebridean Spirit*, formerly the small cruise ship *Megastar Capricorn*. Cruising in the Western Isles is now also supported by Noble Caledonia, with the tiny *Lord of the Glens*, which maintains a ten-day, summer-cruise roster in alternate directions between Inverness and Ullapool, via the Caledonian Canal, calling at Eigg, Rum, Muck and Skye.

Other former members of the Caledonian MacBrayne fleet assumed much more mundane roles, more in keeping with their earlier duties. The *Suilven* was displaced from the Stornoway crossing in 1995 by the new *Isle of Lewis*, and she moved to New Zealand, where she ran for Strait Shipping between Wellington and Picton, and gained a reputation for battling her way through immense waves in stormy conditions. She then moved to Fiji, where she operates for Suilven Shipping. Her arrival led to fare-slashing by rival operators, in a context not entirely dissimilar to that in which other former CalMac vessels found themselves. The pioneering drive-through ferry, *Iona*, completed her service on the Mallaig-Armadale crossing in 1997, and was bought by a new company called Pentland Ferries, who intended to provide a service between St Margaret's Hope in Orkney and Gills Bay in Caithness. For a variety of reasons, the ship, now renamed the *Pentalina B*, was laid up for four years at St Margaret's Hope, pending the start of the new service. She was chartered briefly to the Oban-Craignure service in April 1998 to help Caledonian MacBrayne, when shortage of tonnage (caused partly by the sale of the *Claymore*) and breakdowns almost crippled their main services, while they awaited delivery of the new *Clansman*.

Pentalina B was joined in 2002 by the *Claymore* (no change of name), which, at the insistence of Michael Forsyth, then Conservative Secretary of State for Scotland, had been compulsorily sold by CalMac in 1997 to Sea Containers Limited for their new Campbeltown-Ballycastle service. The idea was that competition should be encouraged, and that such competition would be good for the west coast. Events proved otherwise. Despite appropriate subsidy, the service was withdrawn after only two years. It was re-offered for tender in 2005 – unsuccessfully.

A series of double-ended ('Loch' class) ferries was introduced to take over from the *Kilbrannan* / 'Island' class of landing-craft ferry. The most recent of these is the *Loch Alainn*, which served the Largs-Cumbrae Slip route. Two new ships were built for the Kyle-Kyleakin (Skye) ferry in 1991, the *Loch Dunvegan* and the *Loch Fyne*, both of which have been redeployed since the opening of the Skye Bridge in October 1995, but only after protracted lay-up and attempts to sell them. They are now recognised as valuable fleet units. In the last season before the bridge opened, the Mallaig-Armadale route, operated by the *Iona* between 1989 and 1997, witnessed a huge increase in traffic: 57% in commercial vehicles, and 67% in coaches, in one year. The predictable comment was, of course, that, 'This just goes to prove that people still want to sail over the sea to Skye'.

In 1990, the Scottish Transport Group was dismantled, and Caledonian MacBrayne was transferred to the ownership of the Secretary of State for Scotland and subsequently to the Scottish Executive. In preparation for the demise of the Scottish Transport Group, the Scottish Office had

BUILDING THE CAR-FERRIES

THE SPECIALIST NEEDS of the 1963-64 car-ferries, *Hebrides*, *Clansman* and *Columba*, must have taxed the naval architect dearly. Requirements included the operational use of side-loading hoists (in the days before shore-based end-loading via linkspans), as well as military specification such as reinforced vehicle decks, exterior spray systems and a hermetically sealed citadel within the main superstructure. The latter were not as eccentric as they may now seem, but were incorporated so that the ships (which, after all, belonged to the Secretary of State) could become hospital ships in the event of a nuclear conclusion to the Cold War. For the first time, David MacBrayne Limited forsook the Clyde. It selected the Aberdeen shipbuilders, Hall, Russell. The loss of this contract to Hall, Russell prompted William Denny & Bros. to make the fateful decision to put the company into voluntary liquidation, and close the shipyards and engine works.

As the car-ferry revolution gathered pace, MacBrayne's (operating as Caledonian MacBrayne after 1973) further diversified its shipbuilding strategy. The innovatory *Iona* (1970) was placed with Ailsa

Shipbuilding, Troon. Ailsa also built several of the company's smaller vessels in the 1970s, as well as the fine little *Lochnevis* (2000) for the Small Isles service. The *Pioneer* (1974) and her 'improved sister', the *Claymore* (1978), were constructed by Robb Caledon, Leith. The *Kilbrannan*/ 'Island'-class vessels were all built by James Lamont & Co., Port Glasgow.

When workable car-ferry designs had been well established, the most prominent builder of the company's key vessels in the 1980s and 1990s became Ferguson Shipbuilders, Port Glasgow, who produced the *Isle of Arran* (1984), the *Isle of Mull* (1988), the *Lord of the Isles* (1989), the *Isle of Lewis* (1995) and the *Hebrides* (2001). In virtually all instances, the Ferguson yard developed much enhanced versions of earlier models. These, in turn, influenced the designs of later ships.

Despite its strong connections with Scottish shipyards, however, Caledonian MacBrayne has not restricted its orders to Scotland. In the 1990s and the early 2000s, it chose English shipbuilders for three of its large vessels, namely the *Hebridean Isles* (1985), built by Cochrane's of Selby, the *Caledonian Isles*

(1993), built by Richard Shipbuilders, Lowestoft, and the *Clansman* (1998), built by Appledore Ferguson, Devon. Appledore also produced the innovative *Coruisk* (2003), completed just as the firm was going into liquidation. McTay's of the Wirral built the *Loch Portain* (2003).

Caledonian MacBrayne was now prepared to look beyond Britain. For the first time in its history, it placed an order with the Remontowa Group in Gdansk, Poland, who undertook the construction of the well-appointed car-ferry *Bute* (2005), which operates in the Firth of Clyde. Like the ordering of vessels from English yards, this change of pattern reflects not only the decline of British shipbuilding and the closure of several yards with which Caledonian MacBrayne had previously placed orders – sometimes the last undertaken by these yards – but also the parity and transparency in competition now required by the European Commission. However, Caledonian MacBrayne's order for the *Loch Shira* (2006), for the Largs-Cumbrae Slip service, was placed with Ferguson's, Port Glasgow.

announced in 1989 that the Clyde services would be privatised. This attracted the attention of commercial ferry companies – P&O, Sealink, and, of course, Western Ferries. Since then, the privatisation debate, coupled with European directives that Caledonian MacBrayne should actually be bidding for its own routes, has been recurrent (see Chapter 12).

Nevertheless, in the twenty-one years that the Scottish Transport Group existed, 26 new drive-through ferries had been commissioned, 8 existing vessels converted for roll-on/ roll-off use, and appropriate shore facilities constructed at 19 terminals. Numerous new and diverse routes were introduced by means of the small ferries (the *Kilbrannan* / 'Island' class, and latterly the *Loch* class). These now provide direct connections between islands, and between islands and mainland, furnishing the best network hitherto

to serve islander and tourist alike.

As new car-ferries arrived for the longer crossings, some daring experiments were conducted with the shorter routes in the Clyde estuary and elsewhere. The passenger-only catamaran, *Ali Cat* ('Ali' being the daughter of the owners), entered service on the Dunoon roster on 21 October 2002, to allow two car-ferries to operate on the Wemyss Bay to Rothesay service. The *Ali Cat* is chartered from the Hampshire-based company, Red Funnel, who in turn had chartered her from Solent & Wightline Cruises. Two new services commenced in 1995, between Tarbert and Portavadie on Loch Fyne, and in December between Ballycastle and Rathlin Island in County Antrim. The latter was operated under contract to the Department for Regional Development in Northern Ireland, using the *Kilbrannan* / 'Island'-class vessel, *Canna*.

Recent new additions to the fleet (without exception constructed only after a token Scottish £1 coin has been placed beneath the keel) include the delightful little *Lochnevis* on the Small Isles run out of Mallaig, delivered in 2000, and her rather less delightful, seasonal counterpart on the summer Mallaig-Armadale crossing, namely the *Coruisk*, built in 2003. The latter is a particularly tall vessel, resembling a disproportionately shortened version of one of the 'Raptor' class of ferries currently serving the Isle of Wight. Her motion and performance, controlled by ultra-sophisticated electronic systems, were initially highly unpredictable, to the extent that she struck rocks off Mallaig Harbour in her first week of service, and inspired some disparaging letter-writing in the *West Highland Free Press*. This, together with her 'stacked up and square' appearance, which resembles a Babylonian ziggurat and is not particularly well-suited to West Highland weather, earned her the locally-bestowed nickname, the 'Tower of

Babel'! Since her first embarrassing capers, the 'Tower of Babel' has mended her ways, and has become a reliable, economical and flexible unit. In winter she is deployed to the Clyde, where she provides relief on various routes.

The arrival of the *Coruisk* and the *Lochnevis* coincided with the completion of linkspans at both Mallaig and Armadale. This released the *Lord of the Isles* from her five-year spell on the Mallaig-Armadale crossing, and allowed her to be reassigned to the Oban-Outer Isles and Oban-Inner Isles services, which made much better use of her good facilities. In addition, the *Loch Portain* arrived from her builders, McTay's of the Wirral, in 2003 to take over the Sound of Harris service from the *Loch Bhrùsda*, which was able to move on to the Eriskay-Barra route. The end- and side-loading *Pioneer*, which had served the Mallaig-Armadale crossing between 1979 and 1989, returned briefly to this duty when the *Coruisk* 'misbehaved', and had to be withdrawn for repairs. The immensely versatile

*The **European Trader** was renamed **Taygran Trader** on sale to Taygran Shipping Company for use on the Stornoway to Ullapool night freight ferry service. [NR]*

Pioneer finally left Caledonian MacBrayne in 2004, and, as the *Brenda Corlett*, she is now sailing in West Africa.

As Hebridean routes received new vessels, the replacement of long-serving ferries on the Firth of Clyde continued apace in the early 2000s. The brand-new vessel, *Bute*, designed to run between Wemyss Bay and Rothesay, was delivered from her Polish builders in the summer of 2005, with a sister, *Argyle*, delivered from the same yard in 2007. A third new ship, *Loch Shira*, now serves the Largs-Cumbrae Slip route, replacing the *Loch Riddon*.

Despite such welcome progress, the network developed significant gaps, partly because of the success of car-ferries and the progressive acquisition of expectant and economically powerful custom, especially in heavy haulage. History is a great teacher, provided that the student is willing to listen – and learn. If the student does not listen and learn, history is liable to repeat itself. In 2001, a group of businessmen centred on the Harris Tweed and road haulage industries decided that their pleas for a dedicated night-freight ferry to Ullapool had gone unanswered for long enough, and

took matters into their own hands. Forming the Aberdeen-registered company, Taygran Shipping Limited, they put the chartered freight ferry *White Sea* on the run, replacing her four months later, on 15 June, with the former P&O ferry from Larne, *European Trader*, which had previously been based at Dover.

Under the name *Taygran Trader*, the company's own ship duly arrived at Stornoway. Taygran claimed that they would soon get her up to passenger status and that they would also have a fast craft for cars and passengers available. Taygran also had eyes on what they saw as more profitable routes, such as Ardrossan-Brodick. With alleged debts to Harland & Wolff's shipyard at Belfast and unpaid port dues at both Ullapool and Stornoway, the company inevitably went bankrupt, the end coming at the close of 2001 amid various slanging-matches, not least with one of the major island haulage companies. The matter was politely summed up by the *West Highland Free Press*:

The future of the private ferry operator on the Stornoway-Ullapool route was hanging by a thread this week after

The modern lines of the NorthLink ferry **Hjaltland** are attractive yet functional. [NR]

the company was served with a court order which prevents them from setting sail until pier dues worth £52,000 are paid. The development could deal a fatal blow to Taygran Shipping Limited, who have run a daily cut-price freight service for the last six months in competition with Caledonian MacBrayne.

The writ was served by sheriff officers acting for Stornoway Pier and Harbour Commission on Tuesday afternoon, leaving the **Taygran Trader** stranded at the quayside, with CalMac's **Isle of Lewis** left to accommodate as much of the lorry traffic as possible.

As we went to press yesterday afternoon it emerged that CalMac were ready to carry out an extra run, leaving Stornoway at 2am on Thursday. It is understood that Taygran also owe a significant sum of money to the Ullapool Harbour Trustees, as well as other companies. Further legal action could now follow.

Caledonian MacBrayne responded to the demand by putting the *Isle of Arran* on a night-freight run. Then the newly-acquired NorthLink freighter, the *Hascosay*, which has capacity for carrying 1000 cattle or 3500 sheep, was deployed on the service until required for the new company's own services in October 2002. The former P&O vessel *Belard* (Belfast to Ardrossan) was then chartered, as the permanent Stornoway freight vessel, from Harrison's (Clyde) Limited, who currently also manage the vessel for Caledonian MacBrayne. Renamed *Mùirneag*, she generally leaves Stornoway at 23.30, with additional trips subject to demand.

Caledonian MacBrayne, partnered by the Royal Bank of Scotland, successfully tendered to the Scottish Executive in 2000 to take over the P&O Scottish Ferries services. The latter had maintained the links from Aberdeen to Orkney and Shetland, and between Scrabster in Caithness and Stromness on Mainland Orkney. Prior to the 1970s, these were, of course, the bailiwick of the North of Scotland, Orkney & Shetland Shipping Company (The North Company). Three brand-new ferries were introduced. The *Hjaltland* and *Hrossey*, each with capacity for 600 passengers and 460 lane-metres of vehicle space, plus a small lower deck for a further 25 cars, are based at Aberdeen, and the smaller ferry, *Hamnavoe*, looks after the Scrabster service. The second-hand vehicle ferry, *Hascosay*, formerly deployed at Ullapool, maintains the freight link from Aberdeen. The service started in October 2002, but it was the following April before the £28-million *Hamnavoe* was allowed out of protracted lay-up at Leith Docks to replace the *Hebridean Isles*, which had been maintaining the Scrabster route. The *Hamnavoe* could not be used until linkspan modifications had been introduced.

Competition for the new company was created by – who else? – local hauliers. In an almost identical attempt to that in Harris and Lewis the previous year, entrepreneurs from Orkney and Shetland placed the former Irish Sea ferry, *Merchant Venture*, alongside the former P&O Scottish Ferries' *St Rognvald*, on a nightly freight sailing from Aberdeen, under the banner, Norse Island Ferries. As before, the big company reduced its freight rates. As before, the smaller company slowly ran out of cash. By the summer of 2003, Norse was down to one ship, whose sailings were now integrated into the big company's schedule. In addition, Pentland Ferries had been set up in opposition to Caledonian MacBrayne's Scrabster-Stromness service in October 2001, ironically using the former Caledonian MacBrayne ferries, *Iona* and *Claymore*. However, the Invergordon-Kirkwall service maintained by the *Contender*, and originally established by haulier David Laidlaw of Stromness in 1992, finally ceased at this time.

This early competition, coupled with an over-ambitious business plan, led to a re-tendering exercise for NorthLink. The company declared that there was insufficient funding available to maintain the desired quality of service.

Caledonian MacBrayne was selected as one of three preferred tenderers and was finally awarded the contract. Caledonian MacBrayne had no qualms about tendering for these services, although it too was now subject to tender for its own West Highland routes.

Caledonian MacBrayne currently serves the rural and island communities (22 islands) of the north-west and west of Scotland with a comprehensive and diverse route network (Table 5). The company provides a better quality of service than ever before, and operates a large, modern and diverse fleet of ships which, with few exceptions, have been purpose-built for the work. Caledonian MacBrayne carries over 5 million passengers on its services each year. It is responsible for the conveyance of cars, coaches and lorries which collectively meet the islands' everyday needs. In so doing, the company supports the livelihoods of the island communities, be they fishing, farming, tourism or industry.

In our view, the company discharges its obligations efficiently and economically, although this point may well be disputed by some observers and users who believe passionately that the company 'could do better' on both counts. Despite occasional, and at times well-merited, criticism from its customers as a consequence of mistakes and miscalculations, Caledonian MacBrayne and its Directors deserve, on the whole, both congratulation and encouragement, in the hope that they will continue to maintain such high standards long into the future.

Yet, at the same time as the company renders an ever-improving service to the islands, the volume of passengers and vehicles crossing the linkspans from ship to shore makes increasing demands of the infrastructure of these fragile communities, now deeply and irreversibly dependent on the mainland. Caledonian MacBrayne, in short, contributes not only to the daily lives of islanders, but also to the relentless process of change which has reshaped their habitats, as well as their ways of life, since the first alien steamships anchored in sheltered Hebridean harbours two centuries ago.

Table 5 *The ships of the Caledonian MacBrayne fleet and their normal service routes, 2005*

a) Major units

Vessel	Age in 2005	Normal service route
Bute	0	Wemyss Bay-Rothesay
Loch Portain	2	Berneray-Leverburgh (Harris)
Coruisk	3	Mallaig-Armadale (summer) and Clyde (winter)
Hebrides	5	Uig-Tarbert and Lochmaddy
Lochnevis	5	Mallaig-Small Isles
Clansman	7	Oban-Coll-Tiree-Outer Isles
Isle of Lewis	10	Ullapool-Stornoway
Caledonian Isles	12	Ardrossan-Brodick
Loch Dunvegan	14	Colintraive-Rhubodach
Loch Fyne	14	Lochaline-Fishnish
Lord of the Isles	16	Oban-Inner (including Colonsay) and Outer Isles
Isle of Mull	17	Oban-Craignure
Hebridean Isles	20	Kennacraig-Islay (summer)
Isle of Arran	21	Kennacraig-Islay (summer), relief vessel
*Mùirneag**	27	Ullapool-Stornoway freight
Saturn	27	Ardrossan-Brodick (summer) and Upper Clyde services
Juno	31	Upper Clyde services
Jupiter	31	Upper Clyde services
	Average age 15 years	Total number of major units – 18

On charter from Harrisons (Clyde) Limited.

b) Loch-class drive-through ferries and *Isle of Cumbrae*

Vessel	Age in 2005	Normal service route
Loch Alainn	7	Largs-Cumbrae Slip
Loch Bhrùsda	9	Ard Mhòr (Barra)-Eriskay
Loch Buie	13	Fionnphort (Mull)-Iona
Loch Tarbert	13	Lochranza (Arran)-Claonaig
Loch Linnhe	19	Tobermory-Kilchoan
Loch Ranza	19	Gigha-Tayinloan (Kintyre)
Loch Riddon	19	Largs-Cumbrae Slip
Loch Striven	19	Raasay-Sconser (Skye)
Isle of Cumbrae	28	Tarbert-Portavadie
	Average age 16 years	Total number of small drive-through ferries – 9

c) *Kilbrannan*-class bow loading ferries

Vessel	Age in 2005	Normal service route
Bruernish	36	Spare vessel at Oban
Canna	36	Ballycastle-Rathlin, Northern Ireland
Eigg	36	Oban-Lismore
Raasay	36	Spare vessel on the Clyde

d) Passenger catamaran

Vessel	Age in 2005	Normal service route
Ali Cat*	6	Gourock-Dunoon (passenger only)

*On charter from Red Funnel, but owned by Solent & Wightline Cruises.

*The lounge aboard the new **Coruisk** [NR]*

CHAPTER 11

CHANGING ISLANDS:
THE IMPACT OF THE SHIPS ON PERSPECTIVE,
PEOPLE AND PLACE

The **Dunara Castle** is captured magnificently at Lochmaddy before 1894. Note the horse-drawn cart on the pier, and the two men having a leisurely conversation, as an officer looks over the dodger. [George Washington Wilson. Aberdeen University Archives]

CHANGING ISLANDS:
THE IMPACT OF THE SHIPS ON PERSPECTIVE, PEOPLE AND PLACE

The scenery is most varied, and is unequalled for solitary grandeur, and wild and savage magnificence. It teems with incidents romantic and tragic which have been rendered famous by the pens of the historian, the poet and the novelist. Glimpses are to be had of the primitive ways of life that are fast becoming obsolete.

Cabin Fare for the Round, - - - - - - - - - - - - - £1 15s.
Do.   Do.   (including Meals),   £3   5s.

Occasional Special Trips to the Island of St. Kilda.
Return Cabin Fare, including Meals, £4 4s.

MARTIN ORME & COMPANY ADVERTISEMENT OF 1895 FOR 'CIRCULAR TOURS' ON THE *DUNARA CASTLE.*

Few words ever written on behalf of a West Highland steamer are as significant, and in retrospect as ironic, as those found on Martin Orme's 1895 advertisement. Not only was the *Dunara Castle* arguably the most influential vessel ever to have sailed the Minches, but her role was also inexorably intertwined with the fate of St Kilda, giving the island its first regular steamer service in 1877, and then taking off its remaining sheep, shepherds and mail, just over fifty years later in August 1930. 'The primitive ways of life' found in St Kilda did indeed become obsolete when, a few hours after the *Dunara* had sailed out of Village Bay, the remaining islanders were evacuated by H.M.S. *Harebell*. In due course, these very 'incidents' were to be 'rendered famous by the pens of the historian, the poet and the novelist' – and one might add, for good measure, by the words of the politician, the dramatist, the film-maker and a host of other apologists. Without knowing it, the drafters of the advertisement were trapped within, and contributing to, a self-fulfilling prophecy. Its wider implications would also embrace the Hebrides as a whole – though mercifully not to the point of evacuation – as the century wore on.

In the 1930s, when McCallum and Orme offered 'circular tours' to St Kilda, by then depopulated (although islanders returned in summer to maintain their old homes), they continued to use the language of sublimity to attract custom (see Chapter 4). The evacuation of the island was regarded by them as the consequence of the relentless romantic struggle between man and Nature, with Nature gaining the upper hand: 'the elements', the company noted, '[had] won the battle for supremacy.' While there was a degree of truth in this, some might feel that the real victor, or at least the real catalyst for change, was not the weather, but Martin Orme and his steam-driven wonder-ship, the *Dunara Castle*, with the support of John McCallum's *Hebrides*. Gradually, as commentators like Tom Steel in his important volume(s), *The Life and Death of St Kilda*, have argued, the St Kildans became used to the patronage of the steamship, which underpinned summer tourism and supplemented their way of life. Other aspects of 'mainland' life began to intrude, from gramophones to lollipops, and self-sufficiency declined. Eventually the 'levelling up' process of bringing an outlying island into conformity with external values, coupled with weather-related challenges, tilted the balance in favour of abandoning an archipelago which, paradoxically, had been enormously significant in developing the concept of the multi-purpose Hebridean steamship and its motorised successors. Reaching St Kilda was the ultimate challenge for tourist and steamship owner alike.

McCallum and Orme were particularly important in helping to redraw the map of the Hebrides in relation to the Scottish mainland. The chain of insular interconnection which they provided so effectively between the islands was also a chain of increasing external dependence, with its primary anchor in the Glasgow docklands. Distances began

SELLING THE ISLANDS AND PROMOTING THE COMPANY: ADVERTISING IMAGES SINCE 1930

DAVID MACBRAYNE'S BROCHURES and advertisements, in both art and text, have tended to reflect the prevailing moods of each decade, though some images have lasted much longer than others – notably that of the brawny-kneed Highlander, who now keeps the Caledonian lion at bay, though not always successfully. The Highlander was to be seen in metallic majesty on the quasi-figureheads of the motor-vessels, *Loch Seaforth* (1947) and *Claymore* (1955). Despite being deprived of a significant amount of his dash and colour since those glamorous days, he still takes a bow on the contemporary car-ferries *Clansman* and *Hebrides*, but he has – shamefully! – lost his place to the intrusive Caledonian lion on the noses of both the *Isle of Lewis* and the *Lochnevis*. In post-1930 promotional literature, the Highlander tended to appear in his finest apparel when there was a particularly special event to celebrate, such as the arrival of the car-ferries, *Hebrides*, *Clansman* and *Columba*, in 1963-64. He represented the 'macho' side of the company's self-identity, as well as the warrior ethos of the romantic Highlands and Islands.

Romanticism – most of it rather airy-fairy – tended to be the keynote of the inter-war advertising material. By the later 1930s, the Highlands and Islands were presented to the expectant public as 'The Isles of Youth', a phrase which reflected the dominance in that period of 'Songs of the Hebrides' in the repertoire of the immensely popular singer, Marjory Kennedy Fraser. In Kennedy Fraser's renditions of Gaelic songs, the Hebrides were a mixture of magical sunsets and deep blue skies, and MacBrayne's blurb-writers presented the islands no less idyllically. 'And out there,' gushed the 1939 brochure, 'on the chord of the setting sun, lies a region that is ever new – the Isles of Youth….The Isles of Youth belong to another state of human affairs – another plane of experience – where the burdens of obligation and compulsion are unknown and the eye is satisfied.' This effusion of sunset sentiments, which did nothing to enhance the case for the real-life

Hebrides, was counterbalanced – mercifully – by more believable monochrome photographs in the body of the brochure.

The contribution of Kennedy Fraser's collaborator, the Rev. Kenneth MacLeod, emerged when the company adopted the slogan 'The Road to the Isles' and extolled 'Enchanted Islands' in the 1950s. This slogan – the name of a very popular and 'couthy' song written by MacLeod – was an advertising master-stroke, as it could be invested with even greater meaning when the new car-ferries arrived. Needless to say, it sat rather uneasily with the towering bulks of 'the three fat ladies', as did the concept of 'Hebridean Highways', which emerged at the same time. Whatever the quality of the car-decks, quality highways on the ground were rather hard to find. As always, such slick sloganising tended to conflict with the grim realities of Highland life, including wind and storm, and the appalling state of many Highland and Island roads, which were about to be pot-holed still further by cars rushing to catch the new ships. It also conflicted with the company's rejection of Road Equivalence as a means of setting fares for car- and lorry-owners, though this was debated vigorously, particularly in the 1970s, with the arrival of the no-nonsense, forward-to-basics company, Western Ferries.

Alongside the warm embers of romanticism, the company plugged into the jingoism of emerging nationalism in the decolonising decade of the 1960s. Banners and flags seemed to wave everywhere in MacBrayne's brochures, almost blotting out the sky. The banner-waving image was not, however, new. It first appeared in the 1930s, but it was given contemporary relevance by placing a more modern ship behind the forest of flag-staffs, namely the *Claymore* (1955), rather than the earlier turbine steamer. The brawny-kneed, sword-bearing Highlander was now surrounded by three powerful kilted standard-bearers, raising aloft the Union Jack, the Scottish Saltire, the Scottish lion rampant, MacBrayne's house-flag and

MacBrayne's white name-flag. The old, romantic Highlands were very much in evidence, as the subliminal message nodded retrospectively towards the raising of the standard at Glenfinnan by Prince Charles Edward Stewart in 1745.

Although MacBrayne artists invested much time and effort in the contextual detail of these images, they paid surprisingly little attention to the ships themselves. Brochures usually carried fleet lists, and sometimes photographs of key vessels. Representations in art of the ships were, however, largely conspicuous by their absence. When they did occasionally appear, they were disappointingly poor, and tended to convey the impression of a company out of touch with, and not very interested in, its own ships. Thus the *Claymore* was almost invariably portrayed with her derrick in the 'rest' position, something unknown in the Hebrides throughout her twenty years of service. This misrepresentation was due in large measure to over-use, by armchair artists, of photographs of the vessel running the measured mile on her trials. Apart from particularly significant ships, such as the *Lochfyne*, which appeared on many posters and brochures, commonly alongside MacBrayne buses, the Hebridean motor-vessels were kept firmly in the background. The company never exploited – nor even appeared to recognise – its position as the world leader in the introduction of motor-ships to coastal passenger services. In contrast to the cleverly associational subtexting of David MacBrayne himself, the post-1928 company was also largely oblivious to the selling-point offered by the undeniable parallels between its motor-vessels and the new generation of diesel-powered ocean liners.

Particular occasions might induce a more ship-conscious approach. Thus the *Loch Seaforth* made a special appearance on the company's centenary brochure of 1951. Motor-vessels like the car-ferry *Columba* might also be portrayed in the context of one-off events and accompanying brochures or handbills – most obviously launches, introductions and summer cruises. Overall, however, pride of place in artwork was given to older excursion vessels usually based in the Clyde, such as the *Lochfyne* and the *Saint Columba*. This conveyed the unfortunate impression that the diligent Hebridean motor-ships were but the poor, peripheral and largely forgotten relations of a mainly Clyde-centred core. The only Hebridean motor-vessel which appeared regularly, and was drawn accurately and recognisably, on advertising material was, curiously, the cargo-boat *Loch Carron*, which – tellingly – took the place assigned to the old steamship, *Hebrides*, on the earlier posters of McCallum, Orme & Company.

By the late 1960s, the advertising material of David MacBrayne, like the company itself, was distinctly jaded and in need of a very long rest. Its drab and repetitive motifs contrasted markedly with the sparkling artwork of the Caledonian Steam Packet Company. The CSPC's poster and cover images were generally excellent, and conveyed an impression of firm, knowledgeable management. Because of their emphasis on accurate and powerful drawings and paintings of CSPC ships, they became immediate collectors' items, to be cherished by enthusiasts and saved from the bin at all costs. The Hebridean author of this book remembers his daring 'rescue' of some superlative poster-pictures of the *Queen Mary II* and a turbine *Duchess*. He happened to be passing through a Clydeside railway station at a critical moment when the posters were being pulled off the walls and about to be thrown out! Such sacrilege was halted immediately. CSPC's brochure covers likewise often sported fine line-drawings which were recognisably in the style of the talented marine artist, Alasdair MacFarlane.

With the creation of the Scottish Transport Group in 1969, and of Caledonian MacBrayne in 1973, the combined company was able to breathe new life into the time-stained art and advertising portfolio of David MacBrayne. As a consequence, Caledonian MacBrayne has diversified its advertising material into many appropriately contemporary media, including a very accessible and well-connected website, and it

has placed a strong and very pleasing spotlight on the Highlands and Islands. Earlier images of 'mists and mysticism' still float around the edges, but these are kept under control. Publishing is now much higher on the company's priority-list. Its output includes its well-produced and full-colour *Explore(r)* magazine, which, in addition to carrying articles by Hebridean- and mainland-based authors, gives considerable space to fleet lists and excellent photographs of the ships themselves. The presentational emphasis is on the 'experience' of being on the ships and travelling in the islands, with glimpses of wider contexts and company aspirations. The 2001 *Explorer* magazine, for example, placed the launch of the *Hebrides* by Her Majesty the Queen on its front cover, and concluded with a most useful and pleasantly illustrated article on the *Suilven* (1974) in New Zealand service.

Among the company's most notable self-promotional achievements has been its strong support for the recording of its own history. This is evident in its *Ships of the Fleet* booklets (appearing from 1977), and in Ian McCrorie's 150th Anniversary volume, *Royal Road to the Isles* (2001), which carries a detailed text and a superb selection of prints and photographs. As new ships have been built, recent company policy under Dr Harold Mills CB, Chairman, and Lawrie Sinclair, Managing Director, has ensured a growing connection with the communities served by the ships, by bringing the ships to the communities for their naming ceremonies. Often simultaneously with such events, the indefatigable and immensely knowledgeable Historian of the company, Ian McCrorie, has produced highly esteemed 'spotlight histories'. These include accounts of the three vessels named *Hebrides* (to celebrate the arrival of the new *Hebrides* in 2001), the services to and from Mallaig (to coincide with the introduction of the *Coruisk* in 2003), and a history of the car-ferry *Pioneer* (to mark her retiral from the fleet in 2003).

In such ways, the company in its new guise has reinvented its marketing image, and has got rid of the Highland/Lowland dichotomy which was (paradoxically) much more obvious when David MacBrayne was a 'private' entity. The company's commitment to

Gaelic culture was enhanced by the appointment of a Gaelic-speaking Head of Communications, Dr Hugh Dan MacLennan. Support for Gaelic and Gaelic cultural events, such as the annual Royal National Mod, is now at the heart of the company's marketing strategy. Meaningful symbolic linkages are made whenever the opportunity arises. Most recently, at the time of the 2005 Mod in Stornoway, Caledonian MacBrayne presented the builder's name-plate of the former Lewis mail-ship *Loch Seaforth* to An Lanntair, the Gaelic art-gallery in the town.

All in all, over the last thirty years, and more noticeably in the last five, Caledonian MacBrayne has radically rethought its advertising and communication policies for the greater benefit of both the company itself and the communities dependent upon it.

Ian McCrorie promotes his booklet on (board) the **Pioneer.** *[Caledonian MacBrayne]*

to shrink, and the Hebrides began to move spatially closer to mainland Scotland, in a pattern which went in the opposite direction to what is nowadays known as 'continental drift'. 'Hebridean drift' was centripetal, not centrifugal, with the 'centre' exerting an ever stronger pull on the 'periphery'. The ships of David MacBrayne likewise contributed massively to this service-based reconfiguration of island/mainland relationships. The process continues today, as ever more powerful 'ferries' reduce journey times, and as Hebridean harbours and mainland ports sprout concrete and hydraulic linkspans to ensure that 'turn-around times' are as tight as existing technology and finance can make them.

One might fault Martin Orme and his collaborators for not being sufficiently sensitive to their part in the growing dependency syndrome which led to the death of St Kilda. The same charge could be laid against present-day operators. However, it is not at all easy to see one's own contribution to the life or death of a community, when one is actually 'serving' that community. In retrospect, and only with hindsight, do the consequences of such intervention become clearer. Nor is it the place of service-rendering companies to ponder, to their own detriment, the wider challenges inherent in sustaining the Hebridean environment. It is their duty not only to sustain themselves, but also to respond appropriately to the level of demand from the islanders whom they serve. Steamship services in the past, like ferry services now, were the result of a negotiation between the customer and the supplier, with ever more strident calls from the customers for bigger, better and faster vessels, and a ready response in the mind of the supplier, provided that financial balances were favourable. In future, such services will be secured by commercial contract.

As steamship services to the Hebrides developed in the course of the nineteenth century, the users of the services – who were more detached from business dynamics than the owners of the ships – were forced to reflect on the nature of the ongoing and far-reaching exchange between the islands and the Scottish mainland which the steamship had inevitably initiated. We have already noted (Chapter 1) the response of the Rev. Dr Norman MacLeod to the arrival of the *Maid of Morven*. By the mid-nineteenth century commentators based in Glasgow, such as the Rev. Dr Norman MacLeod of the Barony Church, son of the aforesaid Norman, regarded the Highlands and Islands as a region of 'distance and darkness' prior to the coming of steamships (Chapter 2). At the same time, they lamented the loss of older customs, and blamed iconic writers such as Sir Walter Scott for 'dressing up' the Highlands as a tourist package, but they were prepared to accept the cultural deficit, however reluctantly. The resolution of the dilemma was thus broadly favourable to the promoters of the steamship. A price had to be paid for what was perceived even by Highlanders and islanders themselves as 'progress'. The fact that David Hutcheson and David MacBrayne were later regarded as 'benefactors' of the Highlands and Islands indicates that broadly similar perspectives were widely held at the end of the century, by both businessmen in the cities and islanders in the Hebrides.

Gains and losses, however, could be perceived and quantified in more personal terms. Gaels who were conveyed from the Highlands to the Lowlands by steamship often saw matters from quite the opposite perspective to Norman MacLeod and his peers. For them notions of 'distance and darkness' were to be applied first and foremost to Glasgow and the industrial areas of Scotland, and not to the Highlands and Islands. Indeed, in certain contexts, usually those involving farewell and leave-taking, the dark, smoky steamship herself became synonymous with the loss of innocence, immediacy and brightness, as migrants left their native areas, and prepared to enter the grubby, industrialised Lowlands. The contemporary romantic movement, which encouraged individuals to project their moods on to the landscape, also taught them to relate their emotions to inanimate objects, by way of parallel or contrast. These perspectives are evident in the 1870s and 1880s, but they had begun to emerge much earlier in the century. Indeed, they are foreshadowed to some extent in the older Norman MacLeod's piece on the *Maid of Morven*.

Apart from MacLeod's prose passage, one of the earliest

nineteenth-century allusions to the steamship in the context of separation is contained in a song composed by Dr John MacLachlan of Rahoy (1804-74), apparently on behalf of another man, whose sweetheart had gone off to Glasgow. The song is noteworthy for its thumbnail sketch of the paddle-driven steamship:

'S ann Di-màirt bho cheadha Loch Alainn
A dh'fhalbh mo ghràdh-sa le bàt' na smùid;
Bu luath a ceum dol gu tìr na Beurla,
'S tha mi fo èislean air bheagan sùnnd.

'S gur ann le bàta nan roithean làidir,
'S nan cuibhlean pràis 's iad a-ghnàth cur strì;
Fear ga stiùireadh gu làidir, lùthmhor,
'S e dèanamh iùil dhi gu Diùraidh shìos.

It was on Tuesday from Lochaline pierhead
that my sweetheart left, on the ship of steam;
swift was her step going to the land of English,
and I am dejected with little cheer.

It was on the ship with the powerful paddles,
and the wheels of brass that forever strive;
a man steering her with strength and vigour,
guiding her down towards Jura's isle.

Here the ship is referred to as *bàt[a] na smùid[e]* ('the ship of steam') – her standard appellation in Gaelic – with connotations of dirtiness in the word *smùid*, meaning also 'smoke', 'mist' and 'sweat', as used of the *Maid of Morven* in Norman MacLeod's 1829 essay. Indeed, this may have been the very ship that the poet had in mind. In any event, the metaphor is more important than the detail. Her course away from Lochaline, directed by her steersman, is obviously intended to parallel that of the young lady, who is on her way to Glasgow, portrayed in the song as the city of fashionable, feminine vanity. She was not the only Highland lassie to vanish for ever in a cloud of smoke from a steamship funnel.

The pain of departure to the Lowland city, drawn against the image of the steamship, has seldom been more succinctly expressed than by the Skye poetess, Mary MacPherson, better known as 'Màiri Mhòr nan Oran'(see Chapter 3), who was by this time working in Glasgow, and taking regular holidays in her native island. In her well-known song, 'Nuair bha mi òg' ('When I was young'), probably composed in the late 1870s, she describes how, while holidaying in Ose in Skye, she awoke one day to a beautiful morning. This caused her to admire the countryside around her, but it also forced her to recollect the scenes and circumstances of her girlhood. She reimagines the lost community of her youth, now scarred by emigration and the loss of traditional customs, and she begins to yearn for its recreation.

At the end of the song, however, Mary's arcadian idyll is

*A cauld day on the Clyde: travelling on the **Saint Columba** (Donald B. MacCulloch)*

destroyed by the sudden intrusion of a departing steamship – in all probability the *Glencoe*. She becomes acutely aware of leaving – indeed, having left – the familiar island for the alien city. The main noises of the mechanical ship – shrill hooter and churning motion – are well delineated, while *iùbhrach na smùid* and its implied dirt, foreshadowing the squalor of the city, contrast sharply with the 'fragrant island' and the purity of traditional sail:

Nuair chuir mi cùl ris an eilean chùbhraidh,
  'S a ghabh mi iùbhrach na smùid gun seòl,
Nuair shèid i 'n dùdach 's a shìn an ùspairt,
  'S a thog i cùrsa o Thìr a' Cheò,
Mo chridhe brùite 's na deòir lem shùilean
  A' falbh gu dùthaich gun sùrd, gun cheòl,
Far nach faic mi cluaran no neòinean guanach
  No fraoch no luachair air bruaich no lòn.

When I turned my back on the fragrant island,
and took the smoky vessel that has no sail,
when her whistle blasted and the churning started
and she set her course from the Misty Land,
my heart was crushed and my tears were flowing,
going to the country with no tune or spark,
where I will see no thistle or joyful daisy
or heather or rushes on field or bank.

In this context, the steamship acts as a means of disconnecting the traveller from her homeland and from a range of relationships with the area, including a detailed appreciation of its flora and fauna. The ship helps to create the state of exile, which begins the moment the traveller steps on board.

Mary MacPherson was, however, equally well aware that the steamship could act as a means of reconnecting her with her native island, and she describes the experience of 'reconnection' no less skilfully. In the preface to a song which celebrates her return to Skye on board the *Clansman* (built 1870), she chronicles (for the benefit of the song's recipient) how she was overwhelmed by homesickness, and found solace in the ship:

Is beag a shaoileadh do mhàthair gun robh mi dà fhichead bliadhna agus a h-aon gun ghas fraoich fhaicinn, no uiread agus sguabach a bheireadh sgrìob air an taigh gus an do thachair dhomh air là àraidh foghair a dhol seachad air bùth ann an sràid Earra-Ghàidheal ann an Glaschu. Chunnaic mi bocsa làn fraoich agus eòin a chuir na Sasannaich fhad-chasach, a spùill ar dùthaich àghmhor, a Ghlaschu gan reic. Thug mo chridhe leum às le toil-inntinn. Shaoil leam gum bu leam fhèin am fraoch agus na h-eòin. Dh'fhoighneachd mi dhiubh ann an Gàidhlig an reiceadh iad am fraoch. Fhreagair iad mi ann am Beurla chruaidh nach reiceadh. Thill mi mach, sheas mi air an t-sràid agus thuirt mi na mo chridhe, 'Gheobh mise fraoch agus neo-ar-thaing dhuibh.' Mar a thuirt b' fhìor. Dh'ullaich mi mi fhèin agus thog mi orm gu sunndach air an ath Dhi-luain; ràinig mi am Broomielaw; leum mi staigh do shoitheach na smùide, an Clansman. Cha chreid mi nach abair thu gu bheil an iorram a leanas mar gum b' ann a' freagairt do ghleadhraich a cuid ùpraid.

Little would your mother think that I was forty-one years without seeing a shoot of heather, or as much as a sheaf [of dry heather] that would give the house a lick until one autumn day I happened to go past a particular shop in Argyle Street in Glasgow. I saw a box full of heather and birds [pheasants] that the long-legged Sasannaich, who pillaged our magnificent country, had sent to Glasgow to be sold. I felt that the heather and the birds were my very own. I asked them in Gaelic if they would sell the heather. They answered me in hard English that they would not. I went back out, I stood on the street, and I said in my heart, 'I will get heather, and to pot with you.' As I said, it turned out. I got myself ready, and I set off in good spirits on the next Monday; I reached the Broomielaw; I jumped into the steamship, the Clansman. *I think that you will say that the following rowing-song corresponds, as it were, to the commotion of her noisy movement.*

Here the noise of the ship is regarded as passenger-friendly, positive rather than negative, and in tune with the emotions of the returning exile who has been deprived of her native language and community – in contrast to the picture of departure in 'Nuair bha mi òg'. Mary composes the song verse by verse, as familiar landmarks come into view, and the vistas refresh her body and spirit:

'S ged a tha mo cheann air liathadh,
'S aois a' gealachadh mo chiabhag,
Nuair nochd mi ri Eilean Dhiarmaid,
Dh'fhalbh na striachan às mo mhalaidh.

Nuair chunnaic mi mullach Ghlàmaig,
Taobh Beinn Lì is Ruighe Mhàrsgo,
Shaoil leam fhèin gun d'fhàs mi làidir,
Leis an fhàile thar nam beannaibh.

And although my head has greyed,
and age is whitening my locks,
when I came in view of Isle Ornsay,
the furrows vanished from my forehead.

When I saw the summit of Glàmag,
Ben Lee's slope and the Ridge of Marsgo,
I thought that I had been strengthened
by the waft coming off the mountains.

Mary also sketches the personal links and historical associations of each landmark.

Pèighinn a' Chorrain is an t-Olach,
'S Lag a' Bhaile, 'n t-àite còmhnard,
Far am biodh na gillean òga
'G iomain gu bòidheach le camain.

'S ged a bha mo chridhe leònte,
Snighe bho mo shùil a' dòrtadh,
Faicinn Ratharsair gun Leòdach,
Rinn mi sòlas ri Dùn Cana.

Leagh mo chridhe staigh an Udairn
Sgoireabreac am beachd mo shùilean;

Bha na laoich a dhèanadh taobh rium
Fad' on dùthaich 's iad fon talamh.

Peighinn a' Chorrain and Ollach,
and Lag a' Bhaile, the level region,
where the young fellows once played
beautifully with shinty sticks.

And although my heart was wounded,
tears flowing from my eye,
seeing Raasay with no MacLeod there,
it cheered my spirits to see Dun Can.

My heart melted passing the Udairn,
with Scorrybreck before my eyes;
the heroes who would have helped me
were far from home, beneath the turf.

Mary's technique is reminiscent of the guidebooks for *Summer Tours* which were produced for tourists from the late 1870s by David MacBrayne (see 'Remote and Royal'). These described the main features – geographical, architectural, and maritime – to be viewed on the voyage.

The similarity, however, may be coincidental and superficial. In reality, the steamship is providing a novel platform from which to view the topography of Skye, and to appreciate afresh its physical features in relation to its history. A new bonding between person and place is being nurtured, with a 'value-added' dimension for the 'insider'. The state of exile in the urban Lowlands is being alleviated by panoramic views from the deck of the *Clansman*, while the poetess, like a contemporary tourist, but with deeper knowledge, experiences a new sense of pride in her homeland as she sees it from other angles. Far from being a vehicle of separation, the steamship in this context becomes a means of reintegrating the exile and her native area. The steamship, in short, has two sides to her. On other occasions, the focus of interest was the main deck of the steamship, and especially the company on board, who might merit extended treatment as part of the poet's experience of being in transition between cultures. Lowlandised Highland lassies' enforced re-entry into Gaelic culture, helped along by a storm and the vessel's heavy rolling, is the theme of Neil MacLaine's song on 'The Night on the *Dunara*' (Chapter 4).

By the last quarter of the nineteenth century, the broadly ambivalent role of the steamship, in depriving the Highlands and Islands of their people while helping to sustain the local economy, was accepted as normal. This is indicated in a song by Mary MacPherson about the steamer *Clydesdale*, when the ship was transferred about 1887 to the Oban run from the Glasgow-Skye-Stornoway service. The song demonstrates how, by this stage, a person and probably also a community could identify closely with the vessel concerned, and lament her transfer to another route:

> Farewell to you, O 'Dale of Clyde' -
> many a year you've ploughed the brine,
> leaving great Glasgow of gables high,
>   to head north to my home country.
>
> Many a cold and rainy night,
> with showers of snow and northern blast,
> you rounded the Mull by striving hard,
>   with no food but coal and water.
>
> When the sea would rise in glens,
> you would swim above their heads,
> as your propellers ground the waves
>   like grain inside a hopper.
>
> When the storm would stir the seas,
> and spume would rise about your ears,
> you were like a bird at sea,
>   as you steered your course with rigour.
>
> Many a cargo you conveyed
> which saved us in the hour of need,
> when the folk were kept under heel,
>   through the deeds of the great nobles.
>
> When you would deliver meal and tea,
> you would get butter and some cheese,
> and the produce of land and sea
>   would seek a price in Lowlands.
>
> Many a youthful lad and lass
> you took away from the Isle of Mist,
> as they went to earn their keep,
>   and many did not return there.
>
> And those of them that would come back
> once their pay was safely banked,
> your face would wear a joyful laugh,
>   when they chanced to be on board you.
>
> When some would succumb to haze,
> because of the stuff you had tucked away,
> your knee would not tire in any way,
>   though they should set you dancing.
>
> The friendly 'Clansman' will be sad,
> if you do not meet her in each port;
> without your music or your smoke,
>   they will miss you sorely.
>
> When you both met on ocean's back,
> one from the Clyde on an outward track,
> and the other running in so fast,
>   with cargo from the Highlands;
>
> The kindly 'Clansman' would then call,
> 'Are you all in best of form?
> Do you have any news on board,
>   that would cheer my soul to hear it?'
>
> The 'Dale of Clyde' would then assert,
> 'I do have news to lift your heart -
> There's fine fishing in the Misty Land,
>   and much of it's inside me.'

If you have now turned your back,
and we'll no longer see your smoke,
our thousand blessings in your wake,
wherever you may travel.

In the concluding verse, Mary comments on the *smùid* ('smoke, steam') from the *Clydesdale*'s funnel, but in the ninth verse of the song she also alludes playfully to another form of *smùid*, namely the 'steam of intoxication', which these vessels were able to produce in their passengers. In effect, the steamer functioned as a floating public house or 'drinks cabinet'. By means of commercially available alcohol neatly 'tucked away', she supplemented the variety of beverages available to islanders, in the days before hotels were granted licences. Voyages to and from the islands were thus heaven-sent opportunities to slake thirst with liquor that was to be tasted, savoured and enjoyed at every level – including the horizontal – before the ship reached port. Social drinking, sometimes to excess, in a formal and to some degree 'neutral' context was one of the 'pastimes' that the steamship introduced to the islands.

Alcoholic beverages helped to relieve the pain of leaving one's native island, as well as to stimulate celebration – and even dancing on the ship's deck – on the emigrant's happy return. They also helped to cut time on long voyages. Passengers often arrived at their destinations with remarkable speed, having lost days on their way, and they were sometimes unconscious of – and, of course, on – their arrival. John MacLean, a Tiree bard and later resident in Manitoba, had this experience on one of the early steamships (quite probably the *Dunara Castle*), when he sailed on her from Tiree to Glasgow:

Nuair thàinig an oidhche, cha robh suim do na dh'fhàg
    sinn;
Chuir an dram às ar cuimhn' iad is sinn cruinn anns a'
    chàbin.
Cò nach òladh na fhuair e, 's daoin'-uaisle ga
    phàighheadh?

Nuair a dh'iarradh a-suas sinn, bha is' an Cluaidh aig a
    h-àite
Gar cur a-mach.

When night came, we did not give a hoot for those we had
    left behind;
The dram erased them from our memory when we were
    gathered in the cabin.
Who would not drink what he had received, when
    gentlemen were paying it?
When we were summoned on deck, she was in the Clyde at
    her place,
Disembarking us.

This tasty solution to maritime tedium has retained its popularity to the present day. Over a century later, the *Oban Times* (9 December 2004) told the moving story of passengers 'the worse for drink' who delayed the departure of the car-ferry *Lord of the Isles* by 35 minutes and the consequent arrival of the inbound *Clansman* by 20 minutes:

Ferry pair refused to budge
THE WARM welcome of ferry operator Caledonian MacBrayne is well known, so much so that on Tuesday two passengers did not want to leave when *Lord of the Isles* berthed in Oban at the end of the Coll run.

The man and woman, described as 'the worse for drink', would not budge.

After 20 minutes the lady left, with the help of the crew, but the gentleman was staying put and so the police had to be called.

As a result *Lord of the Isles* sailed 35 minutes late; her delay meant that the single linkspan in Oban was blocked and *Clansman* was unable to berth and she, too, sailed 25 minutes late.

Oban Police confirmed that a man and woman were apprehended and a report would go to the Procurator Fiscal; the pair enjoyed the hospitality of Oban Police Station until sober enough to leave.

*Giving a car a lift in the nets: the **Lochiel** loading at Port Ellen [Margaret Storrie]*

*The **Loch Seaforth** loads bales of tweed at Stornoway. [School of Scottish Studies Archives]*

Continuities from the nineteeth century to the twentieth are evident in other ways too. Present-day islanders, living at the beginning of the twenty-first century, will readily recognise the range of key issues and emotional responses which had appeared before 1900. Although they may have diminished in intensity, these issues have not vanished completely with the arrival of powerful new car-ferries.

From the late nineteenth century until 1960, the carriage of passengers and cargo by sea to and from the Hebrides remained relatively static in its overall method. This is evident in the long careers of the *Dunara Castle* and the *Hebrides*, which, at their time of building, represented the high-water mark of the late Victorian coastal steamer. The *Dunara* lasted until 1948, and the *Hebrides* was able to satisfy demand, alongside the new motor cargo-boats, until the mid-1950s. It could be argued that Martin Orme and John McCallum had picked 'winners' in designing their ships as they did, but against this we must set the generally conservative nature of the area which they served. Ship-board derricks, operated by winches, block and tackle, were the standard means of loading and unloading even when the innovatory, but traditional, mail-ship *Claymore* was built in 1955 (see Chapter 9). Hebridean piers could not cope with any other method at this stage. Other powerful agents of change did, however, appear in this period, among them regular air services to and from Glasgow, and bases and aerodromes constructed during and after the Second World War, with their accompanying personnel. Shipping services alone cannot be held responsible for changing islands.

Although change came slowly to the Hebrides as a whole, its pace varied from island to island. Factors which affected the rate of change included the proximity of each island to the mainland and the size of the island and its population. In the case of St Kilda, change was relatively rapid, partly because the community itself was small, and the environment inhospitable. In addition, the steamship made the community extremely aware of its 'difference' from the rest of mankind. Significant distance from the mainland, which is normally a deterrent to

rapid change, appears to have been a catalyst in the fate of the St Kildan archipelago. By contrast, where populations were relatively large, as in Tiree and the main islands of the Outer Hebrides, which were much closer to the mainland than St Kilda, change was absorbed much more slowly. Older social practices, rooted in Gaelic custom, co-existed alongside the delivery of UHT milk from the mainland, Massey-Ferguson tractors (arriving in the shape of 'little grey Fergies' from the late 1940s) and hay-balers. Overall, as modern practices won out in the long term, the islands became gradually and 'naturally' dependent on the mainland. In such a context, shipping services became 'lifelines', absolutely essential to maintaining the standard of living to which these islands aspired, as well as to preserving the island communities themselves and their economic bases.

One of the principal developments in changing the social life of the Hebrides, as well as the design of vessels and the rationale of shipping services, was the oil engine. The arrival of motor-cars in ever-increasing numbers, offering much more flexible forms of tourism, meant that the ships themselves had to change to become, in effect, 'floating garages'. As has been noted elsewhere (Chapter 6), David MacBrayne was a world leader in introducing the motor engine to coastal vessels. The company's response to the implications of the motor-car and its demands on ferry services was, however, much slower, but it was not alone in that respect. The side-loading car-ferries of 1963-64, *Hebrides*, *Clansman*, and *Columba*, ushered in a new era when they arrived. Their arrival was of great significance for the islands closest to the mainland, which they served in the first instance, namely Skye and Mull, as well as for the Outer Hebrides. Responding

MAKING CONNECTIONS: THE DEVELOPMENT OF LINKSPANS

WEST HIGHLAND PIERS and jetties have given islanders, companies and crews much to think about, and not a few headaches, across the years. At the heart of the availability, maintenance and upgrading of existing facilities has often lain the vexed question of ownership. In cases where the pier has been owned by the local authority, action has occasionally been taken unilaterally and apparently without warning by the pier-owners against individual ships. For example, the *Dumbarton Herald* of 16 October 1901 reported a pier-head boycott of the McCallum steamer, *Hebridean*:

> The steamer *Hebridean*…made a special run to Salen, Loch Sunart, for the purpose of shipping a consignment of about 500 sheep. On approaching the pier recently built there – one of the finest structures of its kind in the West Highlands – the captain was informed by the piermaster that he would not be permitted to put out ropes or gangways. Remonstrance proved fruitless, and the captain was obliged to wait four and a half hours, when the rising tide enabled him to take the stock on board at a neighbouring boat-slip. A few days afterwards the same boat called at Mingary for another consignment of sheep. Here also the captain was prohibited from using the pier, and, no boat-slip being available, the animals had to be taken out to the steamer in small boats. Neither at Salen

nor at Mingary did the piermasters assign any reason for their extraordinary behaviour. Mingary pier was built some eight years ago by a Government grant, and its absolute management is vested in Argyllshire County Council.

Clearly, the policy for the provision of piers – if such existed in Argyll County Council – was put into effect at very different times and places across the county. Tiree had a deep-water pier at Gott Bay by 1912, but the neighbouring island of Coll had to wait until 1965 for its pier. The case for the construction of piers – and, later, linkspans – doubtless depended on the amount of cargo, and then the number of motor vehicles, loaded or unloaded at each mainland port or island. This in itself was also determined by the nature of existing facilities.

Throughout the network served by McCallum and Orme and MacBrayne, standard wooden piers, where they existed, were effective enough for long-established lift-on/lift-off approaches to cargo-handling. However, old-style piers were severely challenged by the arrival of the new ferries from the mid-1960s, as the old structures now had to carry additional weight. The deployment of the new ships themselves, and the modernisation of the network in line with developments elsewhere in Britain, could be stymied by inadequate loading facilities. The issue

of root and branch modernisation had to be faced and reconsidered as the ships were updated. Side-loading, using hydraulic lifts, was a very workable initial solution, as the *Hebrides*, *Clansman* and *Columba* demonstrated, and it served several islands well for most of the 1970s and 1980s. However, this method of loading and unloading was slow, particularly when traffic was heavy, and sheep and cattle had to be carried. Motorised cattle-floats were not yet used, and pier-head rodeos, involving officers, crew and islanders, wasted immense amounts of time, sometimes delaying the departure of the scheduled service by more than an hour. Pressure increased for the deployment of roll-on/roll-off vessels. For this reason linkspans were needed across the network.

Key ports were the first to be furnished with linkspans, much of the work being done by civil engineers, Crouch and Hogg. Thus a linkspan at Oban – the Mecca of MacBrayne – was inaugurated on 15 October 1973 by the *Iona* (1970). The following April, a linkspan was provided for Craignure, making it possible for Mull to receive a modern drive-through service much earlier than most other islands. It was not until the early 1990s that the Inner Hebridean islands of Tiree, Coll and Colonsay eventually received linkspans, thus allowing the use of larger car-ferries such as the *Clansman* and the *Isle of Mull* on these

---

to Western Ferries' pugnacious challenges to their Jura and Islay services, MacBrayne's introduced the *Iona* of 1970, the first of the drive-through vehicular ferries with side-loading capability. Paradoxically, the *Iona* could not serve her design route because of the inadequacy of berthing facilities at West Loch Tarbert. This provided a glimpse of the future. The company's battles with local authorities and public opinion in connection with the Islay route foreshadowed the immense range of difficulties which it would require to confront in the process of improving and (re)building other terminals. The *Iona* irreversibly set the pace for change, and provided the model for the next generation of ships.

Since the introduction of the *Iona*, the Hebrides have, in fact, witnessed a shipping revolution. State-of-the-art car-ferries have appeared consistently during the 1970s, the 1980s and the 1990s. These now serve all of the main Hebridean routes. The old-style, leisurely chaos of loading and unloading tall steamships and prim motor-vessels at wooden piers has been superseded by the disgorging of large, slab-sided, bluff-bowed ferries. The raising of the bow visor or the lowering of the stern ramp is followed by a mechanical stampede over steel linkspans, generating long, snake-like lines of lorries, and then cars, loaded with roof-boxes, surf-boards, bicycles and tents, winding their way past

routes. Of the Outer Islands, the best served was Lewis, which had a linkspan at Stornoway for the use of the enlarged, drive-through *Clansman* and the *Suilven* (1974), which did not have side-loading facilities. The mainland terminal, Ullapool, which had replaced Mallaig as the principal port for Lewis by this stage, was likewise given a linkspan to accommodate these vessels.

The 'Hebridean triangle' was not given full roll-on, roll-off facilities until January 1987, when various difficulties surrounding the pier at Uig, Skye, were finally resolved. The 'mixed' nature of terminal facilities across the network until the early 1990s meant that ships had to be built with the capability for side-loading as well as bow- and/or stern-loading, unless they were for dedicated services with existing linkspans.

Upgrading of facilities, and most commonly the provision of new slipways for the 'Island' and 'Loch' classes of vessels, frequently generated protracted disputes which delayed modernisation still further. This was the case with the Fionnphort-Iona service, as the prospect of new slipways raised fears of a four-wheeled invasion of Iona. In the eyes of some, 'an historical way of life' appeared to be under threat. The provision of terminals at Raasay and Sconser in 1976 was preceded by a long-running wrangle with the obstructive Dr Green, then owner of much of the island of Raasay.

Accompanying the provision of more modern facilities and much larger ships, there were inevitable losses, particularly in the reduction of the number of piers being served. Some well-established and much appreciated 'calls' were eliminated. The loss of the 'call' at Tobermory by the Inner Hebrides ferry, serving Coll and Tiree, was among the long-term casualties of the upgrading of Craignure at the south end of Mull, but the factor which affected it most seriously was the arrival of the new *Clansman* in 1998. The *Clansman* was too large, she had no side-loading capability, and Tobermory had no linkspan. The result was the abandoning of a harbour which is especially well-known for its great natural beauty. One of the authors of this book recollects boarding the *Lord of the Isles* at Tobermory for Tiree on a glorious July morning in the early 1990s. The *Lord of the Isles* looked particularly handsome as she came round Calve Island, and pulled quickly alongside Tobermory pier, at the north end of the brightly coloured town, itself magnificent in the morning light.

Since the mid-twentieth century, many smaller piers, once used by the cargo-boats of both McCallum and Orme and David MacBrayne, have been decommissioned. Cargo-boats used to call at Pooltiel in Skye, and at Kallin and Loch Eport in North Uist. From time to time, vessels such as the *Lochnevis* (1934) would berth at Bunessan in Mull, itself a former haunt of the *Hebrides* (1898) and the *Dunara Castle* (1875). McCallum and Orme specified that their vessels were prepared to call at harbours where there might be 'inducement' in terms of cargo. Now the key 'inducement' is a modern linkspan for larger vessels or a very serviceable slipway for smaller ones.

The **Pioneer** loads MacBrayne lorries at West Loch Tarbert. [DEM]

The **Lord of the Isles** receives a line of cars at Coll pier. [DEM]

the Caledonian MacBrayne office and on to island roads. Essentially the same picture is to be found at Dover, Douglas or Roscoff. The Hebrides are now part of a well-recognised global pattern of ferry operations.

This has brought a wholly new set of challenges to the Hebrides. The infrastructure of roads and pierheads in the islands has generally lagged far behind the development of the new car-ferries. In most of the Hebrides, this infrastructure has had to be repaired or totally rebuilt to cope with growing volumes of traffic. The redesigning of the approaches to Port Askaig in Islay is an example of essential, ferry-driven upgrading. Beyond the pierheads, island roads have been particularly inadequate, and continue to be highly vulnerable to heavy traffic. The arrival of forty-ton fish-lorries has led to complaints of broken culverts and smashed dykes. As roads are single-track in many islands, visiting car-drivers have had to learn to use passing-places, and to reduce speed on sharp bends. Islanders have also had to learn to keep a sharp look-out for drivers who are unskilled in, or unwilling to yield to, island etiquette. So too have the sheep and cattle. Grazing innocently by the road-side and sunning themselves on the warm tarmac, as they have done for the best part of a century, they suddenly find themselves confronted by the blaring horns of alien vehicles and the frustrated gesticulations

*The compact **Lochnevis** manages to squeeze into Canna's beautiful harbour. [Bob Barlow]*

*Although suffering serious vibration problems when first commissioned, the **Loch Alainn** has settled down as a valuable unit on the shorter crossings. [NR]*

*The **Eigg** shows off her new and incongruously high bridge as she approaches the slip at Oban from Lismore. [NR]*

of their awkward, unreasonable occupants, unused to the leisurely conventions of Hebridean animals. Why should animals change their time-honoured ways for the sake of mere humans, whose only interest is speed, even when they are on holiday? Are they, the animals, not the true representatives of old-style island life? Why should *they* yield to 'Jim an' Teeny an' ra weans frae Gleska' or to 'Ralph and Vanessa and the poppets from Surrey'?

Development of passenger services has had equally serious implications for David MacBrayne and his successors, and for the deployment of their vessels. As vessels and services have improved beyond measure, the company has become ever more liable to public criticism over 'quality of service' – a bone of contention which can be traced back to at least 1959, when the *Lochinvar* was redeployed to the Mallaig-Portree service. The mail-ship which had served the Sound of Mull

for almost fifty years was no more than a 'tub' in the eyes of the Skye people. Even Dame Flora MacLeod of MacLeod, the incumbent of Dunvegan Castle and the mother of a huge global family of exiled clansfolk, was momentarily distracted from the onerous task of caring altruistically for the needs of her children, in order to concentrate on her own ugly back-yard, and to fire some verbal torpedoes at the defenceless *Lochinvar*. Clearly, the Mallaig-Portree service had gone up-market since the days of the octogenarian *Glencoe*, and the ageing veteran of Dunvegan was no longer prepared to tolerate her counterpart at sea.

Ageing ships are one problem, and new ships another. Each car-ferry built for Caledonian MacBrayne, with greater capacity and speed than the one before it, has almost invariably attracted an increasing number of cars to the island that it serves. As such custom increases, it is expected by island communities that the economically beneficial upturn will be maintained, if not enhanced, year upon year, particularly in summer. Consequently there can be a vigorous element of competition between islands for the 'best and biggest' ships, as well as heated debates about frequency of service. In Tiree, for example, feelings ran high in 2003 about the inadequacy of the *Lord of the Isles*' car-carrying capacity in comparison with that of the *Clansman*, especially on Saturdays. Caledonian MacBrayne was bombarded with some very sharp complaints from local representatives. As a result of growing demand, the company considered the possibility of extending the *Lord of the Isles* by fifteen metres to bring her car-carrying capacity more closely into line with that of the *Clansman*, but this has been ruled out by increasing costs in other areas, notably fuel.

Upgrading of facilities continues, nevertheless. The company has built its second linkspan at Oban, in order to speed up still further the loading and unloading of several key car-ferries, and it has invested £3.8 million in a new 'flagship' terminal building at the port's Railway Pier. When planning the new linkspan, the company had to deal with considerable opposition from Oban fishermen, who were afraid that the second linkspan would be detrimental to their use of the pier. Clearly, the plans and schedules of Caledonian MacBrayne, as well as the size of the fleet and its individual units, are being challenged ever more strongly, and its public relations are being tested anew, as island demands and aspirations continue to increase.

In such a context, the Inner Isles may be pitched against the Outer Isles in an ongoing series of localised 'ferry wars'. Variants of such wars, which are usually directed at Caledonian MacBrayne but may produce flak which can affect other parties, extend to schedules and timetables, and break out most frequently and violently when a timetable has been published. A common complaint, especially by the population of Barra in the 1980s and 1990s, was that islanders were not consulted sufficiently fully before timetables were introduced. Ferries that sailed at midnight were no longer acceptable by the late 1990s. As a result, consultative groups – Shipping Service Advisory Committees (SSACs) – were formed, in which representatives of the company and of the various island communities discussed timetables and their implications in advance of implementation. Currently, relative peace prevails.

Another stressful field of conflict is the keeping of the Sabbath day in the Outer Isles, especially in Lewis and Harris. 'Sunday ferries' have been a contested area, productive of strong sentiments, since the early 1960s, when the Rev. Angus Smith, then in Skye, lay down in front of the first car to come off the turntable ferry at Kyleakin on a Sunday – and was subsequently dubbed disrespectfully the 'Ferry Reverend'. Sunday sailings have been introduced gradually to Inner Hebridean services, sailings to Barra and South Uist from Oban, and the Uig-Lochmaddy service. There are now Sunday sailings on the Sound of Harris. The more northerly islands of the Outer Hebrides have resisted this development to date, despite a strong interest in Sunday sailings among the younger age-group.

The challenge to Sabbath-keeping, and the erosion of the churches' traditional supremacy in this domain, offer a particularly telling comment on the improvement of transport services to the Hebrides, and the two-way exchange which lies – inevitably – at its heart. The islands are no longer insular, if indeed they ever were. Over the last two centuries, the Hebrides have changed beyond recognition in terms of their social conventions and their ways of life. The steamship, the motor-vessel and the car-ferry have been key factors in such change. They have not, of course, been the only factors, but they have been highly significant, nevertheless. The islands are now more accessible to, and from, the mainland than they have ever been – and more dependent on it.

As the future unfolds, Caledonian MacBrayne will face ever more strident calls for changes in its practices, ship-design and general strategy, in order to meet changing needs. If certain political voices are heeded, the hitherto impregnable Kingdom of MacBrayne may yet have to face some of the toughest challenges in its long, distinguished and complex history.

CHAPTER 12

SURVEYING THE KINGDOM:
PAST, PRESENT – AND FUTURE

*The **Clansman** shimmers in the deep-blue waters of Gott Bay, Tiree, as she turns to the linkspan, and shows her Highlander to advantage. [DEM]*

SURVEYING THE KINGDOM:
PAST, PRESENT – AND FUTURE

There can be few Scots who are not familiar with the name MacBrayne. It is synonymous with communication in the Western Isles, the islands' lifeline and the main factor in enabling some islands to remain inhabited. If ever MacBrayne's ferries are compelled to compete commercially with other operators under a private enterprise system, the less economic routes would simply disappear and the smaller and more remote islands would either become uninhabited, or playgrounds for those wealthy enough to afford motor cruisers or aircraft.

JAMES D.G. DAVIDSON, *SCOTS AND THE SEA* (2003)

James Davidson's sentiments reflect pretty accurately the fears of many islanders as the 'Kingdom of MacBrayne' enters the twenty-first century. Under EC directives relating to marine cabotage and fair competition, Caledonian MacBrayne has had to prepare itself for the challenge of tendering its time-honoured routes to external bidders. Given the chequered history of the 'Kingdom', its peaks and troughs across the best part of two centuries, one would have expected that the message to leave well alone, in the light of past failures and present hard-won successes, would have been the immediate and well-considered response of Scottish politicians to their colleagues in Brussels, but that has not been the case. Caledonian MacBrayne will have to be put out to tender, in line with EC policy on routes which receive government subsidy. At the same time, analysts are considering the services given by Caledonian MacBrayne, the nature of its ships and their suitability to the emerging needs of the islands. It is therefore worth reflecting, in general terms, on the 'ups and downs' and the changing complexion of the 'Kingdom', both ships and services, in order to provide some guidance for the future.

The evidence of this book shows clearly that the legend of David MacBrayne – David the icon, rather than David the man – has been a powerful factor in company identity throughout the twentieth century, giving it a measure of distinctiveness and cohesion in the face of the levelling and integrating effect of successive take-overs and mergers.

In contrast to his own treatment of the Hutchesons, subsequent partnerships did not remove David's name from that of the company. It remained firmly in place. Indeed, it is very largely the name of MacBrayne that has prevented the complete assimilation of the 'Kingdom' within the state-owned company, Caledonian MacBrayne, formed in 1973.

Beyond this company, MacBrayne's name continues to be a connecting force in a scattered community, offering a sense of service, security and dependability. For the external hearer or reader, it immediately raises awareness of the special needs of the Highlands and Islands, which have been at the heart of the company's development throughout its existence. MacBrayne's best-remembered response to these needs came in the shape of sturdy, multi-purpose vessels – mainly pulsating motor-ships, with strongly-rigged derricks always ready for action, until they and their derricks were eliminated by the arrival of the new car-ferries from the 1970s. Their workaday look, with cars, animal-boxes and Pickfords containers resting on their foredecks, distinguished them from the ships of the Caledonian Steam Packet Company, which, for the most part, served the more genteel waters of the Firth of Clyde.

David MacBrayne's supreme contribution, however, was not made as the founder of the fleet, but as the risk-taking developer of a cohesive, modern 'radial service', with ships plying outwards to the islands from a number of mainland 'hubs'. Yet, although David's operating principles have been followed over many years, the MacBrayne family has been 'dead' in commercial terms since 1928. There is no longer a 'real MacBrayne' whose interests require to be protected. What must be protected is not necessarily the name, consoling, cohesive and important as that may be, but the quality of existing services, following major modernisation and improvement in the thirty years since the creation of Caledonian MacBrayne. This requires to be underlined forcefully, given the precarious nature of funding for MacBrayne operations since their inception back in the nineteenth century, and the immense efforts that have been made to maintain, and especially to enhance, all aspects of company practice.

From the moment that David MacBrayne took over the Hutchesons' business in 1878, the company has been no stranger to crises. These have been pre-eminently financial. In broad terms, MacBrayne's has been reconfigured as a commercial enterprise, and/or boosted by means of major capital injections, every twenty-five years or so. By 1905 David Hope MacBrayne had taken his father's place in the business, but by 1928 David Hope's company was in grave difficulties – in effect, bankrupt. Without a consistent policy of replacements, the fleet had aged gradually to the point of becoming a 'working museum'. There was no capital with which to build the new ships which were urgently required. The loss of three ships in 1927 forced the issue. Mercifully, Coast Lines and the London, Midland & Scottish Railway came to the rescue. This is arguably the best thing that ever happened to David MacBrayne, in any of its guises, as the visionary leadership of Sir Alfred Read introduced the succession of modern, diesel-engined vessels which were to provide the back-bone of the MacBrayne fleet until the 1960s. Despite their various design faults and the shortcomings of their machinery, the new ships built between 1930 and 1940 were state-of-the-art, and some were at the cutting edge of contemporary marine technology. Their designs were copied for service elsewhere, from the Northern Isles to the Thames estuary.

Consequently, the *Lochearn,* the *Lochmor* and the *Lochfyne* (see Chapter 7) have a very important place in the history of British maritime development, which is often overlooked.

Twenty years later, after the Second World War, the company again faced similar challenges, as it required replacement tonnage. When the new funding agreements eventually came to fruition with the *Loch Seaforth* (1947) and the *Claymore* (1955), along with their accompanying cargo-vessels, the company was not particularly forward-looking in its specifications. As the *Claymore* demonstrated, it was conservative in its designs and rather sparing, if not mean, in its outlays. The mood of the time also encouraged caution. The implications of the loss of the *Princess Victoria* in 1953 delayed the development of car-ferries in Britain as a whole. Traditional loading by derrick (lift-on/lift-off) was still the norm in the Hebrides throughout the 1950s, and lasted until the 1970s. By the early 1960s, the provision of three new car-ferries was essential, but it was beyond the existing capital assets of Coast Lines and the London, Midland & Scottish Railway to provide sufficient finance. The ships were therefore built by the then Secretary of State for Scotland, and registered in Leith. Compelled by the pressures of rebuilding at critical junctures, the company was edging gradually towards full state-ownership.

Similar stories of gradual attrition, but without the happy ending, can be told of other companies in the West Highland trade, most notably McCallum, Orme & Company (see Chapter 4). Their ships, the *Dunara Castle* and the *Hebrides*, became the undoubted 'old-timers' of the Hebridean service after 1930, while MacBrayne's modernised its fleet and got rid of its ancient veterans. McCallum and Orme were evidently largely dependent on their revenue income, supplemented by a small government subsidy, to keep their ships sailing. They performed admirably with what they had, giving sterling service to the islands for the best part of a century, but they did not have sufficient cash in hand to replace their tonnage. Their ships simply wore out. Their fate represents what would have happened to MacBrayne's in the longer term without the intervention of

Coast Lines and the London, Midland & Scottish Railway, and subsequent government support. When MacBrayne's eventually purchased McCallum, Orme & Company in 1948, it bought goodwill rather than good ships, as both vessels were long past their peak. The *Dunara*, whose advancing years had been of some concern to civil servants twenty years earlier, went to the scrap-heap immediately, but her sister was significantly younger – having been built as recently as 1898! – and therefore adequate for a few more years. By now a Victorian curiosity, the *Hebrides* partnered the cargo-boat *Loch Carron* until the *Loch Ard* arrived in 1955.

Government files, declassified within the last few years, show clearly that, when MacBrayne's was recreated in 1928, McCallum and Orme were under considerable pressure to merge with the new company, in order to create a single operator, responsible for all such transport in the West Highlands. The government of the day was broadly unhappy to contemplate the existence of several small companies, each living on the edge of viability, and constantly making the case for increased subsidy. Political debate since the 1980s seems to have moved in the opposite direction, with consequences which are already becoming apparent, as the Campbeltown-Ballycastle fiasco – with its wholly inadequate single-route subsidy – amply demonstrates.

The overwhelming challenge, then, for Hebridean shipping companies has been how best to stay afloat, and especially how to raise capital to replace ageing vessels. David MacBrayne itself – with a subsidy infinitely larger than that of McCallum and Orme – contended with, or quietly overlooked, this challenge until the early 1970s, as the allegedly very poor condition of the *Loch Seaforth* at the time of her sinking indicated. The company's tendency to retain older vessels longer than their 'sell-by date' also inhibited flexibility, as 'challengers' of various kinds suddenly appeared. In the later 1960s, MacBrayne's had to respond to the example of Eilean Sea Services and Western Ferries in introducing roll-on/roll-off facilities to the Inner Hebrides, an initiative which was later accompanied by

strongly worded and wryly written analyses by Andrew G. Wilson, Chairman of Western Ferries, in his two booklets, *The Sound of Silence* and *The Sound of the Clam*, published in the mid-1970s. Funding difficulties and increasing state support left MacBrayne, and later Caledonian MacBrayne, open to charges of being an inflexible, unaccountable and rather complacent 'fat cat'. The company had to take practical steps to answer its critics, as the wee dog of private enterprise snapped noisily at the 'fat cat's' large stern. It may also be noted, in the bygoing, that Western Ferries was prepared to have its vessels built in Norway, where ship-designs and inter-island services were more progressive and user-friendly than the existing MacBrayne set-up.

The Caledonian lion flies proudly from the mast of the **Lord of the Isles***. [Rhoda Meek]*

LITTLE AND LARGE: *PRIDE OF HULL* AND *CALEDONIAN ISLES*

TODAY, WITH SO many ships flagged-out to foreign registers with poorly paid crews, the flagships of the British and Irish ferry fleets are the P&O North Sea sisters *Pride of Hull* and *Pride of Rotterdam* – the latter flies the Dutch flag – and the Irish Ferries' *Ulysses*. The *Pride of Hull* has a gross tonnage of 59 925 (some 13 000 tons more than the *Titanic*!) and a length overall of 215 metres – big indeed – and has a service speed of 22 knots – fast as well. Her deadweight (the weight she can carry) is 8850 tonnes. The maximum draught of the ship when loaded is an incredible 6 metres, i.e. the keel is 6 metres – only 20 feet – beneath the water. The twin engines collectively provide 37 800 kW of power to twin variable-pitch propellers, each with four high-skew blades.

The *Pride of Hull* represents an investment of £90 million. She offers an impressive 4.5 km lane metres of space on the car deck and three separate freight decks, and can accommodate 250 cars and 400 freight units on her overnight run between Hull and Rotterdam. The ship can accommodate a total of 1360 passengers with a seat for everyone, or a choice of cabin accommodation, all with private facilities, as well as a selection of luxury suites. Facilities include an

à la carte restaurant, a casino, a wine bar, a two-tiered show lounge, a sky lounge with panoramic views and a cyber zone with permanent Internet connection. The ship has a fine art collection specially created by British and Dutch artists.

The *Pride of Hull* is arguably the world's largest ferry, and vies with the *Ulysses* for that privilege. How do they compare with the largest in the CalMac fleet? Well, in terms of safety, all the ships, large and small, are equipped to the same demanding standards, laid down in the Safety Of Life At Sea (SOLAS) regulations and by the licensing authorities. All have the same satellite navigational aids and computer assisted operating systems. The only significant difference is that the CalMac ferries are smaller, both to access confined and shallow harbours and because the available traffic does not require larger ships.

The *Caledonian Isles*, for example, has a gross tonnage of just 5221, is 94 m long (less than half the length of the *Pride of Hull*) and has a service speed of 15 knots. The *Caledonian Isles* can carry 1000 day passengers but only 120 cars and 10 lorries. The slightly larger and younger *Hebrides* and *Clansman* are similar, but are equipped to carry just over 600

passengers, and 110 and 90 cars respectively. They have a service speed of 16.5 knots.

The *Caledonian Isles* was launched at Lowestoft in May 1993, in the style of the finest cruise ship, by the Princess Royal. And like any cruise ship, and for that matter the *Pride of Hull* as well, all of the accommodation is air-conditioned. There is an observation lounge below the bridge, a children's play area and a kiosk. There are two cafeterias, a lounge and a separate bar lounge, and, of course, there is a lift to access the different decks and the vehicle deck.

The first thing you are conscious of when driving aboard the *Caledonian Isles* is that the car deck seems to be massive, complete with a hoistable mezzanine deck for cars that is more reminiscent of the Dover-Calais ferry than the ferry to Arran. In relative terms, of course, the vehicle deck is modest by today's standards, and small by comparison with the *Pride of Hull*. But it is in the passenger decks that the main differences lie, as the accommodation is laid out to a much smaller scale, without the broad corridors, airy plazas and spacious public rooms found on ships such as the *Pride of Hull* and her consorts. The accommodation aboard the *Caledonian Isles* is nevertheless compact

---

The Hebridean leopard began to change its spots slowly but surely, by crossing itself with the Caledonian lion, and producing a new hybrid, which was fated to carry the red lion in a yellow circle on the traditional red-and-black MacBrayne funnel. This mutation caused ship enthusiasts to rub their eyes in disbelief, as some still do, but the consequences of 'mating' the lion and the leopard were broadly beneficial, and good-quality 'cubs' emerged. Following the creation of the state-owned Scottish Transport Group on 1 January 1969 and the full acquisition of David MacBrayne Limited in July of that year, the stage was set for the formation of Caledonian MacBrayne. The company continued under the STG umbrella until 1990, when it was made directly accountable to the Secretary of State for Scotland.

Overall, Caledonian MacBrayne succeeded in turning what had been a very adverse and difficult tide, and, with state backing, it provided excellent vessels for its island services in the thirty years following 1973. Progress, however, has not been entirely spontaneous or on the company's own initiative. The rethinking of Hebridean sea-transport is due in no small part to Eilean Sea Services (now defunct) and Western Ferries, who were the initial, and very necessary, catalysts for the forthcoming revolution. State support has also been essential. Earned revenue alone could not have funded new building.

Once launched on its renewal programme, Caledonian MacBrayne produced good-looking vessels, often defying general global trends towards grossly utilitarian and hideously incongruous ship-designs. The rather ugly *Coruisk* and the

and neat, designed with a light, airy and open style. It is welcoming, yet functional. In addition, there is ample open deck space, always an attractive facility to those keen to watch the passage of the ship from port to port. The ship's crew comprises 23 in winter, with nine additional hands hired during summer to assist with passenger needs and catering. The crews work two weeks on and two weeks off, with a typical working day of 15 hours.

Both the big ferry and the smaller ferry are equipped with all the bells and whistles expected at sea, and both offer numerous sophisticated gadgets as well. The *Caledonian Isles'* equipment is a scaled-down version of that on the mega-ferry. She has twin variable-pitch propellers and twin Becker flap-rudders, and the main engines comprise a pair of Mirrlees Blackstone eight-cylinder units, together developing 4300 kW at 850 revolutions per minute. This is only a fraction of the design output of the *Pride of Hull*, reflecting a much reduced operational speed (15 instead of 22 knots) and a considerably smaller displacement. The *Caledonian Isles'* sophistications also include two Brunvoll bow-thruster units and retractable Brown Brothers fin stabilizers.

The tough, mean days of 'making do' with antiquated technology – such as that fitted to the 1955-built *Claymore*, which, despite her innovative elegance, was given outdated direct-reversing engines with four rattling cylinders each – have long gone. Only the best equipment will suffice for the modern fleet, and quite rightly so in the context of a company which now has the largest number of British-registered ferries to its name, with many of these working in some of the most unpredictable sea conditions around Britain.

The *Pride of Hull* does offer a casino, a plethora of cafeterias, restaurants and bars, and even a night club venue and a cinema, but who needs these on a 55-minute crossing, when there is Holy Isle to watch, along with all the other familiar landmarks of Arran, as the ship makes her approach towards Brodick Bay? Indeed, the comforts of the *Caledonian Isles*, the *Clansman* and the slightly better-appointed *Hebrides* are all that the modern-day traveller could ask for. These contrast with the plain and simple, almost utilitarian, accommodation of their respective predecessors.

Caledonian MacBrayne is to be congratulated on the standards to which it aspires, especially given the extent of the resources at its disposal, compared with the more lucrative cross-channel operating margins available to operators such as P&O and Irish Ferries. No private operator could ever be expected to perform as well as Caledonian MacBrayne. Private companies may well approach cautiously forthcoming invitations to tender for Caledonian MacBrayne's services, but their shareholders will inevitably ask the hard question – 'Could there ever be a dividend?'

*The **Pride of Hull** [P&O Group]*

*The **Caledonian Isles** [NR]*

box-like 'Loch' class ferries are the least attractive, largely because the emphasis in their design has been on providing the best, and most efficient, type of vessel for the route, rather than the most handsome. In general, however, the company's various designers have responded sensitively – within a Hebridean context – to the inevitable angularities and slab-sides imposed by the layout of a large car-ferry, to say nothing of the increasing amount of shape-determining safety regulations with which every shipping company now has to contend since the *Herald of Free Enterprise* disaster at Zeebrugge in 1987.

CalMac ferries have been developed in harmony with the modern era, and, on balance, they meet expectations. There are, inevitably, occasional outbreaks of dissatisfaction with timetables and services (see Chapter 11), and, from time to time, high-profile media publicity is given to the perceived underperformance of certain vessels in bad weather. None of these reactions is unprecedented in company history, nor are the actions of the disaffected. As happened with Western Ferries, disgruntled local merchants and enterprising businessmen are still capable of taking matters into their own hands, and running ventures in effective opposition to Caledonian MacBrayne. Even if these prove to be short-lived, they are often necessary, and make their point forcefully. In early 2001 the *White Sea* and later the *Taygran Trader*, belonging to Taygran Shipping, Aberdeen, began to sail briefly from Stornoway, and compelled CalMac to provide an overnight service for heavy vehicles. Daytime capacity for cars had been restricted severely by heavy haulage, and CalMac had failed to recognise the problem.

A gap in provision had been identified by the competitor. The 'fat cat' was asleep, and the little dog was barking at its stern once again – but on this occasion the little dog barked too loudly, and was seriously damaged by intestinal problems. Enhanced provision for hauliers resulted in a 20% increase in car traffic, as more space was now available on the *Isle of Lewis*.

Car-ferries have come, and are here to stay. With them has also come an ethos which, despite a large state subsidy, has its roots in competition. It proclaims itself in various ways, some of which conflict with the sensitivity shown in ship-design. These include a strong assault on observers' eyes, by employing the ships themselves as floating bill-boards, promoting the name of CALEDONIAN MACBRAYNE in eye-catching letters on their sides. Some logos were neatly placed in red lettering on the white superstructure, as on the 1978 *Claymore*, but the majority were (and are) painted in white letters on black hulls, as on the *Lord of the Isles*, whose sides have been covered between the beltings with disproportionately large and intrusive lettering. The principle behind this practice, now employed globally by ferry-operators, reflects the commercial aspirations of the company, which take precedence over aesthetics. Quite apart from the manner in which bill-boarding disfigures and demeans the ships themselves, it is superfluous in a context in which Caledonian MacBrayne has an outright monopoly of services, and the consumer has no choice in sea-travel. It is more understandable in a competitive environment, such as one might find in the English Channel, but not in the Minches. A neatly-fashioned and tasteful 'board',

Making the message stick: the car-stickers portray three different deisgns of modern car-ferry. [DEM's collection]

or a smaller, less prominent style of lettering (such as that employed by the Isle of Man Steam Packet Company – and even by Cunard!), would surely be preferable.

An unfortunate result of contemporary bill-boarding is that it can distort history. It is sometimes 'read back' by commercial artists (not commissioned by the company), who may disfigure earlier ships unknowingly, or perhaps even wilfully for promotional purposes, by adorning them anachronistically with the company's name. Thus, on the otherwise very attractive promotional display-board produced at the time of the Royal National Mod at Oban in 2003, which shows vessels of the (Caledonian) MacBrayne fleet past and present, the artist's impression of the 1955 *Claymore* carries the Gaelic/English logo *Caledonian Mac a' Bhriuthainn* in bold white letters on her starboard side. While some degree of creativity is understandable in such a context, it is unfortunate that this 'mistake' has been made, as the *Claymore* maintained the best traditions of David MacBrayne Limited until she was sold to Greek owners in 1976 (see Chapter 9). By escaping to the Mediterranean, her sides – mercifully! – avoided the disfigurement inflicted on her Hebridean successors.

This rather gauche literary development has now been supplemented by the addition of the company's URL, in red and black letters on the superstructure. This again seems superfluous, given that most computer-literate passengers will locate the company easily on the Internet by the use of a competent search-engine, if they do not have a current timetable. They will not think readily of nipping along to the quayside – in Oban, Stornoway or Lochboisdale – to check the website address of CalMac before taking up their keyboards!

The nomenclature of Caledonian MacBrayne vessels has likewise changed, at least in presentation. It is now bilingual, with English and Gaelic 'equivalents' on all ships except those originally given Gaelic forms of names. The Gaelicising of English names may seem sensible at first sight, since several of the ships serve Gaelic-speaking areas (for the most part) and Gaelic is part of Scottish life. However, it is questionable whether like is always being matched with like, as the names are transferred from English to Gaelic. As well as literal meaning, such names have onomastic significance and cultural connotations which reflect the circumstances in which they were coined and originally bestowed. As has been indicated elsewhere in this book, the English names chosen for MacBrayne's vessls often reflected the romantic and heroic ethos associated with Highland society and landscapes, and these established a pattern, which, on the whole, has been maintained to the present. In general, the original English/Scots names have been translated in terms of their literal meaning. In the process, however, several key names have lost their broader English/Scots cultural sparkle. *Clansman* has become *Fear-cinnidh* ('Man of Kindred'), which feels wooden and dull, and lacks the swashbuckling romanticism of the sword-bearing Highlander, at the centre of MacBrayne's traditional imagery, while the *Isle of Mull* (normally *Eilean Mhuile*) is equated with *An t-Eilean Muileach*, which Gaelic people know best as the title of a popular song. Paradoxically, the least successful Gaelic transfer of all is the name of the region that the ships actually serve – the Hebrides. *Hebrides* becomes the alien-sounding *Innse Gall* ('Islands of Foreigners'), which is historically correct, but hardly ever used by Gaelic-speakers beyond 'learned' circles. It has no romantic glow, even for native Hebrideans – the opposite, in fact. In cross-cultural exchanges of this kind, there are inevitably gains and losses, and the translation of ship names is no exception. It is a telling comment on the ships' Gaelic nomenclature that it is not normally used in Gaelic news programmes. The *Isle of Lewis*, for instance, which serves the most strongly Gaelic-speaking area of the entire Hebrides, regularly retains her English name in such broadcasts.

In broad terms, nevertheless, Caledonian MacBrayne's use of, and commitment to, Gaelic is greatly appreciated, and it manifests itself at various levels. Three Gaelic-speakers from the islands have recently been among the non-executive members of its Board of Directors. The company now employs a Gaelic-speaking Head of Communications, who is able to address the Gaelic community directly. Through his regular interviews on Gaelic radio, listeners are kept closely in touch with company policy and shipping movements. Largely because of this, the public relations dimension of the company has improved beyond measure in recent years. Before the late 1990s, Caledonian MacBrayne and its predecessors did not engage to any great extent with Gaelic culture, despite the obviously major contribution made by David MacBrayne and his successors to Gaelic demography and the reshaping of the Gaelic world. Admittedly, there is still an element of tokenism in some of the company's policies, as is evident in the extremely brief Gaelic 'welcomes' which precede the Safety Announcements before a vessel sails, but its overall strategy is quite clearly on the right cultural course, and the company has committed itself to the principles of the Gaelic Language Act (2005).

Caledonian MacBrayne also appears to have followed the right course in its provision of services. Those with first-hand experience of the ships and services previously provided by David MacBrayne Limited will readily agree that Caledonian MacBrayne has made great progress with the revitalisation of its fleet since its creation in 1973. This has not been a 'blank cheque job', as the company has had to provide investment plans, and to argue for its levels of funding from government relative to route revenue projections and expenditure such as new building. It has also had to live with the down side of its state-owned position. This appears in various guises, such as intervention in 'its' affairs by Ministers, or 'waiting games' for project permissions, or the imposition of directives from the Scottish Executive, and now from Brussels, which may change the nature of

The **Isle of Lewis** draws alongside at Ullapool, while the **Happy Return** bids her welcome. [Ian MacKenzie]

the company. One of these directives, whose shadow has loomed large over the company for several years, relates to the tendering of subsidised operations.

At the heart of 'tendering' is the principle of inviting other companies, as well as the current operator, to bid for the running of the services presently provided by Caledonian MacBrayne. This is in line with what has happened in other areas of transport (e.g. the railways), and it holds out the possibility that, if the right operator can be found, a reduction may be achieved in running costs and deficit grants, currently amounting to £31.4 million for 2005-6 and 2006-7 (a sum inclusive of the costs of new building).

'Tendering' Caledonian MacBrayne is not a new policy, although it is currently formulated in terms different from those previously employed. The idea is, in fact, almost twenty years old. The option of 'privatising', and even 'splitting up', Caledonian MacBrayne was one of the possibilities raised as far back as January 1988 by the Conservative government of the period. Malcolm Rifkind, then Secretary of State for Scotland, announced that he would be considering 'the best future arrangements' for Caledonian MacBrayne. By November of that year, the government had decided to retain Caledonian MacBrayne as a single entity within public ownership, but to transfer its shares from the Scottish Transport Group to the Secretary of State.

As John Whittle, former Executive Director of Caledonian MacBrayne, indicated in *Speed Bonny Boat*, when summarising views expressed in 1988,

There were some who favoured splitting Caledonian MacBrayne, even down to individual services, while others

THE ART AND CRAFT OF MACBRAYNE

DAVID MACBRAYNE'S SHIPS have been an endless source of pleasure and fascination to writers, artists and model-makers. This book draws on the work of various writers over the last century or so, in both Gaelic and English. Just as MacBrayne's ships continue to live within the written word, they also have an unending life in art and craft. Artists have captured the 'Kingdom' on paper and canvas, and model-makers have ensured that it continues to sail onwards in miniature. Now powered by electric motors and controlled by radio, ships that have long since gone to the scrapyard still cross the duck-ruffled waters of country lochs and city ponds, or grace the static display cases of transport museums and the alcoves of private houses.

Ships that have remained particularly popular among model-makers include the 'favourites', *King George V* (1926), *Lochnevis* (1934), *Lochiel* (1939), and *Claymore* (1955), commonly built to a scale of 1/48. An impressive model of the *Lochfyne* (1931) can be seen in the display cases of the Clyde Room of the Glasgow Transport Museum. More recent

vessels are gradually finding favour. *Model Boats* (July 2005) featured a splendid model of the present *Lochnevis*, built in meticulous detail (including lorries on the car-deck) by Bob Barlow, who described the construction of his model. Builders' models are on display at official centres: the *Claymore* (1955) is in the Caledonian MacBrayne terminal at Oban, and the *Loch Seaforth* (1947) in Stornoway Museum, while the *Clansman* (1998), *Hebrides* (2001), *Loch Portain* and *Coruisk* (both 2003) currently reside at Caledonian MacBrayne's Gourock office.

Artists have depicted the MacBrayne fleet in different styles and in different media across the years. Alasdair MacFarlane (1902-60), a native of Tiree resident in Glasgow, produced a fine series of pen and scraper-board sketches of McCallum Orme vessels (some of which are reproduced in this book from prints in the Glasgow *Evening Citizen* newspaper), as well as depictions of MacBrayne's *Loch Seaforth* (1947), *Loch Ard* (1955) and *Claymore* (1955). His output covered Clyde-built ships serving in home and foreign fleets.

Probably the best known and most distinguished

colour artist in this context in recent years has been the late John Nicholson (1921-2004), an engineering draughtsman based in Leeds, whose paintings feature *Claymore* (1881), *King George V* (1926), *Lochfyne* (1931) and *Columba* (1964), as well as the occasional McCallum Orme vessel, notably the *Dunara Castle*. Nicholson's lively output extended to drawings for dust-jackets and book covers, with sketches of the *Claymore* (1955), in addition to several depictions of Clyde steamers. His artistic endeavours embraced many other fleets, including the Isle of Man Steam Packet, for which he had a special affection.

Officers, engineers and sailors of MacBrayne vessels likewise make an important contribution to maritime art. Tom Robertson, former Chief Engineer of the *Claymore* (1955), produces a wide range of paintings of such ships as *Lochearn* (1930), *Claymore* (1955 and 1978) and *Loch Seaforth*, as well as the more recent ferries, including *Hebrides*, *Clansman* and *Columba* (1963-64), and the *Lord of the Isles* (1989). In contrast to Nicholson, whose paintings generally have fairly romantic and 'stylised' settings, Robertson brings

The **King George V** at Tobermory by John Nicholson [DEM's collection]

Bob Barlow's fully-operational model of the **Lochnevis** [Bob Barlow]

his personal knowledge of Hebridean landscape and weather to bear on his atmospheric compositions, such as 'No Call at Coll', showing the *Claymore* (1955) ploughing through heavy seas close to the island.

Occasional sketches by enthusiasts of various kinds appear in print from time to time, but these seem to be less common now than they were twenty years ago. A generation ago, Glasgow bookshops and newsagents, such as the now defunct Aladdin's cave run by Messrs Porteous of Exchange Place, displayed all manner of delineations, good, bad and indifferent, of MacBrayne and Caledonian Steam Packet ships. At present it is comparatively rare to find good-quality amateur paintings of MacBrayne or CalMac vessels for sale. It seems likely that this is related, in part at least, to the gradual attrition of the romance once associated with 'classic' steamers and motor vessels, as younger generations, turning away from the Clyde and Western Isles, seek the sun-spots of the Mediterranean, or find themselves increasingly preoccupied with mobile phones, DVDs and ipods rather than pen and brush. The changing nature of the ships themselves doubtless also contributes to loss of artistic interest. Contemporary car-ferries, with their biscuit-tin vents, towering sides, angular profiles and intrusive bill-boarding, are hard to present attractively. To most people with vacant space on their walls, they are very much less appealing than the portrayal of elegant 'veterans' such as the incomparable *King George V* slicing at full speed through the Sound of Mull.

Artists who are also talented writers combine their skills in both word and paint to commemorate MacBrayne. This is particularly evident in the work of Mairi Hedderwick, whose years of residence in the island of Coll are the inspiration behind her delightful *Katie Morag* books for a 'younger' readership. These feature a round-faced little lassie in wellington boots, living on the island of Struay, and finding her way between the competing claims of Grannie Island and Grandma Mainland. The 'big boat' which brings mails, cargo and people (including Grandma Mainland) to Struay is unquestionably the *Claymore* (1955), deftly sketched with some artistic licence some twenty years after her departure to Greece. Ship and island are particularly well delineated in *Katie Morag and the New Pier* (1993), in which islanders express their views of the pluses and minuses of this development, which came to Coll in 1965: 'The old ways will be forgotten', [Grannie Island] frowned. 'The place will get too busy; there will be no more jaunts out in the ferryboat to the big boat in the Bay.'

In books set in pre-pier insularity, the Coll ferry appears prominently, and it is possible for those with 'insider knowledge' to identify the principal members of her intrepid crew, among them the former proprietor of Coll Hotel, the kenspeckle Mr Jardine, who always wore his kilt, even when sailing against the cold, stiff, south-easterly breezes of Loch Eatharna in order to make a hazardous rendezvous with the *Claymore*. Thermal underwear was not in fashion, nor indeed required, among such heroic, hot-blooded mariners. Even Grannie Island was cold-resistant: 'Grannie Island often manned the ferryboat on the days that the ferryman was ill or on holiday'.

In the *Katie Morag* books, the essence of island life is conveyed superbly, with an even-handed and gently satirical touch which transcends the age of the readership and defies the passage of time and of ships. In such skilful contexts, the art and craft of MacBrayne – to be variously understood – continues to flourish.

*The builder's model of the **Hebrides** [DEM]*

pointed to the problems of co-ordination and interchange of vessels which this would cause. Island opinion seemed strongest against any significant change with real concern that a privately-owned company would be unable to maintain the same level and quality of service without significant additional subsidy which seemed an unlikely outcome.

Needless to say, the same arguments have accompanied the debate about tendering the company, which has dragged on since the early 2000s, when Sarah Boyack, MSP, announced in January 2001 that the Scottish Executive regarded 'all of the services provided by the company as being consistent with Public Service Obligations and planned to tender them in line with EU regulations'. The Executive rejected the tendering of individual services, however, believing that 'the way forward was to tender the network as a whole rather than by individual routes or areas'. Caledonian MacBrayne would be allowed 'to tender for the operating franchise on the basis that the bid was prepared on a fair and full cost basis and evaluated transparently and equally with bids from other potential operators'. The company was, however, to remain in the public sector.

Thereafter, progress was painfully slow. The debate reached the level of little more than parliamentary farce, seen most obviously when, in December 2004, a bizarre alliance of Conservatives, disgruntled Labour members, Scottish Nationalists and Scottish Socialists defeated *by one vote* the Labour-Liberal Democrat alliance which wished to tender company services. Clearly, the Scottish Parliament had become increasingly wary, but there was little heart in Scottish Labour circles for a prolonged struggle against EC policy. Brussels helped the Executive out of the ditch by indicating in July 2005 that Caledonian MacBrayne must be put out to tender, while conceding that – apart from the Gourock-Dunoon route – it could be tendered as a single entity. In September 2005, the Scottish Parliament voted by a majority of 10 votes to put the company out to tender, and the process was put in hand. Out of twenty who expressed an initial interest, only three potential bidders for the west-coast and Hebridean services were selected and permitted to proceed to the next stage – Western Ferries, V-Ships and Caledonian MacBrayne. The same bidders lodged an interest in the Gourock-Dunoon service.

As the tendering process inched towards a conclusion, Caledonian MacBrayne itself had been bidding for routes formerly maintained by P&O from Aberdeen to Orkney and Shetland. A company called NorthLink, in which Caledonian MacBrayne has been a 50% shareholder with the Royal Bank of Scotland, was able to bid successfully for these services, and to provide three new vessels. In April 2004, however, it was announced that the routes would have to be put out to a new tender earlier than expected, because NorthLink could not meet its costs. By its own claim, it had to contend with unforeseen circumstances, requiring an additional £13.4 million subsidy (over eighteen months) from the Scottish Executive.

This episode raised many questions about the logic of the entire tendering process. Not least perplexing to the outside observer is the fact that a company in the public sector, open to tender and already heavily subsidised, could enter the lists for the acquisition of further subsidised routes. To add to the external observer's perplexity, Caledonian MacBrayne was invited to tender again for the same routes, despite the manifest weaknesses of its earlier, successful bid. Caledonian MacBrayne formed another company to tender for these routes, while the Royal Bank of Scotland retained ownership of the three new NorthLink ships. On 9 March 2006, it was announced by the Scottish Executive that Caledonian MacBrayne had been selected to run the NorthLink service.

Equally complex arrangements – which certainly do not appear to simplify existing practices – were created to handle the west coast routes. Broadly, the developing plan proposed the creation of an asset-owning company, presently called VesCo, to retain control of ships and piers. The Scottish Executive would hold ownership of VesCo, and thus protect the integrity of the fleet. The contract to run the services, which is the subject of the current tendering process, would be operated by a company provisionally known as OpsCo. Two other wholly-owned subsidiaries were formed to prepare for tendering. These are Caledonian MacBrayne Crewing (Guernsey) Limited, who employ the seagoing staff, so that the employer does not require to pay National Insurance, and Caledonian MacBrayne HR (UK) Limited, based in Gourock, who will manage the crewing on behalf of the Guernsey company. One can only imagine what the great David MacBrayne, with his unshakeable belief in a one-man operated company, would have to say if he could be party to the philosophies, political and economic, presently determining the shape of his former enterprise!

To judge by the NorthLink experience, a successful tender for operating its own west-coast routes may not be the end of the story for Caledonian MacBrayne, even in its traditional heartlands. It – or any other company brave enough to undertake these services – will still have to face all the inevitable challenges of its position, in relation to subsidies, fares, timetables and unhappy islanders. Charges may have to be increased to meet the cost of tendering alone, currently estimated to be in the region of £1 million for the existing company. If another operator is given the contract, while retaining the external façade of Caledonian MacBrayne, it will need to embark on a steep 'learning curve' in order to master the complexities of the region. This will introduce the potential for fresh mistakes and miscalculations. As the NorthLink saga demonstrates, it is possible for even an experienced bidder to underestimate basic 'unforeseen' costs, with the result that further subsidy may be required in what is supposed to be an exercise in 'value for money'. If the chosen operator fails to deliver, with the result that an 'operator of last resort' will require to be appointed, or if matters remain much the same as before, the exercise will have been no more than an immense waste of time, money and effort, required primarily to keep the Brussels bureaucrats in business. There may be 'efficiency gains' of a kind, but they are unlikely to cure all ills. Tendering, in short, will not offer the panacea that disaffected critics of the existing system yearn to discover. Unquestionably, it has already caused a great deal of additional work for Caledonian MacBrayne, and it has doubtless diverted energies, as well as financial and managerial resources, which would have been much better used in addressing the needs of the island communities served by the company.

The Kingdom of MacBrayne has weathered many storms, but it has also had to be rescued periodically from impending disaster, and from the slings and arrows of its enemies and detractors. The company is not perfect, and in several instances the actions taken by disgruntled hauliers, carriers and users have been entirely justified. Some have resulted in much-needed improvements to services. The company and its officials are not above contradiction, and, as services diversify, they require to listen ever more intently to the views of their customers, as well as those of policy-makers. At the same time, they have to react to market forces, including the ever-increasing cost of fuel. Idealism on the part of the customer has to be set against realism on the part of the company. The reasoned argument, based on well-marshalled evidence, must also be distinguished from the intemperate noise of the 'CalMac basher', whose kind has existed since the days of David Hutcheson, and whose advice on 'how to run the company properly' is always freely available.

Inevitably, areas of debate are never lacking. These currently include the shipyards which ought to be given contracts to build the company's new vessels. Until recently Caledonian MacBrayne's ships have been built in the United Kingdom or (very occasionally) bought off the stocks from Norway, but European shipyards (and others world-wide) are now firmly in the frame. The building of the *Bute* (2005) in Gdansk by the Remontowa Group in Poland sparked controversy, fomented by those politicians and journalists – among others – who saw it as a sell-out to EC regulations and a betrayal of Scottish interests, particularly those of the Ferguson yard at Port Glasgow, which has already built five of the company's finest car-ferries (*Isle of Arran*, *Isle of Mull*, *Lord of the Isles*, *Isle of Lewis* and *Hebrides*).

Given the decline of British shipbuilding and the closure of several yards which have built its vessels in recent years, the company faces a dilemma in this respect, since, like every other purchaser of its kind, it is obliged in law to obtain the best, the most reliable and the most cost-effective deal.

The problem is made all the more acute by European directives on transparency, and by the company's state-owned position. If it were seen to be 'wasting public money' on expensive contracts and on 'maintaining shipyards', critical voices would be no less strident. National newspapers are, of course, extremely anxious to exploit any supposed 'political mistake' by Caledonian MacBrayne, and they will devote columns to an 'exposé'. The same papers, however, devoted only a few lines to the news that the most recent (December 2005) Caledonian MacBrayne contract had, in fact, been won by the Ferguson yard.

Another area of debate centres on the design of the company's allegedly 'antiquated' car-ferries, in comparison with large, fast or semi-fast, aluminium catamarans and monohulled vessels. As the *Bute* went into service in the Clyde, advocates of the 'fast ferries' were making a case for their use between Gourock and Rothesay – hardly the scene of much success for 'fast ferries' to date. Whatever their potential for the Clyde, the viability of such vessels in Hebridean waters is very much open to question. Their potential is likely to be off-set by the nature of the maritime environment, restrictions on their carrying capability (which would extend to fuel-tankers, for instance), and their very high maintenance and operating costs (estimated to be four times those of conventional ships), especially in the context of ever-increasing fuel bills, which have doubled in the last year alone. Their introduction could

well lead to further increases in fares or subsidies. In any case, given the implications of climate change, and the likelihood of more violent storms in the future, it would seem sensible to consider stronger and more powerful, and somewhat faster, versions of the current *Clansman* and *Hebrides* as the models for the years immediately ahead. It remains to be seen how the 'fast ferries' develop, but, despite their attribute of speed, their arrival in Hebridean waters will be very much subject to MacBrayne's old caveat – 'weather permitting'.

The challenges for Scottish west-coast ferry operations will continue to be many and varied, and there will be no single, easy, all-round answer which will usher in a new era of flawless development. That is made abundantly clear by the patterns of the past. Any new operator who wishes to 'transform the company', or even to maintain existing services, will require a very big bank-balance to fund its responsibilities. It can rest assured that its purse will soon be depleted in the process, and that subsidies of one kind or another will always be required.

The evidence of this book presents the enormous difficulties encountered by David MacBrayne and his successors across more than 150 years, and it shows how these were tackled. Undoubtedly, there have been failures on the part of the company, in its various forms, but there have also been many, very significant, successes. The book, in short, records remarkable progress, especially since 1973, in providing an up-to-date range of ships and services for the Hebrides and the west of Scotland. The Kingdom of MacBrayne has served its subjects well, though never perfectly, and it deserves to be steered carefully as a single, well-protected entity through the choppy seas of change.

*Looking astern: the **Lord of the Isles** leaves the islands in her wake. [Rhoda Meek]*

CHAPTER 13

THE RETURN OF THE KING?
LEASING SHIPS AND DELIVERING SERVICES

*The **Loch Striven** leaves Sconser, and heads for Raasay, in September 2007. [DEM]*

THE RETURN OF THE KING?
LEASING SHIPS AND DELIVERING SERVICES

'We are always aware of the lifeline we provide, and no matter what the structure, we feel that that responsibility never changes…Provided that the present company wins each tender, Caledonian MacBrayne will maintain its services as before, although changes are inevitable as technology advances. The fundamental purpose of serving the islands will always remain, and we must all play our part in providing the services for which we have been renowned over the last 157 years.'

CAPTAIN JOHN A. GILLIES, MASTER, MV *ISLE OF ARRAN*

Just as the first edition of this book was about to be published, Caledonian MacBrayne Limited completed the long, complex and expensive process of restructuring, in order to have the privilege of tendering for its own services in competition with other bidders, and thus satisfying the conditions laid down by the European Commission, as described in the preceding chapter. From 1 October 2006, the single company became three separate companies, in addition to those already established in Jersey and Gourock to handle aspects of crewing and human resources respectively. To the outward eye, nothing had changed; the ships continued to sail on their accustomed routes in accordance with their normal schedules, and the name of Caledonian MacBrayne remained firmly on their sides, with the accompanying branding and house-flag. To all intents and purposes, it was 'business as usual'. Nevertheless, when one scratched beneath the paintwork, the changes were indeed far-reaching, with major implications for the future of Hebridean and related sea-services.

In the new arrangements, ultimate ownership of the entire Caledonian MacBrayne operation was retained by Scottish Ministers. However, from 1 October 2006, ships and piers were put under the banner of Caledonian Maritime Assets Limited (abbreviated to CMAL), which had the same company number and basic assets as Caledonian MacBrayne Limited. In business terms, therefore, CMAL was technically identical with the 'old company', except

that it was given a new name, new staff and a new Board of Directors. The actual operation of the ships became the responsibility of a new company, CalMac Ferries Limited (CFL), who obtained a bareboat charter of their former vessels from CMAL, together with Harbour Access and an Operating Agreement.

Perhaps the most welcome development was 'the return of the King', after a period in unacknowledged exile. David MacBrayne Limited, which had been a dormant company since 1980, was revitalised to become the holding company for the operating 'subsidiary', CalMac Ferries Limited. It also held the crewing and human resource companies, Caledonian MacBrayne Crewing (Guernsey) Limited (operational from 1 February 2006), and David MacBrayne HR (UK) Limited (operational likewise from 1 February 2006), as well as NorthLink Ferries Limited (operational from 6 July 2006), Rathlin Ferries Limited (operational from 1 April 2007) and Cowal Ferries Limited (operational likewise from 1 April 2007). 'King David' thus returned in bureaucratic triumph, but the king's person was, in reality, much less robust than it had previously been. The organic unity of the regal warrior with a raised claymore, who had once held undisputed sway on the bows of ships and the sides of buses, on letter-heads and colourful brochures, was to a large extent a legal convenience. Although the 'brawny-kneed Highlander' was to re-appear as David MacBrayne's identifying device, he too was at best a reconstructed icon with a computer-woven kilt, giving some degree of outward cohesion to the inner complexities of the new world order.

David MacBrayne Ltd
Serving Scotland's Islands

As David MacBrayne made his iconic come-back, Caledonian MacBrayne Limited was, like the once and future king, put to sleep as a dormant company, being retained as a legal entity solely to protect the former name from potential piracy. 'Caledonian MacBrayne' and 'CalMac' were preserved, nonetheless, as the trading names of the enterprise as a whole. Although CMAL was largely a renaming of Caledonian MacBrayne Limited, it lost front-line status. Most customers still regard the familiar faces and voices of the operators, CalMac Ferries Limited, as the 'real' company in practical, day-to-day terms, and refer simply to 'CalMac' or 'Caledonian MacBrayne', rather than the formal business designation of CFL.

The major issue which had set the entire restructuring process in motion – the award of a contract for the operation of the actual services – remained a matter of speculation for another year, and it was finally resolved only with the creation of a Scottish Nationalist administration in Edinburgh following the General Election of May 2007. Although the Nationalists were among those who opposed the EC directive to put Hebridean services out to tender, calling the process 'an expensive exercise in futility from a supine [Scottish] Executive', they were – ironically – fated to receive the poisoned chalice from the previous Labour-Liberal Democrat administration, which is unlikely to have derived much electoral advantage from its rather tardy performance on the 'CalMac issue'.

In contrast to the uncertain sounds and apparent dithering of their predecessors, the Nationalists moved expeditiously to end the long and costly process which had kept both CalMac Ferries Limited and the people of the Hebrides in a state of unhelpful suspense for some

five years. By this stage, however, only CalMac Ferries Limited remained as a serious contender for the contract. Both Western Ferries and V-Ships, which had previously shown interest, had withdrawn. On 20 September 2007 it was announced that CalMac Ferries Limited had been awarded the contract, which had been ratified between the parties at a Completion Meeting in Glasgow on that day. Predictably, this was the cause of further political point-scoring. According to Scottish Conservatives, 'This sorry episode disgrace[d] the previous Liberal Democrat and Labour ministers, who presided over years of chaos and delay since the tendering of these routes was announced. Vast sums of taxpayers' money have been squandered to restore the status quo.'

Regardless of political affiliation, few with any knowledge of the Hebrides and of shipping services to these islands would disagree that the saga had been unncessarily prolonged, extraordinarily costly and rather pointless overall, as anticipated in Chapter 12. Many felt that the money spent on restructuring Caledonian MacBrayne Limited and preparing for the tender would have been much better spent on the services themselves, particularly when it was understood that the final cost of the exercise had reached the region of £15.3 million – more than half the cost of a large new ship, at current values. Of this sum, £11 million consisted of a one-off clawback of tax relief, which had previously been due to Caledonian MacBrayne Limited as owner and operator of the vessels now under the control of CMAL. Less stridently, observers of the process wondered how the creation of several companies, some (principally CMAL) requiring new cohorts of paid directors and staff, with potential duplication of roles, could possibly be a convincing display of cost-effectiveness in anyone's terms. The 'system', it seemed, had become much more expensive to maintain, not less, and potentially much more fraught and complex.

For Caledonian MacBrayne as a whole, but particularly for CalMac Ferries Limited, the award of the contract must have generated mixed feelings. On the one hand, there would have been relief among staff and crews that jobs and investment in time and effort had been safeguarded, but, on the other, there must have been a sense of disappointment that the contract had been won without competition from other contenders, thus calling into question the rationale of the whole process. While many would accept without question that the most appropriate company to run the services offered by Caledonian MacBrayne Limited prior to October 2006 was, unsurprisingly, none other than CalMac Ferries Limited, this could be considered by less sympathetic observers as, at best, the natural default position, or, at worst, a 'fix' intended from the start, facilitated by complexities which led to the withdrawal of rival bidders before they were too deeply enmeshed in the preparation of a costly application. Staff at all levels of CalMac Ferries Limited must have sighed, or even groaned, for more than one reason, despite the company's 'success'.

Now that the fog has cleared on the tender landscape of Caledonian MacBrayne, it is possible to see the conflicting contours of the present operation a little more clearly. The broader picture corresponds to what one finds with transport providers in other domains, such as road, air and rail services. The 'hardware' or 'stock' is leased, in such contexts, from a leasing company, usually an investment company or a bank, by the successful bidder for these services, as happens with NorthLink vessels, which are leased from the Royal Bank of Scotland. In the case of CalMac, what makes the operation particularly distinctive is the fact that Scottish Ministers are the ultimate owners of the ships and piers, even though CMAL is the recognised legal entity in possession of these assets. This means that any operator, present or future, has no choice in what vessels to deploy in terms of the overall fleet, and little, if any, leeway to introduce new vessels which are not approved at the highest level. While this undoubtedly protects the Hebridean and Clyde fleet from being 'seconded elsewhere' at a time when vessels of a similar kind are relatively rare across the globe, it cannot be an attractive proposition to potential service-providers, who may well find it restrictive, if not inhibitive, if they have ideas of their own. It is also evident that, while there is an element of flexibility within the new structure, insofar as new operators can bid for services at the end of the current agreement, the existing structure seems overwhelmingly legal, managerial and bureaucratic, creating a need for a much greater degree of consultation between companies than was necessary under the previous single-company model. In short, the new arrangements are not likely to appeal to bidders with a spirit of innovation or independence, or to those who have little previous experience of operating within and between so many different managerial layers, and all ultimately accountable to the Scottish Government.

Given the outcome, what exactly are the possible advantages and disadvantages of the new arrangement for Hebridean and Clyde ferry services? In theory, if not in practice, the differentiation of roles and responsibilities – between CMAL, CalMac Ferries Limited and the crewing and HR companies – ought to mean that it is now easier for the operators to concentrate on delivering the services, without having to worry directly about the ships themselves, or the ever-present likelihood of contentions

*The **Isle of Mull** in the Sound of Mull [DEM]*

relating to piers and harbours, or crewing issues. This should mean that quality will be enhanced all round. This differentiation of roles, however, is at the price of increased bureaucracy, and potential areas of conflict and misunderstanding could conceivably arise between companies within the group; for example, between CMAL, who 'own' the vessels on behalf of Scottish Ministers, and thus call the shots in real terms, and the operators, CalMac Ferries Limited, if the former do not have the requisite knowledge of maritime management that the latter possess intuitively as long-standing operators. The latter could also request a further vessel, or modifications to vessels, which might not be available or forthcoming from CMAL.

It is not difficult, therefore, to see why CalMac Ferries Limited became the only company to submit a bid for Hebridean and Clyde services. Only they knew the totality of the practical, operating requirements, and only they were already familiar with, and long inured to, the tensions of functioning under government regulation and accountability. Nor is it difficult to understand why there was no offer at all for the Gourock-Dunoon service, which was rendered separately because of the interest of Western Ferries. Can a single service be worth the implicit, and explicit, demands made by the 'leasing structure'? Can the operator of a single route be expected to match, like for like, the terms and conditions which are 'old hat' to the larger company, which has years of experience and a network of well-informed, professional support? And what of the level of deficit grant?

These, and many other questions, are inevitably raised by what appears to be a rather messy political fudge, with a particularly sticky core-relationship between Brussels and Scottish Ministers, who have remained the true owners of the operation, despite the fig-leaf offered to private enterprise. The viability of the supposed 'private-enterprise solution', with smaller operators and an inevitable subsidy, may well be tested soon by the arrangements currently emerging (after some setbacks) for the running of the Ballycastle-Rathlin service, previously maintained by Rathlin Ferries Limited, but assigned on 21 April 2008 to Ciarán O' Driscoll, whose vessels already provide services to Cape Clear Island and Whiddy Island, off County Cork. The contract has been awarded for a six-year period, within which the Department for Regional Development is committed to providing a subsidy totalling just under £4 million. It is intended that the services rendered by the CMAL-owned Island-class vessel *Canna* will be supplemented by those of a high-speed catamaran, capable of carrying 100 passengers, although a smaller mono-hulled vessel has enhanced services since the new operating arrangement came into effect from 1 July 2008.

No sooner had the contract for Hebridean and Clyde services (excluding the now-orphaned Gourock-Dunoon service, for which no bids were received) been granted to CalMac Ferries Limited than the next round in the now customary, if not mandatory, 'ferry wars' exploded in the Hebrides. On this occasion, the matter at issue was the provision of a service from Lochboisdale to Mallaig. In its tender, CalMac Ferries Limited had offered two possibilities for the provision of a service,

*The **Canna** arrives at Rathlin [NR]*

either by building a new £25 million ship for the route, or deploying an existing unit of the fleet. Although mighty salvos have been fired from South Uist and Barra in the direction of Gourock, and an equally robust and targeted response has been launched from the silos of CalMac Ferries Limited, the matter remains unresolved. Post-tender discussion included the possibility of reconfiguring the use of existing CalMac vessels, but the failure to agree timetables with the relevant communities thwarted progress. No ship can be made available full-time from the existing fleet until the new vessel currently being built for the Kennacraig-Islay service has been completed, and the likelihood that a further new vessel will be built diminishes by the day as oil prices soar.

Residents of the Inner Hebrides may raise an eyebrow at the claims of South Uist spokespersons to the effect that they have 'the worst ferry service in Scotland', which involves a five-and-a-half hour sea journey directly from Lochboisdale to Oban, or six-and-a-half hours, if the ship calls at Castlebay. Lengthy this route may be, and storm-tossed too at times, but it is not the only exit from

South Uist. In contrast to the rather poor road and ferry infrastructures of, say, Coll and Mull, the Outer Hebrides, including Barra and South Uist, have benefited from significant investment in causeways and connecting ferries by Western Isles Council to create the so-called 'Spinal Route'. As a result, two major ferry routes (Stornoway-Ullapool and Lochmaddy-Uig, Skye), with state-of-the-art car-ferries, are accessible to them, both being additional to the Oban-Castlebay-Lochboisdale service.

What, one wonders, constitutes 'optimum' service in such circumstances? The people of South Uist would answer that, as the year is 2008 and not 1908, such long journeys by sea are quite unacceptable. They would emphasise that they too are affected by the increasing price of oil, and that car journeys to the 'nearest' ferry terminal can be costly, as can the long drive from Ullapool or Uig to Glasgow or Edinburgh. Mallaig has railway connections, and the stretch of main road to Glenfinnan has been upgraded recently, allowing a journey-time of 45 minutes from Fort William to Mallaig.

*Lochboisdale, seen from the deck of the **Lord of the Isles** [DEM]*

SAILING WITH A MODERN MASTER:
DONALD MEEK INTERVIEWS CAPTAIN JOHN A. GILLIES
ON BOARD THE MV *ISLE OF ARRAN*

IT WAS A rather dull and overcast day, with the threat of rain, somewhat unlike June but not unlike the average Hebridean morning in late spring or early autumn. The wooded landscape on both sides of West Loch Tarbert was rich in dark green, while the waters of the loch itself were a mixture of greys and browns, interspersed with bright reflections from clear patches of sky. As I approached Kennacraig, West Loch Tarbert, I could see the *Isle of Arran* at her berth, preparing to undertake the 1.00 p.m. service to Port Askaig. Her prominent and distinctive funnels, placed midships on each side, gave colour to the day, and her raised bow visor was clearly visible above the rocky hillock to the east of the berth. Cars, coaches and lorries were already in position for loading, and soon they were trundling across the linkspan and into the ship. On this occasion, I was a foot-passenger, going for the sail, and I had no need to worry about loading my car. I greeted the Onboard Services Manager, Farquhar Morrison, in Gaelic, and in no time at all I was on my way to the bridge at Captain Gillies's invitation. The ship was about to leave for Port Askaig, and officers and Quartermaster were on the bridge. Having given the customary welcome to passengers, with the assurance that the bow visor had been secured, Captain Gillies moved to the port console, and guided his ship astern, bringing her bow gently round to starboard to head out of the loch, while the standard safety announcements were broadcast. Within a few minutes the 'Arran' was powering along, steered by the Quartermaster, and navigated by the Second Mate, Iain MacKenzie, with Captain Gillies in attendance.

Now it was time for a therapeutic cup of tea, prepared by the Captain himself, who served his officers and his visitor with a fine brew! It was time too for some good-humoured banter, as I reminded the Second Mate that, on the last occasion that I sailed with him, on the *Isle of Lewis*, he had appeared in a white boiler-suit, as he had been on top of the wheelhouse, adjusting communications antennae! Tales and recollections of former Masters and crew were exchanged, as the *Isle of Arran* throbbed through the still waters of the West Loch. Within half an hour, the loch had been cleared, and the Sound of Islay, separating the bulky profile of Jura from the less mountainous landscape of Islay, became visible through the mist. With the ship firmly on course for Port Askaig, Captain Gillies invited me to his cabin, where I had the privilege of talking to him about his training and his career on very nearly every vessel of the modern CalMac fleet. As a recently-promoted Master, he answered my questions in a way that provided a fascinating first-hand view of contemporary seamanship in the Hebrides.

Where do you come from, and why did you choose to go to sea?

I come from the Island of Raasay, where I still live. I grew up messing about in boats and always having a love of the sea. My father was a fisherman, and both my grandfathers were at sea. I think it was always in my blood.

How did you undertake your training? Combinations of college and deck? Which companies?

I served as a cadet with Denholm Ship Management of Glasgow, where I obtained my Second Mate's Certificate. This was a mix of college phases at Glasgow and sea-time on various types of ships, including their training-ship *Wellpark*. I was then made redundant, and, while at home on Raasay, I was asked to do two weeks' relief work on the Raasay to Sconser ferry (MV *Raasay*). Fourteen years later, married with two children, I was still there. I needed a change, and was asked to do ten days on the *Lord of the Isles*. Eleven years later, and I haven't been back! So in total I have 25 years' service with CalMac.

During the last eleven years, I returned to college in Glasgow, after serving the required sea-time, and I obtained my Chief Officer's Certificate, and then, after more sea-time, my Master's Certificate.

Which CalMac vessels have you sailed on, and at what ranks?

I have sailed on all the current Western Isles vessels except for the *Lochnevis* and the *Caledonian Isles*. I have sailed on all the routes except the Small Isles. I have been Third Mate on the *Lord of the Isles* and the *Isle of Mull*, Second Mate on the *Iona*, Second Mate and Chief Officer on the *Lord of the Isles*, *Isle of Mull*, *Hebridean Isles*, *Clansman*, *Isle of Lewis*, *Hebrides*, and *Isle of Arran*. I have been Master on the *Hebrides*, *Hebridean Isles* and *Isle of Arran*. On the *Raasay*, *Eigg*, *Rhum* and *Loch Striven*, I have been Skipper, Motorman and Seaman/ Purser at some stage.

Which ship was your first command?

The *Raasay*! I was Master for one day on the *Hebridean Isles*, and for one week on the *Hebrides*. The *Isle of Arran* is my first permanent post.

How did you feel when you realized that you were responsible for whatever might happen to that ship on that day?

It was an exciting, but yet lonely, feeling in a way. At the first port, you think, 'It is up to me now.' You know that the crew are a team, and that we all work together to get the job done, but ultimately they are always looking to you for the lead.

Do you have a preference for a particular vessel, and, if so, why?

I have to say the *Isle of Arran* now, as she is my first command on 'my own' ship. The *Clansman* and *Hebrides* are special to me, in that I served on them both at the last stage of building, and on each on the day they entered service.

What does your normal day-routine entail, assuming that there is a 'normal' day for you?

First, I check weather forecasts, check and send crew lists etc., and then prepare for departure. After departure I take a walk around the vessel, and meet heads of department making sure all is in order. Paperwork takes up a large part of the day, signing on and off crew, keeping the ship management up to date, and dealing with company and ship's business as it arises. You always have the next port to think about – weather, tide, berthing plan – which is discussed with the bridge team, and then the berthing ready for the return leg. At the end of the day, again you check forecasts etc. for the next day and overnight, which dictates moorings, service reviews and any special manoeuvres.

On each trip, I try to move the job on, in part with improvements or changes as required, as well as the day-to-day running of the vessel.

Each day is different, which varies between routes and ships. That is one of the most exciting and interesting aspects of the job.

Have you ever had a particularly unusual 'cargo' or 'happening' that caused you and the crew to scratch your heads?

Loading a wind-turbine tower on to the *Hebrides*, which had a clearance of 2 cm at each end, made us scratch our heads, but we managed eventually. On the little *Raasay*, however, almost every commercial vehicle loaded was a head-scratcher. Some very unusual and unique methods had to be used to load and discharge them on the slipways. But sheep-floats always seemed to be a nightmare. At one time, we had to unload the top deck of the sheep-floats for stability purposes. But this meant unloading the lower decks first, so that all the sheep could be on the deck. As a result, the small car deck was full of sheep and a ten-metre float. Reloading was a nightmare, crawling under the lorry, pulling sheep out, and pushing, pulling, lifting and carrying the sheep on to the lorry before we could lower the ramp. Sea School doesn't have that in its syllabus!

Which one 'modern' (post-1970) feature of CalMac ships do you think is the greatest advance in handling the vessel?

The Becker rudder has greatly improved ship-handling, especially combined with variable-pitch propellers.

Is there anything 'special' about being a Master with CalMac Ferries Limited?

I think, to me, having grown up on an island served by Caledonian MacBrayne, I have always been aware of the heritage of the company, and the great Captains who have served the company over the years. To become Master in the company and follow in their footsteps – but, I'm afraid, not fill their shoes – is, in itself, special to me.

The 'company' has been 'restructured' recently, and tendering has been something of an issue. Has that affected Masters and crews in any way, in your opinion, or have they simply got on with the job?

It has affected us in that there is always a greater uncertainty about the future and how ferry services will be operated. But on the ships, Masters and crews have, indeed, simply got on with the job, and tried to carry out the services as efficiently and safely as we always have. We are always aware of the lifeline we provide, and no matter what the structure, we feel that that responsibility never changes. The passengers appreciate the service the ships and crews provide, which makes our lives easier.

As a recently-promoted Master, how do you see the future of 'Caledonian MacBrayne'?

I can see changes ahead, both ashore and afloat. Advances in communications between shore and vessel have already affected how we operate and manage vessels. With further advances, change will continue.

Provided that the present company wins each tender, Caledonian MacBrayne will maintain its services as before, although changes are inevitable as technology advances. The fundamental purpose of serving the islands will always remain, and we must all play our part in providing the services for which we have been renowned over the last 157 years.

Tapadh leibh ('Thank you', in Gaelic).

My time with Captain Gillies passed all too quickly. As the *Isle of Arran* proceeded up the Sound of Islay, I left the Captain and the bridge team in peace, to arrange the berthing at Port Askaig. Below decks, I had the pleasure of talking to other members of the crew whom I had got to know over the years. Banter – in Gaelic and English – flowed liberally, like the tea in the restaurant, alongside serious discussions about demands from different parts of the network for more ferry services. The rain did not dampen the enthusiasm of the crew, who were very obviously part of a happy, well-run ship.

The rain came down heavily as the *Isle of Arran* berthed at Port Askaig at 3.00 p.m. Looking somewhat bedraggled, the blue-hulled ferry to Jura, *Eilean Dhiura*, was churning the water and preparing to leave her jetty as the 'Arran' pulled in to linkspan. When the outgoing traffic had been discharged, cars and lorries from Islay squelched their way over the ramp, and on to the car-deck – a very significant cavalcade of vehicles, which filled the ship and caused her to be slightly late in leaving for the return journey to Kennacraig. I joined the bridge team again when the 'Arran' was safely under way southwards in the Sound of Islay, with Chief Officer, John Hamilton, in charge. She was now contending with a strong head current which reduced her speed to some ten knots. Captain Gillies apologized to passengers for the delay, but felt confident that the ship would make up time. She did. At precisely 5.30 p.m., she was back at Kennacraig.

Despite such deeply-felt campaigns, and the diversions and frustrations of the latest 'waiting-game', employing Hebridean shipping services as the inevitable political football, Caledonian MacBrayne, through its relevant companies, has proceeded steadily with its programme of fleet and service enhancement, focusing latterly on the Clyde estuary and its islands. The *Loch Shira*, the new vessel for the Largs-Cumbrae Slip service, was launched at Ferguson's shipyard at Port Glasgow in December 2006, and is now proving her worth. She was followed in 2007 by the introduction to the Wemyss Bay-Rothesay route of the *Argyle*, sister-ship to the *Bute* and similarly built by Stocznia Remontowa at Gdansk, Poland. Mindful of the ageing condition of the *Isle of Arran* and the *Hebridean Isles*, Caledonian MacBrayne placed a further order with Remontowa for the building of a new car-ferry as a second vessel for the Kennacraig-Islay service. Resembling a cross between the *Lord of the Isles* and the *Clansman* in general design, the new ship will come into service in 2011. The delay in delivery reflects the scarcity of readily-available components, including engines, in Europe. The need

to retain the completed hull until such were acquired meant that Ferguson's of Port Glasgow withdrew from the competition.

The allocation of yet another Scottish order to a Polish shipbuilder was received by the media generally with

An artist's impression of the new vessel for Islay [CalMac Ferries Limited]

*The **Argyle** makes a splash at Gdansk. [CalMac Ferries Limited]*

less hostility than the order for the *Bute*, but Caledonian MacBrayne was perceived by one Scottish newspaper (*The Scotsman*, 5 March 2007) as having merely 'delayed' the anticipated 'closure' of Ferguson's, because of its lack of 'more enterprising leadership' which could have helped to sustain 'a thriving "high-end" shipbuilding industry in Scotland'. Caledonian MacBrayne, it was claimed, ought to be ordering more than one ship at a time, thus making use of 'economies of scale like any properly-run operator'. Although the article did show some awareness of global patterns affecting shipbuilding in Britain, it failed to define what it meant by the 'proper running' of Caledonian MacBrayne, and its case for batch-ordering of new vessels in order to save Scottish shipyards, rather than to meet the needs of the islands, seemed ill-founded, given operational constraints. The implication that Caledonian MacBrayne had been in large measure responsible for the plight of Ferguson's (which remains operational) ignored the long-

standing and mutually beneficial relationship between the two bodies. Overall, however, it is fair to conclude that the volume of press speculation, and particularly of poorly-informed elbow-jerk journalism about Hebridean ferry services, has now diminished since CalMac Ferries Limited secured the contract.

Alongside the building of new ships, the refurbishment of existing vessels has continued, and is seen most obviously in the £165,000 programme of improvement of passenger accommodation aboard the *Isle of Lewis* in 2007. A steady programme of upgrading is evident with other ships, such as the *Clansman* and the *Isle of Mull*. Redundant tonnage has also been disposed of. The Island-class vessel, *Bruernish*, was sold to Irish operators in September 2006, and crossed the water to join her sister-ships, the former *Kilbrannan*, *Coll*, *Rhum* (now with Arranmore Island Ferry Services) and *Morvern* (now with Bere Island Ferries). Enhancement of routes has also remained a priority for CalMac Ferries

*Refurbished accomodation on board the **Isle of Lewis** [CalMac Ferries Limited]*

Limited since the Operating Agreement was signed, as is indicated by the provision (outside the contract) of a second vessel for the winter schedule of the service to Islay, largely to cater for the needs of the island's thriving whisky industry, and a second vessel, *Saturn*, for summer service to Arran.

More significantly and certainly more contentiously as a broader form of 'route enhancement', the Scottish Government declared its intention to establish a pilot scheme for the application of Road Equivalent Tariff (RET) to ferry services in the Hebrides. The pilot will be conducted from October 2008 until Spring 2011, and will cover the Ullapool-Stornoway, Uig-Tarbert-Lochmaddy and Oban-Castlebay-Lochboisdale routes, as well as Oban-Coll-

Tiree. Within the pilot area, charges will be reduced in such a way as to include a 'core rate' and an RET rate (per mile) for the categories of passengers, cars and commercial vehicles. In areas outwith the pilot zones, fares will remain as published by CalMac, and will be subject to annual increases in line with the conditions applying in the Clyde and Hebrides contract. Such differentiation, nevertheless, divides the Hebrides into the 'haves' and the 'have-nots', the latter including Sound of Harris, Sound of Berneray, Mull-Craignure and Kennacraig-Islay, and discordant voices have been raised. Accusations of favouritism have also been made with reference to SNP political representation in the 'favoured' areas, particularly by representatives of Orkney and Shetland, which are served by another

company within the custody of David MacBrayne Limited, namely NorthLink.

Unquestionably, the concept behind RET is one of 'favour' for islands, and for that reason it is to be welcomed in principle, but it may involve considerable cost to the nation. If the full scheme is implemented, this will probably mean an immense – additional – bill for the Scottish Government, through a major increase in the annual deficit grant awarded to Caledonian MacBrayne, perhaps to a sum in the region of £100 million, which is more than double the current allocation.

The RET experiment will indeed yield interesting results on completion, and these will require to be considered most carefully not only by the Scottish Government, but also by the islands. For the present, it can be regarded as one of the boldest steps yet taken to address the issue of expensive fares on Hebridean routes and the alleged disincentive to inward investment which they create, but evaluation must be close and critical (in the best sense). The proposal was greeted with general approval, if not delight, in the areas designated for the experiment, but, in the longer term, its implications for the islands require extremely cautious evaluation, rather than innocent acceptance and adulation. First and foremost, the accommodation and, particularly, transport infrastructures of the islands will require to be assessed and kept under review. While some islands, most notably those of the Outer Hebrides, have good roads and will probably take increased traffic in their stride, several Inner Hebridean islands (such as Tiree and Mull) have comparatively poor roads, some of which consist of nothing more than

CALEDONIAN MACBRAYNE –
A UNIQUE COMPANY WITH A UNIQUE HERITAGE?

TEMPTING AS IT is to view the Caledonian MacBrayne story as unique because of its specialist trade, there have been some surprising parallels with other short-sea companies over the years. Survival of the vicissitudes of boom and bust or war and peace is a common thread, but some of the moves made by respective Chairmen and their Boards, and even by government, offer a number of similarities.

However odd the late-1880s move by David MacBrayne into deep-sea operation, with second-hand 'tramp' steamers, may seem nowadays, it may not be so peculiar in the light of other ship-owning activities at that time. The London-based General Steam Navigation Company looked out from its established 'Home Trade' to run ships down to West Africa and later the Americas, using specially-bought second-hand tonnage in the mid-1890s. At the same time, the Wilson Line of Hull was trying its luck with a route to India, and the Moss Steamship Company, like General Steam engaged in near-European routes, but based at Liverpool, tried to offer a service to north-east Canada. In each case, dire financial circumstances or tragic loss of vessels in unfamiliar seas brought urgent retrenching – for Moss (later Moss Hutchison) the wrecking of the brand-new steamer *Mareotis* on the Canadian run in 1900 was the last straw. Could it be that, in all instances, expansion was considered to be achievable only by moving into pastures new?

There are also clear parallels between the MacBrayne heritage and that of its North Sea counterpart, the Edinburgh-based North Company. Both suffered from lack of capital in the early twentieth century, although the North Company was expanding its services into the 1890s with new ships and routes to Orkney and Shetland, and pioneering the cruise industry, with Norwegian coastal excursions offered in season. The North Company then set about consolidating its services and assets, only to be upset by the onset of World War I. But it was cash-strapped thereafter, and in the market for second-hand ships. It was surprisingly keen to take over MacBrayne's *Chieftain* despite the ship's obvious unsuitability to a cargo- (particularly livestock-) intensive route. It is interesting too that

both companies were destined to become partner-subsidiaries within the Coast Lines group, and that the services formerly offered by the North Company would ultimately fall under the management of NorthLink, a subsidiary of David MacBrayne Limited.

The nation could not afford the MacBrayne business to cease trading when it faced bankruptcy in 1928, and it needed to find a way round its financial difficulties. On a much larger scale at about this time, the government had to save what it could of the mighty Royal Mail Group, which was so large that its downfall could directly influence the nation's GDP. Lord Kylsant's accounting indiscretions within the Royal Mail Group, of which Coast Lines was a part, brought it down, along with its subsidiary companies and the shipbuilding interests on the rivers Lagan and Clyde. So frightened was government of the collapse of Royal Mail that it ordered an audit of the P&O and British India complex of companies, to satisfy itself that they were not destined for the same fate. Although the MacBrayne operation was minute compared with Royal Mail interests, government was conscious of the need to service the transport requirements of the islands, and was forced to intervene with a recovery package. In the Depression that followed, other impressive companies foundered, including Glasgow's cherished Anchor Line, although that too was later rescued, but not by the

state, while the names of many lesser companies are now all but forgotten. It is worth remembering that government put the MacBrayne Kingdom into the category of 'a business of national importance', along with British India and other mighty names.

Caledonian MacBrayne continues to provide the vital lifeline to the islands. It retains the subsidies from the state initiated in 1928, and these ensure that a proper service, fit for the purpose but modern and comfortable, is maintained for the benefit of the economy of Scotland and its many-west coast island communities. In this capacity, Caledonian MacBrayne is now unique, together with its associated Northern Isles services to Orkney and Shetland.

For its survival, Caledonian MacBrayne is not wholly dependent on income from its share of either the freight market or the passenger market, as are other ferry operators in cross-channel business or in the UK domestic sector (e.g. Isle of Wight or Channel Islands). Rather, it depends more on serving the precise needs of island communities, and on satisfying the demands and whims of its political masters in both Edinburgh and Brussels. Caledonian MacBrayne recognises that it holds a position of privilege, but careful application of its now unique knowledge and long-standing experience, coupled with the provision of first-class service using first-class assets, will ensure its future.

The NorthLink cargo-vessel **Hascosay** *[NR]*

*Traffic comes off the **Coruisk** at Armadale.[DEM]*

successive – and now seriously fractured – layers of asphalt on top of the original dirt-tracks. On these roads, which barely cope with current demands, the principles of the nineteenth-century engineer, Thomas Telford, have yet to make any noticeable impact, and they are scarcely adequate for large-lorry traffic and increased numbers of visitors' cars. Capacity on existing vessels too will require careful monitoring, lest it be oversubscribed to the disadvantage of the islands. It is possible that the volume of tourists and their cars heading for the islands may leave little space for island residents and their vehicles. Will this require the building of larger vessels, or the more frequent deployment of the existing ships, perhaps using shorter routes (for example, Tobermory-Coll-Tiree, rather than Oban-Coll-Tiree)? Will the convenience of lower fares not also make it easier for people, and perhaps even for investment, to *leave* the islands? RET, in short, could be a double-edged weapon, as is argued in Arran, Bute and Mull.

RET is also likely to have consequences for customs and cultural traditions, sacred and secular, as well as the survival of the Gaelic language, in the islands. If the overall aim of RET is to normalise fares on, and access to, car-ferries relative to the costs of road-travel, this will inevitably affect the perception of the existing six-day service on the Ullapool-Stornoway route, which is currently the subject of debate, with significant decisions awaited from CalMac Ferries Limited. If roads are open and available to all on Sundays, why should car-ferries not be available likewise? After all, nobody is required by law or custom or belief to travel on cars and buses on Sundays, but many – including, presumably, Sabbatarians – do just that. The same element of personal choice – to travel or not to travel – would be expected on the part of those wishing, or not wishing, to travel on car-ferries on the Sabbath. The further 'levelling up' (or 'down') of island expectations and requirements (see Chapter 11) to accord with mainland and Scotland-wide practices is implicit, it would seem, in RET. It is true that this is not the first priority of the scheme, but it must inevitably form part of the wider package.

As for Gaelic, the condition of the language in the Hebrides – even the Outer Hebrides – remains a cause for concern, and can best be described as 'fragile'. Greater access to the Hebrides, particularly by non-Gaelic-speakers, will do little to allay current anxieties, even if the ferry company takes supportive action. In recognition of the value of the distinctive culture of the region, which must be one of its attractions to tourists, CalMac Ferries Limited acknowledges the central importance of Gaelic, and has produced an excellent Gaelic Plan, in response to the burden placed on public bodies, through Bòrd na Gàidhlig, by the Gaelic Language (Scotland) Act of 2005. Indeed, in this respect, as in many others, the company has performed in exemplary fashion, acting more quickly than almost all other public bodies in Scotland, and being the first public transport operator in Scotland to have such a plan. CalMac Ferries Limited has also co-operated with the Red Cell and Creative Cell, Glasgow, to produce two very attractive, colourful 'companions' for Hebridean passengers, within the Gaelic Rings project, *Cearcaill na Gàidhlig*. In the most recent volume, launched on board the *Isle of Mull* in March

*Launching **Cearcaill na Gàidhlig** on board the **Isle of Mull** are (from left to right) Donald Meek, Jane Cheape, Hugh Cheape and Brian Wilson. [Oban Times]*

2008, well-known writers have described their 'personal journeys' on different routes. The bilingual nature of the volume is an important reminder of, and contribution to, the maintenance of Gaelic awareness and normalisation of language use. During the summer, this is complemented by another Gaelic-awareness project, *Gàidhlig air a' Bhàta*, 'Gaelic on the Boat', which takes place on selected vessels with the support of Comunn na Gàidhlig. These initiatives, however, have to be seen in the context of broader transport developments which may not aid the survival of the language, while providing important and much-needed services to the Hebrides. Conflicts and contradictions abound in life, and are reflected in the practical steps taken to facilitate and maintain its distinctive colours.

In summary, it can be said that the two years since the completion of the first edition of this book have been momentous for Caledonian MacBrayne – now divided into several companies – and for its 'customers' in the Highlands and Islands, who, like Caledonian MacBrayne itself, are fated to be participants in a seemingly never-ending range of 'experiments' for the provision of adequate transport service. When, one asks, will the 'experiments'

and the 'political football' cease? When can the residents of the Hebrides reasonably expect a settled policy for car-ferry services, which will lay out principles for the operation of such services beyond 2013, when the current operating contract, held by CalMac Ferries Limited, comes to an end? How will the quality of existing services – maintained by fine ships, devoted crews, and managers who have sailed the 'choppy seas of change' with admirable skill and patience – be preserved? What programme will there be for replacing some of the best-known ships in the fleet, now approaching or well into their third decade of service, among them the *Isle of Arran,* the *Hebridean Isles,* the *Isle of Mull,* and the *Lord of the Isles*? This, in itself, will be a costly investment even at current prices – probably in the region of £200 million.

It is to be hoped – most earnestly – that the award of the next contract will not be subject to the delays, uncertainties and compromise solutions which have been so evident in the course of the last few years. The islands – not to mention Caledonian MacBrayne, and the nation itself – deserve better. At the same time, it is important that the islands, and especially their spokespersons, understand that the funds available to the Scottish Government for the maintenance and development of Hebridean shipping services are not bottomless. Given current economic forecasts, some very hard choices lie ahead for both the communities and the sea-transport providers. Reasoned argument and well-considered strategy are required at every level of Scottish life, including Hebridean 'lifeline' provision, if the nation is to prosper in all its dimensions.

Despite the buffetings, the MacBrayne story continues, seemingly driven by politicians, while the operators are left to worry about the day-to-day issues of maintaining the largest ferry network in Britain. The real business of the network depends, not on politicians, nor on tourists and day-trippers taking advantage of sunny days and glorious scenery, but on the risk assessment made by the Master at the start of each stormy voyage, overshadowed by grey skies and a bad forecast for 'Rockall, Malin, Hebrides'. That the Irish Sea freight-ferry *Riverdance,* sailing from Warrenpoint

to Heysham, ended up so easily on the beach at Cleveleys on 1 February 2008, and was later dismantled where she lay, is reminder enough of the continuing dangers of the seas around our shores. We, the travelling public, are grateful to the crews and the management of the MacBrayne heritage, with its outstanding safety record, for bringing us unscathed to the present day.

While it is tempting to ask what the next chapter will report, it will, no doubt, focus on the continued smooth-running of a highly professional operation and its dedicated workforce. And it is thanks to the Masters, officers and ratings, the engineers, the catering staff, the shore workers and the management in its various manifestations, that the Hebrides are what they are today. These islands would be much the poorer, if it were not for the *Lord of the Isles*, the *Clansman*, the *Isle of Lewis* and the *Isle of Mull* and their numerous sisters. The Kingdom, despite being under the weather occasionally, is alive and well, and long may it flourish.

APPENDIX A

Deck Arrangements

1930s Motor-ship
and
1990s Car-ferry

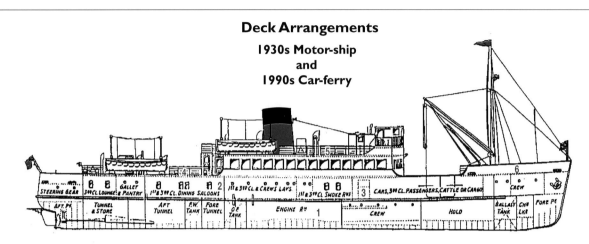

MV *Lochiel* (1939)

1. Lower Deck
2. Main Deck
3. Tween Deck (part of Main Deck)
4. Promenade or Upper Deck
5. Boat Deck
6. Forecastle Deck

MV *Isle of Lewis* (1995)

1. Lower Deck
2. Main or Car Deck
3. Mezzanine Deck (for cars)
4. Upper Deck (with restaurant)
5. Boat Deck (with Observation Lounge)
6. Bridge Deck

PROFILES AND DESIGNS

The accompanying profiles represent part of the changing visual picture of David MacBrayne Limited and Caledonian MacBrayne, as reflected in the designs of the companies' ships. The ships selected begin with the *Glencoe* (originally the *Mary Jane*) of 1846, and conclude with the *Clansman* of 1998, whose sister-ship *Hebrides* entered service in 2001. The pages illustrate the principal eras in company history, namely those of the steamship (1846-1929), the diesel passenger-cargo vessel, culminating in MacBrayne's first side-loading car-ferries (1930–1964), and the contemporary car-ferry, with two broad phases, the first 'foundational and experimental' (1970–78), and the second 'established and mainstream' (1980–).

Two general points are worth making. The first is that, across the years, the MacBrayne kingdom has used a rich variety of ship designs, though these are based on key models (paddle-steamer, motor-ship etc.). MacBrayne and his successors have not been constricted by loyalty to one blueprint. In fact, a very considerable amount of experimentation is evident even in the case of individual ships. The second point is that MacBrayne's designs throughout the period 1846–1998 have been consistent with, and have borrowed from, contemporary patterns in naval architecture in the wider maritime world. These patterns have been modified skilfully to produce the smaller, distinctive 'Hebridean ship'.

Even in the era of the steamship, it is clear that the 'Hebridean' designs offered considerable room for flexibility and adaptation. Thus the *Glencoe*, frugal in all respects but also highly functional, was lengthened as part of her metamorphosis from the *Mary Jane*. She was able to serve almost the entire Hebrides (at different stages)

for an astonishing eighty-five years, partly because of her spacious forward capacity, which was well suited to cargo of all kinds, from loose bulk to animals. Her use of a derrick on the foremast anticipated the pattern of the following hundred years. She maintained to the end the arrangement of a platform placed over each sponson, which was used by the Master when conning the ship.

By the mid-century, the screw-driven steamship was making its appearance, and had become the principal model for Hebridean service by the mid-1870s. The *Claymore* of 1881 represented the 'two-derrick' ship, carrying derricks on both the fore- and mainmasts. This was characteristic of most such vessels in this period. The location of holds fore and aft appears to have been determined in part by the placement of the machinery, which, with boilers, bunkers and engine, occupied a large proportion of the midships section. The profile shows the *Claymore* in her early stages carrying gaff-rig, with sails furled vertically on the mainmasts, and a furled fore staysail (as is attested in contemporary photographs). As confidence in steam propulsion increased, her rig was modified to reduce sail-support. Further modifications also appear to have been made to the *Claymore*, either at building or early in her career. Her midships lifeboats were raised, and a shelter-deck was provided around the engine casing. In contrast to the ornate *Claymore*, John McCallum's *Hebrides* of 1898 represents the 'plainly functional' style of steamship, which was also found in the *Dunara Castle* of 1875. She had a straight stem, and her forecastle looked stunted compared with the fine clipper bow of the *Claymore*. In practice, both vessels, with their sharp entries, could be 'wet' and 'bumpy'. The basic steamship design, with holds and derricks fore and aft, was represented finally by the *Lochness* of 1929.

The *Lochness* was, however, the obvious precursor of the new post-1928 era of development for David MacBrayne, with its dominant motor-ships. Her high forecastle head was intended to reduce ingress from heavy seas over the bow, a characteristic of earlier, sharp-bowed steamships. The *Lochness* was clearly influential in the making of the diesel-engined *Loch Seaforth* in 1947. The new ship had a similar forecastle head, and also two derricks, although in this case the smaller derrick was mounted (initially) ahead of the foremast, as shown in the profile. Diesel engines occupied less space, and could be placed further aft, thus allowing more space forward. The *Loch Seaforth* had long, flowing lines, but the *Lochearn* and *Lochmor* of 1930 established a trend towards 'dumpy diesels'. Low funnels, often obscured by the bridge superstructure, were characteristic of many early diesel vessels, as is evident with the *Loch Seaforth*, and also the *Lochearn* and *Lochmor*, following their 1948 refits. Their earlier, taller funnels were closer to those of the last generation of steamships such as the *Lochness*. The *Lochearn* and *Lochmor* were subjected to minor modifications across the years, including extension of bridge accommodation, lowering of funnels, and moving of the aft jackstaff to the boat-deck, to function partly as a radio aerial. Their rather ugly stovepipes were also moved around. The profile shows their final configuration. The 1955 *Claymore* was another 'dumpy diesel', but greater care was taken to incorporate more in the way of sheer-line and curve, and she was given a very conspicuous funnel. She remained largely unchanged throughout her MacBrayne career, apart from the addition of life-rafts. The plump, high-sided *Hebrides*, *Clansman* and *Columba* of 1963-64 reflected the effect of a 'garage', occupying most of the main deck, on the position of passenger accommodation. Minor modifications to the

class included the (very late) provision of a tripod support for the forward navigating light, previously hoisted just ahead of the hydraulic car-lift.

How to place passenger accommodation relative to the car-deck is one of the key issues for car-ferry designers. Initial under-provision of accommodation made the first vessels rather cramped (see 'The Post-1970 Car-ferries'). The profile of the *Iona* of 1970 shows her as she was in the mid-1970s, with additional cabin accommodation and side vents, and even stern-cranes. The high forward superstructure and long open decks of oil-rig supply vessels contributed to the design of the *Pioneer* of 1974 and the *Claymore* of 1978. The former is shown before she was given side-loading facilities. The drive-through *Suilven*, built in Norway in 1974, was of a much more assured and elegant design, with a handsome curved bow and a cleverly positioned funnel. The *Suilven* had a subtly formative effect on post-1980 car-ferry profiles.

The second phase of car-ferry development showed 'hybridisation' between the earlier designs of the 1978 *Claymore* and the *Suilven*. This produced significantly larger and better-looking vessels with much superior passenger facilities. The *Isle of Mull* of 1988 had an enclosed car-deck. The forward section of the *Lord of the Isles* of 1989 is very similar indeed to that of the *Isle of Mull*, but her after section is closer to the 'open tail' of the *Claymore*. The sophisticated *Isle of Lewis* of 1995, modelled on the *Lord of the Isles*, is the largest of the current car-ferries. Despite her long sweep of white superstructure, she looks rather 'blunt', and has a tendency to sit awkwardly on the water. The handsome *Clansman* of 1998, followed by the *Hebrides* of 2001, reverted to single-funnel design. These vessels appear to be the 'ultimate' (to date) in the evolution of a highly seaworthy type of car-ferry for the Hebrides.

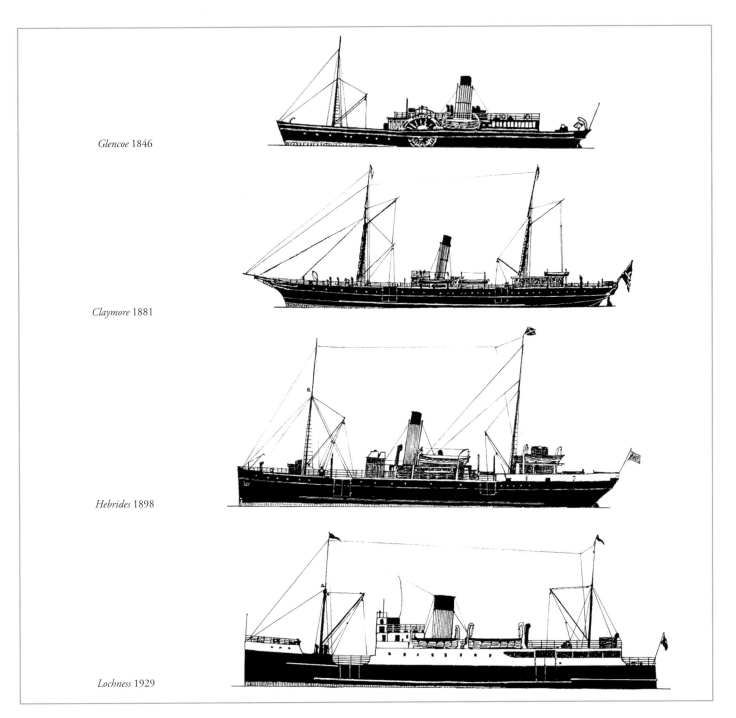

Glencoe 1846

Claymore 1881

Hebrides 1898

Lochness 1929

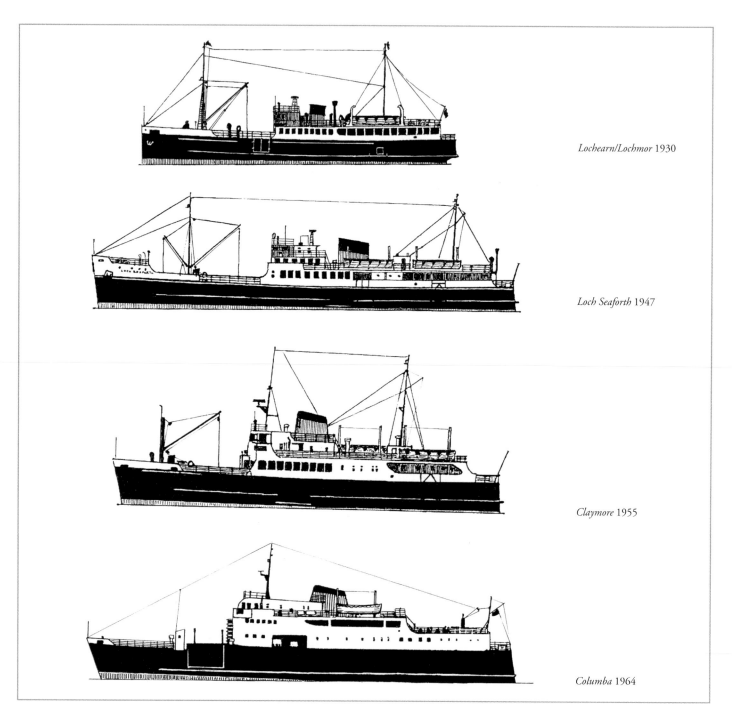

Lochearn/Lochmor 1930

Loch Seaforth 1947

Claymore 1955

Columba 1964

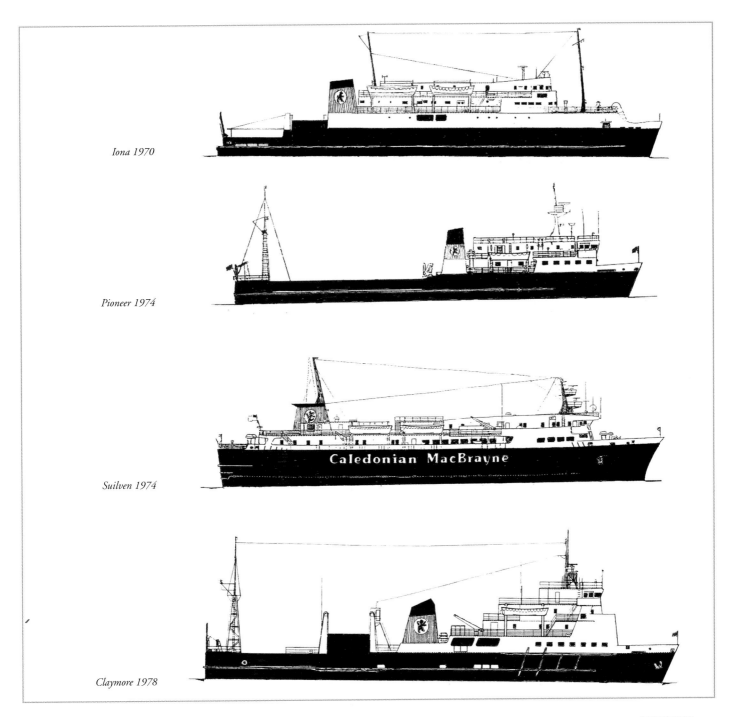

Iona 1970

Pioneer 1974

Suilven 1974

Caledonian MacBrayne

Claymore 1978

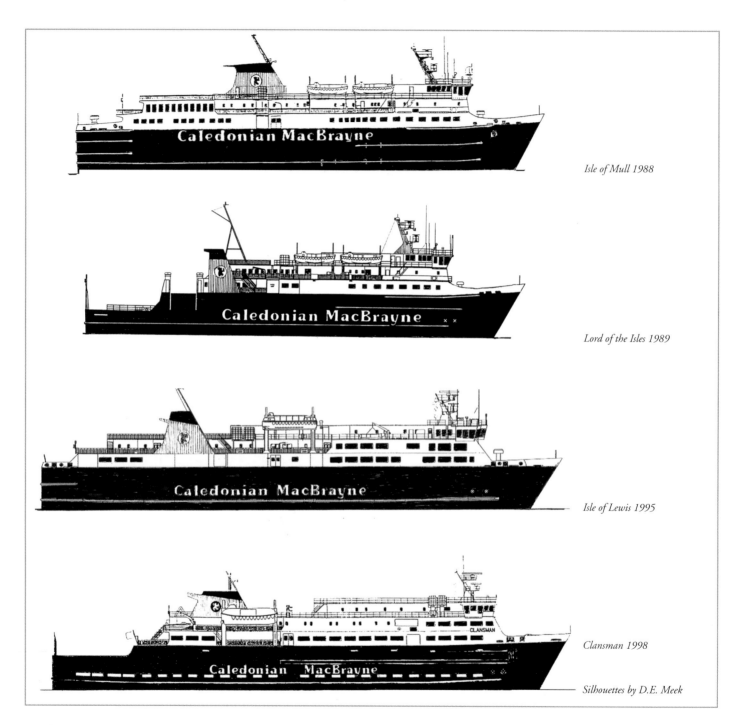

Isle of Mull 1988

Lord of the Isles 1989

Isle of Lewis 1995

Clansman 1998

Silhouettes by D.E. Meek

APPENDIX B

ALL FREIGHT, PASSENGERS, GOODS AND LIVE STOCK CARRIED SUBJECT TO CONDITIONS SPECIFIED ON
THE COMPANY'S SAILING BILLS.

GLASGOW & WEST HIGHLANDS

McCALLUM, ORME AND COMPANY LTD

*Tours through
Hebridean Islands
and to*
St KILDA

ALO/NJ.

TELEGRAPHIC ADDRESS
McCALLUM GLASGOW
TELEPHONE "CENTRAL"
7126 (3 LINES)

45 UNION STREET,
GLASGOW, C.I.

28th December, 19 37.

Messrs. R. McAlister & Co.,
    Boat Builders,
        Sandpoint,
            DUMBARTON.

Dear Sirs,

We are on the lookout for a second-hand wooden square
sterned boat of strong build, suitable for a cargo ferryboat,
dimensions about 34'-0" x 10'-3" x 3'-9", with or without engine.

If you happen to have such a craft for sale we shall be
glad to have particulars, price and information as to where it can
be seen.

Yours faithfully,

McCALLUM, ORME & CO., LTD.

A.L. Orme

Director.

WESTERN FERRIES (ARGYLL) LIMITED

16 WOODSIDE CRESCENT
GLASGOW G3 7UT

Directors:
K. C. Cadenhead
I. V. R. Harrison
A. G. Wilson
P. J. Wordie

Secretary:
K. C. Cadenhead, C.A.

Tel.: 041-332 9766
Tlx.: 77203

Registered Number
44778 Scotland

AGW/CCM

Sea Breezes
202 Cotton Exchange Building
Old Hall Street
LIVERPOOL
L3 9LA

9th December 1987

Dear Sirs

<u>Islay Ferry Service</u>

Mr. Robins' article in the December issue, entitled "Back When MacBraynes Really Were MacBraynes", goes slightly wrong on the history of Western Ferries' service to Islay.

Western Ferries never received any government subsidy despite carrying the majority of vehicular traffic from 1969 to 1975, and had, as a result, to reduce the service and eventually to withdraw under government pressure in 1981. The Monopolies Commission in 1983 reported as follows:

"By 1973 Western Ferries had established itself as by far the largest carrier of cars and commercial vehicles on the route. David MacBrayne's belief that it could operate a profitable service was conditioned by unreasonable optimism about the rate of growth of revenue and the extent to which costs could be reduced.

The second crucial factor was the decision by the Secretary of State in 1975 to increase the subsidy given to STG's ferry services, and not relate it to operating results on individual routes. David MacBrayne was able to offer a level of services to passengers, including car passengers which could not be matched by Western Ferries. If David MacBrayne had been required to break even or make a profit on the route we do not believe the company could have continued to operate the service. Because the granting of subsidy gave David MacBrayne the ability to follow a long-term policy we believe that Western Ferries, under financial pressure, took the decisions to sell the Sound of Jura, and to sell the lease of the pier at Kennacraig. This hastened the process of the withdrawal of the service in 1981."

Yours faithfully
WESTERN FERRIES (ARGYLL) LIMITED

A.G.Wilson
Director

BIBLIOGRAPHY

PRINCIPAL WORKS OF REFERENCE (IN ENGLISH)

Official records
Dissolved company papers relating to the Islay Steam-Packet Company, David MacBrayne Limited, McCallum, Orme & Co. Limited, and the Western Isles Steam Packet Company Limited (West Register House, Edinburgh).

Submissions to government by shipping companies (West Register House, Edinburgh).

Periodicals
Annual *Newsletter* of the West Highland Steamer Club.
Annual *Review* of the Clyde River Steamer Club.
Motor Ship.
Newspapers as quoted in the text.
Paddle Wheels.
Sea Breezes.
Transactions of the Gaelic Society of Inverness.
Transactions of the Highland and Agricultural Society of Scotland.

Books
Atkinson G. C. 2001. *Expeditions to the Hebrides*, edited by D.A. Quine. Maclean Press, Skye.
Bowman J. E. 1986. *The Highlands and Islands: A Nineteenth-Century Tour.* Alan Sutton, Gloucester.
Brown A. 1979. *Craigendoran Steamers.* Aggregate Publications, Johnstone.
Duckworth C.L.D. and Langmuir G. E. 1977. *Clyde and Other Coastal Steamers.* T. Stephenson and Sons, Prescot.
Duckworth C. L. D. and Langmuir G. E. 1967. *West Highland Steamers.* 3rd edition. T. Stephenson & Sons, Prescot.
Duckworth C. L. D. and Langmuir G. E. 1972. *Clyde River and Other Steamers.* 3rd edition. Brown, Son and Ferguson, Glasgow.
Fox S. 2003. *The Ocean Railway.* HarperCollins, London.
Henry F. 1987. *Steam Packet Ships.* Brown, Son and Ferguson, Glasgow.
Kemp P. 1988 edn. *The Oxford Companion to Ships and the Sea.* Oxford University Press, Oxford.
MacBrayne Centenary: One hundred years of progress, 1851-1951. David MacBrayne Limited, Glasgow.
Memoirs and Portraits of One Hundred Glasgow Men. Glasgow Digital Library. http://gdl.cdlr.strath.ac.uk/100men/gm46.htm.
Oxford Dictionary of National Biography. 2004-5. Oxford University Press, Oxford.
Osborne B. D. 2001. *The Ingenious Mr Bell: A Life of Henry Bell (1767-1830), Pioneer of Steam Navigation.* Argyll Publishing, Glendaruel.
Patton B. 1999. *Scottish Coastal Steamers 1918-1975: The Lines that Linked the Lochs.* Silver Link Publishing, Kettering.
Robins N. S. 1995. *The Evolution of the British Ferry.* Ferry Publications, Kilgetty.
Robins N. S. 1999. *Turbine Steamers of the British Isles.* Colourpoint Books, Newtownards.
Robins N. S. 2003. *Ferry Powerful: A History of the Modern British Diesel Ferry.* Bernard McCall, Portishead.
Robson M. 2005. *St Kilda: Church, Visitors and 'Natives'.* Islands Book Trust, Isle of Lewis. 2005.

Sinclair R. C. 1990. *Across the Irish Sea: Belfast-Liverpool Shipping since 1819.* Conway Maritime Press Ltd., London.

Stewart G. 1881. *Curiosities of Glasgow Citizenship.* James MacLehose, Glasgow.

Stromier G. and Nicholson J. 1967. *Steamers of the Clyde.* Scottish Field, Glasgow.

Thornton E. C. B. 1968. *Clyde Coast Pleasure Steamers.* T Stephenson & Sons Ltd., Prescot.

Weyndling W. 2005. *West Coast Tales: Riveters, Wrecks and Ring-netters.* Birlinn, Edinburgh.

Whittle J. 1990. *Speed Bonny Boat: The Story of Caledonian MacBrayne Ltd. under Scottish Transport Group, 1969-90.* Saltire Communications, Edinburgh.

Williamson J. 1904. *The Clyde Passenger Steamer: Its Rise and Progress during the Nineteenth Century.* James MacLehose and Sons, Glasgow.

FURTHER READING

Anderson I.F. 1937. *Across Hebridean Seas.* Chatto and Windus, London.

Atkinson, R. 1949. *Island Going.* Collins, London.

Carmichael A. 1974. *Kintyre.* David and Charles, Newton Abbott.

Charnley B. 1993. *A Voyage to St Kilda.* Maclean Press, Skye.

Cooper D. 2002. *Road to the Isles: Travellers in the Hebrides 1770-1914.* MacMillan, London.

Cowshill M., Hendy J., and Macduff L., [c.1995], 1999 (twice), *Caledonian MacBrayne: the fleet.* Ferry Publications, Narberth.

Davidson J.D.G. 2003. *Scots and the Sea: A Nation's Lifeblood.* Mainstream. Edinburgh

Deayton A. 2001. *MacBrayne Steamers.* Tempus Publishing Limited, Stroud.

Durie A. 2003. *Scotland for the Holidays: Tourism in Scotland c.1780-1939.* John Donald, Edinburgh.

Hutton G. 2003. *Crinan Canal: The Shipping Short Cut.* Stenlake Publishing, Catrine.

Hutton G. 1998. *The Caledonian Canal: Lochs, Locks and Pleasure Steamers.* Stenlake Publishing, Catrine.

Hutton G. 1994. *The Crinan Canal: Puffers and Paddle Steamers.* Stenlake Publishing, Catrine.

Leach N. 1998. *Lifeboats.* Shire Publications Ltd, Princes Risborough.

MacGregor A. A. 1931. *A Last Voyage to St Kilda.* Cassell and Company, London.

MacLean A. 1984. *Night Falls on Ardnamurchan: The Twilight of a Crofting Community.* Gollancz, London.

Macpherson J. 1996. *The Poems of Ossian and Related Works,* edited by H. Gaskill. Edinburgh University Press, Edinburgh.

McCrorie I. 2003. *M.V. Pioneer.* Caledonian MacBrayne, Gourock.

McCrorie I. 2003. *Sea Routes from Mallaig.* Caledonian MacBrayne, Gourock.

McCrorie I. 2001. *Royal Road to the Isles.* Caledonian MacBrayne, Gourock.

McCrorie I. 2001. *The Three Ships 'Hebrides'.* Caledonian MacBrayne, Gourock.

McCrorie I. 1987. *Steamers of the Highlands and Islands: An Illustrated History.* Orr, Pollock and Co. Ltd, Greenock.

McCrorie, I. 1977, 1980. *Ships of the Fleet.* Caledonian MacBrayne, Gourock.

McCrorie I. [c. 1987] *Glen Sannox.* Caledonian MacBrayne, Gourock.

McCutcheon C. 2002. *St Kilda: A Journey to the End of the World.* Tempus Publishing Limited, Stroud.

Meek D. E. 2000. *The Quest for Celtic Christianity.* Handsel Press, Edinburgh.

Moir P. and Crawford I. 2003. *Argyll Shipwrecks.* Moir Crawford, Wemyss Bay.

Moir P. and Crawford I. 2004. *Clyde Shipwrecks.* Moir Crawford, Wemyss Bay.

Shaw M. F. 1999. *From the Alleghenies to the Hebrides: An Autobiography.* Birlinn, Edinburgh.

Smith C. J. 1999. *In Fair Weather and in Foul: 30 years of Scottish passenger ships and ferries.* Ferry Publications, Narberth.

Steel T. 1994. *The Life and Death of St. Kilda.* HarperCollins*Publishers*, London.

Thornton E. C. B. 1968. *Clyde Coast Pleasure Steamers.* T. Stephenson and Sons, Prescot.

Vallance, H.A. 1996. *The Highland Railway.* House of Lochar, Colonsay.

Watson D. 1999. *From Comet to Caledonia: General Arrangement Drawings of 30 Clyde River Paddle Steamers from 1812 to 1934.* Brown, Son and Ferguson, Glasgow.

GAELIC SOURCES

Periodicals

Gairm.

Books

Boyd A. 2006. *Na Nuadh Bhàtaichean 1928-60.* [*The New Ships 1928-60.*] Acair, Stornoway. [Gaelic text with English summaries.]

Dùghalach A. 1829. *Orain, Marbhrannan agus Duanagan Gaidhealach.* Inverness.

Lamont D. 1960. *Prose Writings of Donald Lamont.* Scottish Gaelic Texts Society, Edinburgh.

MacLeod N. 1910. *The Gaelic Writings of Norman MacLeod,* edited by A. Clerk. John Grant, Edinburgh.

Meek D. E. 1977. *An t-Aiseag an Iar* [*The Passage West*]. Clò Beag, Glasgow.

Meek D. E. 2003. *Caran an t-Saoghail: The Wiles of the World: Anthology of 19th Century Scottish Gaelic Verse.* Birlinn, Edinburgh.

Meek D. E. 1998. *Màiri Mhòr nan Oran.* Scottish Gaelic Texts Society, Edinburgh.

ACKNOWLEDGEMENTS

The authors are very grateful indeed to many individuals who, over the last forty years, have provided photographs, records, insights, anecdotes and memorabilia. Through the publication of this book, a substantial proportion of these items has now been made available to the wider public, and we feel privileged to discharge our responsibilities in this way. We also owe considerable debts to generous people who have come to our aid in the course of writing this book.

Donald Meek would like to thank the following:

Alan Boyd, whose sketches of the motor-vessels, *Lochearn*, *Claymore* and *Loch Seaforth*, provided a basis for the silhouettes of these ships in Appendix A;

Iain Hope, for his kindness in obtaining information about Captain John McCallum in the Captains' Register in the Guildhall Library, and for his account of his voyage on the SS *Hebrides* in 1952;

the late Graham Easton Langmuir, whose work (and that of Christian Duckworth) laid the foundation of this book, and who supplied, many years ago, several excellent photographs;

Dr William Lind and the Ballast Trust for very generous assistance in tracing Captain John McCallum, and for providing MacBrayne memorabilia, the McCallum and Orme letter in Appendix B, photographs of the *Plover*, and photocopies of articles by Donald McLeod and others which first appeared in the *Dumbarton Herald*;

Jack Livingstone, who passed on a fine collection of photographs and MacBrayne memorabilia made by his father, formerly piermaster at Kyle of Lochalsh;

Dr Mairi MacArthur, for a collection of photographs of Clyde and West Highland ships taken by Donald B. MacCulloch, and previously held by her father, the late Dugald MacArthur;

Ian C. McCrorie, whose warm-hearted enthusiasm over many years has been an immense encouragement, and whose regular publications have sustained informed interest in West Highland shipping;

Rhoda Meek, for photographs of several Caledonian MacBrayne ships in the Sound of Mull and at Oban;

Dr Harold H. Mills, CB, recently Chairman of Caledonian MacBrayne, for copies of relevant writings, and for his warm personal support;

Jim Murray, Librarian, The Royal Highland and Agricultural Society of Scotland, for locating an article in an early volume of the Society's *Transactions*;

Tom Robertson, formerly Chief Engineer of the *Claymore*, for generously supplying reminiscences of his time on the ship, and for photographs of the *City of Hydra*, and reproductions of a selection of his paintings;

Michael Robson, for permission to use material on the St Kilda steamers conveniently assembled in his new book;

The School of Scottish Studies Archives, University of Edinburgh, and the Director of Archives, Dr Margaret A. Mackay, for several fine photographs, and for access to the splendid photographic collection as a whole, under the supervision of the current photographer, Ian MacKenzie, who has also provided material for this book;

The Scottish Gaelic Texts Society, for permission to quote, in English translation, from the Gaelic essays of the Rev. Donald Lamont;

Mrs D. Seddon, Leeds, and latterly of Achnasheen, who, in the mid-1960s, provided a Tiree schoolboy with a rare set of her own photographs and other items relating to her tours to St Kilda in 1936–37 on the SS *Hebrides*, now reproduced in Chapter 4;

Dr Donald William Stewart, University of Edinburgh, for copies of cartoons relating to travel in the nineteenth-century Highlands and Islands;

Ms Alma Topen, Glasgow University Archives, who also searched for information about Captain John McCallum. In the 1970s, before Glasgow University Archives were fully developed as custodians of Clyde shipbuilding records, photographs were obtained for use in a 'forthcoming' book on West Highland shipping. These are reproduced in this book, which has 'forthcome' at last.

Nick Robins wishes to thank:

Alistair Deayton, for information on the fate of the *Lochearn* and *Lochmor*;

Malcolm McRonald, for advice on Coast Lines' activities in the 1930s and 1950s;

John Stevenson, for advice on machinery in post-war motor-vessels.

Both authors wish to thank the following:

Caledonian MacBrayne, and especially Dr Hugh Dan MacLennan, for their warm enthusiasm for the project as a whole, and for supplying General Arrangements of the company's most recent (post-1970) vessels, which provided the basis of the silhouettes in Appendix A;

Richard Danielson, Onchan, Isle of Man, for his fine sequence of photographs of the *Columba* (1964);

Harold Jordan, formerly Purser on the *King George V* and other MacBrayne ships, for his anecdotes of these vessels and their crews, and for supplying several fine photographs;

the External Readers of the book, Richard Danielson, Dr Hugh Dan MacLennan, and Ian Ramsay, for their willingness to undertake this additional task, and for their invaluable assistance;

Dr Rachel J. Meek, for editing successive drafts, and steering the authors through difficult literary channels;

and, last but by no means least, Birlinn Limited, for their readiness to publish this book, and for their enthusiasm and support throughout.

Mòran taing dhuibh uile.

INDEX OF SHIPS

INDEX OF SHIPS